Life-Cycle Savings and Public Policy

Life-Cycle Savings and Public Policy

A Cross-National Study of Six Countries

EDITED BY

Axel Börsch-Supan

Mannheim Research Institute for the Economics of Aging
University of Mannheim, Germany

ACADEMIC PRESS

An imprint of Elsevier Science

Amsterdam   Boston   London   New York   Oxford   Paris
San Diego   San Francisco   Singapore   Sydney   Tokyo

Copyright 2003, Elsevier Science (USA).

Academic Press
An imprint of Elsevier Science
525 B Street, Suite 1900, San Diego, California 92101-4495, USA
http://www.academicpress.com

Academic Press
84 Theobald's Road, London WC1X 8RR, UK
http://www.academicpress.com

Library of Congress Control Number: 2002116253

International Standard Book Number: 0-12-109891-5

PRINTED IN THE UNITED STATES OF AMERICA

Contents

3 Household Saving in Germany

Axel Börsch-Supan, Anette Reil-Held and Reinhold Schnabel

4 Household Saving Behavior and Pension Policies in Italy

Agar Brugiavini and Mario Padula

5 Household Savings and Wealth Distribution in Japan

Yukinobu Kitamura, Noriyuki Takayama, and Fumiko Arita

6   *Savings and Pensions in the Netherlands*

Rob Alessie and Arie Kapteyn

7   *Pensions and Life-Cycle Savings Profiles in the UK*

James Banks and Susann Rohwedder

8   *Household Saving Behavior and Pension Policies in the United States*

Orazio P. Attanasio and Monica Paiella

Contributors

Numbers in parentheses indicate pages on which the authors' contributions begin.

Rob Alessie (205)
Department of Economics
Free University Amsterdam
Amsterdam
The Netherlands

Fumiko Arita (149)
Department of International
    Social Science
Toyo Eiwa Women's University
Yokohama
Japan

Orazio P. Attanasio (315)
University College
London
and
Institute for Fiscal Studies
London
UK

James Banks (257)
Institute for Fiscal Studies
London
UK

Axel Börsch-Supan (1, 57)
Mannheim Research Institute for the
    Economics of Aging (MEA)
Universität Mannheim
Mannheim
Germany
and
National Bureau of Economic Research
    (NBER)
Cambridge, Massachusetts
USA

Agar Brugiavini (33, 101)
Departimento di Economia
Università Ca'Foscari di Venezia
Venezia
Italy

Arie Kapteyn (205)
RAND Corporation
Santa Monica
California
USA

Yukinobu Kitamura (149)
Institute of Economic Research
Hitotsubashi University
Tokyo
Japan

Annamaria Lusardi (1)
Department of Economics
Dartmouth College
Hanover
New Hampshire
USA

Mario Padula (101)
CSEF – Department of Economics
  and Statistics
Università di Salerno
Fisciano (SA)
Italy

Monica Paiella (315)
Ufficio Studi
Banca d'Italia
Roma
Italy

Anette Reil-Held (57)
Mannheim Research Institute for the
  Economics of Aging
Universität Mannheim
Mannheim
Germany

Susann Rohwedder (257)
RAND Corporation
Santa Monica
California
USA

Reinhold Schnabel (57)
Fachbereich Wirtschaftswissenschaften
Universität Essen
Essen
Germany

Noriyuki Takayama (149)
Institute of Economic Research
Hitotsubashi University
Tokyo
Japan

Guglielmo Weber (33)
Department of Economics
University of Padova
Padova
Italy

Preface

Saving remains an elusive topic. Saving behavior encompasses not only the sober economic thinking by perfectly informed planners but also (often only seemingly) unstructured reactions deeply rooted in human psychology and socio-cultural norms. These reactions, whether soberly planned or driven by intuition and conventions, are shaped by the institutional and political environment, notably the social safety net, tax rules and capital market regulations. This book acknowledges and exploits this: It compares saving behavior in six countries shaped by very different pension, tax and capital market policies.

It is therefore not by chance that the "International Saving Comparisons Project", on which this book is based upon, is an offspring of a Training and Mobility of Researchers' network sponsored by the European Union, led by Arie Kapteyn, and devoted to "Structural Analysis of Household Savings and Wealth Positions over the Life Cycle" (code ERBFMRXCT960016). We are grateful for the financial support by the European Union. It has sparked – so far – four years of intensive cooperation; certainly a success story of an open minded and therefore fruitful research and teaching cooperation.

This book was a major effort in data preparation. It needed more endurance and resilience than anticipated. Quite a few research assistants have spent long days (and some nights) on a host of data sets. Some have become co-authors. We are grateful to all of them and appreciate their hard work. Stefan Hoderlein in Mannheim has supervised the final production of this book. I owe him many thanks for the tedious work. Scott Bentley from Academic Press and Stuart Giblin from Keyword Publishing Services Ltd have accompanied and produced this project with patience and good humor – which was at times necessary in our group of typical academics. We appreciate their efforts.

Axel Börsch-Supan

CHAPTER 1

Saving: A Cross-National Perspective

Axel Börsch-Supan

Mannheim Research Institute for the Economics of Aging (MEA), University of Mannheim, Germany, and National Bureau of Economic Research (NBER), Cambridge, Massachusetts

Annamaria Lusardi

Department of Economics, Dartmouth College, Hanover, New Hampshire

1.1 INTRODUCTION

Household saving is still little understood, and even the basic facts – for instance: How does saving change over the life cycle? Does saving turn negative in old age? – are controversial. Understanding saving behavior is not only an important question of economic theory because the division of income in consumption and saving concerns one of the most fundamental household decisions but is also of utmost policy relevance. One reason is that private household saving as a private insurance interacts with social policy as public insurance. Population aging and its threat to the sustainability of the public insurance systems have put the spotlight back on own saving as a device for old-age provision. Solving the pension crises therefore requires understanding saving. Another reason is growth: capital accumulation through saving increases economic growth directly, and indirectly through changes in labor productivity.

The topic of household savings is by no means uncharted territory. Recent comprehensive surveys of the work on saving include Deaton (1992), Browning and Lusardi (1996), and Attanasio (1999). These surveys illustrate the many challenges the theory faces in matching the empirical facts about saving as well as the need to use micro data to understand saving behavior.

This volume adds a distinctive international dimension to these studies of saving. It presents the results of the "International Savings Comparison Project" – a project performed under the auspices of a European Union sponsored network of researchers.[1] The main focus of this project is the interaction of household saving with public policy, notably the generosity of public pension systems. In this sense, our work is very much in the tradition of Feldstein's (1974) seminal study. However, we transpose the inference from time series data to a set of international panel data drawn from six country studies. These studies analyze household saving in four European countries – Germany, Italy, the Netherlands, and the United Kingdom – and in Japan and the United States.

1.2 THE VALUE OF CROSS-NATIONAL COMPARISONS

The cross-national aspect of this volume is important. The synthesis of the six country studies – this is the conviction underlying this book – is far more than the sum of the parts. The reason for this conviction is the insight that we can learn from observing and exploiting differences. Hence, understanding saving behavior requires differences in the determinants of saving, including household size and composition, age, lifetime income, and many other variables at the household level, plus the influence of public policy, such as the structure of the pension system and the general social safety net, plus capital market features. Although we generally observe a large variation in household-level variables, studies within a single country often lack the necessary variation in public policies and institutional background.[2] This is most germane for cross-sectional data from a single country, which often fail to have any policy variation. Hence, little can be learned about the impact of public policy on savings because the counterfactual is missing.

Traditional studies of household saving, such as Feldstein (1974) for the United States and Kim (1992) for Germany, have therefore exploited the time-series

---

[1] The TMR (Training and Mobility of Researchers') network on "Structural Analysis of Household Savings and Wealth Positions over the Life Cycle."

[2] As notable exceptions, see Attanasio and Rohwedder (2001) and the references therein.

variation in aggregate data. Such studies, however, cannot really account for changes in the composition of a heterogeneous population. One obvious solution is to use panel data, which combine the cross-sectional variation within a country with the time-series variation of that country. Unfortunately, however, national panel data sets that contain saving data are usually short and therefore rarely include sufficient policy changes and "historical experiments." This particularly applies to one potentially very important determinant of saving: namely, public pension policy. For good reasons, pension systems are not changed frequently, and short national panel data will not identify the impact of public pensions on saving with sufficient precision. The main idea behind the International Savings Comparison Project is to exploit cross-national differences that provide an additional source of variation in policy variables because countries have substantially different social policies, capital taxation regimes, etc.[3]

Whereas the benefits of comparative international research for policymaking become increasingly clear, the conduct of such research poses a number of challenges. The basic challenges for cross-national research are the development of research questions and designs that can be readily adapted to different social and cultural settings, and the harmonization of concepts and measures that provide a reasonably acceptable level of cross-national comparability. Up to now, there is little coordination of data collection and analysis across countries. Whereas recent decades have seen heightened sensitivity to, and substantial technical advances in, the validation of measures in different cultural settings, many problems remain, and we have encountered many such challenges in this project. Data on the same variable or process may differ in myriad small ways. The analysis of data without shared protocols can easily lead to misleading conclusions. This project therefore spent considerable effort in harmonizing the measurement and analysis of household saving. Indeed, we believe that one of the valuable outcomes of this project is the provision of statistics and data that can be compared across countries and that can be used by other researchers.[4]

This volume is in the tradition of earlier cross-national studies, and we are happy that we can leverage earlier work to new connections and insights. Particularly noteworthy are the age–saving profiles for the G-7 countries (except France) that have been presented in the volume edited by Poterba (1994), which analyses savings data from the mid-1970s through the mid-1980s. Almost in parallel to this cross-national study of household savings, a cross-national study of household portfolio choice and stock holdings has been completed (see Guiso *et al.*, 2001). The analyses in these two volumes nicely complement our studies of household savings, and we draw some of the institutional descriptions from their work, in particular descriptions of capital taxation and saving subsidies. Kapteyn and Panis

---

[3]The various aspects of the power of cross-national comparisons are discussed in National Research Council (2001).

[4]The data are available in tabular form by age category at www.mea.uni-mannheim.de/iscp

(2002), very much in parallel to this project, compare Italy, the Netherlands, and the United States in terms of household saving.

We have also been inspired by the cross-national analysis of pension policies in the volume edited by Gruber and Wise (1999). Their analyses are a particularly good example of the power of cross-national comparisons, relating labor force partici- pation of older persons to the incentives in the pension systems to retire early. In addition to the general philosophy, our volume also draws from the institutional descriptions of the pension systems contained in Gruber and Wise (1999).

Several other international comparisons help us to augment such institutional background data. There are several studies on the sources of retirement income, which provide summary data on the generosity of public pension systems, the relative size of pay-as-you-go and funded pillars, and similar system parameters. Most notable is the OECD-commissioned study edited by Disney et al. (1998) and the follow-up study by Disney and Johnson (2001). Health insurance coverage, the second major piece of the savings-related safety net, is documented in the OECD Health Data (2001), and we use a host of other data compiled by the OECD for background information on social expenditures and capital market features.

1.3 THE IMPORTANCE OF PANEL DATA

The research pursued in this volume departs from previous projects in several ways. For example, not only do we try to get data on wealth and saving which are comparable across countries but we also use different measures of saving and devote much atten- tion to the methodological issues involved in studying saving.[5] Most importantly, we try to purge the age–wealth and age–saving profiles from cohort effects exploit- ing the longitudinal dimension of our data sets. This cohort correction is extremely important because apparent life-cycle effects in cross-sectional data are severely con- founded by changes from cohort to cohort. Researchers looking at cross-sectional data may only learn very little about the behavior of saving over the life cycle.

This point is quite vividly shown by the sequence of Figures 1.1 through 1.3, taken from an earlier version of the German country study. Figure 1.1 begins with a set of conventional cross-sectional age–wealth profiles. Each of the four cross sections appears to depict a hump shape, quickly increasing between age 25 and 50, reaching a peak around age 50, and then slowly declining.

Saving behavior, however, does not only change by age, but also from cohort to cohort. Younger cohorts have experienced peace and stability, whereas the cohorts that are now in retirement have lived through one or even two World Wars and the Great Depression. In addition, cohorts have been exposed to different changes in the pension system and some of them lived in a period without any social security (see Alessie et al., 1998). Cohorts have also been exposed to different rates of

[5]See, in particular, the first chapter of the book by Brugiavini and Weber (2001).

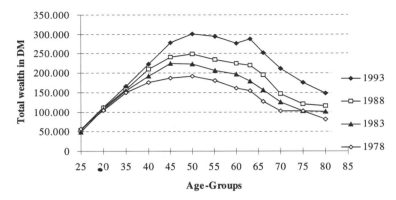

FIGURE 1.1   Wealth by cross section. *Notes and source:* See Chapter 3. All amounts in 1993 DM. 1 DM in 1993 corresponds to a purchasing power of 0.57 Euro in 2001.

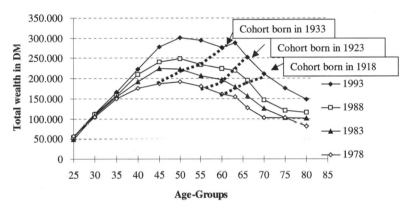

FIGURE 1.2   Age and cohort-time effects in wealth. *Notes and sources:* See Figure 1.1.

productivity growth and to different conditions in the real estate market or the stock market.

Household saving, moreover, reacts to the business cycle and similar factors at any given point in time. Thus, in addition to age and cohort effects, there are also time effects to be taken into account. One of the great challenges of saving research is to distinguish these effects.

In Figure 1.1, each age category also represents a cohort. Comparing points on one of the cross-sectional lines drawn in Figure 1.1 does not depict life-cycle changes since one compares households that are simultaneously in different age categories and cohorts. Hence, the apparent hump shape of wealth in Figure 1.1 is a combination of age, time, and cohort effects, not the life-cycle change created by age. A better approximation of life-cycle effects is to compare the 45- to 49-year-old persons in 1978 with the 50- to 54-year-old persons in 1983 (i.e., follow individuals

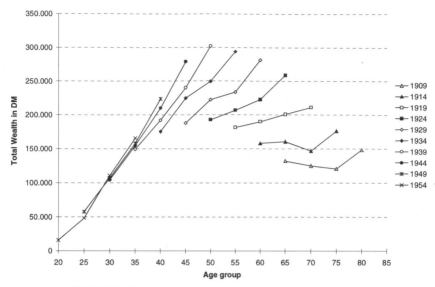

FIGURE 1.3   Wealth by cohorts. *Notes and sources:* See Figure 1.1.

of similar age over time), the 55- to 59-year-old persons in 1988, and the 60- to 64-year-old persons in 1993, and so forth. This procedure amounts to reconnecting the points of Figure 1.1 in a different fashion (see Figure 1.2) and identifies changes over time of a given cohort with life-cycle changes. Technically speaking, this procedure assumes the time effects away, and therefore this identification assumption ignores that not all changes over time for a given cohort are life-cycle changes – some may be changes in the economic and social environment that affect all ages and all cohorts at the same calendar time. There are several more sophisticated methods to separate age, cohort, and calendar-time specific effects (some of them are discussed in Chapter 2), but Figure 1.2 suffices to make a crucial point: cross-sectional data may be grossly misleading in the analysis of life-cycle savings behavior.[6] Rather than being hump-shaped, wealth steadily increases with age even after retirement, which is, on average, just before age 60 in Germany.

This finding comes out even more clearly in Figure 1.3, which simplifies Figure 1.2 by extracting only the dotted lines. Based on the assumption of no time effects, it depicts the life-cycle profiles of wealth by cohorts, starting at the left side with the youngest cohort in our data, born between 1954 and 1958, and proceeding to the oldest cohort, born between 1909 and 1913.

The lesson of this exercise is that there are strong differences between the shape of the life-cycle savings profile drawn from cross-sectional and panel data. The cohort-corrected profiles in Figure 1.3 leave nothing of the apparent hump shape

---

[6]See also the approaches by Deaton (1985), Attanasio (1994), Deaton and Paxson (1994), and Alessie *et al.* (1998).

that was suggested by the cross-sectional data in Figure 1.1. All age profiles mono-tonically increase with age, except a little blip among the very old. In addition, we see that each consecutive cohort has accumulated slightly higher wealth levels. It is therefore crucial to analyze saving behavior using panel data. Some of the countries in this study provide genuine panel data of household saving; for other countries, we have to resort to Deaton's (1985) methodology and create synthetic panel data from repeated cross sections.

1.4   A TYPICAL PITFALL IN THE ANALYSIS OF CROSS-NATIONAL SAVING BEHAVIOR

The fact that life-cycle saving patterns are the primary object of analysis in this book also points to a challenge for this cross-national analysis of saving. The already-mentioned cross-national analysis of pension policies by Gruber and Wise (1999) produced a truly amazing outcome: namely, a very tight correlation between an aggregated measure of old-age labor force participation and a summary measure of early retirement incentives. In that study, it was relatively easy to identify the reasons for the differences in retirement age across countries.

Saving, however, appears to be a much more complex subject than labor force participation. One of the reasons is that there are many motives for saving. Thus, the decision to save depends on a large set of determinants, all of which can vary across countries. Saving for retirement is certainly an important motive, but it is not the only one, and we should not expect a simple alignment of national saving rates with the generosity of national public pension systems, as a naïve and quick interpretation of Feldstein's substitution hypothesis would predict. Among the motives to save that have been suggested by many researchers are the precautionary and the bequest motives. Most importantly, these and other motives to save interact and are affected by the degrees of imperfections in the financial and insurance markets and by public policies.

We will discuss this multitude of motives and determinants in more detail later when we review what an extended model of life-cycle saving can teach us. Let us consider just one of these other determinants – the degree of imperfections in financial markets – in order to demonstrate that, without properly accounting for other saving determinants, one can easily jump to the wrong conclusions. Table 1.1 shows aggregate household saving rates in our six countries together with two other aggregate statistics: the replacement rates of these countries' public pension systems at their average retirement ages and the average down payment required to buy a house in the time period under consideration – a rough measure of financial market imperfections.

Figure 1.4 shows that the simple correlation between saving and the replace-ment rate of pension is positive, not negative as predicted by Feldstein's (1974) substitution hypothesis. This simple *positive* correlation is often used as an argument

TABLE 1.1   Saving Rates, Replacement Rates, and Down-payment Ratios

	Germany	Italy	Japan	Netherlands	United Kingdom	United States
Saving rate	10.1	12.7	13.1	10.6	6.2	2.4
Replacement rate	66.8	86.3	56.8	50.2	27.2	39.6
Down-payment ratio	35	50	35	25	19	20

Sources: Household saving rates: OECD Economic Outlook (2001). Replacement rates of public pension at average retirement age: OECD Ageing and Income (2001; Table A10, p. 172). Down-payment ratios for owner-occupied housing: Chiuri and Jappelli (2000).

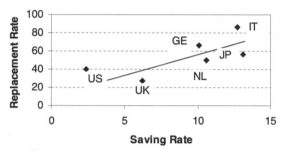

FIGURE 1.4   Saving rates and replacement rates. *Sources*: See Table 1.1.

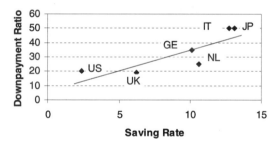

FIGURE 1.5   Saving rates and down-payment ratios. *Sources*: See Table 1.1.

against funded pension systems.[7] Saving, however, is not only influenced by the tightness of the social safety net, represented here by the replacement rate of the public pension system, but also by the degree of imperfections in financial markets, represented in Figure 1.5 by the down-payment ratio.

Figure 1.5 shows two important facts. First, down-payment requirements are correlated with saving rates. Countries which have less-developed financial markets

[7]Examples are statements found regularly in European newspapers such as "funded pensions depress rather than encourage saving as the comparison of saving rates between continental European and Anglo-Saxon countries shows."

TABLE 1.2   Regression[a] of Saving Rate on Replacement Rate and Down-payment Ratio

	Coefficient	Standard error	t-Statistic
Replacement rate	−0.148	0.265	0.56
Down-payment ratio	5.18	4.68	1.11
Constant	10.3	40.1	0.26

[a]This regression has only 4 degrees of freedom. The R-squared is 0.63, and the adjusted R-squared is 0.38.

also display higher saving rates, a finding documented in several other studies on saving.[8] Secondly, down-payment ratios and replacement rates show a very similar pattern across countries, so much so that Figures 1.4 and 1.5 are almost identical. Hence, both bivariate correlations are deceiving due to missing variable bias.

Unfortunately, we have only six countries in our study, which is too few for a proper multidimensional analysis. Accounting for the down-payment requirement in a trivariate regression that has both the replacement rate and the down-payment ratio as explanatory variables provides a hint of how treacherous the bivariate correlation in Figure 1.4 is: it turns the sign of the relation between the saving rate and the generosity of the public pension system from a positive into a negative one, now conforming to Feldstein's crowding-out hypothesis (Table 1.2).

Quite clearly, with only six countries in our sample, we have too few degrees of freedom in this regression to obtain significance. Thus, this exercise is simply a suggestive one. The challenge of this book is to go deeper and to study life-cycle saving patterns rather than cross-sectional snapshots. In addition, we aim to account for the many determinants of saving by using micro data rather than aggregate statistics.

1.5 GOALS OF THIS BOOK

Although the main goals of this book are to collect and to analyze data on saving across countries, our work is guided by the theoretical work on saving originating in Modigliani and Brumberg (1954) and Friedman (1957) and some of its extensions which incorporate other motives to save and make the standard textbook life-cycle model more realistic – see Browning and Lusardi (1996) for a review.

It is important to incorporate uncertainty in income and in other aspects of life, notably in health and, even more fundamental, in the length of life. It is also important to recognize that insurance markets are imperfect and that constraints abound in financial markets. Thus, the possibilities of shifting resources over time is often rather limited. What we particularly would like to take into account is the fact that countries have long recognized the importance of saving for retirement and institutionalized it by devising social security and pension systems designed to provide income support after retirement. In addition, many countries have adopted policies that aim to encourage saving: for example, via tax incentives or education policies.

Ideally, we would estimate a structural model of such an extended life-cycle model of saving as a function of pension policies, tax rules, and all the other many determinants of saving at the household level. While estimating such a dynamic life-cycle optimization model on cross-national data is not a realistic goal for this International Savings Comparison Project, our work has been guided by such a frame of thinking.

More modestly, this volume fulfils two tasks. The first is descriptive: the country chapters (Chapters 3–8) collect the main saving measures by age and cohort, subject to a common treatment of time effects and a common definition of the various saving components. This provides very valuable data, which we make available to other researchers and/or policymakers. The second task is interpretation: we will try to link saving patterns to country-specific policies, such as pension policies, other parts of the social safety net, financial market features, and capital taxation.

1.6 MEASURING LIFE-CYCLE SAVING

The first task of measuring saving in each stage of the life cycle is based on the definitions and procedures described in Chapter 2. Each country team collected data on saving and related measures according to a tightly specified "template." Although these accounting definitions may appear tedious, they are a crucial necessity for a meaningful cross-national comparison.

In principle, there are three different ways of measuring saving:

- by comparing asset holdings at the beginning and at the end of a period;
- by adding inflows and outflows of wealth accounts during one period;
- by taking the difference between income and consumption expenditures in a period.

There are several measurement issues to deal with when examining saving; for example, should wealth and income incorporate unrealized capital gains? Which measure is more appropriate to use depends ultimately on the research question under consideration, but also data availability. Given that our focus is to study life-cycle saving, all resources that can be used to support households over the life cycle are relevant for our analysis. We will therefore work with the most comprehensive measure of saving which differs from aggregate statistics from the national income and product accounts that exclude many components of saving, most notably, unrealized capital gains on assets.

To measure and study saving behavior, when possible, we distinguish between active and passive saving. *Passive saving* is capital gains that are automatically reinvested – the most salient example is the increase in assets value due to stock market appreciation. *Active saving* is everything else. Of particular importance for our analysis of household saving behavior is another distinction: discretionary versus mandatory saving. *Discretionary saving* is completely under the control of the households. Households choose its value as well as its portfolio composition, given their budget constraints and applicable incentives, such as tax relief and mandatory contributions to funded and unfunded pension schemes. In turn, *mandatory saving* is beyond the control of the household. The most important example is mandatory contributions to funded occupational pension plans. Here, the volume is prescribed (e.g., a fixed absolute sum or a fixed percentage of gross income) and frequently even the portfolio composition is outside the control of the household (e.g., the employer provides workers with a single pension plan). Where possible, we also distinguish between *financial* and *real saving*.

A broader definition of saving also includes the addition of claims on unfunded pension benefits (Jappelli and Modigliani, 1998). Under such a broad view, contributions to pay-as-you-go financed pension schemes are considered as saving. We will use the term "*notional saving*" for these contributions although we are aware that the term "saving" may be confusing since these contributions do not contribute to the physical capital stock. Consequently, receiving pension benefits is "*notional dissaving*," and the current present value of pension benefit claims is dubbed "*notional wealth*," "*unfunded pension wealth*," or "*social security wealth*."

In practice, not only definitional but also measurement issues are extremely difficult, in particular when considering micro data. It is well known that wealth, consumption, and income data are severely affected by measurement error and taking first differences (as when using wealth) makes the measurement error problem even more dramatic. Econometric techniques have to be chosen wisely when examining saving data, even though data limitation is often a major constraint. Although we would like to report all three measures of saving in order to learn how reliable our measurements are, the data sources available to the six country studies do not allow this. In many countries, only two measures can be computed, in some countries only one. Frequently, capital gains are not measured or have to be imputed using data on rates of return that are likely to produce additional measurement error.

As an illustration of the serious problems we face when calculating saving data, Table 1.3 reports the saving rate in the United States calculated from three different data sets: the Consumer Expenditure Survey (CEX), the Panel Study of Income Dynamics (PSID), and the Survey of Consumer Finances (SCF). Whereas saving is calculated subtracting consumption from income when using CEX data, saving is calculated by first differencing wealth when using PSID and SCF data.

Differences among data sets are startling. First, saving rates are much higher when using the CEX than the other two data sets. This has to do with a plurality of reasons: measures of income and consumption considered in the calculation; the severity of

TABLE 1.3   Household Saving Rates in the United States

	CEX 1982–89 Y−C	SCF 1983–89 ΔWealth	PSID 1984–89 ΔWealth	PSID 1984–89 Active
Age 30–39				
Median	0.27	0.05	0.04	0.04
Mean	0.30	0.03	0.17	0.15
Age 40–49				
Median	0.26	0.08	0.03	0.04
Mean	0.30	0.29	0.33	0.15
Age 50–59				
Median	0.26	0.05	0.07	0.04
Mean	0.30	0.24	0.32	0.11
All ages				
Mean	0.25	0.18	0.17	0.08
National income and product accounts for corresponding period	*0.09*	*0.09*	*0.08*	*0.08*

Source: Dynan *et al.* (2002).

measurement error, in particular in the income data in the CEX; and differences in survey design and selectivity of the chosen samples. Secondly, active saving is a large proportion of total saving among the young, but at older ages, when it is more likely that household portfolios include stocks and housing, passive saving becomes also important. This highlights the importance of unrealized capital gains in deriving saving. Thirdly, as already mentioned before, saving measures calculated from micro data do not match well with aggregate statistics. For the United States, saving from the national income and product accounts (NIPA) is much lower than reported in the CEX, PSID, and SCF. Again, this has much to do with the fact that NIPA saving does not include unrealized capital gains on existing assets.[9]

The various saving measures and their components are displayed in graphical form in Chapters 3–8. In addition, the data are available on our internet site.[10] This internet site represents a machine-readable appendix to this volume that enables readers to generate alternative specifications of saving aggregates and to apply alternative assumptions for the separation of age, cohort, and time effects in saving behavior. The saving data is augmented by summary data on pension systems and other national policies.

[9]See also the discussion of saving measures in the United States in Lusardi *et al.* (2001).
[10]The URL of this site is www.mea.uni-mannheim.de/iscp

The data were collected to analyze our main working hypothesis, namely that a major part of the differences in the age–saving patterns observed across European countries, Japan, and the United States is generated by differences in national policies. The main results are summarized in the sequel of this introduction. We begin by collecting the main results from economic theory, and then structure the sequel by three questions:

- What are the main institutional differences across the six countries in our study and what do they imply in light of the extended life-cycle theory of saving?
- What do we observe empirically?
- Are these observations consistent with the predictions of extended life-cycle models of saving?

1.7   WHAT DOES AN EXTENDED LIFE-CYCLE MODEL OF SAVING PREDICT?

As mentioned previously, our point of departure is the traditional life-cycle model by Modigliani and Brumberg (1954) and Friedman (1957). The main saving motive in this model is consumption smoothing due to a declining marginal utility of consumption, and the fact that income after retirement is generally lower than before. The resulting textbook life-cycle profile of saving is well-known and illustrated for convenience in Figure 1.6. With relatively low earnings at the beginning of the career, consumption is smoothened by borrowing (via financial markets or a loan from the family) (area A). Increasing earnings makes saving possible (area B), which is then decumulated after retirement (area C).

This profile, however, rests on a large number of simplifying assumptions that do not fit many of the institutional peculiarities present in the countries we consider in this volume. For example, the introduction of uncertainty and market imperfections changes the simple predictions of the simple life-cycle model in a substantial

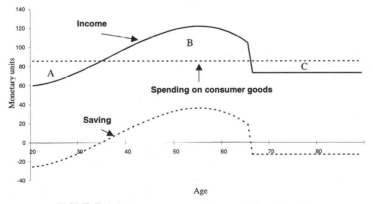

FIGURE 1.6   Income, consumption, and life-cycle saving.

way. Much can be gained by considering more realistic features of the economy, and in particular by capturing features that vary across countries.

As a first example, mentioned before, we note that borrowing constraints are likely to prevent young households from smoothing consumption before the symbolic age of 35 in Figure 1.6 (see Jappelli and Pagano, 1989, 1994; Alessie *et al.*, 1997). Thus, one needs to model more complex budget constraints than the simple intertemporal one that is underlying Figure 1.6. We also would expect higher saving rates (especially at younger ages) in countries with more stringent borrowing constraints.

Figure 1.6 assumes that the time of death is known for the life-cycle computation. In fact, there is uncertainty about the time of death (see Davies, 1981; Rodepeter and Winter, 1998). In addition, there is a great deal of income uncertainty over the life course. Thus, saving not only serves to offset the decline of income after retirement but also to shield households against shocks to income (see Deaton, 1992, Chapter 6; Caballero, 1990; Carroll, 1994, 1997; Zeldes, 1989). Uncertainty becomes particularly relevant when households face borrowing constraints (see Deaton, 1991), so there is often an interaction between uncertainty and imperfections in financial markets. Individuals face uncertainty not only in income and in the length of life but also in all kinds of future economic circumstances: for example, in the size of health costs they may face, in particular in old age (see Palumbo, 1999; Hubbard *et al.*, 1995; Kennickell and Lusardi, 2001). Thus, there exists a precautionary motive to save and not just a retirement motive. Countries with a higher degree of uncertainty in income and other future economic circumstances will feature higher saving rates in the presence of a precautionary saving motive.

Probably because of the pervasiveness of uncertainty and imperfections in the insurance and financial markets, there exist public and social safety nets. These safety nets may in turn replace the need for savings, for example by reducing the gap between earned and actual income that needs to be filled in Figure 1.6 and by insuring against shocks. Countries with a high replacement of earnings by pension annuities are therefore likely to feature lower wealth at retirement, and less decumulation of wealth after retirement. Similarly, the increased annuitization of wealth because of the growing importance of social security and pensions during the last two to three generations is likely to have reduced the amount of precautionary savings (see Browning and Lusardi, 1996, and the references therein).

The same logic holds for unemployment benefits (see Engen and Gruber, 2001; Lusardi, 1998) and other welfare policies (see Hubbard *et al.*, 1995), which aim to reduce changes and shocks to lifetime income. In addition to public safety nets, individuals may also rely on the network of relatives and friends to offset shocks (see Lusardi, 2000). Such informal borrowing opportunities may replace formal capital market interactions and reduce further the need to save.

There are more cross-national differences than those cast into institutions. Anybody working with micro data recognizes the extent of heterogeneity in household behavior and the importance of modeling differences in individual preferences. Some of the preference parameters, such as the degree of risk aversion and the willingness to substitute consumption over time, play a pivotal role in affecting saving decisions. It is certainly restrictive to assume that these preferences do not change across individuals and across countries.

Individuals may, for instance, differ in the extent they care about their children and, more generally, for future generations and thus in the strength of their bequest motive. We expect countries with a more pronounced bequest motive to accumulate higher wealth at retirement than countries with a less pronounced bequest motive. It has been hard, however, to assess empirically the strength of this motive, as the fact that wealth is left over at the end of life and the existence of transfers per se does not necessarily mean that one generation cares for the next. Bequest can be accidental (Davies, 1981; Abel, 1985), strategic (Bernheim et al., 1985) or the result of decreased consumption due to an unexpected deterioration of health (Börsch-Supan and Stahl, 1991b). The existence and strength of a bequest motive is, in turn, critically important to evaluate the effects of public policies on saving. For example, the increased annuitization of wealth through social security is likely to reduce accidental bequests.

Furthermore, households may be more short-sighted than modeled by traditional models of saving, and this tendency may vary across countries. For example, households may display varying rates of impatience (see Lawrence, 1991; Carroll, 1992). They may also have preferences that are inconsistent over time because they lack self-control, and therefore procrastinate saving (see Thaler and Shefrin, 1981; Laibson, 1997; O'Donoghue and Rabin, 1999a, 1999b). In addition, households may simply lack financial literacy and information on the many variables that are needed to make saving plans for the future and face high planning costs and/or limited opportunities to overcome these costs (see Bernheim, 1995, 1998; Lusardi, 2001). Such planning restrictions have become particularly apparent in countries like the United States, where there has been much discussion about privatizing social security and where firms have increasingly shifted from defined benefits to defined contribution pension plans. We have little data on informational differences across countries. In recent years, particularly in the UK and the United States, firms have become concerned about the amount of information, literacy, and planning skills of workers. Many firms, in particular large ones, have started offering retirement seminars to their workers and there is some evidence that this type of financial education has an impact on saving (see Bernheim and Garrett, 1999).

The lack of data that permit researchers to compare preferences across countries forces us to leave those differences in the residuals. Nevertheless, since many of the deviations from Modigliani–Friedman's idealized world are observable and do vary across countries, cross-national comparisons help us to identify their impact on saving behavior. We now review these major observable differences among the countries considered in this volume and then examine how these differences affect saving behavior.

1.8 SOME INSTITUTIONAL DIFFERENCES ACROSS COUNTRIES AND WHAT THEY MEAN FOR SAVING

We begin with the institutional environment, since this is our main interest, and then add general statistics on income and demographics. Table 1.4 shows that among the six countries under consideration, Italy has the most generous social security system, which is essentially pay-as-you-go. It has both a very early retirement age and a rather high replacement rate. Pay-as-you-go systems also dominate retirement income in Germany and Japan. Social security benefits in the United States are less generous than in the preceding three countries, but all four countries have earnings-related benefits: this is different in the UK and in the Netherlands, where the basic pension is flat. In the Netherlands, all earnings-related retirement income comes as private sector savings, mostly as occupational pensions. In the UK, the situation is complicated since the long string of pension reforms has generated large differences across cohorts. The older cohorts have earnings-related public pensions on top of their basic state pension, resembling the US Social Security system, while the younger cohorts have occupational pensions, resembling the Dutch pension system.

The needs to fill income gaps after retirement with private pensions is much larger in the United States and the UK than in Italy and Germany, since the former have much lower public pension replacement rates than the latter. This is the core of Feldstein's (1974) argument. All other things equal, we would therefore expect the United States and the UK to have a more pronounced hump-shaped life-cycle saving profile than Italy or Germany.

TABLE 1.4   Pension Systems

	Germany	Italy	Japan	Netherlands	UK	USA
Public pension spending as percentage of GDP (1999)	11.8	14.2	7.9	5.2	4.3	4.4
Replacement rate of public pension at average retirement age (1998)	66.8	86.3	56.8	50.2	27.2	39.6
Average retirement age (1998)	60.3	58.8	68.5	60.4	62.6	64.6
Percent of workers covered by occupational pensions (mostly 1998)	46	5	50	91	46	45
Financial assets of pension funds as percentage of GDP (1998)	3.3	3.2	18.9	106.1	83.7	86.4
Average public pension income as percent of total pension income (1998)	94.5	94.7	96.3	48.9	42.6	58.8

Sources: OECD Ageing and Income (2001).

TABLE 1.5   Health Care Systems

	Germany	Italy	Japan	Netherlands	UK	USA
Health care spending as percentage of GDP (1998)	10.3	8.2	7.4	8.7	6.8	12.9
Public health care spending as percent of total health care spending (1998)	75.8	67.3	78.5	68.6	83.3	44.8
Percent of households covered by public health insurance (1997)	92.2	100	100	74.6	100	45.0
Private health care spending as percentage of GDP (1998)	2.5	2.7	1.6	2.7	1.1	7.1
Male potential years of life lost per 100,000 males and females (1997)	5500	4860	4000	4300	4900	6850

Sources: OECD Health Data (2001).

As shown in Table 1.4, pension fund assets – savings in the economic sense – are much higher in the Netherlands, the UK and the United States than in Germany, Italy and Japan, where most retirement income is pay-as-you-go.

In turn, the possibility of retiring at a very early age, which the public pension systems in countries such as Italy provide and even encourage (Gruber and Wise, 1999), is likely to increase savings before and wealth at retirement age.

Countries also differ in their exposure to risk: for example, unemployment risk and, more generally, income risk, as well as longevity and health risk, just to mention some of the important sources. More income uncertainty increases savings in the early and medium age ranges, and increases dissaving at old age, holding all other determinants constant (see, among others, Rodepeter and Winter, 1998).

Some of the largest uncertainties in life concern health shocks. Some countries, such as the United States, do not have a national health system and a considerable share of their population does not have public health insurance coverage (see Table 1.5). The average size of out-of-pocket health costs is quite different among the six countries and again the United States displays a high average cost for medical expenses that individuals have to pay. Measured relative to GDP, Americans have to pay more than 7% of GDP as private health expenditures, while the figure is about 1% in the UK. Given this coverage, we would expect that US households save more for health reasons than households in the other countries, notably in the UK. Interestingly, health risks as measured by "potential years of life lost" (i.e., the number of life years lost due to death before age 70 among male residents in each country) are substantially higher in the United States and Germany than in the other countries, supposedly reducing lifetime resources and amplifying the need for precautionary saving for surviving spouses and other family members, all other things equal.

Other important risks are unemployment and, more generally, poverty. While the United States, the UK, and Italy offer a relatively low replacement rate for

TABLE 1.6   Other Social Safety Nets

	Germany	Italy	Japan	Netherlands	UK	USA
Unemployment compensation spending as percentage of GDP (1998)	1.32	0.71	0.50	2.60	0.32	0.25
Unemployment rate (1999)	8.6	11.3	4.7	3.3	6.1	4.2
Replacement rate of unemployment insurance (single person/married couple, two children)	60/73	36/54	63/59	75/85	50/64	60/61
Maximum duration of unemployment compensation (1998)	32 months[a]	6 months	n.a.	5 years	1 year	26 weeks
Percent of households below OECD poverty line (1993)[b]	9.7	18.4	n.a.	11.2	9.1	22.1

Sources: OECD Economic Outlook (various issues), OECD Employment Outlook (various issues), OECD Benefit Systems and Work Incentives (1997), OECD Social Expenditures (various issues).

[a]After 7 years of work experience.

[b]Earning less than 2/3 of median earnings.

unemployment benefits, countries such as the Netherlands and Germany offer a rather generous unemployment insurance scheme (see Table 1.6). Replacement rates are only one part of the story. In addition, the probability of entering unemployment is rather different across countries. Thus, whereas the United States has the lowest unemployment rate, it has nevertheless the highest percentage of population below the poverty line.

It is difficult to measure the overall income risk, not to mention comparing it across countries. Several innovations, however, have been made in the data available in some of the countries under consideration. For example, Italy, the Netherlands, and the United States all have surveys that report subjective expectations of future changes in income from which it is also possible to derive a subjective measure of the variation in income. Das and Donkers (1999) have compared these subjective measures across these three countries and found that the perceived variation in income is higher in the United States than in Italy and the Netherlands. Thus, precautionary motives for saving caused by income risks should be higher in the United States than in the two European countries.

Compared with Germany and Italy, the Netherlands, the United States, and Japan are wealthier in terms of per capita GDP, while the UK has the lowest GDP per capita (Table 1.7). Whereas wealthier individuals tend to have a higher saving rate than poorer ones, this does not necessarily translate to the aggregate. An offsetting effect, for instance, comes through the income distribution, which is more unequal in the United States than in countries such as the Netherlands (Table 1.7).

TABLE 1.7   Income, Income Distribution, and Income Uncertainty

	Germany	Italy	Japan	Netherlands	UK	USA
GDP per capita worker in US$ at PPP (2000)	24,900	24,500	25,600	27,500	23,900	30,600
Earnings of average production worker in US$ at PPP (1998)	29,600	24,000	25,800	27,800	26,600	29,100
Income distribution (Gini coefficient for disposable income)	28.2	34.5	26.0	25.5	32.4	34.4
Income uncertainty	Low	Low	n.a.	Low	n.a.	High

Source: Own calculations based on OECD Economic Outlook (2001). Income distribution: OECD Economic Outlook (1997) and Förster (2000). Income risk: Das and Donkers (1999).

TABLE 1.8   Capital Market Features

	Germany	Italy	Japan	Netherlands	UK	USA
Down-payment ratio (1970–79)	35	50	35	25	19	20
Stock market capitalization (in percent of GDP; 1998)	51	49	66	158	175	163
Corporate income tax (*=double taxation)	1.4	4.0	4.7 DT[a]	4.1 DT	3.8	2.7 DT
Capital gains tax	Exempt	12.5	26	n.a.	INC[b]	20
Taxation of interest income	31.5 WC[c]	27 WF[d]	20 WF	n.a.	20 WC	INC

Sources: Down-payment ratios for owner-occupied housing: Chiuri and Jappelli (2000). Stock market capitalization: WDI 2000. All else: OECD Economic Surveys – Poland (2000).
[a]DT = Double taxation of dividend income.
[b]INC = Taxes as ordinary income.
[c]WC = Withholding tax with a tax credit.
[d]WF = Withholding tax payable in full.

Hence, one may expect most saving in the United States to come from relatively few households, and indeed, this is the finding in most micro data analyses (Avery and Kennickell, 1991; Carroll, 2000; Dynan *et al.*, 2002).

Cross-country capital market differences are also likely to shape differences in saving patterns. We have already pointed out the large differences in borrowing constraints, repeated in Table 1.8. Borrowing constraints are particularly large in Italy with its traditionally very high down-payment requirements. We expect that these constraints increase saving in younger ages, particularly during the time span in which households have to save for their own home. In turn, the ease at which money can be borrowed in the United States should reduce the US saving rate accordingly.

TABLE 1.9   Demographic Features

	Germany	Italy	Japan	Netherlands	UK	USA
Life expectancy at birth (male/female; 1998)	74.5/80.5	75.3/81.6	77.2/84.0	75.2/80.7	74.8/79.7	73.9/79.4
Life expectancy at 65 (male/female; 1998)	15.3/19.0	15.8/20.2	17.1/22.0	14.7/18.8	15.0/18.5	16.0/19.1
Share of population aged 65 and over (1998)	16.4	18.2	17.1	13.8	16.0	12.5

Sources: OECD Health Data (2001).

Some countries, such as the United States, but also Germany and Japan, have pursued policies to encourage saving. The United States, for example, offers several tax incentives (IRAs, 401(k)s) to promote saving. Japan, after the Second World War, launched a major educational campaign to promote saving (Bernheim, 1991). Germany has traditionally subsidized saving for a down payment in building societies (Börsch-Supan and Stahl, 1991a) as well as saving through whole life insurance (Walliser and Winter, 1999). Countries also differ in their capital taxation, in particular the taxation of interest income and wealth, which include inheritance taxes – see Table 1.8. Countries with low rates of capital taxation, such as Germany, supposedly save more than countries with high capital taxation, such as Japan – and again we need to stress: all other things being equal.

Another source of cross-national differences in saving rates are demographic differences, although the direction of causality is difficult to determine (see Cigno and Rosati, 1996). Some of the core differences are collected in Table 1.9.

In a deterministic world, a longer life span for given retirement age increases saving before retirement, provided that the replacement rate of retirement income is less than unity. Uncertainty about the length of life increases this effect (see Davies, 1981). Although Japanese persons have considerably longer life expectancies than Dutch or British people, the differences are probably too small to make a discernible difference. Moreover, it is the difference in actual duration of retirement that should matter according to economic theory. This is the longest in Germany and Italy, which therefore are expected – all other things being equal – to have higher wealth at retirement, in particular compared to the United States (see Gruber and Wise, 1999).

Reviewing Tables 1.4 through 1.9 delivers a rather complicated and multidimensional picture of cross-national differences. Table 1.10 makes an attempt to summarize and to conclude what economic theory predicts about saving behavior in our six countries.

As we see from Table 1.10, there are many opposing effects. In Italy, for instance, we would expect lower saving due to its generous public pension

TABLE 1.10   Expected Effects on Savings Behavior

Cause	Germany	Italy	Japan	Netherlands	UK	USA
Wealth at retirement						
Public pension replacement rate	Low	Low	Low	High	High	High
Retirement age	Intermediate	High	Low	Intermediate	Intermediate	Low
Income risk		Low		Low		High
Longevity and health risk	Low	Low	Low	Low	Low	High
Saving at younger ages						
Public pension replacement rate	Low	Low	Low	High	High	High
Retirement age	Intermediate	High	Low	Intermediate	Intermediate	Low
Income risk		Low		Low		High
Down-payment ratio	Intermediate	High	Intermediate	Low	Low	Low
Dissaving at older ages						
Public pension replacement rate	Low	Low	Low	Low	High	High
Longevity risk	High	High	High	High	High	Low
Health risk	High	High	High	High	High	Low

replacement level, but higher saving because of the early retirement age and, particularly at younger ages, the strict down-payment requirements. The Netherlands has lower income uncertainty than the United States but their public health care system coverage is more generous. The United States has many reasons to save much – in particular precautionary motives – but it also has a capital market that makes borrowing much easier and a relatively short duration of retirement since people retire much later than in most European countries. In addition, it is hard to predict an overall effect, as we do not have good and comparable data across countries for preferences. For example, we do not have a good idea which country has the strongest bequest motive.

There are, however, some relatively clear patterns. A good case in point concerns the neighbors Germany and the Netherlands. The Netherlands with its small pay-as-you-go system, but otherwise relatively similar background, should feature higher wealth at retirement and more dissaving after retirement than Germany. Another example of a relatively clear case concerns the strict borrowing constraints in Italy, which should increase saving in young ages, whereas the generous pension replacement rate should lower wealth at retirement, thereby flattening out the life-cycle profile compared with, for instance, the Netherlands and the United States.

1.9 WHAT DO WE OBSERVE EMPIRICALLY?

Figures 1.7 and 1.8 present the median saving rates in the six countries described in this volume. Figure 1.7 plots the raw data by cohort and age, subsuming all time effects into age and cohort effects. This is the simple methodology shown earlier in Figures 1.1 through 1.3. Figure 1.8 uses a more sophisticated methodology developed by Deaton and Paxson (1994), regressing median saving rates on age, cohort, and time dummies restricted by the identifying assumption that time effects sum up to zero and are uncorrelated with any linear trends in the data. Neither of the two identifying assumptions is uncontroversial, and both are certainly restrictive. It is possible to think of cases where time effects do not follow the pattern we assume in the data. For instance, it is possible that there is an interaction between time and cohort effects or time and age effects. The model with uncertainty would predict such interaction.

Unfortunately, the separation of age, cohort, and time effects cannot be data-driven, since any two of these effects determine the linear part of the third. Hence, it is not possible to separately identify age, time, and cohort effects without imposing some a priori assumptions. Only higher-order effects can be separated by the data (Fitzenberger et al., 2001), but not the basic linear trends. Assuming that time effects sum to zero and are orthogonal to a linear time trend essentially reduces time effects to cyclical variation, which we regard as the most meaningful and most useful a priori assumption. Figures 1.7 and 1.8 must be interpreted taking these a priori restrictions into account.

Since Figure 1.8 is regression-based, it is smoother than the raw data depicted in Figure 1.7. Figure 1.8, on which we focus our analysis, shows the age profiles for three representative cohorts: born around 1920, 1935, and 1950.

Differences in the saving profile across countries are striking. Whereas we observe a pronounced hump-shaped profile in the Netherlands, and a bit in Germany and the United States, saving increases with age almost throughout the entire life course in Japan and the UK. Moreover, Italy has essentially a flat saving profile (Figure 1.8).

The most striking communality in Figures 1.7 and 1.8 is that (maybe except for the Netherlands) we do not observe dissaving in old age.[11] While we may face the problem of differential mortality in old age (poorer individuals tend to die younger, see Hurd, 1990) and therefore figures for very old ages have to be interpreted with caution, it is hard to reject a pattern of substantial positive saving between retirement and age 70.

---

[11]Findings for the Netherlands in Figure 1.8 are consistent with the empirical estimates of Alessie et al. (1995).

1.10 ARE THESE OBSERVATIONS CONSISTENT WITH OUR EXPECTATIONS?

What explains these startling differences? Do they match our theoretical predictions? The honest answer is that the pattern is much too complicated in order to tell a simple story. However, one important part of the explanation seems to be the pension system. Let us focus on the three continental European countries. Germany and Italy have pay-as-you-go financed public pensions with very high replacement rates. They generate net retirement incomes that are almost 70% of pre-retirement net earnings in Germany and almost 90% in Italy. In addition, the public pension systems in Germany and Italy provide generous survivor benefits that constitute a substantial proportion of total unfunded pension wealth, and disability benefits at similar and often even higher replacement levels than old-age pensions. Pensions are important not only for providing support at retirement but also for providing insurance against the risks of disability and survivorship. As a result, public pensions are by far the largest pillar of retirement income in these countries and constitute more than 80% of the income of households headed by persons aged 65 and older, whereas funded retirement income, such as asset income from private saving or firm pensions in which the employer saves on behalf of the worker, plays a much smaller role. This is quite different from the Netherlands, which only provides a flat base pension on a pay-as-you-go basis with a replacement rate that is very low for households above median income. All other retirement income is withdrawals from mandatory occupational and individual pension accounts. Hence, a crucial difference between the three countries is that saving for old age is unlikely to be the main savings motive in Germany and Italy, whereas it is necessary for Dutch households. The famous hump shape of savings predicted by the life-cycle hypothesis – negative, positive, and negative again, see Figure 1.6 – therefore applies to Dutch households much more than to the other two continental European countries. This finding is broadly confirmed in Figures 1.7 and 1.8.

If this explanation of the observed cross-national saving differences were correct, it would have important implications for the future. If indeed most of the saving patterns currently observed in Germany and Italy were caused by generous retirement benefits from their pay-as-you-go pension systems, we should expect distinct changes in saving patterns when the pension reforms in these countries are put in place. The introduction of multi-pillar systems with a substantial portion of funded retirement income will revive the retirement and precautionary motive for saving. In fact, these reformed systems will look very similar to the current Dutch system. Hence, it is likely that saving rates among the young Germans and Italians will increase (to accumulate retirement savings), and saving rates among the elderly will decline sharply (because they will decumulate their retirement savings).

Another one-dimensional element of explanation is the stringency of borrowing constraints. Germany, Italy, and Japan feature much more restrictive down-payment requirements for housing – the single largest budget item for

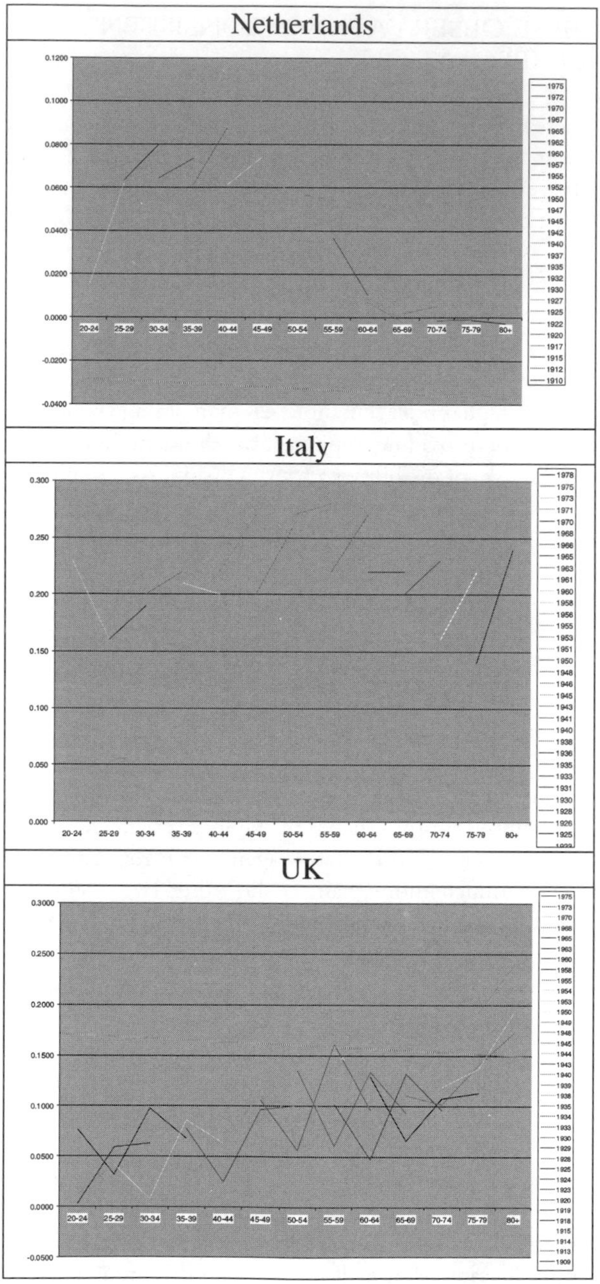

FIGURE 1.7   Cohort-corrected saving rates by age (medians, raw data). *Source*: Derived from Chapters 3–8. Average saving rates have been roughly adjusted to match aggregate household saving rates at corresponding year: see OECD Economic Outlook (various issues).

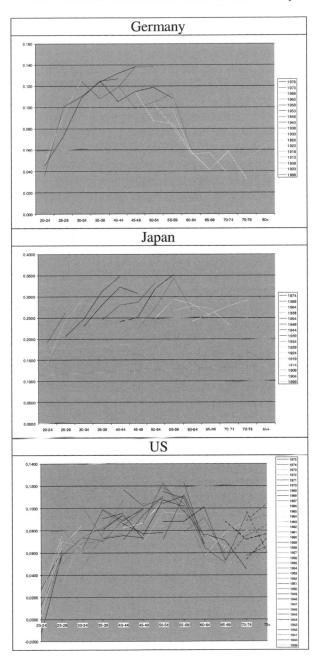

FIGURE 1.7 *Continued*

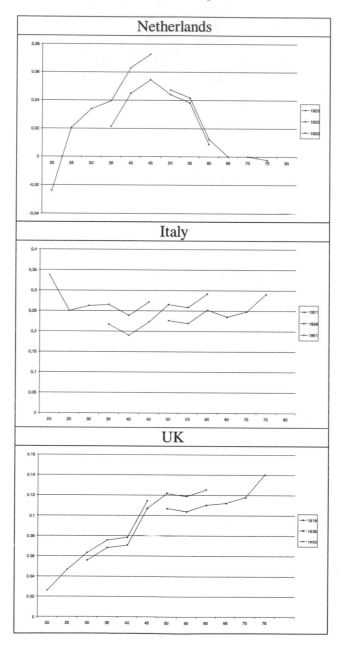

FIGURE 1.8 Saving rates by age (medians, Deaton–Paxson decomposition). *Note*: Age profiles for three representative cohorts, born around 1920, 1935, and 1950. *Source*: Derived from Chapters 3–8. Average saving rates have been roughly adjusted to match aggregate household saving rates at corresponding year: see OECD Economic Outlook (various issues).

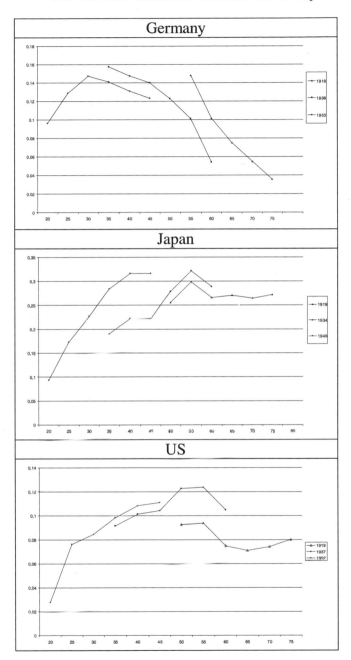

FIGURE 1.8 *Continued*

almost all households – than the Anglo-Saxon countries and the Netherlands. This appears to drive up savings in young age, as can be seen in Figure 1.8, and also increases aggregate saving in general (see Table 1.1). Again, the ongoing changes in the financial markets, particularly in Italy, are likely to change this pattern and have the potential to make Italy, Germany, and Japan look more like the Netherlands, the UK, and the United States.

Pension replacement rates and down-payment ratios are just two determinants. The experience of the six countries we have considered is rather complex and requires the consideration of many variables. As we have demonstrated, many other factors, from uncertainty through preferences – what econometricians call "unobserved heterogeneity" – confound simple comparisons.

This International Savings Comparison Project, therefore, ends on the note that we need to go one step further than comparing savings data on the aggregate level, even if derived from carefully compiled micro data. One of the lessons of this project is that research on saving behavior is still severely hampered by the lack of suitable data. Most of the age–saving profiles in Figures 1.7 and 1.8 were based on synthetic panels constructed from cross-sectional micro data. To purge unobserved heterogeneity, however, a genuine panel of individual households is required, with sufficient length to capture individual specific effects. Without proper longitudinal data on savings and wealth, it appears impossible to establish causal linkages, and we will keep making pension, tax, and other public policy decisions without understanding the most basic behavioral effects of such policies.

ACKNOWLEDGMENT

The authors would like to thank Al Gustman, Stefan Hoderlein, Anette Reil-Held, Jon Skinner, Steven Venti and Joachim Winter for suggestions and comments. Mathias Sommer provided very able research assistance. We received financial support from the Deutsche Forschungsgemeinschaft (Sonderfor schungsbereich 504) the Gesamtverband der Deutschen Versicherungswirtschaft (GDV), and the European Commission (TMR contract no. ERBFMRXCT960016). The first author very much enjoyed the hospitality of Dartmouth College when writing this article.

REFERENCES

Abel, A. (1985). Precautionary saving and accidental bequests. *American Economic Review* 75, 777–791.

Alessie, R., A. Lusardi, and A. Kapteyn (1995). Saving and wealth holdings of the elderly. *Ricerche Economiche* 49, 293–315.

Alessie, R., M. Devereux, and G. Weber (1997). Intertemporal consumption, durables and liquidity constraints: A cohort analysis. *European Economic Review* 41, 37–59.

Alessie, R., A. Kapteyn, and A. Lusardi (1998). Explaining the wealth holdings of different cohorts: Productivity growth and Social Security. CentER Discussion Paper, Tilburg University.

Attanasio, O. (1994). Personal saving in the United States. In: J. Poterba (ed.), *International Comparisons of Household Savings*. Chicago: University of Chicago Press, 57–124.

Attanasio, O. (1999). Consumption. In: J. Taylor and M. Woodford (eds), *Handbook of Macroeconomics*. Amsterdam: Elsevier Science.

Attanasio, O. and S. Rohwedder (2001). The impact of pension reform on household saving behaviour. Working Paper 01/21, Institute for Fiscal Studies, London.

Avery, R. and A. Kennickell (1991). Household saving in the US. *Review of Income and Wealth* 37, 409–432.

Bernheim, D. (1991). *The Vanishing Nest Egg: Reflections on Saving in America*. New York: Priority Press.

Bernheim, D. (1995). Do households appreciate their financial vulnerability? An analysis of actions, perceptions and public policy. *Tax Policy and Economic Growth*. Washington, DC: American Council for Capital Formation, 1–30.

Bernheim, D. (1998). Financial illiteracy, education and retirement saving. In: O. Mitchell and S. Schieber (eds), *Living with Defined Contributions Pensions*. Philadelphia: Pension Research Council: 38–68.

Bernheim, D. and D. Garrett (1999). The effects of financial education in the workplace: Evidence from a survey of households. Mimeo, Stanford University.

Bernheim, D., A. Schleifer, and L. Summers (1985). The strategic bequest motive. *Journal of Political Economy* 93, 1045–1075.

Börsch-Supan, A. (1992). Saving and consumption patterns of the elderly: The German case. *Journal of Population Economics* 5, 289–303.

Börsch-Supan, A. (1994a). Savings in Germany—Part I: Incentives. In: J.M. Poterba (ed.), *Public Policies and Household Saving*. Chicago: University of Chicago Press, 81–104.

Börsch-Supan, A. (1994b). Savings in Germany—Part II: Behavior. In: J.M. Poterba (ed.), *International Comparisons of Household Saving*. Chicago: University of Chicago Press, 207–236.

Börsch-Supan, A. and A. Brugiavini (2001). Savings: the policy debate in Europe. *Oxford Review of Economic Policy*, 17(1), 116–143.

Börsch-Supan, A. and K. Stahl (1991a). Life-cycle savings and consumption constraints. *Journal of Population Economics* 4, 233–255.

Börsch-Supan, A. and K. Stahl (1991b). Do dedicated savings increase personal savings and housing consumption? An analysis of the German Bausparkassen system. *Journal of Public Economics* 44, 265–297.

Börsch-Supan, A., A. Reil-Held, R. Rodepeter, R. Schnabel, and J Winter (2001). The German savings puzzle. *Research in Economics* 55(1), 15–38.

Browning, M. and A. Lusardi (1996). Household saving: macro theories and micro facts. *Journal of Economic Literature* 34, 1797–1855.

Brugiavini, A. and G. Weber (2001). Household savings: Concepts and measurement. In: A. Börsch-Supan (ed.), *International Comparisons of Household Saving*. New York: Academic Press.

Caballero, R. (1990). Consumption puzzles and precautionary savings. *Journal of Monetary Economics* 25, 113–136.

Carroll, C. (1992). The buffer-stock theory of saving: Some macroeconomic evidence. *Brookings Papers on Economic Activity* 2, 61–156.

Carroll, C. (1994). How does future income affect consumption? *Quarterly Journal of Economics* 59, 111–148.

Carroll, C. (1997). Buffer-stock saving and the life-cycle/permanent income hypothesis. *Quarterly Journal of Economics* 62, 1–56.

Carroll, C. (2000). Why do the rich save so much? In: J. Slemrod (ed.), *Does Atlas Shrug? The Economic Consequences of Taxing the Rich*. Cambridge, MA: Harvard University Press.

Chiuri, M. C. and T. Jappelli (2000). Financial market imperfections and home ownership: A comparative study. CSEF Working Paper No. 44, University of Salerno, Italy.

Cigno, A. and F.C. Rosati (1996). Jointly determined saving and fertility behaviour: Theory, and estimates for Germany, Italy, UK, and USA. *European Economic Review* 40, 1561–1589.

Das, M. and B. Donkers (1999). How certain are Dutch households about future income? An empirical analysis. *Review of Income and Wealth* 45, 325–338.

Davies, J. (1981). Uncertain lifetimes, consumption and dissaving in retirement. *Journal of Political Economy* 89, 561–578.

Deaton, A. (1985). Panel data from time-series of cross-sections. *Journal of Econometrics* 30, 109–124.

Deaton, A. (1991). Saving and liquidity constraints. *Econometrica* 59, 1221–1248.

Deaton, A. (1992). *Understanding Consumption*. Oxford: Oxford University Press.

Deaton, A. and C. Paxson (1994). Saving, aging and growth in Taiwan. In: D. Wise (ed), *Studies in the Economics of Aging*. Chicago: The University of Chicago Press.

Deutsches Institut für Altersvorsorge (DIA) (1999a). *Die Deutschen und Ihr Geld*. Köln: Deutsches Institut für Altersvorsorge.

Deutsches Institut für Altersvorsorge (DIA) (1999b). *Reformerfahrungen im Ausland: Ein systematischer Vergleich von sechs Ländern*. Köln: DIA.

Disney, R. and P. Johnson (eds) (2001). *Pension Systems and Retirement Incomes across OECD Countries*. Cheltenham: Edward Elgar.

Disney, R., M. Mira d'Ercole, and P. Scherer (1998). Resources during retirement. OECD Ageing Working Paper AWP 4.3, Paris.

Dynan, K., J. Skinner, and S. Zeldes (2002). Do the rich save more? Mimeo, Dartmouth College.

Engen, E. and J. Gruber (2001). Unemployment insurance and precautionary saving. *Journal of Monetary Economics* 47, 545–579.

Eymann, A. and A. Börsch-Supan (2001). Household portfolios in Germany. In: L. Guiso, M. Haliassos, and T. Jappelli (eds), *Household Portfolios*. Cambridge, MA: MIT Press.

Feldstein, M. (1974). Social Security, induced retirement and aggregate capital accumulation. *Journal of Political Economy* 82(5), 905–926.

Fitzenberger, B., R. Hujer, T.E. MaCurdy, and R. Schnabel (2001). Testing for uniform wage trends in West Germany: A cohort analysis using quantile regression for censored data. *Empirical Economics* 26(1), 41–86.

Friedman, M. (1957). *A Theory of the Consumption Function*. Princeton: Princeton University Press.

Gruber, J. and D. Wise (eds) (1999). *Social Security and Retirement Around the World*. Chicago: The University of Chicago Press.

Guiso, L., M. Haliassos, and T. Jappelli (2001). *Household Portfolios*. Cambridge, MA: MIT Press.

Hubbard, G., J. Skinner, and S. Zeldes (1995). Precautionary saving and social insurance. *Journal of Political Economy* 103, 360–399.

Hurd, M. (1990). Research on the elderly: Economic status, retirement, and consumption and saving. *Journal of Economic Literature* 28, 565–637

Jappelli, T. and F. Modigliani (1998). The age-saving profile and the life-cycle hypothesis. CSEF Working Paper No. 4, University of Salerno.

Jappelli, T. and M. Pagano (1989). Consumption and capital market imperfections: An international comparison. *American Economic Review* 79, 1088–1105.

Jappelli, T. and M. Pagano (1994). Saving, growth and liquidity constraints. *Quarterly Journal of Economics* 109, 83–109.

Kapteyn, A. and C. Panis (2002). The size and composition of wealth holdings in the United States, Italy, and the Netherlands. Mimeo, The RAND Corporation.

Kennickell, A. and A. Lusardi (2001).Wealth accumulation and the importance of precautionary saving. Mimeo, Dartmouth College.

Kim, S. (1992). Gesetzliche Rentenversicherung und Ersparnisbildung der privaten Haushalte in der Bundesrepublik Deutschland von 1962 bis 1988. *Zeitschrift für die gesamte Versicherungswirtschaft* 81, 555.

Laibson, D. (1997). Golden eggs and hyperbolic discounting. *Quarterly Journal of Economics* 112, 443–478.

Lawrence, E. (1991). Poverty and the rate of time preference: Evidence from panel data. *Journal of Political Economy* 99, 54–77.

Lusardi, A. (1997). Precautionary saving and subjective earnings variance. *Economics Letters* 57, 319–326.

Lusardi, A. (1998). On the importance of the precautionary saving motive. *American Economic Review Papers and Proceeding* 88, 449–453.

Lusardi, A. (2000). Precautionary saving and the accumulation of wealth. Working Paper, Dartmouth College.

Lusardi, A. (2001). Explaining why so many households do not save. Working Paper, Dartmouth College.

Lusardi, A., J. Skinner, and S. Venti (2001). Saving puzzles and saving policies in the United States. *Oxford Review of Economic Policy* 17, 95–115.

Modigliani, F. and R. Brumberg (1954). Utility analysis and the consumption function: An interpretation of cross-section data. In: J.H. Flavell and L. Ross (eds.), *Social Cognitive Development Frontiers and Possible Futures*. Cambridge, NY: University Press.

National Research Council (2001). *Preparing for an Aging World: The Case for Cross-National Research*, The National Research Council, Washington, DC.

O'Donoghue, T. and M. Rabin (1999a). Doing it now or later. *American Economic Review* 89, 103–124.

O'Donoghue, T. and M. Rabin (1999b). Procrastination in preparing for retirement. In: H. Aaron (ed.), *Behavioral Dimensions of Retirement Economics*. Washington, DC: Brookings Institution and Russell Sage Foundation, 125–156.

Organization of Economic Cooperation and Development (OECD) (2001). *Health Data*. Paris: OECD.

Organization of Economic Cooperation and Development (OECD) (1998–2001). *Social Expenditure*. Paris: OECD.

Organization of Economic Cooperation and Development (OECD) (2001). *Ageing and Income*. Paris: OECD.

Organization of Economic Cooperation and Development (OECD) (1998–2001). *Economic Outlook*. Paris: OECD.

Organization of Economic Cooperation and Development (OECD) (1998–2001). *Employment Outlook*. Paris: OECD.

Organization of Economic Cooperation and Development (OECD) (1998–2001). *Benefits Systems and Work Incentives*. Paris: OECD.

Palumbo, M. (1999). Uncertain medical expenses and precautionary saving near the end of the life-cycle. *Review of Economic Studies* 66, 395–421.

Poterba, J. (ed.) (1994). *International Comparisons of Household Savings*. Chicago: University of Chicago Press.

Reil-Held, A. (1999). Bequests and aggregate wealth accumulation in Germany. *The Geneva Papers on Risk and Insurance* 24, 50–63.

Rodepeter, R. and J. Winter (1998). Savings decisions under life-time and earnings uncertainty: Evidence from West German household data. Discussion Paper No. 98–58, Sonderforschungsbereich 504, Universität Mannheim.

Thaler, R. and H. Shefrin (1981). An economic theory of self-control. *Journal of Political Economy* 89, 392–406.

Venti, S. and D. Wise (1990). But they don't want to reduce housing equity. In: D. Wise (ed.), *Issues in the Economics of Aging*. Chicago: University of Chicago Press, 13–29.

Venti, S. and D. Wise (1998). The cause of wealth dispersion at retirement: Choice or chance? *American Economic Review Papers and Proceedings* 88, 185–191.

Walliser, J. and J. K. Winter (1999). Tax incentives, bequest motives and the demand for life insurance: Evidence from Germany. Discussion Paper No. 99–28, Sonderforschungsbereich 504, University of Mannheim.

Zeldes, S. (1989). Optimal consumption with stochastic income: Deviations from certainty equivalence. *Quarterly Journal of Economics* 104, 275–298.

CHAPTER 2

Household Saving: Concepts and Measurement

Agar Brugiavini

Dipartimento di Economia, Università Ca'Foscari di Venezia, Italy

Guglielmo Weber

Department of Economics, Università di Padova, Italy

*Heaven can be hell for the unprepared. Eternity is
a very long time to have no savings for!*

Nick Waplington, Private Fantasy/Public Domain,
2001 Venice Biennial Arts Exhibition

2.1 INTRODUCTION

Households save for a large number of reasons (see Browning and Lusardi, 1996, for a comprehensive list). Prominent among them are

- to smooth (the marginal utility of) consumption over time (life–cycle saving);
- to (self) insure against longevity risk, health risk, unemployment risk (precautionary motive);
- to bequeath wealth to their heirs (dynasty motive).

The first motive listed above has some short-run implications on the way consumption growth reacts to the interest rate (intertemporal substitution), but is also capable of explaining saving and dissaving behavior over the whole life cycle. If resources are front-loaded, i.e., if labor income accrues early in life, consumers will save when young and dissave in their old age. This is known as Modigliani's life-cycle theory, which emphasizes the retirement motive of saving.

The second motive relates to the way prudent consumers behave when facing uncertainty: even in the extreme case when income is evenly spread over the life cycle and the market discounts future flows the same way as individual consumers, consumers will save to buffer unexpected losses (unemployment risk) or surges in necessary spending (health risk). A further risk that may generate this type of precautionary saving is longevity risk if the annuity market is imperfect.

The third motive instead relates to the utility of final wealth: if consumers are not selfish (and do not expect to live forever – or need wealth after their death, contrary to what is assumed by the quoted artist, Nick Waplington), they may plan to leave bequests to their heirs. The importance of this motive in explaining wealth holdings is hard to deny (especially for the very rich), but its implications for the age profile of saving (i.e., for the change of wealth over time) may well be relatively minor.

A fourth motive has attracted attention: namely, liquidity constraints. Liquidity constraints take two forms: first, they require consumers to repay all their debts with probability one by the time of their death; secondly, they further prevent current wealth from falling below a given threshold. The first type of constraint is fully equivalent to a stronger precautionary motive (the individual needs to self-insure more). The second type of constraint may generate excess sensitivity of consumption to income, but is unlikely to be an important factor over long periods of time (Deaton, 1991). It may also generate extra saving to purchase bulky durable items (saving for down payment, as in Jackman and Sutton, 1982).

In this book, survey data on household income, consumption, and wealth are used to analyze the way saving evolves with age, accounting for differences across generations (cohort effects) and business-cycle effects. The underlying theoretical model is a modified life-cycle theory, where saving for retirement is the key motive, but precautionary and bequest motives are also allowed to play a role. The theory clearly implies that institutions such as pension and insurance schemes and, more generally, welfare provisions are crucially important in shaping individual saving behavior. The data refer to a number of countries that share high living standards but differ in important respects, not least their public pension system ("social security"). This source of international variability makes the data particularly attractive, but poses some formidable challenges in terms of comparability.

This chapter reviews a number of methodological issues. First, it addresses the controversial issue of whether and how the definition of saving can take into account social security wealth. It also proposes a convenient definition of the saving rate and discusses how this relates to the aggregate saving rate. We further deal with a number of potentially relevant problems, such as the treatment of durable goods (and housing in particular) and how the analysis can cope with the multiple-adult households, where the definition of head is nontrivial.

This chapter is organized as follows. In Section 2.2 we show how saving is defined in a simple one-asset world, then extend the analysis to a number of financial assets, and to social security. We also discuss advantages and drawbacks of focusing on saving rates as opposed to saving levels, particularly when the data are repeated cross sections. In Section 2.3 we review some identification issues typical of cohort analysis, whereas Section 2.4 addresses data requirements and explicitly includes in the analysis real (housing) wealth. It also provides a more thorough discussion of how the analysis should deal with the various types of pension assets. Section 2.5 is devoted to aggregation and estimation problems, and Section 2.6 concludes.

2.2 HOW CAN WE MEASURE HOUSEHOLD SAVING?

To understand the basic issues we can start from the very simple budget constraint (all in real terms):

$$A_{t+1} = (1 + r_t)A_t + y_t + b_t - \tau_t - C_t \tag{2.1}$$

where t denotes the time period (normally a year) and A is wealth (financial and real; does not include social security wealth[1]); r is "the" interest rate (inclusive of capital gains and dividends, net of inflation); y is earned income (i.e., labor income net of income tax); C is consumption (i.e., expenditure on goods and services); τ is social security contributions; and b is social security benefits.

This budget constraint assumes the existence of one (perishable) good and of a single interest rate on private wealth holdings. In this context, disposable income is earned income plus social security benefits minus social security contributions $(y_t + b_t - \tau_t)$.

Let us now consider how the budget constraint is modified when different assets yield different returns. If there are J assets, we can define

$$A_t = \sum_{j=1}^{J} A_{t,j} = \sum_{j=1}^{J} \omega_{tj}A_t$$

where $A_{t,j}$ denotes the holding of the jth asset at time t and ω_{tj} the corresponding portfolio share. Then the budget constraint, Eq. (2.1), becomes

$$A_{t+1} = \sum_{j=1}^{J}(1 + r_{t,j})\omega_{t,j}A_t + y_t + b_t - \tau_t - C_t \tag{2.2}$$

and this highlights that the real interest rate in Eq. (2.1) is a weighted average of individual asset rates, where the weights are choice variables (portfolio shares) likely to differ across households and over time.

[1]We use social security wealth in the US tradition, even though we refer to any form of pay-as-you-go (PAYG) public pension system delivering old age, invalidity, and survivor benefits.

Traditional Definition

Saving is normally considered a choice variable of the household. For this reason, its standard definition takes into account changes in that part of the wealth that is under direct household control. In our notation, the *traditional way* to define saving (also known as discretionary saving) is simply the change in wealth:

$$S_t = A_{t+1} - A_t = y_t + r_t A_t + b_t - \tau_t - C_t$$

and this can be measured if data are available on wealth holdings $(A_{t+1} - A_t)$ or if data are available on income (inclusive of asset income: $y_t + r_t A_t + b_t$) and consumption (C_t).

A third way to compute discretionary saving requires knowledge of net purchases of assets. This method draws on the distinction between passive and active saving: the former corresponds to changes in wealth due to unrealized capital gains and unspent dividends $(= r_t A_t)$. Active saving is then the net purchases of saving instruments. Then, discretionary active saving is $D_t = y_t + b_t - \tau_t - C_t$; this is invested in the various assets in such a way that $\sum_j D_{jt} = D_t$, where D_{jt} denotes the net investment in asset j at time t.

It follows that total discretionary saving is

$$S_t = A_{t+1} - A_t = r_t A_t + D_t \tag{2.3}$$

In actual survey data, these three methods may deliver different measures of saving for a number of reasons that mostly relate to data quality. Equality of these measurement concepts is only achieved when the variables involved – stock of wealth, flows into and out of accounts, income, and expenditures – are consistently defined. This is particularly hard to obtain in a single survey, where respondents are unlikely to be asked all relevant questions, and where their ability to recall or even calculate detailed measures of their wealth and income may be genuinely limited.

Alternative Definition

The traditional definition of saving treats social security contributions as taxes, and social security benefits as income. By construction, it underestimates the amount of financial resources set aside for retirement (Jappelli and Modigliani, 1998). For this reason, an *alternative definition* can be considered that treats the accumulation of contributions and the present value of claims to the public pension system as an asset (social security wealth).

On the assumption that current and future contributions and benefits are known to the household, for a given certain end-of-life T, we can define social security wealth (SSW) as

$$SSW_{t+1} = (1 + \rho_T)SSW_t + \tau_t - b_t \tag{2.4}$$

where ρ_T is the internal rate of return of investing in social security wealth for the household.

If we add A_{t+1} to SSW_{t+1} we obtain

$$A_{t+1} + SSW_{t+1} = (1 + r_t)A_t + (1 + \rho_T)SSW_t + y_t - C_t \qquad (2.5)$$

and the corresponding saving measure becomes

$$\tilde{S}_t = A_{t+1} + SSW_{t+1} - A_t - SSW_t = y_t + r_tA_t + \rho_TSSW_t - C_t \qquad (2.6)$$

Total saving, $\tilde{S}_t$, is the sum of discretionary saving, S_t, and mandatory social security saving $(SSW_{t+1} - SSW_t)$. Its calculation requires knowledge of S_t and either estimates of social security wealth in both periods (left-hand side) or an estimate of SSW_t and of its household-specific internal rate of return (right-hand side).[2]

The sum of A_t, financial and real wealth, and SSW_t, social security wealth, generates a useful measure of total household wealth if social security wealth is as fungible as private wealth. The household must be similarly able to realize its cash value for consumption purposes: i.e., by borrowing against future social security benefits at the appropriate rate ρ_T. It must therefore be the case that the social security system is viable, so that future contributions and benefits anticipated by the household are credible because the overall social security system is balanced in the long run. If this condition is not met, the internal rate of return ρ_T, computed by the household in Eq. (2.4), will differ from the borrowing rate. For at least one use, A_t and SSW_t are unlikely to be close substitutes, though – contrary to financial and real wealth – pension wealth is by definition non-bequeathable. If the focus of the analysis were on bequests, it would make little sense to sum the two.

It is worth pointing out that ρ_T is a hard-to-measure rate: even if the household knows the value of T, and there is no uncertainty on survival and on future contributions and benefits, the econometrician is unlikely to share this knowledge and will at best be able to compute a measure based on cohort-specific life expectancy. Similarly, future contributions and benefits must be imputed on the basis of eligibility and assumptions on the prevailing social security rules. This has prompted many studies (including those in this volume) to set $\rho = 0$ as a first approximation.

Even in ideal conditions, using $\tilde{S}_t$ to measure saving is questionable: according to Eq. (2.6) contributions to the social security system increase saving and benefits decrease it. This latter implication is controversial. In fact, if the person knows her time of death, the present value of her future benefits decreases over time and reaches zero in the end, but if she faces uncertainty on the date of death, then it is

---

[2]We are not considering here private pensions, contributions to which may be either fully discretionary or compulsory. This latter case is particularly relevant for occupational pensions, which are widely used in the UK and in the Netherlands.

hard to see in what sense enjoying an extra year of benefit should be regarded as dissaving (this point applies to any annuity-type asset).[3]

We have so far argued that summing financial and real wealth to social security wealth may be undesirable because the two are not perfect substitutes. However, they are likely to have some degree of substitutability for most individual households and this strongly suggests that both must be measured when evaluating saving behavior.[4]

Saving Rates

The various measures of saving described so far are *absolute* measures. If we want to allow for differences in household lifetime resources or size we normally divide by a measure of current income. This defines the *saving rate*.

We can define the following saving rates:

$$s_t = \frac{S_t}{y_t + r_r A_t + b_t - \tau_t}$$

and

$$\tilde{s}_t = \frac{\tilde{S}_t}{y_t + r_r A_t + \rho_T \text{SSW}_t}$$

Each of these measures is internally consistent, but they are hard to compare because of the differences in the denominator. Also, they are not defined or ill-defined for zero or negative "income" (respectively: $y_t + r_r A_t + b_t - \tau_t$ or $y_t + r_r A_t + \rho_T \text{SSW}_t$), a rare but not impossible occurrence in household level data (e.g., a self-employed individual may suffer losses in any one year; an unemployed individual may receive no income over a period, if she does not qualify for welfare benefits).

Even for positive income, individual saving rates can be quite volatile because of variability in the denominator. For this reason the analysis is sometimes focused on median saving rates, rather than mean saving rates.[5] However, the relation between median saving rates and the corresponding aggregate measure is by no means straightforward.

A better alternative (Attanasio, 1998) that gets round the problem of non-positive income observations consists of dividing saving by C_t (consumption), as a simple common proxy for lifetime resources. The resulting saving rates are a monotonically increasing function of the saving rates as defined above (for positive income). This measure is particularly useful when consumption data are known to be of

---

[3]It is worth noting that despite these considerations, National Accounts treat annuity income as dissaving.

[4]This issue is also discussed in Jappelli (2001) and Börsch-Supan (2001b).

[5]The use of medians and other quartiles in the analysis of wealth accumulation age profiles is first advocated in Attanasio (1993).

relatively high-quality compared with income data, as in diary-based surveys. When consumption is instead known to be affected by major underreporting, the traditional measure may be preferable. In fact, households who underreport their expenditure most will appear to save more, and their saving rate will be further inflated if the denominator is C_t rather than income.

One drawback of working with saving rates is the nontrivial relation between the individual level data and the corresponding aggregate variable. Suppose we plot the mean saving rate for a given age group against time, i.e., we take means of the saving rates of individual households h of age a at time t. The resulting statistic is *not* the average (or aggregate) saving rate of the a age group in period t, defined as:

$$s_t^a = \frac{S_t^a}{Y_t^a} = \frac{\sum_{h \in a} S_t^h}{\sum_{h \in a} Y_t^h}$$

where Y denotes either "income" or consumption, according to the chosen measure. The two are related as follows:

$$s_t^a = \sum_{h \in a} \omega_t^h s_t^h$$

where $\omega_t^h = Y_t^h / Y_t^a$ is the "income" or consumption share of household h within the age group. If we want to study the time pattern for s_t^a we must weigh the individual saving rates by ω_t^h.

An approximation that works well at the aggregate level is sometimes used (Deaton and Paxson, 1994):

$$s_t \simeq \ln(Y_t) - \ln(C_t)$$

This approximation is again not defined for negative or zero income and can be quite inaccurate at the individual level, but has the advantage of being less sensitive to outliers. The relation between the average saving rate and the corresponding aggregate variable is known and exact when both income and consumption are lognormally distributed.

2.3 WHY COHORT ANALYSIS?

We are interested in the age profile of household saving (or of the saving rate). But we don't normally observe the same individuals through time long enough to be able to plot individual age profiles. Sometimes we only have wealth at a moment in time (individual saving cannot be computed); some other time we observe income and consumption flows for a single period (individual saving can be computed, but only for a particular age).

If we plot saving against age in a cross section, the resulting profile will link individuals born in different years. This may produce misleading evidence on age effects if individuals born in different years are different in their resources or preferences (Shorrocks, 1975). If we have access to several cross sections over time, we can address this issue by using cohort analysis.

We define a *cohort* as a group of individuals born in the same calendar year. By construction, cohort members age together (in this sense a cohort can be considered as a synthetic individual). Note there is no within-cohort age variability over any one observation year. Wider cohorts can be defined, including all individuals born within a certain year band (5-year cohorts, for instance), but care must be taken to define the age of each individual as the cohort mid-age. Narrower cohorts can be defined, by selecting individuals who meet certain time-invariant criteria (race, sometimes education and region).

When dealing with households, cohorts are normally defined on the basis of the year of birth of the household head. This is correct if the head does not change over time. Within couples the head is often the male, but this choice is of little consequence if the age difference between spouses is not large. However, the presence of more than one adult within the household does raise the issue of who takes the relevant consumption/saving decisions. There can be doubts on the ability of the unitary model to interpret the data, particularly when both spouses work. A simple example is provided in Browning (1995): given that women survive longer, there will be disagreement within married couples on saving. The higher the bargaining power of wives, the higher the household saving rate will be.

The case of multiple-adult (or composite) households poses further important problems, discussed in Deaton and Paxson (2000). At the very least, household income and consumption should be attributed to the various household members, and not just to the head, before age profiles can be drawn. As we show in Table 2.1, the presence of young adults living with their parents is extremely common in at least two of the countries studied in this book (Italy and Japan). If the choice of leaving home relates to wealth, income, or consumption, we face a problem of

TABLE 2.1   Proportion of Young Adults Living with Parent(s)

Country	Male aged 25–29	Female aged 25–29	Male aged 30–34	Female aged 30–34
Germany	32	12	14	3.5
Italy	76	50	32	19.5
Japan	59	48	37	28
Netherlands	27	6	6	1.5
UK	21	9.5	6.5	4
USA	19	12	8	5.5

Source: OECD (2000).

endogenous household formation, and age profiles of saving may be severely altered by composition effects.

Observed saving behavior of nuclear and composite households is indeed different. In Figure 2.1 we show the discretionary saving rate age profiles by each type of household in Italy: the nuclear household in the top panel, the composite household in the bottom panel (these are estimated age profiles, as detailed in Brugiavini and Padula, 2001). We see that composite households typically save more and that their saving age profile slopes up after retirement age, whereas nuclear

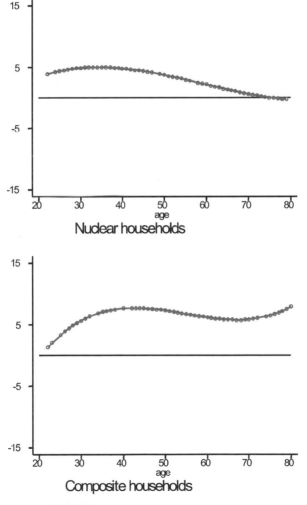

FIGURE 2.1   Discretionary saving rates in Italy.

households display a monotonically decreasing profile after age 35. We should be careful not to interpret these findings as relating to two mutually exclusive groups: the same household is likely to be classified as nuclear at certain ages and as composite at other ages. For instance, households with teenage children will move from the former to the latter group as soon as one of the children becomes of age. Insofar as these changes in household type by age correlate with income, consumption, and wealth, we can expect the saving rate age profiles for each group to reflect composition effects.

A related conceptual problem is created by nonrandom attrition (differential mortality by wealth, or wealth-related household dissolution). As already noted in Shorrocks (1975), if there is differential mortality by wealth (wealthy individuals live longer), the average wealth of survivors may increase with time, even if each surviving individual is decumulating. This may therefore produce false evidence against decumulation if one looks at one or more cross sections of individual- or household-level data, because for any age group the wealthier survive while the less wealthy die and therefore disappear from the sample. The solution to this problem requires assumptions on the relation between mortality and wealth (see for instance Attanasio and Hoynes, 2000).[6]

In the context of consumption/income or saving levels, cohort differences may reflect differential access to economic resources (life-cycle theory) or differences in preferences (if later-born generations are more impatient, or prudent). In the context of saving rates, cohort differences are less likely to reflect differences in opportunity sets, but may still arise because of differences in preferences (the baby boomers may be more impatient than their parents, say).

In Figures 2.2 and 2.3 we show cohort age profiles for (average) disposable income and consumption for the UK. The data source is the Family Expenditure Survey, one of the very few household surveys that contains high-quality data on both. Also, the low incidence of composite households in the UK makes the definition of household head less problematic.[7] Cohorts are defined on the basis of 5-year birth intervals (see Banks and Rohwedder, 2001, for further details). The data cover a very long time period (1974–95), including a period of stagflation (the 1970s), two recessions (1981–2 and 1992), and two booms (the mid-1980s and 1993–5).

Vertical distances in these graphs can be interpreted as cohort effects if there are no time effects at play (of course two year-of-birth cohorts will have the same age at different points in time). A single age profile is normally hard to detect, even though for both income and consumption we can see the familiar hump shape emerge.

---

[6]Even with genuine panel data this source of nonrandom attrition makes it hard to infer the population-wide wealth–age profile. The best one can do is to look at profiles of survivors up to a certain age, thus discarding information on those who die earlier.

[7]In the FES sample only 8% of all households can be classified as composite households. Banks and Rohwedder (2001) therefore drop them altogether when drawing age profiles.

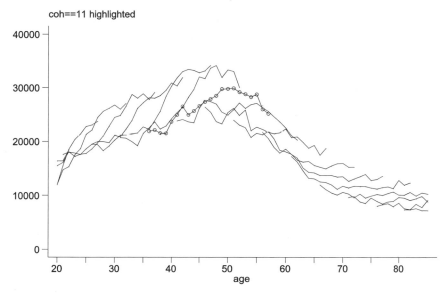

FIGURE 2.2   UK disposable income (1998 euros).

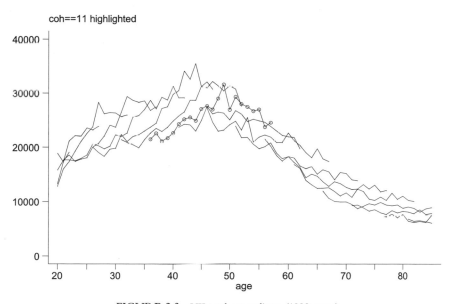

FIGURE 2.3   UK total expenditure (1998 euros).

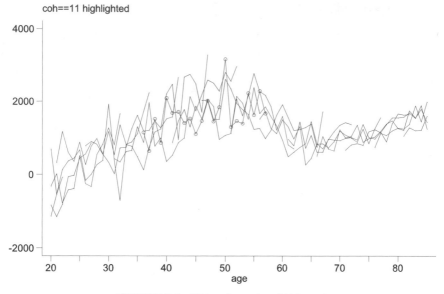

FIGURE 2.4   UK median savings (1998 euros).

Time effects are likely to play an important role with saving: by definition savings buffer shocks. Also, saving changes in response to interest rate changes and to changes in pension legislation. In Figure 2.4 we show UK household saving (in the traditional definition). Because extreme outliers are not uncommon with saving, median saving is plotted against age. As we can see, some age pattern can be detected (first a hump, then a gentle rise past retirement age), but no eyeball impression of cohort or year effects emerges from this graph.

If we want to go beyond simple pictures or graphs, we need to address this as a formal estimation problem. A general specification for the age profile by household h in period t is

$$S_t^h = f(\text{age}_t^h; \ \text{yob}^h; \ t) + \varepsilon_t^h$$

where yob denotes year of birth and the dependent variable could be any one of the saving measures/rates defined above. As usual, ε_t^h is a disturbance measuring the distance between the conditional expectation of S_t^h and its observed value.

An identification problem arises because

$$\text{age}_t^h = \text{yob}^h + t$$

and this lies at the core of the interpretation difficulties we mentioned in discussing the cohort age profiles above.

Ways to solve the identification problem typically rely on separability assumptions, plus restrictions on time effects or specification of a model for year effects or cohort effects as functions of observables.

MaCurdy and Mroz (1989) and Attanasio (1998) make the following separability assumption:

$$S_t^h = g(\text{age}_t^h) + h(\text{yob}^h) + k(t) + \varepsilon_t^h \tag{2.7}$$

where $g(.)$, $h(.)$, and $k(.)$ are finite-order polynomials and some convention is used for the linear terms (such as no linear time effects). This assumption treats the three explanatory variables symmetrically, by restricting their cross effects on the saving rate (direct cross terms in age, yob, and t are ruled out). Depending on the structure of the problem, further restrictions may also be imposed.

Restrictions on Time Effects

Deaton and Paxson (1994) specify the following equation:

$$S_t^h = l(\text{age}_t^h) + \beta D_c^h + \gamma D_t + \varepsilon_t^h \tag{2.8}$$

where $l(\text{age}_t^h)$ is a polynomial in age, D_c^h is a set of cohort (or year of birth) dummies, and D_t is a set of time dummies. To avoid the noted collinearity problems, the γ coefficients are suitably constrained: time effects sum to zero and are orthogonal to a time trend.

This is equivalent to saying that *any time trend in the data is attributed to the interaction of cohort and age*, and that time effects are computed as deviations from the mean. In this sense, the γ parameters measure cyclical variability alone. This is the solution to the identification problem adopted in the book.

As a way to assess the relevance of this assumption in the context of saving, we show in Figure 2.5 the results of the analysis for the UK (see Chapter 7). The NW quadrant shows the estimated age profiles when the assumption is made of no time effects. Thus, in Eq. (2.8) the γ parameters are set to zero and $l(\text{age}_t^h)$ is a fifth-order polynomial. The remaining quadrants show instead the results of estimating Eq. (2.7) under the minimal set of restrictions described above. The NE quadrant shows cohort effects, the SE quadrant year effects (that sum to zero and are orthogonal to the time trend by construction), and the SW quadrant shows the age profile. Comparing the NW and SW quadrants we notice that the apparently different patterns tell a similar story: the saving age profile increases up to age 60 and then flattens out. Comparing the NW and NE quadrants we detect positive cohort effects for younger cohorts, with the sole exception of some of the youngest households.

In Figure 2.6 we show similar graphs for the saving rate. Here we see that the age profile is broadly similar for age between 30 and 50, but that there are remarkable differences between the NW and SW quadrants for young ages and again over the 60–70 age range. Cohort effects are also more pronounced in the NE quadrant than in the NW quadrant (in both cases we see a certain amount of noise for the most recent cohorts).

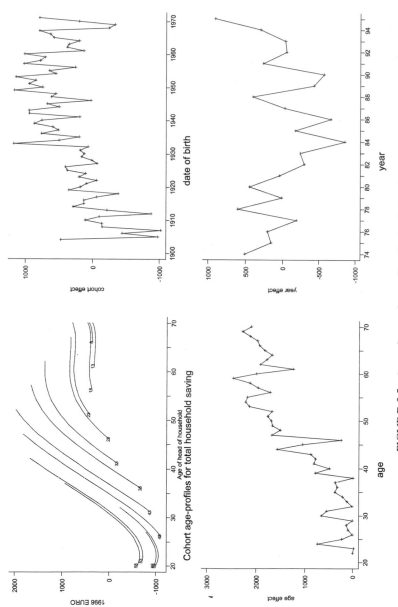

FIGURE 2.5   Age, cohort, and year effects for (median) saving.

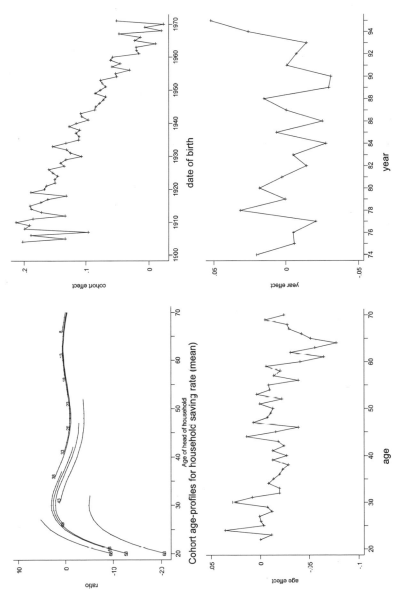

FIGURE 2.6   UK median saving rate.

The assumptions made on time effects can be given a theoretical justification when the dependent variable is consumption. In a rational expectations framework, rational consumers choose their consumption today along the path chosen yesterday if no new information accrues. If there is news, their actual consumption will differ from their planned consumption in a way that is uncorrelated with any information they had when they formed their original plan. If their planned consumption is represented by $l(\text{age}_t^h) + \beta D_c^h$, then the error term $\gamma D_t + \varepsilon_t^h$ must be orthogonal to the constant and the time trend (as indeed any other known function of calendar time).[8] For this argument to carry over to saving, one must assume that the corresponding error term of the income process is negligible or, anyhow, completely unpredictable.

To better assess the plausibility of the Deaton–Paxson restrictions we show in Figure 2.7 the results of the analysis on UK consumption data. As above, the NW quadrant is estimated on the assumption of no time effects and smooth age effects, whereas the other quadrants show cohort, age, and restricted year effects. The striking feature here is that cohort effects are monotonically increasing in year of birth and the age profile displays a smooth hump shape. This contrasts sharply with the evidence shown earlier for saving.

Modeling Time or Cohort Effects

An alternative to the above is to assume that time or year of birth matter for well-specified reasons. Indeed, Heckman and Robb (1985, p. 139) argue that an equation like Eq. (2.7) for earnings "should be seen as a crude approximation of what we are really interested in. The approximation is so crude that it creates a problem of its own."

In the case of saving, time effects in Eq. (2.7) may capture interest rates changes or pension reforms. If we can observe or construct variables for these, call them x_t, the equation becomes

$$S_t^h = m(\text{age}_t^h; \text{yob}^h; x_t) + \varepsilon_t^h$$

and no further restrictions need to be imposed.

The same applies to the year of birth variable: given that the life cycle predicts that cohort effects in consumption and income are due to productivity growth, an argument can be made for explicitly modeling this dependence. Recent applications of this method are Kapteyn et al. (1996) and Jappelli (1999).

Kapteyn et al. (1996) for instance assume that cohort effects in income and wealth solely reflect productivity growth, in the sense that earlier born generations are lifetime poorer (this is a standard assumption of the stripped-down version of the life-cycle theory, see Deaton, 1992). Then they model cohort effects by

---

[8]We are grateful to Rob Alessie for suggesting this interpretation to us.

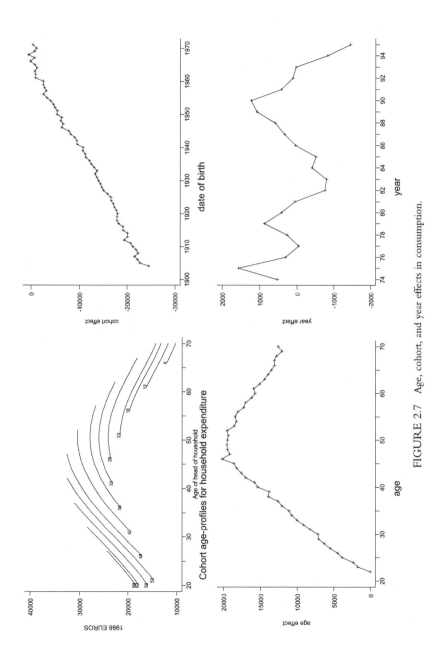

FIGURE 2.7 Age, cohort, and year effects in consumption.

creating a variable that is a function of real per-capita gross domestic product at the time individuals entered the labor force. This way they can be fully flexible in their specification of age and time effects.

An extreme assumption on cohort effects is made in Paxson's (1996) analysis of the *saving rate*: they are set to zero. This is equivalent to assuming that consumption and income cohort effects exactly cancel out.[9]

2.4 DATA REQUIREMENTS

Equations (2.6) and (2.3) show that there are three different ways of measuring saving (defined in the traditional way, that does not include changes in social security wealth):

- first, by comparing asset holdings at the beginning and at the end of a period: $A_{t+1} - A_t$
- secondly, by adding inflows and outflows of wealth accounts during 1 year: $\sum_j (r_{jt} A_{jt} + D_{jt})$
- thirdly, by taking the residual of income minus consumption expenditures: $y_t + r_t A_t + b_t - \tau_t - C_t$.

Equality of these measurement concepts is only achieved when the variables involved – stock of wealth, flows into and out of accounts, income and expenditures – are consistently defined. Ideally, one would like to report all three measures in order to learn how reliable actual measurements of all variables involved are.

As noted above, household saving is the sum of discretionary and mandatory saving. Discretionary saving (active and passive) is completely under the control of the household. Households choose its absolute value as well as its portfolio composition, given their budget constraints and applicable incentives such as tax relief and mandatory contributions to funded and unfunded pension schemes. Instead, mandatory saving is beyond the control of the household.

So far, we have taken social security contributions as the only type of mandatory saving. However, other forms of retirement saving are sometimes seen as part of mandatory saving. For instance, according to Börsch-Supan (2001a):

> the most important example are mandatory contributions to funded occupational pension plans. Here, the contributions are prescribed (e.g., a fixed absolute sum or a fixed percentage of gross income) and frequently even the portfolio composition is outside the control of the household (e.g., the employer provides a single pension plan).

---

[9]Kapteyn et al. (1996) derive sufficient conditions for Paxson's assumption to hold. They show that in a model with quadratic preferences, time preference equal to the interest rate and productivity growth that has only a one-off proportional impact on income, cohort effects are the same on wealth, consumption, and income.

In theory, all private pensions are under the household control, and therefore contributions to pensions should be part of discretionary saving. This is indeed the case for private annuities and individual retirement accounts (IRAs in the United States, personal pensions in the UK). In practice, in some countries (notably the UK and the Netherlands) there are mandatory occupational pension schemes, and contributions to these schemes cannot be considered part of discretionary saving. Thus, the distinction between mandatory and discretionary saving does not fully overlap with the distinction between funded and unfunded schemes (or private schemes versus public schemes).

In all cases where retirement saving is mandatory, contributions are anyhow hard to measure, because household survey data do not normally record employer's contributions or the taxpayer's contributions to the unfunded schemes. For this reason, the analysis normally focuses on discretionary saving only. This is also the emphasis in this book, even though an attempt is made at measuring social security wealth as well as other forms of pension insurance wherever possible.

Within discretionary saving, the distinction is often made between financial and real saving. To understand the way real saving can be computed, consider again the budget constraint when the household can either rent or buy housing stock. Let H_t denote the real value of the housing stock, M_t the outstanding mortgage, and r_{tH} their (common) rate of return. Then Eq. (2.1) becomes

$$A_{t+1} + (H_{t+1} - M_{t+1}) = (1 + r_t)A_t + (1 + r_{tH})(H_t - M_t)$$
$$+ y_t + b_t - \tau_t - C_t \tag{2.9}$$

where consumption C_t is the sum of expenditure of nondurable goods and services and the actual or notional rental value of housing services. The rate of return on housing equity $(H_t - M_t)$ then reflects nominal price changes (capital gains) net of capital depreciation as well as its rental value. When C_t does not include imputed rent, then the rate of return is made simply of capital gains minus depreciation, as in the standard neoclassical model of durable goods. In the case of housing, we believe it is convenient to use an all-inclusive consumption measure.

As previously mentioned, discretionary financial saving is the sum of active and passive financial saving. Active financial saving is

- Deposits into, minus withdrawals from, saving accounts, mutual money market accounts, and other money-like investments
- plus purchases of, minus sales of, bonds
- plus purchases of, minus sales of, stocks
- plus contributions to, minus outpayments from, whole life insurance
- plus contributions to, minus outpayments from, dedicated saving plans (defined by a contract that determines for which purpose withdrawals may be made, e.g., building societies, individual health spending accounts, etc.)

TABLE 2.2   Macroeconomic Indicators for Italy

	1995	1996	1997	1998
Long-term (10-year) interest rate[a] on government debt	12.21%	9.40%	6.86%	4.88%
CPI inflation	5.2%	4.0%	2.0%	2.0%
Personal sector saving rate	19.4%	19.1%	17.2%	15.4%
Personal sector saving rate (inflation adjusted)	14.4%	14.8%	14.2%	14.2%
Disposable income growth	4.7%	5.5%	2.8%	2.2%

Source: Bank of Italy — Relazione del Governatore 1998
[a]All interest and growth rates are nominal.

- plus voluntary contributions to, minus payments from, individual retirement accounts and pension funds where withdrawals may be made only after retirement or a pre-specified age
- plus amortization of, minus take-up of, consumer loans.

In turn, active discretionary real saving consists of

- Purchases of, minus sales of, real estate (including owner-occupied housing)
- plus expenditures in upkeep and improvement of housing, minus depreciation
- plus amortization of, minus take-up of, mortgages
- plus purchases of, minus sales of, gold and other jewellery.[10]

Finally, a word on inflation. In the budget constraint, Eq. (2.1), we have defined all variables in real terms. This includes the return on financial assets, $r_t A_t$. Normally, disposable income is defined as net labor income plus total (net) asset income, but this grossly overstates the true measure and can provide a misleading picture of current trends. In Table 2.2 we show the importance of this issue for Italy in the recent past (1995–1998), when nominal returns fell from 12.2% to 4.9% and inflation fell from 5.2% to 2%: the aggregate, uncorrected personal saving rate appears to be falling from 19.4% in 1995 to 15.4%, but once the disposable income measure is corrected for inflation the saving rate is in fact quite stable over time.[11]

2.5 AGGREGATION AND ESTIMATION

When we plot the saving age profile by cohort, we are effectively estimating the equation

$$S_t^h = f(\text{age}_t^h; \text{yob}^h; t) + \varepsilon_t^h$$

[10]See Börsch-Supan (2001a).
[11]This adjustment is routinely carried out by the Bank of Italy.

by instrumental variables (two–stage least squares), where the set of instruments includes all nonredundant year-cohort dummies. Thus, in the first stage the estimator works out cohort averages for each year and in the second stage these are regressed on the explanatory variables (that are perfectly fitted by the instruments: by construction there is no within-year cohort cell variability in age, year of birth, or time).

If further regressors are considered, the cohort averaging technique fails to exploit all available information in estimation (on this point, see Attanasio, 1998) and is in fact less widely used (see Attanasio and Weber, 1994). Suppose, for instance, we wish to control for the effects of education, but do not wish to define cohorts on the basis of both year of birth and education. We could for instance specify

$$S_t^h = l(\text{age}_t^h) + \beta D_c^h + \gamma D_t + \delta \text{Educ}^h + \varepsilon_t^h$$

where Educ^h represents the years of education (that we assume not to vary over time). This equation can be estimated on individual data or on average cohort data: estimates will not be identical because cohort averaging does not exploit within-cell variability in education.

A natural and sometimes useful extension of this is to add further time-varying explanatory variables that reflect household structure (number of household members, number of children, and so on). The estimated age profile will now have a different interpretation because it is conditional on no demographic changes taking place.

Let us now look at

$$s_t^h = f(\text{age}_t^h; \text{yob}^h; t) + \xi_t^h$$

where the dependent variable is

$$s_t^h = \frac{S_t^h}{Y_t^h}$$

i.e., the saving rate (where the denominator can be either an income measure or a consumption measure).

If we use average cohort techniques in this context we estimate the age profile for the average saving rate within each cohort. This is *not* the cohort saving rate, defined as

$$s_t^c = \frac{S_t^c}{Y_t^c} = \frac{\sum_{h \in c} S_t^h}{\sum_{h \in c} Y_t^h}$$

As we have seen, the two are related as follows:

$$s_t^c = \sum_{h \in c} \omega_t^h s_t^h$$

where $\omega_t^h = Y_t^h / Y_t^c$ is the income or consumption share of household h within the cohort.

If we want to estimate the age profile for s_t^c we can weigh the individual saving rates by ω_t^h. Note that $\sum_{h \in c} \omega_t^h = 1$, so that weighing does not affect the values taken by the explanatory variables (age_t^h; yob^h; t). Therefore, the cohort-averaging technique applies in this case, except that weighted averages replace simple averages. If further explanatory variables are considered, their values will need to be weighted.

Cohort averaging is convenient for computational and graphical purposes, but not necessary for estimation, when the dependent variable can be computed for each household in the sample. When this is not the case – either because saving is computed as the difference between wealth at two different periods and the data are not a panel or because income and consumption are drawn from different surveys – cohort averaging is instead necessary for estimation.

2.6 CONCLUSION

In this chapter we have addressed some methodological issues that underlie the study of household saving presented in this book. We have showed how saving is defined in a simple one-asset world, then extended the analysis to a number of financial assets, to pension wealth (social security, occupational pensions, private annuities), and to real wealth. We have also discussed advantages and drawbacks of focusing on saving rates as opposed to saving levels, particularly when the data are repeated cross sections. We then reviewed some identification and aggregation issues typical of cohort analysis.

ACKNOWLEDGMENT

We are grateful for helpful discussions with Rob Alessie and Axel Börsch-Supan.

REFERENCES

Attanasio, O. P. (1993). An analysis of life-cycle accumulation of financial assets. *Research in Economics* 47(4), 323–354.

Attanasio, O. P. (1998). Cohort analysis of saving behaviour by U.S. households. *Journal of Human Resources* 33, 575–609.

Attanasio, O. and H. W. Hoynes (2000). Differential mortality and wealth accumulation. *Journal of Human Resources* 35(1), 1–29.

Attanasio, O. P. and G. Weber (1994). The UK consumption boom of the late 1980's: aggregate implications of microeconomic evidence. *The Economic Journal* 104, 1269–1303.

Banks, J. and S. Rohwedder (2001). Life-cycle saving patterns and pension arrangements in the U.K. *Research in Economics* 55(1), 83–107.

Börsch-Supan, A. (2001a). Introduction to 'International Comparison of Household Savings Behaviour: A Study of Life-Cycle Savings in Seven-Countries'. *Research in Economics* 55(1), 1–14.

Börsch-Supan, A. (2001b). Rejoinder to Tullio Jappelli's comments. *Research in Economics* 55(2), 185–187.

Browning, M. (1995). Saving and the intra-household distribution of income: An empirical investigation. *Research in Economics* 49(3), 277–292.

Browning, M. and A. Lusardi (1996). Household saving: micro theories and micro facts. *Journal of Economic Literature* 34(4), 1797–1855.

Brugiavini, A. and M. Padula (2001). Too much for retirement? Saving in Italy. *Research in Economics* 55(1), 39–60.

Deaton, A. (1991). Saving and liquidity constraints. *Econometrica* 59(5), 1221–1248.

Deaton, A. (1992). *Understanding Consumption*. Oxford: Oxford University Press.

Deaton, A. and C. Paxson (1994). Intertemporal choice and inequality. *Journal of Political Economy* 102, 437–467.

Deaton, A. and C. Paxson (2000). Growth and saving among individuals and households. *Review of Economics and Statistics* 82(2), 212–225.

Heckman, J. and R. Robb (1985). Using longitudinal data to estimate age, period and cohort effects in earnings equations. In: W. M. Mason and S. E. Fienberg (eds), *Cohort Analysis in Social Research. Beyond the Identification Problem*. New York: Springer Verlag, 137–150.

Kapteyn, A., R. Alessie, and A. Lusardi (1996). Explaining the wealth of different cohorts: productivity growth and social security. Mimeo (revised: 2000).

Jackman, R. and J. Sutton (1982). Imperfect capital markets and the monetarist black box: Liquidity constraints, inflation and the asymmetric effects of interest rate policy. *Economic Journal* 92, 108–128.

Jappelli, T. (1999). The age–wealth profile and the life-cycle hypothesis: A cohort analysis with a time-series of cross-sections of Italian households. CSEF WP 14, University of Salerno.

Jappelli, T. (2001). Comment on the International Savings Comparison Project. *Research in Economics* 55(2), 173–184.

Jappelli, T. and F. Modigliani (1998). The age–saving profile and the life-cycle hypothesis. CSEF WP 4, University of Salerno.

MaCurdy, T. and T. Mroz (1989). Measuring macroeconomic shifts in wages from cohort specifications. Mimeo, Stanford University.

Organization of Economic Cooperation and Development (OECD) (2000). *Reforms for an Ageing Society*. Paris: OECD.

Paxson, C. (1996). Saving and growth: evidence from micro data. *European Economic Review* 40, 255–288.

Shorrocks, A. (1975). The age–wealth relationship: A cross-section and cohort analysis. *The Review of Economics and Statistics* 57, 155–163.

CHAPTER 3

Household Saving in Germany

Axel Börsch-Supan

*Mannheim Research Institute for the Economics of Aging (MEA) and
Sonderforschungsbereich 504, University of Mannheim, Germany and
National Bureau of Economic Research (NBER), Cambridge, Massachusetts*

Anette Reil-Held

*Mannheim Research Institute for the Economics of Aging (MEA) and
Sonderforschungsbereich 504, University of Mannheim, Germany*

Reinhold Schnabel

Department of Economics, University of Essen, Germany

3.1. INTRODUCTION

Household saving is still little understood, and answers even to the most basic questions – e.g., How does saving change over the life cycle? – are controversial. Understanding saving behavior is not only an important question because the division of income into consumption and saving concerns one of the most fundamental household decisions but it is also of utmost policy relevance since private household saving as a private insurance interacts with social policy as a public insurance.

In accordance with the general aims of this book, this chapter has two main purposes and is structured accordingly. In the first part, we describe how German households save. We investigate cross-sectional as well as longitudinal patterns of household saving in Germany. In the second part, we link the saving patterns of German households to public policies in Germany, most notably the generous German public retirement insurance. Other policies include the lenient taxation of capital in Germany and subsidies to specific forms of savings which have been popular in the 1970s and early 1980s.

Our main finding is a hump-shaped age–saving profile. However, Germans of all ages save a lot. Savings remain positive in old age, except for very low income households. Somewhat ironically, the generous mandatory German public pension system is a prime candidate to explain the German savings pattern. We face a "German savings puzzle": Germany has one of the most generous public pension and health insurance systems of the world, yet private savings are high until old age. We provide a complicated answer to the questions raised by that puzzle, combining historical facts with capital market imperfections, and housing, tax, and pension policies.

The first and descriptive part of this chapter is set up as follows: Section 3.2 describes our data source. Section 3.3 presents cross-sectional and longitudinal profiles of various saving measures by age and birth cohort. Finally, Section 3.4 looks at financial, real, and pension wealth. The second interpretative part of the chapter starts with Section 3.5, in which we briefly describe the institutional background for saving in Germany. Section 3.6 links the observed saving and wealth patterns to this background, and Section 3.7 concludes.

3.2. DATA

We base our description of savings behavior in Germany on five waves of the German Income and Expenditure Survey ("Einkommens- und Verbrauchsstichproben," EVS). The EVS has been collected by the Federal Statistical Office every 5 years since 1963. The main purpose of the EVS is to comprehensively examine the economic and social situation of private households in order to construct statistical measures for the government, such as various price indexes, poverty measures, and measures of wealth accumulation (Euler, 1992). Data on income, expenditures, homeownership, wealth, and debt are collected.

The EVS 1993 included for the first time the new Eastern states and foreign households. The EVS 1993 includes the main socioeconomic characteristics of all household members, whereas earlier surveys carry information only about the head of the household. Assigning incomes to individual household members is possible to some extent, although dividing up a household's stock of wealth is not. The EVS 1993 is provided to researchers as a "*scientific use file*" that contains nearly 80% of the original sample (the basic and the final interview as well as the summarized diaries for the surveyed period are included): this comprises 40,230 households. Selected information on income, wealth, and expenditure from the upper and bottom decile were made coarser than originally surveyed.[1] Further selected discrete characteristics were summarized in a sophisticated manner so that no univariate distribution consists of less than 5000 cases.

The EVS 1998 has also been released as a "scientific use file," although at substantially higher costs than the EVS 1993. Unfortunately, the EVS 1998 suffers from some deficiencies compared with the EVS 1993, since variables necessary to construct savings and portfolio measures comparable over time were deleted from the 1998 survey instrument.

Earlier surveys (1978, 1983, and 1988) are provided only in aggregate form: for example, as special tabulations by the Federal Statistical Office. We used such data to construct a synthetic panel by the use of grouped data.

Representativity

The EVS is claimed to be a representative sample of Germany's private households. Since taking part in the EVS is voluntary for the interviewed households, the Federal Statistical Office applies quota sampling to reach proper representation. This stratified sampling of households is carried out on the basis of the micro-census of the preceding year. The social position of the head of household (unemployed persons are also classified according to age and marital status as the head of household even though the head earns no income), household size, and household income are taken into account. The stratified sample is used for the calculation of a target number of interviews and to compute the final weights (Pöschl, 1993).

The EVS does not include segments of the population living in institutions and households with very high incomes. In the EVS 1993 and 1998, the monthly net household income was limited to DM35,000, (about €18,000). Since the highest income bracket of the micro-census is only DM7500 or more, the weights are not guaranteed to represent the upper-income segment (Laue, 1995). There is also doubt about the representativity of the bottom income segment (Börsch-Supan et al., 1999a). Comparisons of the EVS with other data sources indicate too much weight given to middle-income brackets. Table 3.1 presents some evidence to this effect in terms of homeownership. It shows ownership rates on the basis of the EVS 1978–93 and compares them with ownership rates on the basis of the GSOEP and the German housing censuses ("*Gebäude- und Wohnungszählung*"). The comparison shows that the number of households who own a home or an apartment is overestimated by the EVS. The same holds for the number of

---

[1]This coarsening was developed in two steps: a 1% error on each information in these deciles. Moreover, each of the five lowest and highest characteristics were replaced by their mean. See also Helmcke and Knoche (1992) for the method of anonymization.

TABLE 3.1   Coverage of Homeownership: EVS versus GWZ and GSOEP

	Source	1978	1983	1988	1993
HH owns real estate	EVS	43.3%	46.0%	47.4%	50.7%
HH lives in own home/condominium	EVS	41.8%	43.9%	45.7%	46.7%
HH lives in own home/condominium	GSOEP[a]		39.8%	40.2%	40.4%
HH lives in own home/condominium	GWS/GWZ[b]	37.6%	38.3%	39.1%	40.9%

Note: [a]First figure for 1984. [b]Figure for 1993 interpolated. All figures based on EVS and SOEP have been weighted by sampling weights.

Source: Own calculations based on EVS 1978–93, GSOEP 1984–93; Gebäude- und Wohnungszählung (GWZ) 1987; Ein-Prozent-Gebäude- und Wohnungsstichprobe (GWS) 1993.

households owning property. The bias in the scientific use file is even larger than in the full data set.[2]

Method of Data Acquisition

During the survey period each household keeps a monthly diary in which all income sources and expenditures for the most important areas are recorded. Around 70% of total expenditures are accounted for, without encumbering households with too much detailed bookkeeping (Lang, 1997). In addition, for 1 month in the year, a detailed recording of all expenditures helps to account for the remaining 30%.[3] In 1998, the procedure was changed, and the households recorded their diaries during one-quarter of the year on a rotating basis.

The records in the household diaries are complemented by two interviews. In the "basic interview" the composition of the household, socioeconomic characteristics, as well as equipment with durable goods, and living conditions are recorded. Changes during the survey period are noted in the monthly reports. Until 1998 the survey ended with the "final interview", during which the household is asked for its financial circumstances and public transfer payments. This interview also permits a control of the information given during the sample period. For example, it is possible to deduce interest income from the information about the household's stock of wealth. To avoid inconsistencies, the different reporting dates and periods have to be considered during the evaluation of the data (e.g., a change in the composition of the household or acquisition of property).

[2]See also Lang (1997) for an elaborate critical analysis of the EVS, and Börsch-Supan (1999) for a survey on suitable data sources for household saving in Germany.

[3]To exclude seasonal effects, the "Detailed Record Months" are equally distributed across households: thus, each month 1 out of 12 households records in detail.

Coverage

The coverage of EVS income has been checked against the national income and product accounts (Hertel, 1997). Such a comparison is only meaningful if methodological differences are accounted for. The national accounts statistics include private non-profit organizations, whereas the EVS includes only private households. Another important difference is the treatment of employers' contributions to social security insurance. Although the national accounts statistics include these contributions in the total payroll, the EVS does not.[4] Nevertheless, if one compares the disposable income of the national accounts statistics with the calculations of the EVS, the coverage is 93.5%. In 1988, this ratio was only around 86% (see Table 3.2).[5]

The high coverage of income in the EVS 1993 results from an almost complete coverage of the total of wages and salaries (97.6%) and a satisfying coverage of income from property and entrepreneurship (92.7%):[6] 94.3% of households in 1993 received current transfer payments with lower coverage than in 1988, but transfer payments carried out were overestimated in comparison to the national accounts.

TABLE 3.2   Coverage of Income by Sources: EVS versus NIPA

	NIPA	EVS 1993	
	Amount (DM)	Amount (DM)	Coverage (%)
Gross labor income	43,200	41,300	97.6
Gross capital and self-employment income	16,500	15,300	92.7
Transfers received	19,200	18,100	94.3
−Transfers given	22,900	23,200	101.3
Disposable income	55,100	51,500	93.5

Note: All figures refer to households. Coverage is defined as ratio of column (2) to column (1). Amounts in DM. US$1.00 corresponds to DM2.05 in purchasing power parity.

Source: Hertel (1997), p. 29.

[4]Further differences exist regarding the registration of profit retentions in the EVS, for example. Moreover, activities referring to the housing sector are classified as belonging to the corporate sector in the national accounts statistics. Contrary to this, the rental value of apartments used by taxpayers (*Mietwert der Eigentümerwohnung*) is regarded as capital assets income (*Einkünfte aus Kapitalvermögen*) (net of depreciation) in the EVS.

[5]See Lang (1997) for a detailed comparison of the EVS data 1978–88 with official statistics.

[6]Here, one has to consider that the EVS does not register any depreciation on facilities. Thus, rental and lease income (*Einkünfte aus Vermietung und Verpachtung*) as part of property income is upward biased.

TABLE 3.3   Coverage of Financial Wealth

	Germany: households excluding non-profit organizations		
	1993 Bundesbank estimates (1)	1993 income and expenditure survey (EVS) (2)	Percent of assets reported in EVS as compared to Bundesbank estimates (2)/(1)
Financial assets			
Checking, deposit, and savings accounts	41,222.7	14,157.6	34.3
Bonds	19,503.1	11,716.7	60.1
Stocks	6,295.9	2,522.4	40.1
Mutual funds and managed investment accounts	6,768.7	2,789.1	41.2
Building society savings contracts	6,765.1	4,214.5	62.3
Insurance and pension wealth	22,702.1	17,129.0	75.5
Other financial assets	8,067.9	6,320.6	78.3
Total financial assets	**110,220.8**	**58,849.9**	**53.4**
Non-financial assets			
Real estate wealth	167,132.2	181,939.4	108.9
Stock of durable goods	38,617.1	n.a.	n.a.
Total non-financial assets	**205,749.3**	**181,939.4**	**88.4**
Debt			
Mortgage loans	28,109.3	27,412.8	97.5
Consumer credit	8,951.1	2,990.4	33.4
Total debt	**37,060.0**	**30,403.2**	**82.0**
Total net wealth	**277,253.6**	**210,386.1**	**75.9**

Source: Eymann and Börsch-Supan, 2002, based on Deutsche Bundesbank (1994a,b,c; 1999a,b).

The coverage of financial wealth is harder to assess. Comparing the EVS wealth with the flow-of-funds statistics by the German Bundesbank shows that the extent of underreporting has varied over time. The total net worth of financial assets reported amounts to slightly less than 50% of the total net worth reported by Deutsche Bundesbank in 1978 and decreased to slightly less than 40% in 1988 (Lang, 1998). Table 3.3 shows that this trend has been reversed in the last wave (Guttmann, 1995): in 1993, the average value of financial assets per household amounted to 53.4% of the average financial wealth reported by Deutsche Bundesbank (1999b), and net worth is covered at about 75%.

There are several reasons for the discrepancy between survey and flow-of-funds data. First, assets of non-profit organizations are included as private households in the national accounting definition of the Bundesbank. This implies that the above coverage rates are substantial underestimates of the true coverage rates.

Secondly, major financial asset categories have not been covered at all in the survey instruments, including cash, checking accounts, and employer-based pension claims. According to the *Finanzierungs- und Geldvermögensrechnung* 1983 by the Bundesbank, these unreported assets represent about 15% of all financial assets held by private households (7.7% in cash and checking accounts, and 7.5% in occupational pension funds not under the financial control of the employee).

Thirdly, stocks reported by the EVS cover only about 40% of stocks held by private households (Lang, 1993). The remaining unaccounted 60% represent most likely the wealth of the upper 2% tail of the income distribution, which is not sampled in the EVS. Because the wealth distribution is much more skewed than the income distribution, far more than 2% of wealth remains unreported in the EVS.

Coding Changes

The Federal Statistical Office carries out several checks for plausibility of the EVS. Obvious coding errors are corrected. Information about wealth is estimated to correct for missing or implausible information. For example, if households offer only information about the sum of their equity wealth, this sum is distributed equally across the different kinds of equities, not a breakdown by type (Lang, 1997; Euler, 1985). Unfortunately, an external user cannot distinguish between the original information and the changes undertaken by the Federal Statistical Office. Our analysis largely avoids the use of such contaminated data.

Construction of Longitudinal Data

Each wave of the EVS represents a separate cross section. Even if a household has participated in two or more surveys, identification is not possible, though it is possible to construct a synthetic panel for the five EVS waves 1978 through 1998. Households of each survey are divided up into as many homogeneous household types ("cells") as possible. Next, these cells are identified across time. Such a panel does not consist of households but household groups as sampling units. On the one hand, the statistical analysis of such synthetic panels is eased by reducing the unobserved heterogeneity: this is accomplished by taking means within household types. On the other hand, neglecting movements between household types across time may lead to biases (Deaton, 1985). As long as there is no panel of individuals with savings data, we will have to live with a conflict between stability and homogeneity of the cells.

To obtain consistent variable definitions across cross sections, one has to take into account the differences between surveys; the EVS 1993 contains much more detailed information than earlier surveys and the 1998 survey; many variable definitions change from survey to survey. A consistent definition of variables across all the five surveys makes it necessary to make compromises. Thus, it is not always possible to use the detailed information contained in the EVS 1993 for the comparative analysis.[7]

Earlier Work Using the EVS

The previous subsections have shown that the EVS are by no means ideal data sets to study savings. To this date, however, they represent the best data to study household savings in Germany (Börsch-Supan, 1999). The German Federal Statistical Office publishes regular evaluations of savings and wealth based on the EVS: e.g., Euler (1985, 1990) and Guttmann (1995) for financial wealth and Laue (1995) for land property in 1993. The latest wave is presented in Statistisches Bundesamt (2001a), and Statistisches Bundesamt (2001b) reports financial wealth, Statistisches Bundesamt (1999) land property in 1998.

Börsch-Supan and Stahl (1991) deduce saving profiles from cross-sectional data of the EVS 1983 that are in sharp contrast to the predictions of the life-cycle hypotheses. As a possible explanation, they suggest health constraints on consumption in the face of a guaranteed high annuity income. Using a synthetic panel of the EVS 1978 and 1983, Börsch-Supan (1992) confirms the results of this study. Taking the EVS 1988 as additional data, Lang (1996) works out saving profiles and detailed forecasts of future income and wealth circumstances of senior citizens. Schnabel (1999) presents first evaluations of empirical saving profiles on the basis of the EVS 1978–93. Rodepeter and Winter (1998) as well as Börsch-Supan et al. (1999b) stress the importance of detailed micro data for differentiated hypotheses testing: various extensions of the pure life-cycle hypotheses, such as liquidity constraints, income uncertainty, and increasing risk aversion, yield age–savings profiles that resemble each other and are very similar to evaluated savings profiles of the EVS. Such longitudinal savings patterns have been constructed and interpreted by Börsch-Supan et al. (1999c, 2001b). This paper adds the 1998 wave to their synthetic panel.

There are only a few empirical studies of German households' portfolio choices. Schlomann (1992), Grimm (1998), and Lang (1998) have used the EVS to analyze the socioeconomic determinants of household portfolio choice, whereas Eymann

---

[7]A detailed account of cross-sectional and longitudinal variable definitions can be found in Börsch-Supan et al. (1999c). An English translation can be found on the web under www.mea. uni-mannheim.de

and Börsch-Supan (2002) provide an econometric analysis of East and West German households' portfolios. Börsch-Supan and Essig (2002) analyze stock holding in Germany.

In addition to studies on savings and investment behavior, there is a wide range of literature on other household characteristics and decisions. For the definition of household income we build on the work of Becker (1997) and Hauser and Becker (1998). They observe that the distribution of household income was relatively stable in spite of large economic fluctuations. The income structure of low-income households is analyzed by Hauser and Neumann (1992) and Hauser (1997). Münnich (1997), Börsch-Supan et al. (1999a), as well as Börsch-Supan and Reil-Held (1998) examine the income structure of households of retired couples. Our definition of households' stock of wealth is based on the contribution of Schnabel (1999). Furthermore, there is a range of studies that help us to resolve some problems in detail: Reil-Held (1999) examines the influence of inheritances on the accumulation of aggregate wealth. Walliser and Winter (1999) study the determinants of the demand for life insurance contracts. Fachinger (1998) investigates the measurement of wealth distribution on the basis of the EVS and additional data sets.

3.3   THE FLOW OF HOUSEHOLD SAVING

The data permit two measurements of savings. The first measure is based on changes in the stock of assets and is computed as the sum of purchases of assets minus sales of assets. Changes in financial assets reported in the EVS (see Table 3.4) are deposits to and withdrawals from the various kinds of savings accounts; purchases and sales of stocks and bonds; deposits to and withdrawals from dedicated savings accounts at building societies ("Bausparkassen") which are an important savings component in Germany; and contributions to life insurances and private pension plans minus payments received. New loans are subtracted and repayments are added to net savings. Not reported are changes in cash and checking accounts. Changes in real assets reported in the EVS are purchases and sales of real estate and business partnerships. Not reliably reported are changes in durables (other than real estate). Unrealized capital gains are unreported. To arrive at saving rates, household saving is divided by disposable household income, consisting of labor, asset, and transfer income minus taxes and social security contributions.

The second definition of saving is the residual of income minus consumption. We will show that both definitions are very close on average, although there is substantial discrepancy for some households. This definition requires several adjustments to the income and expenditure components (see Tables 3.5 and 3.6). The most important adjustments are voluntary contributions into the public pension system. If these contributions are regarded as savings, they must not be subtracted

TABLE 3.4   Asset Components in the EVS

Component	Subcomponent
Gross financial wealth	Passbook savings
	Savings in building societies
	Bond-like passbook savings
	Municipal bonds
	Government bonds
	Stocks
	Real estate funds
	Investment funds
	Other bonds
	Resale value of life and similar insurances
	Other financial wealth
−Loans	Consumer loans
	Mortgages
+ Real estate	Sales value of:
	One and two family homes
	Multi-family houses
	Condominiums

Note: The EVS provides no data on checking accounts and no reliable data on business property.

from gross income in order to obtain disposable income. However, if they are regarded as taxes paid for future transfer income, they decrease gross income, but have no effect on wealth accumulation. We take the first road. Transfers of other private households are another, less important example. We consistently regard them as income components rather than wealth transfers.

A third definition, the difference between initial and end of period stocks of wealth, cannot be computed from the data since stocks are measured only once in each wave.

We distinguish three components of household savings:

A. *Discretionary saving* is defined as changes in financial and real wealth that are under the control of the household as it concerns the absolute volume and its portfolio composition.
B. *Mandatory saving* is defined as changes in financial wealth that are beyond the control of the household, either in terms of volume (e.g., a fixed percent of gross income) or in terms of portfolio composition (e.g., the employer provides only one pension plan).
C. A third component – sometimes dubbed *"notional" saving* – comprises contributions to pay-as-you-go systems such as public pensions, health, and long-term care insurance that may substitute for actual saving.

TABLE 3.5   Income Components in the EVS

Income component	Subcomponent
Gross income	Labor income
	Self-employment income
	Capital income (interest, dividends, capital withdrawals)
	Rental income (excl. imputed rent for owner-occupied home) minus expenses (mortgage interest, utilities, maintenance)
	Public transfer income
	Private transfer income
	Irregular transfer payments below DM2000 received minus such transfers given
−Taxes and contributions	Income tax
	Property tax
	Church tax
	Mandatory contributions to public retirement, health, and unemployment insurance
	Voluntary contributions to public retirement insurance
+ Inheritances and gifts	Irregular transfer payments above DM2000 received minus such transfers given

The distinction between categories A and B can only be made when we have a detailed account of how total saving is split among different usages. This is obviously not possible for a residual saving measure when consumption is subtracted from income. We will therefore begin by concentrating on the first saving measure: the sum of purchases of assets minus sales of assets.

The crucial difference between categories B and C is that contributions under category B are funded whereas contributions under category C will not add to the capital stock of the economy. We will present a measure of "social security wealth" generated by the contributions to the German public pension system in Section 3.4.

Discretionary Saving in EVS 1978–98

Figure 3.1 shows mean total discretionary saving by age in the five cross sections 1978–98. On the vertical axis, amounts are given in real terms, converted to 1993 euros.[8] On the horizontal axis, we have age, generally in 5-year intervals. Each

[8]All amounts were deflated using the German consumer price index.

TABLE 3.6   Expenditure Components in the EVS

Components	Subcomponents
Consumption	Food
	Clothing
	Housing (excl. imputed rent for owner occupancy)
	Utilities
	Durables
	Health
	Transportation
	Education and leisure
	Valuables, other
Other taxes	Inheritance and gift taxes
	Car taxes
Insurance premiums	Voluntary contributions to public health insurance
	Premiums to private health insurance
	Premiums to car insurance
	Premiums to liability and similar insurances
	Other insurance premiums
Fees and charities	
Interest for overdrafts	
Expenditures for owner-occupied homes and condominiums (mortgage interest, utilities, and maintenance)	

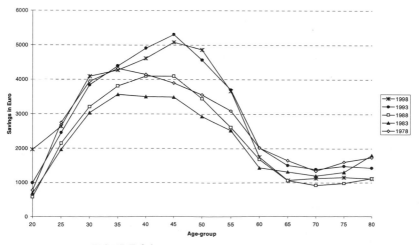

FIGURE 3.1   Mean discretionary saving in 1978–98.

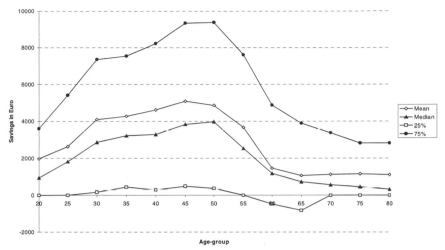

FIGURE 3.2   Mean and median discretionary saving in 1998.

age category also represents a cohort, and following points on one of the cross-sectional lines drawn in Figure 3.1 compares households that are simultaneously in different age categories and cohorts.

The shapes are roughly similar. Changes across years are far from a simple shift of each profile: for the younger age groups, 1993 and 1998 were the years with the highest saving, whereas there is less of a clear picture for the older ones. There are two main features: first, saving exhibits a hump shape, reaching a peak at the age/cohort group around age 45; secondly, saving remains positive, even in old age. These features are astoundingly similar for all income groups except the lower income quarter of the German households, see Figure 3.2. Median and mean saving have the same hump shape as Figure 3.1, and remain positive for all age groups, except for the lower quartile.

Whereas Figures 3.1 and 3.2 were calculated as purchases minus sales of assets during one calendar year, the EVS also permits the computation of a second savings measure: namely, the residual from subtracting all consumption expenditures from disposable income.[9] Figure 3.3 depicts the comparison of both measures and shows that our saving measure is robust. The figure also gives an impression of the sampling error of our saving measure, which is relatively small due to the large cell sizes.

The first measure is almost always within the 2σ confidence bands of the second measure. Using confidence bands for both measures, the difference is not

---

[9]Disposable income is gross income minus direct taxes and contributions to mandatory social security systems. Consumption expenditures are reported in great detail in the EVS, based on weekly diaries. For precise definitions, see Börsch-Supan et al. (1999c).

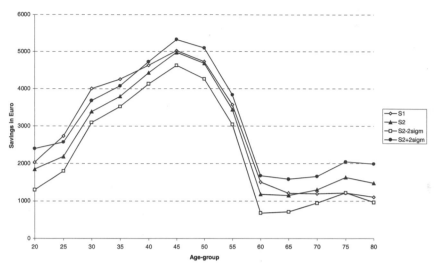

FIGURE 3.3   Mean discretionary saving by two different definitions, 1998.

significant.[10] This is an important result as it strengthens the belief in the internal consistency of the data, even though there are some large deviations between the two measures for a few households which are masked by the averages depicted in Figure 3.3.

Cohort Analysis of Discretionary Saving

Figures 3.1–3.3 display cross-sectional variation across age/cohort groups and do not identify life-cycle changes. In order to understand life-cycle behavior, we need to follow households over time. As pointed out in Section 3.2, we lack longitudinal data on savings in Germany and therefore combine the data of the available five EVS cross sections from 1978 to 1998 to a synthetic panel of household groups. Figure 3.4 displays cohort-specific age–savings profiles from this synthetic panel under the identifying assumption that time effects are zero, starting on the left with the youngest cohort in our data, born between 1964 and 1968, and proceeding to the oldest cohort, born between 1904 and 1908.[11] Saving increases until it reaches a peak in the age range 45–49, then declines until the 65–69 age group. It then remains essentially flat. As pointed out previously, saving remains positive even in old age.

[10]The bands are computed under the assumption that the quota sample can be treated as a random sample.
[11]Identifying assumptions in genuine and synthetic panels (Deaton, 1985) are discussed by Brugiavini and Weber (2001).

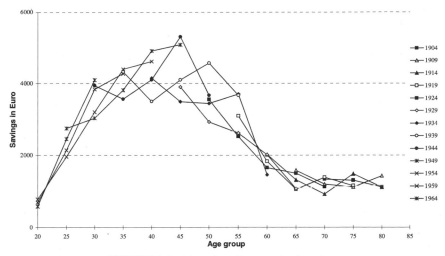

FIGURE 3.4 Mean discretionary saving by cohort.

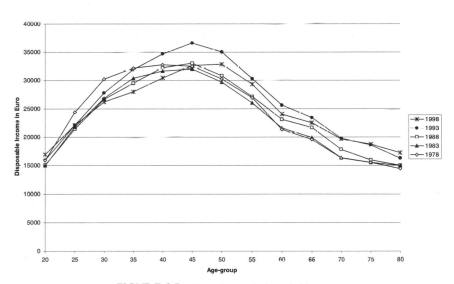

FIGURE 3.5 Mean disposable household income.

Total savings in Figure 3.4 can be split up into two components: disposable household income times saving rates. Disposable household income has a pronounced hump-shape pattern: see Figure 3.5. Hence, savings rates, to which we will turn now, are likely to be flatter over the life cycle than total savings.

Saving Rates

Because mean saving rates are very sensitive to changes in nominator and denominator, we focus on the median and quartile saving rates in each age category. We only show the 1998 cross section, since the others have a very similar shape. Figure 3.6 shows that the age/cohort pattern is rather stable across income quartiles. The differences (pronounced hump shape for the richer, fairly flat for the poorer households) are thus mainly due to differences in income profiles, as speculated above. The increase in mean saving rates at very old age is interesting. Quite clearly, it is due to households in the upper part of the income distribution. Remember, however, that the data only cover households, not the elderly in institutions. Thus, the sample selects those who are less likely to dissave. A back-of-the-envelope calculation (Börsch-Supan, 1992) shows that the institutionalization rates are much too low to create a selection effect that could by itself turn the high saving rates in old age to dissaving. A more precise analysis of this selection effect, however, should be based on genuine longitudinal data, which is currently not available.

If we combine the data in Figure 3.6 with the other waves and disentangle age and cohort effects, we obtain the life-cycle profiles of Figure 3.7. Saving rates are fairly stable and around 12% for all young and middle-aged groups until around age 45–49. They then decline and stabilize around age 65–69, when they remain at about 4%.[12]

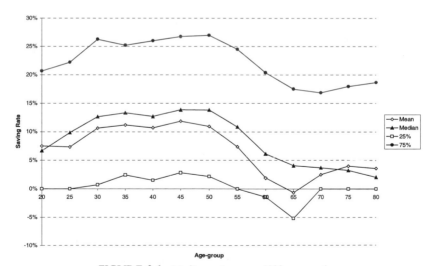

FIGURE 3.6   Median saving rates, 1998 cross section.

---

[12]The data suggest an increase for the 1988 wave for all older cohorts. We have no satisfactory explanation for this effect, particularly, because the pension level decreased between 1983 and 1988.

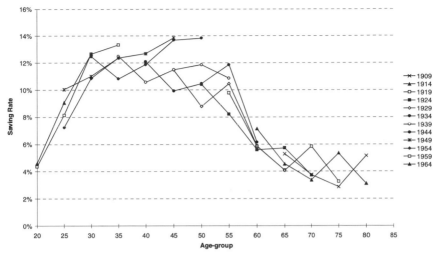

FIGURE 3.7   Median saving rates by cohort.

Composition of Discretionary Saving: Real and Financial Saving

Real estate saving is depicted in Figure 3.8. It mainly consists of purchases minus sales of owner-occupied housing, and it subtracts applicable mortgage payments.[13] We did not add upkeep and subtract depreciation, because we have no reliable estimate of depreciation, or of house value appreciation; we have simply assumed that the three components cancel each other out, which is roughly the case on average, since housing values are more stable than in other countries, e.g., the United States. Figure 3.8 shows the five cross sections of real saving, 1978–98. Because homeownership in Germany is only about 40%, much lower than in most other countries, the median is mostly zero and not shown. The means depicted in Figure 3.8 quickly reach a sizable magnitude for the age/cohort groups around age 35 and then decline steadily, reflecting much less housing wealth among the households which are older and born earlier. Note that this graph is particularly prone to misunderstanding: the pattern visible in Figure 3.8 does not necessarily reflect a life-cycle change in which households decumulate housing wealth as they age. It may also represent a generational change from cohort to cohort: households in younger cohorts experienced wealthier times and could generally afford more expensive homes than their parent generation.

[13]Other real wealth is not well measured. For example, the EVS data do not permit a sensible measurement of changes in wealth that is invested in business partnerships. This affects only a few households significantly, but not the average: see Börsch-Supan et al. (1999c). We also do not have the regional information necessary to impute capital gains in housing, which were large in some places such as Munich.

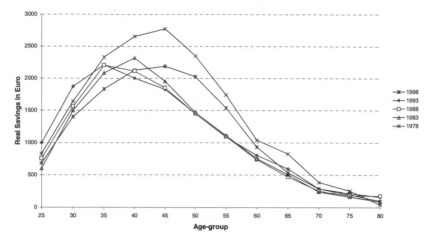

FIGURE 3.8   Mean real saving, 1978–98.

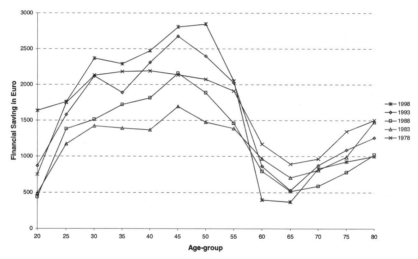

FIGURE 3.9   Mean financial saving, 1978–98.

The counterpart to real saving is financial saving; depicted in Figures 3.9, 3.10 and 3.11. Figures 3.9 and 3.10 show means and medians for all five cross sections; Figure 3.11 shows mean, median, and quartiles for 1998.

Mean and median financial saving are very close, and the median is positive even in old age. This is quite different from US observations, where most households do not accumulate financial assets over most parts of their life cycle, and points to the more equal income distribution in Germany than in the United States (see Table 3.7): more than 90% of all households have incomes between 0 and only twice the average income.

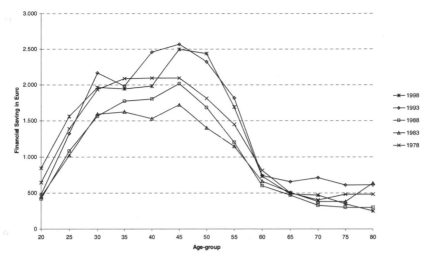

FIGURE 3.10   Median financial saving, 1978–98.

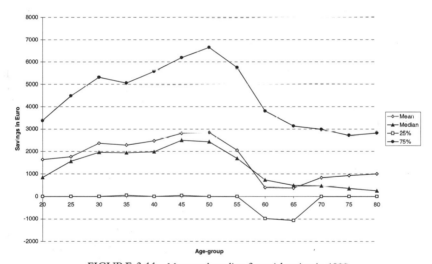

FIGURE 3.11   Mean and median financial saving in 1998.

Financial saving is relatively flat between age 30 and 40, then reaches a peak between age 40 and 45.[14] The flat part is most likely to be due to the slow build-up or even withdrawal of financial assets during the ages when many households purchase a house. It is noteworthy that financial saving remains positive

[14]Our measure of financial saving includes the conventional financial saving categories, such as consumer loans, but excludes mortgages and capital gains or losses. Capital gains to the consumer have been small in Germany relative to the UK and the United States, see Eymann and Börsch-Supan (2002).

TABLE 3.7   Income Distribution (EVS 1993)

	Percentile									
	1%	5%	10%	25%	50%	75%	90%	95%	99%	Mean
Gross income	11,199	16,792	21,614	34,542	58,809	91,451	128,798	157,023	234,882	69,478
Disposable income	10,678	15,827	20,027	29,989	46,692	70,107	98,423	120,705	179,986	54,743
Disposable labor and transfer income	9,504	14,712	18,515	28,060	43,452	66,151	92,294	111,556	163,725	51,094

Note: Calculations for West Germany only. All figures weighted. The 99th percentile in the EVS corresponds to the 97th percentile in total population because of sample truncation at monthly net incomes above DM35,000.

Source: Own calculations based on EVS 1993.

even for those households that are age 70 and older. Mean financial saving substantially increases during old age. Since the median stays flat, this must mainly be a phenomenon among richer households.

Figure 3.11 shows some more distributional details of the 1998 wave. The main increase at old age appears to come from the richest upper 10% or so of households, since the 75% percentile is still relatively flat. Note however, as mentioned in Section 3.2, that our data excludes the upper 2% of the income distribution and thus misses households that deviate even further from the median.

Mandatory Saving

Mandatory contributions to public funded pension plans are negligible in Germany. Only a minority of civil servants are required to contribute a small percentage of their salary increases to funds that are effectively invested in government bonds. The contributions amount to roughly 0.5% of salary.

Contributions to private pension plans are not negligible in Germany, but they are much smaller, for example, than in the Netherlands or in the Anglo-Saxon countries. Slightly more than 50% of workers are covered by a firm pension at least part of their career, but these pensions are small and provide only about 6% of total average retirement income. In many cases, these pension plans are mandatory in the sense that they come as a package deal with the employment contract and offer no opting-out possibility.

Because mandatory occupational pensions play such a small role in Germany, the related saving flows have been subsumed in the discretionary saving category discussed earlier.

"Notional Saving": Mandatory Contributions to Pay-As-You-Go Systems

Germany has very large pay-as-you-go systems that finance old age and health care. Almost all dependent employees and their employers must contribute to the German public retirement insurance. In our view (Börsch-Supan, 2001a,b), these contributions are not saving in a narrow sense. However, they are a functional equivalent of saving and are thus regarded by some authors to be savings in a broader sense, see, e.g., Jappelli (2001). We refer to them as "notional savings." They are certainly a potentially important determinant for discretionary saving, as discussed in Section 3.6.

For an overwhelming portion of the population, contributions (or "notional savings") are proportional to gross income. As detailed in Section 3.5, the contribution rate to the public retirement insurance in 2001 was 19.1% of gross earnings[15] up to an upper earning threshold which is about 1.8 times the average income, about the 85th percentile of the earnings distribution. In addition, an estimated 8.5% of gross earnings is levied indirectly via other taxes, mainly VAT and the new ecology tax. Opting out of the public retirement system is impossible. Due to the upper earnings threshold, high wage earners pay a lower percentage of their income into the pay-as-you-go system and receive a correspondingly lower replacement rate. The contributions add up to a claim on public pensions that is substantial when compared to actual financial and real wealth. We consider this point in Section 3.4 on wealth.

Other branches of the German social insurance system include health, long-term care, and unemployment insurance. For the average worker, the contributions to these branches add up to another 21% of gross income.[16] For the public health and long-term care insurance, the tax base is capped at about 1.6 times the average earnings. Workers above this threshold can opt out. The contribution base for the unemployment insurance is capped at about 1.8 times the average earnings. Opting out is impossible.

In sum, these social insurance contributions by far exceed discretionary savings for all dependent employees below the earnings cap – about 85% of all workers.

3.4 THE STOCK OF WEALTH BY AGE AND BIRTH COHORT

The EVS also provide data on the stocks of financial, real, and total discretionary wealth in a separate interview at the end of each survey year. We use these data

---

[15]More precisely: gross earnings include net earnings, income taxes, and the employee's share (one-half) of social security contributions. Total labor compensation includes gross earnings as defined plus the second half of social security contributions, the so-called employer's share.

[16]See footnote 15.

to crosscheck our findings on saving flows and to obtain a picture of total resources at the disposal of a household when the household reaches retirement.

Discretionary Real and Financial Wealth

Figure 3.12 depicts total discretionary wealth, defined in accordance to the flow measure of discretionary saving in Section 3.2. It consists of gross financial and real wealth, minus outstanding consumer loans and mortgages.

Figure 3.13 takes the same data and arranges it by cohorts using the synthetic panel approach described earlier.

We see that total discretionary wealth increases until late in life, and there is only a brief (and statistically insignificant) indication of a flat episode for the 1904, 1909, and 1914 cohorts, and even at the oldest cohorts the change between the first and the last observation is positive.

West German private households possessed an average total wealth of €122,000. At the time of the head's retirement, an average German household owned around €138,000 of total wealth in 1993. This is 12.5 times the annual public pension of an average employee with 45 years of service in 1993: net €11,000. The median wealth at that age is €100,000, which is lower than the mean but still relatively high. Thus, drawing down wealth could quite substantially contribute to consumption (Schnabel, 1999). Nevertheless, accumulation of even more wealth in the form of financial wealth takes place on average in old age, as was illustrated in the savings profiles presented earlier. This is a surprising departure from the life-cycle hypothesis.

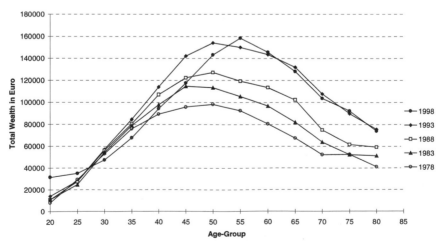

FIGURE 3.12   Mean total discretionary wealth, 1978–98.

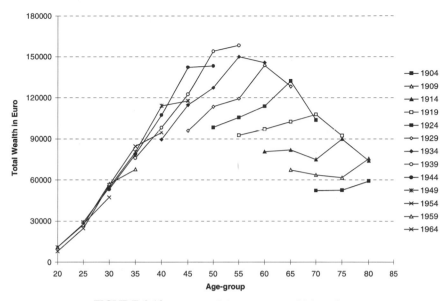

FIGURE 3.13   Mean total discretionary wealth by cohort.

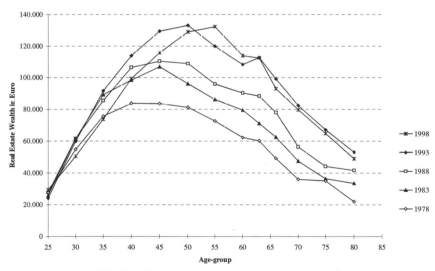

FIGURE 3.14   Mean gross real estate wealth, 1978–98.

The largest part of total discretionary wealth is real estate – in particular owner-occupied housing: compare Figures 3.14 and 3.16, for the life-cycle profiles Figures 3.15 and 3.17. For the group aged 30–59, real wealth amounts to 80–90% of total wealth. Mean gross real wealth increased substantially from 1978 to 1993. A more detailed analysis shows that this is mainly caused by an increase in

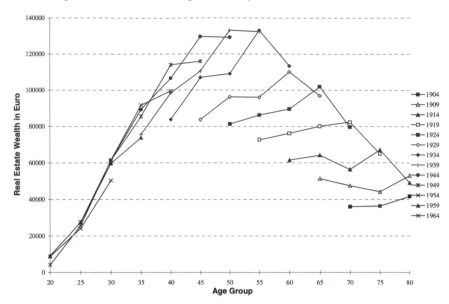

FIGURE 3.15   Mean gross real estate wealth by cohort.

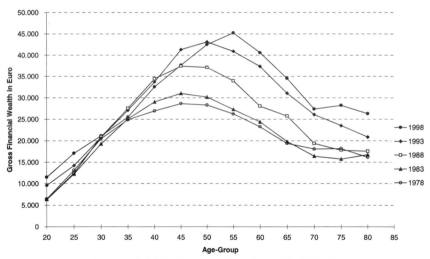

FIGURE 3.16   Mean gross financial wealth, 1978–98.

homeownership from cohort to cohort, whereas ownership rates remained essentially constant with increasing age after age 60 for any given cohort (Schnabel, 1999).

Financial wealth increased by almost 40% between 1978 and 1993. This increase was mainly caused by a wealth expansion of the middle-age classes.

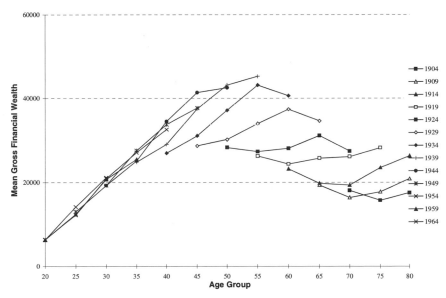

FIGURE 3.17   Mean gross financial wealth by cohort.

The expansion of financial wealth is particularly striking between 1983 and 1993. The reason is a large increase in securities ownership for all age classes. Between 1993 and 1998, we observe a structural shift: financial wealth in the younger-age classes/birth cohorts slightly decreased, while it slightly increased for the older households.

Pension Wealth

The life-cycle pattern of discretionary wealth in Germany – almost always increasing, at most flat – is in contrast to the hump-shaped pattern of unfunded ("notional") pension wealth that trivially emerges from the sequence of first paying pension contributions and then receiving pension benefits. Figure 3.18 shows how notional pension wealth builds up and is drawn down in a synthetic life cycle. The representative worker underlying this simulation has an earnings history of the average age-specific wage between ages 20 and 60, then retires at the average retirement age and draws the statutory pension benefits. Notional pension wealth, social security wealth or SSW, at time t is then computed as[17]

$$SSW\ (t) = (1 + \rho)\,SSW\ (t-1) + \text{contributions}\ (t) - \text{benefits}\ (t)$$

[17] See Brugiavini and Weber (2001) for a discussion of this measure.

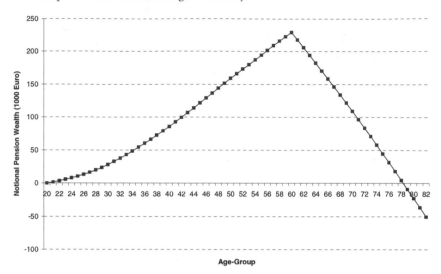

FIGURE 3.18   Life-cycle build-up of notional pension wealth.

where ρ is the internal rate of return that equalizes the present value of contributions and benefits for the above 40-year contribution history and a duration of benefits corresponding to average life expectancy. At retirement, notional pension wealth of the representative worker is about €200,000, which is 30% more than the sum of average financial and real wealth shown in Figure 3.12. By definition, notional pension wealth is drawn down after age 60 and becomes negative after age 78 (average life expectancy): see Figure 3.18. In contrast, financial and real wealth increases until age 70 for the 1919 cohort (see Figure 3.13), and increases between age 60 (65) and age 75 (80) for the 1914 (1909) cohort. This contrast is not by chance. Rather, it reflects the influence of pension policies on discretionary saving. We will analyze this link in this chapter, which starts with Section 3.5.

3.5 THE INSTITUTIONAL BACKGROUND FOR SAVING IN GERMANY

We begin the second part of this chapter by a description of the institutional background that is likely to influence saving decisions of German households. We first sketch the German pension system as it relates to savings. Börsch-Supan and Schnabel (1999) provide a more extensive description as part of the international comparison of retirement behavior in Gruber and Wise (1999). We then deal with other savings incentives – mainly, the German system of capital taxation and dedicated savings incentives.

The German Pension System

Germany has a contribution-based pay-as-you-go (PAYG) system. It is monolithical, covering almost all workers and providing almost all retirement income in a single system with relatively transparent rules. Until recently, it had been successful in providing a high and reliable level of retirement income and was praised as one of the reasons for social and political stability in Germany. It has survived two major wars, the Great Depression and, more recently, unification. However, times have changed, and a flurry of reforms since 1992 have not succeeded in stabilizing contribution rates, public support, and system enrollment. There are two main reasons for the increasing difficulties of the German public pension system: population aging and negative incentive effects on labor supply.

As opposed to other countries such as the UK and the Netherlands, which originally adopted a Beveridgian social security system that provided only a base pension, public pensions in Germany were from the start designed to extend the standard of living that was achieved during working life to the time after retirement. Thus, public pensions are roughly proportional to labor income averaged over the entire life and feature only few redistributive properties. Benefits include old-age pensions, survivor benefits at 60% of old-age pensions, and disability benefits exceeding old-age pension benefits before age 65.

Benefits are computed on a lifetime contribution basis. They are the product of four elements: (1) the employee's relative wage position, averaged over the entire earnings history, multiplied by (2) the number of years of service life and (3) adjustment factors for pension type (old-age and two disability pension types) and retirement age (since the 1992 reform), both in turn multiplied by (4) the average pension level that is indexed "dynamically" (i.e., during the entire retirement period) to the current average net wage of the working population. Until 1992, indexation was to gross wages. The first three factors make up the "personal pension base," whereas the fourth factor determines the income distribution between workers and pensioners in general. Wage indexation has kept the income distribution between workers and pensioners constant, as it has automatically transferred productivity gains also to pensioners.

The German retirement insurance system has a high replacement rate, generating net retirement incomes that in the 1990s were about 70% of pre-retirement net earnings for a worker with a 45-year earnings history and average lifetime earnings.[18] This is substantially higher than, for example, the corresponding US net replacement rate of about 53%.[19] In addition, the German retirement insurance system provides generous survivor benefits that constitute

[18]This replacement rate is defined as the current pension of a retiree with a 45-year average earnings history divided by the current average earnings of all dependently employed workers. This concept is different from the replacement rate relative to the most recent earnings because these are usually higher than the lifetime average.

[19]Using the same replacement rate concept as in footnote 18.

a substantial proportion of total unfunded pension wealth, and disability benefits at similar and sometimes even higher replacement levels than old-age pensions.

Because of this high replacement rate, public pensions are by far the largest pillar of retirement income, much more so than in many other countries.[20] Public pensions constitute more than 80% of the income of households headed by persons aged 65 and older, whereas funded retirement income, such as asset income or firm pensions, plays a much smaller role than, for example, in the Netherlands or the Anglo-Saxon countries. Pension funds are largely unknown in Germany, although an increasing number of workers, in particular young ones, have bought whole life insurance. As a result, Germany has few institutional investors and stock market capitalization is very low in international terms.

Adding to the generosity are the early retirement provisions. The 1972 pension reform introduced the opportunity to retire at different ages ("flexible retirement") during a "window of retirement." This window began at age 60 for women, the unemployed, and for workers who could not appropriately be employed for health or labor market reasons. It began at age 63 for workers with a long service history (35 years, including higher education, military service, a certain number of years for raising children, etc.). Normal retirement age was (and still is) age 65. The 1972 reform did not introduce an actuarial adjustment. The reforms in the 1990s will shift the window of retirement for all workers to age 62 and will include an adjustment of benefits. However, this adjustment will be about half of the actuarially fair adjustment.

The introduction of early retirement in 1972 had a huge impact on retirement age. Within a few years, average retirement age among men dropped by about 3 years below age 60.[21] The resulting distribution of retirement ages became marked by distinct "spikes" at ages 60, 63, and 65. The retirement age of 65 now mostly applies to women with a very short earnings history, whereas the most popular retirement age among men became age 60. Since average life expectancy of a male worker at age 60 is about 18 years, the earlier retirement age amounts to an increase in pension expenditures of about 15%. The effect is smaller, but still significant, for women.

Disability status is granted for medical reasons. In this case, no actuarial adjustments apply, even after the 1992 reform. Moreover, pensions received before age 60 are calculated as if the worker had worked to age 60. Incentives to take up disability pensions are thus strong if one manages to claim full disability status. Disability status is also given for economic reasons: e.g., when a worker could not find a job at all, or no appropriate job. In the latter case, a lower replacement rate applies.

The German public pension system provides two floors for retirement income. First, contributions below a certain minimum have ex post been topped to lie

---

[20]See the international comparisons in Gruber and Wise (1999) and OECD (1998).

[21]Averaged over new recipients of old-age and disability pensions. Results for women are similar.

between 50 and 75% of average contributions. Although not an entitlement by the law, the Bundestag has enacted such ex-post adjustments to poor workers' earnings histories, and has thereby effectively introduced a minimum pension. Secondly, social assistance provides a minimum income to which all Germans are entitled. Older households receive a higher minimum income than younger households (about €600 for single elderly, €900 for an elderly couple, including housing assistance).

The topping-up mechanism has generated a redistributive element along the income scale into the German retirement insurance. However, quantitatively this intragenerational redistribution is small relative to the other intragenerational redistribution through early retirement (Börsch-Supan and Reil-Held, 2001). Social assistance is quantitatively more important, and has shielded the elderly from poverty. Indeed, poverty rates are much lower in Germany than in the United States and in the UK.

Savings Subsidies and Taxation

Germany has a tradition of promoting the formation of household wealth. It rests on two pillars — favorable tax treatment of asset holdings and direct savings subsidies. Starting in the 1950s, German tax and subsidy policies were initially set up to foster the formation of industrial capital and housing in the early post-war years. In the 1960s and 1970s, the focus was gradually shifted to low- and medium-income earners with children.[22] In the wake of reunification, subsidies and tax exemptions were temporarily expanded to promote industry, infrastructure, and housing construction in East Germany, much in the spirit of the policies of the early 1950s.

Three different systems of subsidies for long-term saving plans were introduced in the late 1950s and 1960s.[23] Subsidies to undedicated long-term saving contracts ("*Sparprämie*"), subsidies to contributions to building society saving contracts ("*Wohnungsbauprämie*"), and subsidies to employer-sponsored saving plans ("*Arbeitnehmer-Sparzulage*"). Subsidy rates varied over time and were generally higher for dedicated saving plans.

The inflation of the 1970s seriously eroded the accessibility of the subsidies because income limits and contribution caps remained unadjusted. In the 1980s and 1990s, the scope of assets was narrowed to building society saving contracts, stocks, stock-based mutual funds, and loans to the employer, further reducing the attractiveness. The accessibility of *Wohnungsbauprämie* and *Arbeitnehmer-Sparzulage* was widened again during the 1990s, however. Subsidies to building society saving contracts were a key element in housing construction programs

---

[22]For a detailed description of savings subsidies and taxation in Germany, see Börsch-Supan (1994a).
[23]A recent history is detailed in Eymann and Börsch-Supan (2002).

for Eastern Germany. Germany may soon see yet another shift in the use of dedicated saving subsidies: it is now planned to funnel most saving subsidies to mutual funds dedicated to retirement income as an individual or company-sponsored supplement to the public pension system.

Savings subsidies were available to lower-middle-income households and amounted to less than €100/year during the 1980s and 1990s.[24] The successive policy changes have left their traces on households' portfolio choice (see Table 3.8). The decrease in long-term saving contracts in the 1980s is most likely due to the decrease in real after-tax yields of long-term saving contracts compared to bonds. Another piece of evidence is the diverging trends in ownership rates and portfolio shares of building society saving contracts between Eastern and Western Germany (see Eymann and Börsch-Supan, 2002). Obviously, a growing number of eligible households took out building society saving contracts during the 1990s, but held their investment to roughly €500/year, the ceiling for the subsidies.

As we have seen, it seems questionable whether policy shocks were the sole cause of changes in portfolio composition. Rather, changes in the relative yields of assets and savings policy shocks are likely codetermined by common underlying factors (notably the determinants of increasing budget deficits) and mutually reinforcing.

The favorable tax treatment of rented and, to a lesser degree, owner-occupied housing[25] as well as of life insurance contracts forms the second and strongest pillar of German saving policy. Like the subsidies described above, tax exemptions generally favor low- and medium-income employee households with children.[26]

Stocks, mutual funds, and housing were also implicitly tax-favored in that capital gains were not taxed if assets were held beyond the "speculation period" which was 6 months and 1 year, respectively; these were lengthened to 1 year and 10 years in 2000, significantly reducing this incentive.

The attractiveness of owner-occupied housing is further reduced because interest payments for mortgages are not tax-deductible. However, mortgage interest was made tax-deductible in 1991 for a restricted period of 3 years. In line with a general expansion of tax breaks for housing in Eastern Germany, this measure was introduced in order to increase the incentives for housing construction. It seems likely that the increase in the ratio of new mortgage loans to real estate formation reported by Deutsche Bundesbank (1999b) for the early 1990s is related to this policy change.

---

[24]A maximum subsidy of €100 on a maximum contribution of €500.

[25]See Börsch-Supan (1994a).

[26]Life insurance contracts are a noteworthy exception to this rule. The tax treatment of interest and capital gains favors the rich. Moreover, contributions to life insurance contracts are (partly) tax exempt for civil servants and the self-employed (see Brunsbach and Lang, 1998).

TABLE 3.8   Asset Shares According to Aggregate Financial Accounts (in %)

	West Germany: households incl. non-profit organizations					Germany: households incl. non-profit organizations		Germany: households excl. non-profit organizations			
	1975	1980	1985	1990	1992	1990	1992	1990	1993	1995	1997
Financial assets											
Checking, deposit, and savings accounts	51.6	46.7	39.6	37.1	35.4	37.8	35.4	37.8	38.0	35.7	33.6
Bonds (incl. mutual funds on bonds)	12.0	17.3	21.5	22.8	26.2	22.8	26.2	n.a.	n.a.	n.a.	n.a.
Stocks (incl. mutual funds on stocks)	7.3	4.8	7.0	6.4	5.2	6.4	5.2	n.a.	n.a.	n.a.	n.a.
Bonds	n.a.	n.a.	n.a.	n.a.	n.a.	n.a.	n.a.	20.0	18.0	18.9	17.1
Stocks	n.a.	n.a.	n.a.	n.a.	n.a.	n.a.	n.a.	5.5	5.8	5.5	8.3
Mutual funds and managed investment accounts	n.a.	n.a.	n.a.	n.a.	n.a.	n.a.	n.a.	3.9	6.2	7.6	8.6
Building society savings contracts	7.8	7.3	5.5	4.1	3.7	4.1	3.7	3.7	3.7	3.4	3.4
Insurance and pension wealth	13.2	14.5	16.3	18.6	18.6	20.9	18.6	20.9	20.9	21.8	22.5
Other financial assets	8.1	9.6	10.0	11.2	11.1	7.8	11.1	7.8	7.4	6.9	6.6
Total financial assets	**n.a.**	**n.a.**	**n.a.**	**n.a.**	**n.a.**	**37.5**	**n.a.**	**37.5**	**39.2**	**40.4**	**42.8**
Non-financial assets											
Real estate wealth	n.a.	n.a.	n.a.	n.a.	n.a.	83.0	n.a.	83.0	82.4	82.7	81.9
Stock of durable goods	n.a.	n.a.	n.a.	n.a.	n.a.	17.0	n.a.	17.0	17.6	17.3	18.1
Total non-financial assets	**n.a.**	**n.a.**	**n.a.**	**n.a.**	**n.a.**	**62.5**	**n.a.**	**62.5**	**60.8**	**59.6**	**57.2**
Debt											
Long-term bank loans	57.4	65.2	63.0	68.0	69.0	n.a.	n.a.	n.a.	n.a.	n.a.	n.a.
Short-term bank loans	31.3	27.5	28.0	22.6	22.3	n.a.	n.a.	n.a.	n.a.	n.a.	n.a.
Other loans	11.3	7.3	9.0	9.4	8.7	n.a.	n.a.	n.a.	n.a.	n.a.	n.a.
Mortgage loans	n.a.	n.a.	n.a.	n.a.	n.a.	76.6	n.a.	76.6	75.8	78.1	79.6
Consumer credit	n.a.	n.a.	n.a.	n.a.	n.a.	23.4	n.a.	23.4	24.2	21.9	20.4
Total debt	**n.a.**	**n.a.**	**n.a.**	**n.a.**	**n.a.**	**13.1**	**n.a.**	**13.1**	**13.4**	**14.2**	**14.8**

Source: Deutsche Bundesbank (1994b, 1999b), and own computations.

Three major changes in the German tax code in the late 1980s and 1990s are likely to have substantially changed the after-tax yields of some asset categories:

- In 1989 a 10% withholding tax on interest income (*"Kleine Kapitalertragsteuer"*) was introduced, reflecting political efforts to increase the tax base and after prior announcement in 1988. It was abolished within a span of just 6 months.
- In 1991, a ruling by the Supreme Court (*"Bundesverfassungsgericht"*) forced the government to rule out tax discrimination between labor and capital income and to reinstate the withholding tax on interest: a 30% tax on interest income above €3000 (€6,000 for couples) was introduced in 1993.[27] In September 1994, the withholding tax was extended to interest income on foreign assets that are transferred to Germany (*"Zwischengewinnbesteuerung"*). The introduction of the withholding tax was accompanied by a drive to curb tax evasion. Audits of income tax statements became more frequent, and several major German banks were accused of helping their customers to evade tax payments in the late 1990s. The planned income tax reform in 2000 aims to further reduce loopholes in the personal income tax code and to reduce tax exemptions for interest income by 50%.[28]
- In 1995, another Supreme Court ruling targeted the discriminatory tax treatment of housing against financial assets in 1995. So, in 1996, the government abolished the wealth tax, which had favored housing and penalized stocks. This ruling also necessitated reform of the bequest and gift tax. The revised tax code, however, still allows for tax exemptions for housing up to the price of an average family home for children and an average townhouse for grandchildren.

The wealthier German households have reacted sharply to changes in the tax code and the introduction of the withholding tax, although this is hard to see in the financial accounts and the survey data (Tables 3.1 through 3.3), since the macro-data sources do not include housing wealth by region and the survey data have only been collected at 5-year intervals. However, the Deutsche Bundesbank (1994a,c) reports that the turnover rate of cash increased by 30% in 1992 and that investments in foreign mutual funds sky-rocketed to €6.6 billion in 1988 and a total of €50.8 billion[29] between mid-1991 and November 1993. Shortly after the first withholding tax was abolished, net investment in foreign mutual funds turned negative. The same happened when the tax was extended

---

[27]The Ministry of Finance estimated that the tax exemptions were high enough to free four-fifths of the German population from paying income tax on interest (see Deutsche Bundesbank, 1994c). The tax-free amount was halved in 2000.

[28]For a survey of loopholes in Germany, see Lang *et al.* (1997).

[29]Investments in Luxembourg-based mutual funds only.

to income from foreign mutual funds ("*Zwischengewinnbesteuerung*") in the second half of 1993. Interestingly, and unlike the situation in 1988, the net capital outflow in the period 1991–93 was small. Three-quarters of the "foreign" investments consisted of investments in Luxembourg mutual funds, which were largely based on German bank bonds and (to a smaller extent) German government bonds.[30]

3.6 LINKS BETWEEN SAVING PATTERNS AND PUBLIC POLICY

We have now collected the main elements to link saving patterns of German households with public policy in Germany. These saving patterns can be summarized in the three points:

- Saving rates are high and stable until around age 45–49.
- Saving is lower but still positive even in old age. There is depreciation drawing down real wealth, but virtually no signs of drawing down financial wealth.
- Until age 35, saving is mainly invested in owner-occupied housing, whereas it is mainly financial saving at older ages.

These observations pose a host of questions: How can we explain a life-cycle profile of discretionary household saving in Germany that is much flatter than, for example, in the United States? Specifically: Why does saving remain positive in old age, even for most low-income households? And what explains the "German savings puzzle", the puzzling fact that pensions and health insurance are generous and likely to have large crowding-out effects, yet German households accumulate so much real and financial wealth and do not appear to draw it down?

We need a complicated answer to resolve this puzzle. We obviously need to distinguish between the older and the younger generation because they appear to save for different purposes. Moreover, our data on the flat and positive savings in old age only pertain to the cohorts born before the 1930s; we do not yet know whether that pattern will also hold for the younger generation.[31] We then distinguish among three effects of public policies: effects on the level of savings, essentially by crowding-out mechanisms mainly through social insurance; effects on the life-cycle pattern of savings, flattening the age–savings profile; and effects on the portfolio composition of savings, mainly through differential taxation.

---

[30]See Deutsche Bundesbank (1994c).

[31]We refer to the generation now aged between about age 30 and 50. There is also a third generation, the "really young," but we have little data on their saving and consumption habits.

Crowding-out Effects of Public Pensions

We start with an analysis of the older generation in our data. Their members were born between 1910 and 1930 and they retired until about 1995 – this is today's generation of German retirees. Their current income is dominated by public pension income, much more than in many other countries (see Table 3.9).

About 85% of retirement income stems from the public mandatory retirement insurance, and only 15% comes from private sources such as funded firm pensions, individual retirement accounts, and other asset income, and only a little from remaining labor income and family transfers.

The international comparison in Table 3.9 suggests a strong substitution between the provision of pay-as-you-go pensions and other income sources in old age. This crowding-out result is in line with a careful time-series analysis carried out by Kim (1992). He links changes in the retirement system to the savings rate and shows that the German pay-as-you-go system has crowded out saving to a significant extent. Cigno and Rosati (1996) confirm these findings but explain the crowding-out effect unconventionally by repercussions on fertility rather than through the familiar channels stressed by Feldstein (1974).

The crowding-out result as it pertains to current retirement income is also at odds with the fact that Germany has such a high saving rate, and in particular, that German elderly have on average real and financial wealth levels that would suffice for about 10 years of their retirement income (see Figure 3.12). This is of course the core of the "German savings puzzle." We need three elements to explain it.

First, a part of the apparent contradiction between stocks of wealth (almost equally divided between notional pension wealth and tangible real and financial wealth) on the one hand and current income (85% pensions, 15% other income) on the other hand is resolved by realizing that Table 3.9 only reports current money income, not the imputed rent from homeownership, and that most wealth held by the elderly is owner-occupied housing (Figures 3.14–3.17). Hence, Table 3.9 exaggerates potential crowding-out effects. However, the omission of imputed rent cannot fully explain the puzzle. The German

TABLE 3.9   Retirement Income by Pillar (percentages)

	Germany	The Netherlands	Switzerland	UK	USA
State	85%	50%	42%	65%	45%
Employer	5%	40%	32%	25%	13%
Individual	10%	10%	26%	10%	42%

Notes: Income composition of two-person households with at least one retired person. UK: "State" includes SERPS. USA: "Individual" includes earnings (25%).
Source: DIA (1999b), compiled from Gruber and Wise (1999) and OECD (1998).

homeownership rate is much lower than in the Netherlands, the UK, and the United States. For the generation born between 1910 and 1930, it is just above 50%.[32] Moreover, flat and positive saving rates in old age are also prevalent among elderly German renters (see Figure 3.6).

Schnabel (1999) provides the second element of our explanation. It is a story of ex-ante versus ex-post savings plans. He shows that the growth of income during the German economic miracle years and up to the 1970s was so large and unprecedented that the elderly could just not have anticipated it. Hence, they saved more than if they had known how miraculous a growth rate they would experience.

Figure 3.19 displays the growth of earnings during the work history of a typical worker who retired in 1970, the drop due to the 70% replacement rate after retirement, and then the subsequent increase in pension income due to gross indication. All numbers are in real terms. After less than 10 years into retirement, the average worker had essentially recouped the former income level. The process was only stopped in the early 1980s, when economic growth slowed down to normal also in Germany. Since such an income path could hardly be anticipated, workers consumed too little and ended up with too large a stock of wealth around retirement.

Whereas Schnabel's (1999) story is plausible, it does not explain why this wealth has not been spent at higher rates in old age. This is the third element of our explanation of the "German savings puzzle". First, habit formation may

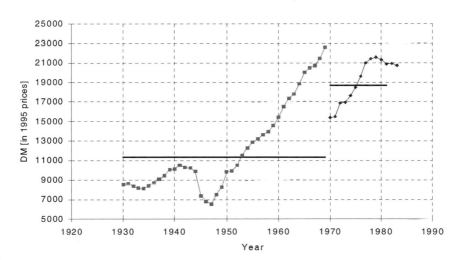

FIGURE 3.19   Life-cycle income path of the 1910 cohort. *Source:* Schnabel (1999).

[32]This lower homeownership rate is only partially offset by the fact that the average home in Germany is more expensive than in the Netherlands, the UK, and the United States (see later).

play a role. The elderly do not want to change the accustomed level of consumption which they have learned some 50 years ago, not even increase it in the face of accumulated financial wealth. There is some new evidence on the importance of habit formation (Dynan, 2000). Secondly, Börsch-Supan and Stahl (1991) provide a complementary explanation. They argue that due to deteriorating health conditions, the elderly are less able to spend as much as they would need to make saving negative. Both lines of argument are strengthened by capital market imperfections since annuitized pension income cannot be borrowed against. Hence, even if the current generation of the elderly had anticipated their unwillingness or inability to draw down wealth at later ages, they could not have responded by dissaving faster as long as their annuity income exceeds the planned consumption level. Evidence for this effect is provided by Börsch-Supan (1992).[33]

Life-Cycle Saving Patterns

Whereas the older generation may have had a retirement savings motive, but was surprised by the high retirement income and could not draw the accumulated wealth down, the younger generation – now aged between about 30 and 50 years – has learned that retirement will not be a time of scarce resources. For them, the high replacement rates of the German public pension system have made additional private retirement provision largely unnecessary. Saving for retirement, the only motive under the pure life-cycle hypothesis, is of secondary importance. Other saving motives dominate, most importantly saving for homeownership, as Figures 3.8–3.10 have shown. In addition, there are motives such as high-frequency precautionary saving, high-frequency saving for durables such as cars, and saving for intergenerational transfers. In fact, inter-vivos transfers are high in Germany and survey questions on savings motives show an almost equal spread between the aforementioned saving motives (DIA, 1999a).

The mechanisms pertaining to both generations generate much flatter age–saving profiles than under the retirement-saving oriented life-cycle hypothesis. The older generation still has positive saving rates because of the unwillingness or inability to draw down wealth at later ages which they accumulated in lack of anticipation of the spectacular economic growth. The young generation has a flat saving profile because the slow process of owning a home and short-frequency saving motives generate a flat saving rate over a long period.[34]

---

[33]We know very little about bequests which may, in theory, contribute to the observed flat age–saving profiles in old age. Cross-sectional regressions of wealth levels on number of children do not produce significant results. This finding, however, does not necessarily rule out an operative bequest motive. Only longitudinal data will clarify this matter.

[34]Conventional mortgages in Germany have a term of 30 years.

Hence, the generous public pension system in Germany appears to be the main cause for a relatively flat age–saving profile. It has made the retirement savings motive relatively irrelevant for the younger generation, and it has led to overannuitization among the elderly. We are aware that this line of argument is vulnerable because it lacks a counterfactual. The international comparisons in this book help in this respect. For instance, among the countries represented, the hump-shaped life-cycle savings pattern is most pronounced in the United States where the replacement rate of the public pension systems is lower – and thus the retirement savings motive is more important – than in continental Europe.

If a substantial portion of the saving patterns currently observed in Germany is caused by the public pension system, we should expect substantial changes in saving patterns in the future. Growth rates have declined and the dependency ratio is deteriorating rapidly. The current generosity of the social insurance system is unlikely to prevail. A major pension reform is under way which will cut benefits substantially and, in effect, introduce more prefunding. This will revive the retirement motive for saving. Hence, saving rates among the young are likely to increase, and saving rates among the elderly are likely to decline sharply because they have to rely more on their retirement savings to finance consumption. We will have to wait for this counterfactual to obtain a clearer explanation of what caused the puzzling German savings behavior.

Portfolio Composition

Public policies appear also to have shaped the composition of tangible household wealth.[35] As pointed out in Section 3.3, the largest part is real estate, mainly owner-occupied housing. For the group aged 30–59, this makes 80–90% of total wealth. Whereas ownership rates are lower than in most other European countries, the United States, and Japan, both land and housing construction is relatively expensive in Germany. This book is not the place to analyze why this is the case, but there is some evidence pointing toward restrictive land regulation.[36] In addition, saving for down payment in building societies (*"Bausparkassen"*) is tax privileged.

German tax policy, described in Section 3.5, appears to have shaped the composition of financial wealth, which is displayed in Table 3.10.

---

[35]For a detailed study of German household portfolio choice, see Eymann and Börsch-Supan (2002).

[36]Börsch-Supan *et al.* (2001a) claim that housing policies explain a significant share of the price differences among Germany, Japan, and the United States, such as restrictive land development by local governments, excessive building codes and insufficient legislation to avoid monopolization of the construction industry.

TABLE 3.10   Composition of Household Wealth, Germany, 1978–98

	1978	1983	1988	1993	Share in 1993	1998	Share in 1998
Savings accounts	7.907	6.247	6.789	5.673	17.5%	7.200	22.2%
Building societies	3.168	3.044	2.554	2.420	7.5%	2.417	7.5%
Stocks and bonds	3.782	4.578	5.304	10.178	31.4%	7.901	24.3%
Life insurance (cash value)	8.510	8.596	11.434	10.786	33.3%	9.959	30.7%
Other financial wealth	–	926	912	3.374	10.4%	4.978	15.3%
Gross financial wealth	23.367	23.391	26.993	32.431	100.0%	32.455	100.0%
−Consumer loans	815	1.125	1.337	1.025		1.223	
Net financial wealth	22.552	22.266	25.656	31.406		31.232	

Note: Household data from the Einkommens- and Verbrauchsstichprobe (EVS). All figures in 1993 Euro.
Source: Börsch-Supan *et al.* (1999c) and own computations.

The most important component is whole life insurance, about one-third of gross financial wealth. The central reason for the important role of whole life insurance in German households' life-cycle savings decisions is its favorable tax treatment, as shown by Brunsbach and Lang (1998) and Walliser and Winter (1999). Stocks and bonds are the second most important category. Bonds make up the "lion's share" in this category, whereas stocks are less than 10% of the average household portfolio. This fact is also significant for financial markets, as life insurance companies have not been allowed to invest significantly in stocks in the past, which in turn is one of the main reasons for thin capital markets in Germany. Stocks and bonds are tax privileged in so far as capital gains are tax exempt if the underlying asset has been held for longer than 1 year.[37] The lenient taxation of capital income may be another explanation for the high saving rate in Germany, but we are not aware of a reliable time-series analysis that links the level of tax relief to the aggregate household saving rate.

It is highly speculative how the portfolio composition in Table 3.10 would change in the wake of a major change of the German social insurance system, notably a partial transition to prefunding pensions. If there was no substitution between new retirement saving and current saving, the household saving rate would increase by 2–4% (see Birg and Börsch-Supan, 1999). If these new savings were channeled into pension funds, which only recently have been introduced in Germany and still do not receive preferential tax treatment similar to whole life insurance, pension funds would amount to between 15 and 18% of households' portfolios, comparable to the UK, the United States, the Netherlands, and Switzerland. Substitution between new retirement saving

---

[37]This has recently been changed to 2 years.

and current saving would increase this share, but part of new retirement saving may also be done as whole life insurance. Households' direct and indirect exposure to stock markets then depends on future investment decisions of life insurance companies who only recently began to increase their portfolio share of stocks. Judging from the international experience in countries as diverse as the UK, the United States, the Netherlands, and Switzerland, a more prominent role of equities seems very likely when more of the German retirement income is prefunded.

3.7   CONCLUSIONS

Although using the EVS data has several disadvantages (e.g., limited representativity and a missing panel structure), they allow for an elaborate cross-sectional analysis and a restricted longitudinal analysis of saving behavior. Advantages are the large sample sizes and the detailed collection of flow variables (e.g., income and its disbursal). The lack of representativity created by neglecting that portion of the population living in institutions and households with very high incomes leads to underestimating financial wealth. However, age and cohort profiles seem to be qualitatively unaffected. The construction of a synthetic panel is possible as an approximation of the missing panel structure.

Empirical analysis of saving behavior is only possible under the precondition of a consistent definition of saving, wealth, and income. Large parts of this chapter were dedicated to this arduous task. On average, we succeeded: our two saving definitions (residual between income and expenditures, and difference between sales and purchases of assets) yielded very similar mean and median figures. Moreover, errors resulting from comparability problems across waves appeared to be small. However, both are valid only on average, while individual variation is high.

With regard to economic substance we achieved two very robust results pertaining to the saving behavior of German households. First, there is nearly no dissaving in old age. While the age–cohort profile of discretionary saving is indeed hump shaped, it is fairly flat after the age of 65 and does not become negative except for the lowest income quartile. This does not correspond to the predictions of the traditional life-cycle hypothesis. Secondly, there is a time effect for all age groups: saving was especially high in 1993. Since age and cohort profiles can only be separated by the use of individual longitudinal data, a more detailed analysis of this finding is not possible with the EVS synthetic panel.

The flat age–savings profile presents an interesting "savings puzzle." On the one hand, saving rates are high and stable until around age 45–49, and remain positive even in old age. Whereas depreciation draws down real wealth among elderly homeowners, we find virtually no signs of drawing down financial wealth. On the other hand, Germany has a very generous public pension system. "Notional pension wealth" provided by the pay-as-you-go social insurance system is larger than real wealth and much larger than financial wealth.

Our explanation is cohort-specific. Our data on the flat and positive savings in old age only pertain to the cohorts born before the 1930s; we do not yet know whether that pattern will also hold for the younger generation. The older generation was surprised by an unprecedented income growth in the 1960s and 1970s. Households born between 1910 and 1930 were saving for retirement but ended up being overannuitized. Habit formation and ill health then prevented the older generation from spending down their unexpected wealth.

What will happen, when younger cohorts reach retirement, is likely to depend on future pension policy. Pension reform is under way in Germany. It will shift a significant share – between one-quarter and one-third – of retirement income from the pay-as-you-go pillar to a funded pillar. Most likely, this will increase saving in younger ages, and induce dissaving among the elderly. We will have to wait for this "experiment" to obtain a clearer explanation of what had caused the puzzling German savings behavior.

ACKNOWLEDGMENT

We have profited greatly from many discussions with many colleagues. We especially thank Agar Brugiavini, Stefan Hoderlein, Mike Hurd, Tullio Jappelli, Jim Smith, Gert Wagner, and Joachim Winter. We are grateful to Florian Heiss, Simone Kohnz, Melanie Lührmann, Gerit Meyer-Hubbert, and Konrad Menzel for their able research assistance, and to the Deutschen Forschungsgemeinschaft for financial support through the "Sonderforschungsbereich 504," and the EU for financial support through the TMR-Project on "Savings, Pensions, and Portfolio Choice."

REFERENCES

Becker, I. (1997). Die Entwicklung von Einkommensverteilung und Einkommensarmut in den alten Bundesländern von 1962 bis 1988. In: I. Becker und R. Hauser (eds), *Einkommensverteilung und Armut. Deutschland auf dem Weg zur Vierfünftel-Gesellschaft?* Frankfurt: Campus Verlag.

Birg, H. and A. Börsch-Supan (1999). *Für eine neue Aufgabenteilung zwischen gesetzlicher und privater Altersversorgung.* Berlin: GDV.

Börsch-Supan, A. (1992). Saving and consumption patterns of the elderly: The German case. *Journal of Population Economics* 5, 289–303.

Börsch-Supan, A. (1994). Savings in Germany–Part I: incentives. In: J M. Poterba (ed.), *Public Policies and Household Saving.* Chicago: University of Chicago Press, 81–104.

Börsch-Supan, A. (1999). Data and research on saving in Germany. In: *Preparing for an Aging World,* Washington, DC: National Academy of Sciences.

Börsch-Supan, A. (2001a). International comparison of household savings behaviour: A study of life-cycle savings in seven countries. Introduction to a special issue of *Research in Economics* 55, 1–14.

Börsch-Supan, A. (2001b). Rejoinder to Tullio Jappelli's comments. *Research in Economics* 55(2), 185–187.

Börsch-Supan, A. and L. Essig (2002). Stockholding in Germany. In: L. Guiso, M. Haliassos, and T. Jappelli (eds), *Stockholding in Europe*. New York: Palgrove MacMillan.

Börsch-Supan, A. and A. Reil-Held (1998). Retirement income: level, risk, and substitution among income components. *OECD Ageing Working Paper AWP 3.7*, Paris.

Börsch-Supan, A. and R. Schnabel (1999). Social security and retirement in Germany. In: J. Gruber and D. Wise (eds), *International Comparison of Social Security Systems*. Chicago: The University of Chicago Press.

Börsch-Supan, A. and K. Stahl (1991). Life-cycle savings and consumption constraints. *Journal of Population Economics* 4, 233–255.

Börsch-Supan, A., Y. Kanemoto, and K. Stahl (2001a). *Housing Markets in Germany, Japan and the United States*. Unpublished manuscript, University of Mannheim.

Börsch-Supan, A., A. Reil-Held, and R. Schnabel (1999a). Pension provision in Germany. In: P. Johnson (ed.), *Pensioners' Income: International Comparisons*. Cambridge, MA: MIT Press.

Börsch-Supan, A., R. Rodepeter, and J. Winter (1999b). The empirical identification of life-cycle savings patterns. Unveröffentlichtes Manuskript, Universität Mannheim.

Börsch-Supan, A., A. Reil-Held, R. Rodepeter, R. Schnabel, and J. Winter (1999c). Ersparnisbildung in Deutschland: Meßkonzepte und Ergebnisse auf Basis der EVS. *Allgemeines Statistisches Archiv* 83, 385–415. The English version of this paper is available as a Discussion Paper (No. 99-02, Sonderforschungsbereich 504, University of Mannheim).

Börsch-Supan, A. and A. Reil-Held (2001). How much is transfer and how much insurance in a pay-as-you-go system? The German Case. *Scandinavian Journal of Economics* 103, S. 505–524.

Börsch-Supan, A., A. Reil-Held, R. Rodepeter, R. Schnabel, and J. Winter (2001b). The German Savings Puzzle. *Research in Economics*.

Brugiavini, A. and G. Weber (2001). Household savings: concepts and measurement. In: A. Börsch-Supan (ed.), *International Comparisons of Household Saving*. New York: Academic Press.

Brunsbach, S. and O. Lang (1998). Steuervorteile und die Rendite des Lebensversicherungssparens. *Jahrbücher für Nationalökonomie und Statistik* 217, 185–213.

Cigno, A. and F.C. Rosati (1996). Jointly determined saving and fertility behaviour: theory, and estimates for Germany, Italy, UK, and USA. *European Economic Review* 40, 1561–1589.

Deaton, A. (1985). Panel data from time-series of cross-sections. *Journal of Econometrics* 30, 109–124.

Deutsche Bundesbank (1994a). Entwicklung und Bedeutung der Geldanlage in Investment-zertifikaten. *Monthly Reports* October 1994, 49–70.

Deutsche Bundesbank (1994b). Ergebnisse der gesamtwirtschaftlichen Finanzierungsrechnung für Westdeutschland 1960 bis 1992.

Deutsche Bundesbank (1994c). Aufkommen und ökonomische Auswirkungen des steuerlichen Zinsabschlags. *Monthly Reports* January 1994, 45–57.

Deutsche Bundesbank (1999a): Ergebnisse der gesamtwirtschaftlichen Finanzierungsrechnung für Deutschland 1990 bis 1998.

Deutsche Bundesbank (1999b). Zur Entwicklung der privaten Vermögenssituation seit Beginn der Neunziger Jahre. *Monthly Reports* January 1999, 33–50.

Deutsches Institut für Altersvorsorge (DIA) (1999a). *Die Deutschen und Ihr Geld*. Köln: Deutsches Institut für Altersvorsorge.

Deutsches Institut für Altersvorsorge (DIA) (1999b). *Reformerfahrungen im Ausland: Ein systematischer Vergleich von sechs Ländern*. Köln: DIA.

Dynan, K. (2000). Habit formation in consumer preferences: Evidence from panel data. *The American Economic Review* 90, 391–406.

Euler, M. (1985). Geldvermögen privater Haushalte Ende 1983. *Wirtschaft und Statistik* 5, 408–418.

Euler, M. (1990). Geldvermögen und Schulden privater Haushalte Ende 1988. *Wirtschaft und Statistik* 11, 798–808.

Euler, M. (1992). Einkommens- und Verbrauchsstichprobe 1993. *Wirtschaft und Statistik* 7, 463–469.

Eymann, A. and A. Börsch-Supan (2002). Household portfolios in Germany. In: L. Guiso, M. Haliassos, and T. Jappelli (eds), *Household Portfolios*. Cambridge, MA: MIT Press.

Fachinger, U. (1998). Die Verteilung der Vermögen privater Haushalte: Einige konzeptionelle Anmerkungen sowie empirische Befunde für die Bundesrepublik Deutschland. ZeS-Arbeitspapier Nr. 13/98, Zentrum für Sozialpolitik, Universität Bremen.

Feldstein, M. (1974). Social security, induced retirement and aggregate capital accumulation. *Journal of Political Economy* 82(5), 905–926.

Grimm, M. (1998). Die Verteilung von Geld- und Grundvermögen auf sozioökonomische Gruppen im Jahr 1988 und Vergleich mit früheren Ergebnissen. *Discussion Paper No. 14*, University of Frankfurt (Main).

Gruber, J. and D. Wise (eds) (1999). *Social Security and Retirement Around the World*. Chicago: The University of Chicago Press.

Guttmann, E. (1995). Geldvermögen und Schulden privater Haushalte Ende 1993. *Wirtschaft und Statistik* 5, 391–399.

Hauser, R. (1997). Armut, Armutsgefährdung und Armutsbekämpfung in der Bundesrepublik Deutschland. *Jahrbücher für Nationalökonomie und Statistik* 216, 524–548.

Hauser, R. and I. Becker (1998). Die langfristige Entwicklung der personellen Einkommensverteilung in der Bundesrepublik Deutschland. In: H.P. Galler und G. Wagner (eds), *Empirische Forschung und wirtschaftspolitische Beratung*. Frankfurt: Campus Verlag.

Hauser, R. and U. Neumann (1992). Armut in der Bundesrepublik Deutschland. Die sozialwissenschaftliche Thematisierung nach dem Zweiten Weltkrieg. In: *Armut in modernen Wohlfahrtsstaaten*. Sonderheft 32/1992 der Kölner Zeitschrift für Soziologie und Sozialpsychologie.

Helmcke, T. and P. Knoche (1992). Zur faktischen Anonymität von Mikrodaten. *Wirtschaft und Statistik* 3, 139–144.

Hertel, J. (1997). Einnahmen und Ausgaben der privaten Haushalte 1993. *Statistische Bundesamt, Fachserie* 15, 4, 28–41.

Jappelli, T. (2001). International comparison of household savings behaviour: A critique. *Research in Economics* 55(2), 180–184.

Kim, S. (1992). Gesetzliche Rentenversicherung und Ersparnisbildung der privaten Haushalte in der Bundesrepublik Deutschland von 1962 bis 1988. *Zeitschrift für die gesamte Versicherungswirtschaft* 81, 533–578.

Lang, O. (1996). Die Einkommens- und Vermögensverhältnisse künftiger Altengenerationen in Deutschland. In: Deutscher Bundestag (ed), *Herausforderungen unserer älter werdenden Gesellschaft an den einzelnen und die Politik*. Studienprogramm der Enquete Kommission "Demographischer Wandel."

Lang, O. (1997). Steueranreize und Geldanlagen im Lebenszyklus. Dissertation, Universität Mannheim.

Lang, O. (1998). *Steueranreize und Geldanlagen im Lebenszyklus: empirische Analysen zu Spar- und Portfolioentscheidungen deutscher Privathaushalte*. Baden-Baden: Nomos Verlag.

Lang, O., K. H. Nöhrbaß, and K. Stahl (1997). On income tax avoidance: The case of Germany. *Journal of Public Economics* 66, 327–347.

Laue, E. (1995). Grundvermögen privater Haushalte Ende 1993. *Wirtschaft und Statistik* 6, 488–497.

Münnich, M. (1997). Zur wirtschaftlichen Lage von Ein- und Zweipersonenrentnerhaushalten. *Wirtschaft und Statistik* 2, 120–135.

Organization of Economic Cooperation and Development (OECD) (1998). *Family Resources During Retirement*. Paris: OECD.

Pöschl, H. (1993). Werbung und Beteiligung der Haushalte an der Einkommens- und Verbrauchsstichprobe 1993. *Wirtschaft und Statistik* 6, 385–390.

Reil-Held, A. (1999). Bequests and aggregate wealth accumulation in Germany. *The Geneva Papers on Risk and Insurance* 24, 50–63.

Rodepeter, R. and J. Winter (1998). Savings decisions under life-time and earnings uncertainty: evidence from West German household data. Arbeitspapier Nr. 98-58, Sonderforschungsbereich 504, Universität Mannheim.

Schlomann, H. (1992). *Vermögensverteilung und private Altersvorsorge*. Frankfurt (Main): Campus.

Schnabel, R. (1999). *Ersparnis und Vermögen im Lebenszyklus in Westdeutschland*. Habilitation, Universität Mannheim.

Statistisches Bundesamt (1999). Haus- und Grundbesitz sowie Wohnverhältnisse privater Haushalte. *Fachserie* 15, Sonderheft 1, Wiesbaden.

Statistisches Bundesamt (2001a). Aufgabe, Methode und Durchführung der EVS 1998. *Fachserie* 15, Heft 7, Wiesbaden.

Statistisches Bundesamt (2001b). Geldvermögensbestände und Schulden privater Haushalte, *Fachserie* 15, Heft 2, Wiesbaden.

Velling, M. (1991). *Ersparnisbildung in Westdeutschland*. Diplomarbeit, University of Mannheim.

Walliser, J. and J. Winter (1999). Tax incentives, bequest motives and the demand for life insurance: evidence from Germany. Discussion Paper No. 99-28, Sonderforschungsbereich 504, University of Mannheim.

CHAPTER 4

Household Saving Behavior and Pension Policies in Italy

Agar Brugiavini

Università Ca' Foscari di Venezia, Italy, and IFS, London

Mario Padula

Università di Salerno CSEF, Italy

4.1 INTRODUCTION

This chapter provides a description of household saving behavior using Italian microeconomic data surveyed at the household level. We present a collection of stylized facts and try to relate them to both the standard motives for saving and the existing institutional setup, particularly pension arrangements.

Italy is a particularly interesting case because a large part of saving is "mandatory." During their working life, individuals must contribute to the public social security system. This is based on a pay-as-you-go (PAYG) financing method: while contributing to the program, workers build up their rights to social security benefits, a process which can be described as accumulation of public social security wealth. Employees also contribute to a severance pay fund, which pays a lump sum at retirement, or at the time of detachment from the firm. The levels of contributions (either to the social security system or to the severance pay fund) and the corresponding level of retirement benefits represent a large portion of household resources. Current contributions in various forms are over one-third of pretax income for employed workers and over 15% for the self-employed. At retirement, employees receive a lump sum payment from the severance pay fund, which typically amounts to 3 or 4 times annual earnings. During retirement pension benefits are in the order of 60–70% of pre-retirement after-tax income. Since these welfare programs are so relevant, Italy provides the clearest example of the importance of accounting for the various pension and insurance arrangements in assessing the overall saving behavior of the household.

Given the format of the data at our disposal we can measure saving by adopting two measures: a residual measure obtained as the difference between income and consumption and a measure based on the difference between wealth levels at two points in time.[1] However, whereas the residual measure can be computed for all households in the sample and for all years, the measure based on wealth differences can be obtained only for a small subsample of households, which is regularly re-interviewed (an actual panel). Hence, the emphasis in this book is on the residual measure of saving, only for financial saving and real saving we resort to computing differences in wealth.[2]

We distinguish between *discretionary saving* (the difference between the conventional measure of disposable income and consumption) and *mandatory saving* (the difference between mandatory contributions and social security benefits). The distinction draws on two alternative (but consistent) definitions of income: disposable income and earned income. Earned income is equal to disposable income plus social security contributions minus benefits. Discretionary and mandatory saving are defined as residual: discretionary saving is obtained as disposable income minus consumption; mandatory saving as earned income minus consumption.[3]

We provide a systematic analysis of saving trends, controlling for the possible impact of cohort effects. Age profiles of individual variables, such as income, consumption, or saving, cannot be estimated with cross-sectional data because the presence of cohort effects produces a bias. For instance, since younger generations

---

[1]See Chapter 2 for a discussion on the different measures.

[2]Jappelli and Modigliani (1998) provide a more complete accounting exercise of stocks and flows and of the fact that total household wealth is allocated in what can be termed as discretionary wealth (real plus financial assets) and mandatory wealth (of which the largest components in Italy are social security wealth and severance pay).

[3]Some aspects of this discussion are also presented in Chapter 2. Note that in the remainder of this book the term "mandatory saving" refers to saving which is out of the control of the household, whereas "notional saving" is confined to the accumulation of pay-as-you-go (PAYG) contributions and other contributions. Because in this chapter we consider both the contribution to the Italian PAYG social security system and the contribution to a severance pay fund existing at a firm level, we extend the term "mandatory" for both types of retirement saving (and these are both compulsory contributions for employees).

are lifetime richer than older ones, in pure cross-sectional data their income is biased upward. By making use of recent methodological developments in this area of research, we disentangle the age effect from the cohort effects and estimate individual age–saving profiles relying on a time series of cross sections of Italian households.

In Section 4.2 we describe our sample, which is drawn from the 1984–98's waves of the Survey of Household Income and Wealth (SHIW), a total of eight cross sections representative of the Italian population spanning 15 years of data. In Section 4.3 we tabulate our measures of consumption, income, financial and real wealth, and financial and real saving. Furthermore, we compute saving rates and the two proposed measures of saving: discretionary saving and mandatory saving. One puzzling result is that the stock and the flow measure of discretionary saving do not match and we simply list a number of possible explanations for this finding. In Section 4.4 we report cohort-adjusted age profiles for the same variables, whereas Section 4.5 focuses on saving by different population groups. We describe saving patterns by education, employment status, family type, and homeownership and summarize the evidence by regression analysis. Section 4.6 discusses the importance of pension arrangements and computes an estimate of the social security wealth. Section 4.7 tackles the potential impact of measurement error in consumption for our measure of private saving. For this purpose we use data from the ISTAT Survey of Household Budgets. Overall, we find that the level of private saving in the SHIW is upward biased, but that the general pattern is consistent between the two surveys: private saving does not decline in old age. Section 4.8 concludes.

4.2   THE DATA

We use a time series of Italian surveys collected by the Bank of Italy (the SHIW, Survey of Household Income and Wealth). The purpose of this survey is to provide detailed data on wealth, demographics, consumption, income, and households' balance sheets. The data set used in this study includes eight independent cross sections (1984, 1986, 1987, 1989, 1991, 1993, 1995, and 1998), a total of 60,077 observations.[4]

To gauge the quality of the saving data, it is useful to compare the SHIW measures of the private saving rate with the national accounts aggregate data.[5] Table 4.1 indicates that the survey measure of saving is substantially higher than the national account measure in all years. The reason is that income in the SHIW is more accurately reported than consumption. In fact, Brandolini and Cannari (1994) show

---

[4]See Brandolini and Cannari (1994) for further details on the survey.

[5]Saving rates are computed as 1 minus the ratio of consumption on disposable income. In the aggregate defining saving as earned income minus consumption or as disposable income minus consumption does not make a notable difference. As it will be made clear below, it is the age profile of the two saving measures that differs.

TABLE 4.1 A Comparison between Measures of Aggregate Saving from National Accounts and Survey Data[a]

	Saving rate		Observations in the SHIW surveys	
Year	National accounts data	SHIW survey data	Total	Used
1984	20.2	31.5	4,172	3,878
1986	17.6	30.3	8,022	7,593
1987	17.6	25.6	8,027	7,602
1989	16.3	26.4	8,297	8,040
1991	16.5	24.0	8,188	7,947
1993	14.5	25.0	8,089	7,931
1995	14.0	23.4	8,135	7,959
1998	10.0	28.5	7,147	6,930

[a]The aggregate saving rate in the first column is the household saving rate ratio computed on the basis of the 1999 Annual Report of the Bank of Italy and the 1998 OECD Economic Outlook. The aggregate saving rate in the second column is computed using the SHIW and dividing total household saving by total household disposable income. The survey estimates use sample weights and the entire data set for each survey year.

that disposable income is underreported by 25% with respect to the national account data, whereas consumption is underreported by 30%. This should be kept in mind when evaluating the results.

Although the saving levels differ, the time pattern of the saving rate in the SHIW is similar to that of the national accounts. Both measures show a decline of about 6 percentage points between 1984 and 1995, and in both cases the bulk of decline occurs in the second half of the 1980s. The decline in saving is not peculiar to our sample period: a steady reduction of over 10 percentage points starts just after the "growth years" (1950s and early 1960s). This trend may be explained by several facts: a fall in the productivity growth rate, the transition to an unfunded social security system, the change in the population structure, the development of credit markets, and the reduced need for precautionary saving, due to the increased availability of social insurance programs. Here we do not try to sort out these explanations; rather, we limit ourselves to a description of the age–saving profiles and wealth patterns of Italian households.

The general features of our sample are described in Table 4.2: household size has the typical life-cycle pattern; the bulk of retired households is between the ages of 55 and 100. It should be noted that almost 40% of households have their head retired between age 55 and age 59; this is a reflection of the generosity of the early retirement option in terms of replacement rates and in terms of eligibility criteria. Roughly 40% of households are homeowners as from age 35 to 40; before then, the proportion is slightly lower – indeed part of the saving observed at younger ages is needed to build up a down payment for home purchase.

TABLE 4.2   Sample Characteristics[a]

	Household size	Head employed	Head retired	Homeowner	Marginal tax rate	Has health insurance
Age 20–24	2.40	0.69	0.00	0.31	0.37	0.04
Age 25–29	2.61	0.72	0.00	0.35	0.38	0.07
Age 30–34	3.09	0.72	0.00	0.42	0.39	0.12
Age 35–39	3.46	0.73	0.00	0.53	0.41	0.12
Age 40–44	3.69	0.73	0.02	0.63	0.40	0.11
Age 45–49	3.77	0.69	0.04	0.67	0.41	0.12
Age 50–54	3.59	0.58	0.15	0.71	0.41	0.10
Age 55–59	3.21	0.37	0.39	0.71	0.41	0.08
Age 60–64	2.67	0.14	0.70	0.73	0.39	0.06
Age 65–69	2.27	0.02	0.91	0.70	0.37	0.04
Age 70–74	1.95	0.00	0.96	0.67	0.37	0.03
Age 75–79	1.79	0.00	0.98	0.61	0.35	0.02
Age 80+	1.64	0.00	0.98	0.56	0.34	0.02

[a]The table reports means of some covariates by age.

4.3 CROSS-SECTIONAL AGE PROFILES OF INCOME AND SAVING

This section describes the cross-sectional age profiles of financial and real saving, financial and real wealth, and income. We base our analysis mainly on a residual definition of saving (income minus consumption). However, our samples contain a small panel component: only for these households can we compute financial saving and real saving by taking differences in financial and real wealth at different points in time. Before presenting the evidence on these different measures of saving it is worth discussing in more detail the definition of income we propose when making use of the residual measure of total saving and the reasons why this distinction is relevant for the present study.[6] We adopt two definitions of income – earned income and disposable income – which allows us to compute two measures of saving, i.e. mandatory and discretionary saving, respectively.

Following Jappelli and Modigliani (1998), we define *earned income* as total labor income (net of taxes) and asset income (net of capital income taxes), which is different from *disposable income*, the more conventional measure of income. The latter is equal to earned income minus social security contributions, plus pension

[6]See footnote 3.

benefits. Disposable income treats contributions to pension funds and social security contributions as taxes, and pension benefits as income. If we take the view that households build up social security wealth while contributing to the mandatory pension system, then contributions represent additions to social security wealth, whereas benefits represent depletion of pension wealth. Thus contributions, but not benefits, are part of earned income.

In the SHIW, earnings are reported net of taxes and contributions, and contributions are a flat tax for individuals, increasing gradually from 24% of gross earnings in 1984 to 33% (approximately) in 1998 for employment income, and from 15% to 20% on self-employment income.[7] It is therefore straightforward to rescale income in proportion in order to obtain the grossed-up figure, which we use for computing "earned income".[8] Whereas we impute social security contributions on the basis of after-tax income and the relevant contribution rate, we have directly available from the survey pension benefits as a separate component of income.[9] Our procedure of adding workers' contributions and subtracting retirees' old-age benefits would correspond to a change in "pension wealth", i.e. to a change in the stock of wealth that households notionally build up by contributing to a pension program and by acquiring rights toward that program.

We also carry out an imputation for contributions paid by Italian workers in a severance pay fund (known as TFR).[10] By law, in Italy, the employer must pay a fraction of the wage bill of his work force into a TFR fund. The accumulation of the fund is only notional because the employer retains the full amount of this contribution from his workers' wage and because firms are not required to accumulate reserves, but only to meet payments. The severance pay fund is totally regulated by legislation.[11] In our exercise we estimate TFR contributions by grossing-up labor income in proportion to the contribution rate.

[7]In Italy, part of the contributions are paid by the employee, and part by the employer. But clearly this distinction is immaterial as in both cases contributions are part of an employee's total compensation.

[8]One of the key advantages of the SHIW is that it reports a breakdown of income by income source. This breakdown is not available in the ISTAT survey (see Section 4.6). Thus, for estimating mandatory saving one must rely on SHIW data.

[9]Note that we were forced, in order to make the computation tractable on the basis of the available data, to compute contributions on after-tax earnings, whereas contributions to social security are normally paid before any income tax is due.

[10]TFR stands for *Trattamento di fine rapporto*. The mandatory contribution to TFR is 7.4% of gross earnings, but 0.5% of this is transferred to INPS (the social security agency) to finance other provisions; hence, 6.9% is the effective contribution rate.

[11]Since 1982 severance pay is computed as 6.9% of the gross yearly salary for each year worked. Past contributions are capitalized each year at a rate equal to $(0.015+0.75\pi)$, where π is the rate of change of the consumer price index. This implies that the worker's real return on the fund is negative for inflation rates above 6%. Employees cannot withdraw the full value of their fund until termination of their employment contract; hence, severance pay is rather illiquid and can actually be regarded as forced saving. The only form of flexibility is that workers can dispose of part of the severance pay for exceptional medical expenses or for the purchase of their first home. Partial withdrawal is allowed only once during the employment contract and only for a small fraction of each firm's work force at the same time.

The two income definitions just described allow us to obtain two saving measures: both are obtained subtracting total consumption expenditures from income.[12] We define as *discretionary saving* the difference between disposable income and consumption. This is the conventional definition of saving. We then define *mandatory saving* as the sum of social security contributions, contributions in the form of severance pay minus social security benefits (under the assumption that cashing 1 year of benefits reduces pension wealth by an equal amount). Juxtaposing discretionary and mandatory saving is crucial to the understanding of the interplay between private saving and pension policy. To the extent that households smooth their lifetime consumption profile through pension wealth and that social security wealth exhibits a hump shape, the absence of a hump shape in private wealth is more easily understood.

Turning now to the actual saving measures: we break discretionary saving into financial and real discretionary saving by making use of the panel component of the sample. Tables 4.3 and 4.4 report financial and real saving by age group for four years: 1991, 1993, 1995, and 1998. By making use of the panel subsample and by dropping households headed by individuals aged less than 20, we restrict the actual sample to around 2000 households, who are followed from 1989 through to 1998.[13] Because the time span between two waves is usually 2 years, saving is computed as the end of the period financial wealth in year t minus the end of the period financial wealth in year $(t-2)$ divided by 2. Tables 4.3 and 4.4 show that both financial and real saving are somewhat imprecisely estimated, mostly due to the small cell size.

Financial discretionary saving does not display a clear age profile in any of the 4 years of the survey, whereas real saving exhibits, in all the four waves, a modest hump, peaking at around age of 50. Table 4.4 also provides weak evidence of real wealth decumulation at older ages. This finding is roughly consistent with the results of Jappelli and Modigliani (1998), who show that the total discretionary saving, computed as difference of the stocks of financial and real wealth, is somewhat hump shaped and negative at old ages: a result probably dominated by the real component of saving rather than financial saving.

Unfortunately, we cannot rely too much on the results obtained from the panel observations: the core of our application relies on cross-sectional data, which allows for a reasonable cell size. Cross-sectional information is used both to provide evidence on life-cycle profiles of wealth holdings and to derive a residual measure of saving.

---

[12]Our conclusions do not depend on the definition of consumption (including or excluding durables). We use total consumption expenditures because expenditure on durable goods was not collected in the 1986 SHIW.

[13]Very few households in the survey are headed by individuals aged less than 20 and are likely to be outliers.

TABLE 4.3   Financial Saving: 1991, 1993, 1995, and 1998[a]

		Number of observations	Mean	Standard deviation of mean	Median
1991	Age 20–24	1	−3.49	–	−3.49
	Age 25–29	16	−0.11	0.86	0.37
	Age 30–34	37	−3.38	3.78	0.97
	Age 35–39	60	−0.21	2.86	0.73
	Age 40–44	62	−2.10	2.17	0.99
	Age 45–49	60	−2.82	1.98	−1.04
	Age 50–54	57	6.56	6.78	−0.35
	Age 55–59	46	1.24	2.03	0.00
	Age 60–64	58	−4.37	7.73	0.04
	Age 65–69	42	−1.42	2.85	−0.23
	Age 70–74	20	−8.36	0.12	−3.63
	Age 75–79	15	0.12	2.69	2.06
	Age 80+	10	−1.04	0.58	−1.63
1993	Age 20–24	1	0.07	–	0.07
	Age 25–29	13	−0.68	2.04	0.27
	Age 30–34	26	7.75	6.56	1.08
	Age 35–39	59	5.63	3.16	1.89
	Age 40–44	62	0.70	1.33	0.57
	Age 45–49	68	0.72	0.99	0.97
	Age 50–54	52	6.41	4.35	1.44
	Age 55–59	46	2.92	6.02	1.92
	Age 60–64	50	1.04	2.27	0.00
	Age 65–69	50	1.98	1.61	1.58
	Age 70–74	35	0.48	4.06	1.58
	Age 75–79	11	−6.35	4.14	−0.54
	Age 80+	11	−0.67	0.63	−0.27
1995	Age 20–24	–	–	–	–
	Age 25–29	6	0.21	1.00	0.38
	Age 30–34	20	−3.70	7.91	0.01
	Age 35–39	54	4.57	1.89	2.86
	Age 40–44	54	2.15	1.73	0.28
	Age 45–49	67	2.01	1.25	0.45
	Age 50–54	59	0.43	4.62	0.08

(Continues)

TABLE 4.3   (*Continued*)

		Number of observations	Mean	Standard deviation of mean	Median
	Age 55–59	54	−3.77	5.59	0.55
	Age 60–64	50	−0.29	2.00	−0.53
	Age 65–69	50	2.27	1.45	0.20
	Age 70–74	36	2.90	2.87	0.00
	Age 75–79	19	3.33	3.60	−1.96
	Age 80+	15	−0.92	0.33	−0.17
1998	Age 20–24	–	–	–	–
	Age 25–29	1	0.87	–	0.87
	Age 30–34	12	0.27	1.83	1.72
	Age 35–39	31	2.27	1.05	0.52
	Age 40–44	61	1.49	1.64	1.46
	Age 45–49	61	2.69	1.12	1.27
	Age 50–54	68	2.82	1.31	0.92
	Age 55–59	53	2.36	2.67	0.35
	Age 60–64	46	11.07	5.50	2.26
	Age 65–69	55	0.84	1.39	0.00
	Age 70–74	46	1.87	2.05	0.03
	Age 75–79	30	13.39	13.18	1.08
	Age 80+	20	0.24	0.81	−0.27

[a]The table reports for 1991, 1993, 1995, and 1998 the financial saving by age brackets. Financial saving is defined as the difference of financial wealth in 2 years, converted into yearly figures. We use the panel component of the SHIW. This leaves 1936 households. Figures are expressed in 1998 euro.

Sample statistics are computed using sample weights. Households headed by individuals younger than 20 are excluded. In the first column we report the age group of the head of the household, in the second column the number of observations, in the third column the mean, in the fourth column the standard deviation of the mean, and in the last column the median.

In Tables 4.5 and 4.6 we present the cross-sectional age profile of financial and real wealth. As shown in Table 4.5, mean and median financial wealth peak at median ages (around 45–55), in all years. The distribution of financial wealth by age is characterized by a mean higher than the median; hence, the upper tail of the distribution is thick. We provide illustrations of these findings in Figure 4.1. The top-left panel of Figure 4.1 shows the cross-sectional age profile of

TABLE 4.4   Real Saving: 1991, 1993, 1995, and 1998[a]

		Number of observations	Mean	Standard deviation of mean	Median
1991	Age 20–24	1	0.10	–	0.10
	Age 25–29	16	18.02	9.02	13.05
	Age 30–34	37	−3.32	10.04	4.92
	Age 35–39	60	23.82	7.31	13.55
	Age 40–44	62	19.33	7.08	1.51
	Age 45–49	60	22.39	5.86	8.04
	Age 50–54	57	17.67	7.02	1.56
	Age 55–59	46	42.15	27.88	5.07
	Age 60–64	58	19.95	8.1	9.10
	Age 65–69	42	−1.45	7.1	0.15
	Age 70–74	20	1.23	8.85	2.82
	Age 75–79	15	1.14	6.24	2.21
	Age 80+	10	−0.83	5.5	4.20
1993	Age 20–24	1	188.38	–	188.38
	Age 25–29	13	41.57	32.97	2.48
	Age 30–34	26	22.15	6.31	19.40
	Age 35–39	59	23.90	8.57	6.88
	Age 40–44	62	15.79	11.55	10.81
	Age 45–49	68	3.69	9.28	−0.09
	Age 50–54	52	40.10	19.34	12.44
	Age 55–59	46	0.34	27.25	4.83
	Age 60–64	50	25.83	11.8	2.04
	Age 65–69	50	16.31	8.44	5.31
	Age 70–74	35	23.94	24.89	−2.02
	Age 75–79	11	−4.27	9.6	8.34
	Age 80+	11	0.17	2.85	0.88
1995	Age 20–24	–	–	–	–
	Age 25–29	6	−0.10	12.17	0.02
	Age 30–34	20	−21.73	21.8	0.53
	Age 35–39	54	1.58	5.53	0.78
	Age 40–44	54	5.13	7.91	1.80
	Age 45–49	67	4.28	9.56	2.17
	Age 50–54	59	6.01	19.1	0.17

(*Continues*)

TABLE 4.4   (*Continued*)

		Number of observations	Mean	Standard deviation of mean	Median
	Age 55–59	54	−7.87	10.14	−1.58
	Age 60–64	50	13.36	12.78	3.95
	Age 65–69	50	5.84	4.72	−0.01
	Age 70–74	36	−7.81	8.43	0.05
	Age 75–79	19	−13.88	18.37	1.03
	Age 80+	15	5.13	12.46	3.46
1998	Age 20–24	–	–	–	–
	Age 25–29	1	−96.87	–	−96.87
	Age 30–34	12	−5.26	10.81	−0.06
	Age 35–39	31	16.77	7.62	1.83
	Age 40–44	61	0.11	3.97	0.13
	Age 45–49	61	46.93	37.83	−1.11
	Age 50–54	68	1.12	10.03	−0.34
	Age 55–59	53	14.48	14.87	0.52
	Age 60–64	46	−1.95	7.80	0.03
	Age 65–69	55	−1.76	5.00	−0.17
	Age 70–74	46	−12.13	9.34	−0.17
	Age 75–79	30	6.71	8.31	0.34
	Age 80+	20	2.55	8.80	−8.10

[a]The table reports for 1991, 1993, 1995, and 1998 the real saving by age bracket. Real saving is defined as the difference of real wealth in 2 years, converted into yearly figures. We use the panel component of the SHIW. This leaves 1936 households. Sample statistics are computed using sample weights. Households headed by individuals younger than 20 are excluded. In the first column we report the age group of the head of the household, in the second column the number of observations, in the third column the mean, in the fourth column the standard deviation of the mean, and in the last column the median.

financial wealth for the different years.[14] Mean financial wealth shows the distinctive hump-shaped profile and the median (shown in the top-right panel) is below the mean at all ages.[15] The distribution of real wealth by age is left-skewed (Table 4.6) – older people seem to hold a substantial amount of real wealth. In 1991,

[14]In this and in the following figures we use a cubic spline to smooth the raw data. We used 9 knots, corresponding to the deciles of the data, and smooth the data using linear (mean) and quantile (median) regression.

[15]Mean financial wealth at the ages 45–49 and 50–54 in 1991 are not statistically different, so are the mean financial wealth at ages 50–54 and 55–59 in 1993, at the ages 55–59 and 60–64 in 1995 and 1998.

TABLE 4.5 Financial Wealth: 1991, 1993, 1995, and 1998[a]

		Number of observations	Mean	Standard deviation of mean	Median
1991	Age 20–24	71	9.90	2.99	5.35
	Age 25–29	305	9.32	2.45	3.41
	Age 30–34	663	10.33	1.02	5.14
	Age 35–39	721	10.50	0.89	3.87
	Age 40–44	902	14.65	1.23	5.33
	Age 45–49	861	18.27	2.51	6.17
	Age 50–54	940	17.90	1.60	8.55
	Age 55–59	834	17.22	1.37	6.00
	Age 60–64	877	17.27	1.73	7.08
	Age 65–69	752	13.97	1.40	4.25
	Age 70–74	489	10.91	1.23	4.67
	Age 75–79	437	14.59	2.74	4.04
	Age 80+	332	10.65	2.23	2.54
1993	Age 20–24	50	10.07	2.76	7.00
	Age 25–29	304	10.69	1.63	3.81
	Age 30–34	592	14.04	1.59	4.81
	Age 35–39	725	15.92	2.39	4.10
	Age 40–44	793	15.39	1.57	6.01
	Age 45–49	858	18.41	2.85	5.96
	Age 50–54	879	24.38	2.45	6.63
	Age 55–59	828	22.34	1.99	8.41
	Age 60–64	838	23.71	4.33	6.68
	Age 65–69	798	17.80	2.04	5.39
	Age 70–74	680	13.26	1.26	4.02
	Age 75–79	360	13.10	2.05	3.64
	Age 80+	383	9.91	1.38	1.75
1995	Age 20–24	53	8.65	2.07	5.07
	Age 25–29	259	9.56	2.93	3.52
	Age 30–34	593	14.39	1.34	5.38
	Age 35–39	707	11.60	1.13	4.30
	Age 40–44	755	17.24	2.08	4.33
	Age 45–49	942	18.90	1.97	6.49
	Age 50–54	818	20.94	1.89	6.96
	Age 55–59	903	24.99	2.36	7.71

(Continues)

TABLE 4.5   (*Continued*)

		Number of observations	Mean	Standard deviation of mean	Median
	Age 60–64	796	23.45	2.67	6.53
	Age 65–69	825	21.74	2.19	5.18
	Age 70–74	691	13.69	1.50	3.46
	Age 75–79	344	16.32	2.43	3.52
	Age 80+	446	10.45	1.12	2.77
1998	Age 20–24	39	3.62	1.04	1.03
	Age 25–29	193	9.65	2.26	3.70
	Age 30–34	493	13.87	1.60	6.20
	Age 35–39	660	19.71	2.50	8.01
	Age 40–44	733	17.64	1.49	7.75
	Age 45–49	824	23.38	2.96	8.34
	Age 50–54	858	19.79	1.53	8.68
	Age 55–59	739	34.45	7.09	9.30
	Age 60–64	705	30.31	3.87	8.77
	Age 65–69	633	25.77	3.73	7.00
	Age 70–74	563	17.50	2.27	5.32
	Age 75–79	384	29.12	6.30	5.17
	Age 80+	318	18.98	5.09	4.13

[a]The table reports for 1991, 1993, 1995, and 1998 the financial wealth by age bracket. Financial wealth is defined as financial assets minus financial liabilities excluding mortgages and are expressed in thousands of 1998 euro. Sample statistics are computed using sample weights. Households headed by individuals younger than 20 are excluded. In the first column we report the age group of the head of the household, in the second column the number of observations, in the third column the mean, in the fourth column the standard deviation of the mean, and in the last column the median.

at the age of 80, real wealth is around 70% of the level prevailing around the age of 65. These findings are confirmed in the bottom-left and right panel of Figure 4.1, where we plot the cross-sectional age profile of mean and median real wealth.

Turning to the residual measure of saving (based on income and consumption), we present in Table 4.7 results for total disposable income.[16]

[16]We do not show data for total gross income as we have available in the survey only net incomes (after income tax and contributions). While we do attempt an imputation of contributions used to compute earned income and these are shown in Table A.4.1 in the Appendix, the tax system is highly nonlinear in Italy and we rather avoid making an imputation for income taxes in this study.

TABLE 4.6 Real Wealth: 1991, 1993, 1995, and 1998[a]

		Number of observations	Mean	Standard deviation of mean	Median
1991	Age 20–24	71	41.30	8.87	4.12
	Age 25–29	305	76.36	16.66	6.69
	Age 30–34	663	69.39	6.20	24.08
	Age 35–39	721	89.74	6.34	55.51
	Age 40–44	902	114.16	7.41	75.58
	Age 45–49	861	135.93	9.34	82.27
	Age 50–54	940	134.45	6.90	88.95
	Age 55–59	834	132.26	7.89	87.28
	Age 60–64	877	135.85	9.62	84.46
	Age 65–69	752	100.28	7.60	56.18
	Age 70–74	489	71.79	5.30	47.49
	Age 75–79	437	71.66	6.98	40.80
	Age 80+	332	72.87	10.23	27.42
1993	Age 20–24	50	87.95	23.09	12.30
	Age 25–29	304	85.74	13.47	19.48
	Age 30–34	592	90.68	10.76	30.59
	Age 35–39	725	107.48	6.41	67.38
	Age 40–44	793	134.34	8.19	86.74
	Age 45–49	858	150.59	12.51	92.22
	Age 50–54	879	185.11	13.81	115.04
	Age 55–59	828	147.13	8.82	91.30
	Age 60–64	838	138.36	12.43	73.10
	Age 65–69	798	107.65	6.58	62.09
	Age 70–74	680	92.10	7.87	46.87
	Age 75–79	360	77.20	10.56	18.87
	Age 80+	383	55.74	7.54	3.26
1995	Age 20–24	53	46.76	13.24	1.11
	Age 25–29	259	83.01	17.14	27.80
	Age 30–34	593	88.80	7.13	36.77
	Age 35–39	707	103.87	6.84	67.05
	Age 40–44	755	118.44	5.82	86.17
	Age 45–49	942	149.93	8.85	101.74
	Age 50–54	818	176.49	10.12	112.58

(*Continues*)

TABLE 4.6   (*Continued*)

		Number of observations	Mean	Standard deviation of mean	Median
	Age 55–59	903	175.06	10.51	102.30
	Age 60–64	796	151.17	9.4	86.73
	Age 65–69	825	115.42	6.92	61.15
	Age 70–74	691	87.18	5.93	55.60
	Age 75–79	344	72.20	6.86	36.69
	Age 80+	446	74.34	14.96	11.12
1998	Age 20–24	39	37.87	12.48	1.03
	Age 25–29	193	75.40	10.74	18.08
	Age 30–34	493	92.30	9.90	51.65
	Age 35–39	660	112.18	9.88	67.67
	Age 40–44	733	126.03	8.12	86.26
	Age 45–49	824	167.11	16.49	94.52
	Age 50–54	858	154.32	11.35	101.11
	Age 55–59	739	176.95	20.52	103.41
	Age 60–64	705	158.88	11.05	103.41
	Age 65–69	633	129.29	10.35	77.74
	Age 70–74	563	111.51	12.06	52.69
	Age 75–79	384	84.74	8.64	41.32
	Age 80+	318	80.54	10.23	41.32

[a]The table reports for 1991, 1993, 1995, and 1998 the real wealth by age bracket. Real wealth is defined as real assets minus mortgages and are expressed in thousands of 1998 euro. Sample statistics are computed using sample weights. Households headed by individuals younger than 20 are excluded. In the first column we report the age group of the head of the household, in the second column the number of observations, in the third column the mean, in the fourth column the standard deviation of the mean, and in the last column the median.

In particular, Table 4.7 shows that the distribution of disposable income by age is not skewed. Mean disposable income and median disposable income are not statistically different. Earned income (Table 4.9) exhibits a markedly different age profile vis-à-vis disposable income: it drops after the age of 65–69 by a significant amount. This difference is clearly due to the fact that, unlike earned income, disposable income includes pension benefits at older ages. The mirror image of this pattern can be found in Table 4.8, where we present annuitized retirement income (in Italy this is almost exclusively social security benefits), which obviously grows in old age. Figure 4.2 displays the cross-sectional age profile of disposable and earned

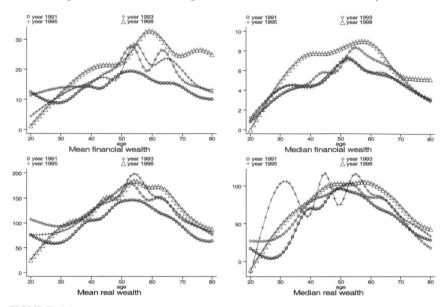

FIGURE 4.1   Cross-sectional age profile of financial and real wealth (thousands of 1998 euro). The figures plot the cross-sectional age profile of mean and median financial and real wealth for the years 1991, 1993, 1995, and 1998. Raw data are smoothed using a cubic spline with 9 knots, each corresponding to a decile.

income. In the top-left panel of Figure 4.2 we plot the cross-sectional age profile of mean disposable income. The concavity of the cross-sectional profile of disposable income is a common finding in micro data and is consistent with the theory of human capital. Table 4.10 (and Figure 4.3) display the cross-sectional age profile of consumption expenditure, which is increasing for young households and starts decreasing at mid-ages; this pattern is more pronounced in mean consumption than in median consumption. This feature of the consumption data is not unique to the Italian data set[17] and is due to a number of reasons, including precautionary motives for saving, demographics, liquidity constraints, and intertemporal and intratemporal non-separabilities.

Equipped with a preliminary analysis on income and consumption patterns, we present in Table 4.11 the cross-sectional age profile of discretionary and mandatory saving. Discretionary saving is computed as disposable income minus consumption expenditure. Mean and median discretionary saving are both hump shaped: a reduction in mean discretionary saving occurs between ages 55–59 (in 1991) and ages 65–69 (in 1998). However, discretionary saving (whether mean or median) never becomes negative, which means that wealth decumulation is not observed at later ages. At first this result may seem inconsistent with what was found for real saving (see Table 4.4); however, it should be noted that the stock measure

[17]US data, for instance, display a similar pattern.

TABLE 4.7 Total Disposable Income: 1991, 1993, 1995, and 1998[a]

		Number of observations	Mean	Standard deviation of mean	Median
1991	Age 20–24	75	17.00	1.63	16.06
	Age 25–29	305	23.19	1.31	19.08
	Age 30–34	663	23.92	0.79	21.46
	Age 35–39	721	24.71	0.65	22.27
	Age 40–44	902	27.60	0.63	25.40
	Age 45–49	861	30.77	1.09	26.21
	Age 50–54	940	30.35	0.78	26.91
	Age 55–59	834	27.86	0.83	23.44
	Age 60–64	877	25.46	0.83	22.15
	Age 65–69	752	21.07	0.88	17.16
	Age 70–74	489	17.32	0.75	13.64
	Age 75–79	437	16.98	1.24	13.55
	Age 80+	332	14.54	0.89	10.83
1993	Age 20–24	51	17.20	1.73	16.66
	Age 25–29	304	20.10	1.01	18.60
	Age 30–34	592	24.03	0.85	20.57
	Age 35–39	725	25.25	0.82	22.46
	Age 40–44	793	27.44	0.91	24.18
	Age 45–49	858	28.26	0.95	24.12
	Age 50–54	879	31.02	0.92	27.02
	Age 55–59	828	28.45	1.12	22.15
	Age 60–64	838	23.39	0.75	18.30
	Age 65–69	798	20.62	0.75	16.20
	Age 70–74	680	17.43	0.58	14.45
	Age 75–79	360	16.23	1.17	12.27
	Age 80+	383	13.83	0.78	10.82
1995	Age 20–24	56	17.52	2.49	15.94
	Age 25–29	259	20.78	1.02	19.45
	Age 30–34	593	22.91	0.87	20.12
	Age 35–39	707	23.14	0.67	21.30
	Age 40–44	755	25.05	0.83	22.48
	Age 45–49	942	28.69	0.72	25.18
	Age 50–54	818	29.32	0.93	24.51

(*Continues*)

TABLE 4.7 (*Continued*)

		Number of observations	Mean	Standard deviation of mean	Median
	Age 55–59	903	28.83	1.07	24.20
	Age 60–64	796	26.33	1.10	20.01
	Age 65–69	825	21.87	0.83	16.71
	Age 70–74	691	17.11	0.56	13.82
	Age 75–79	344	15.98	0.85	11.31
	Age 80+	446	15.00	1.09	11.50
1998	Age 20–24	44	13.01	1.57	10.28
	Age 25–29	193	18.96	0.95	17.93
	Age 30–34	493	22.69	1.07	19.49
	Age 35–39	660	25.30	0.93	21.52
	Age 40–44	733	26.55	0.76	24.65
	Age 45–49	824	31.35	1.55	27.08
	Age 50–54	858	29.50	0.70	26.95
	Age 55–59	739	30.35	1.33	25.63
	Age 60–64	705	28.32	1.37	22.29
	Age 65–69	633	22.14	1.06	16.57
	Age 70–74	563	19.55	0.82	15.70
	Age 75–79	384	18.02	1.44	13.23
	Age 80+	318	16.03	1.05	12.13

[a]The table reports for 1991, 1993, 1995, and 1998 the disposable income by age bracket; figures are in thousands of 1998 euro. Sample statistics are computed using sample weights. Households headed by individuals younger than 20 are excluded. In the first column we report the age group of the head of the household, in the second column the number of observations, in the third column the mean, in the fourth column the standard deviation of the mean, and in the last column the median.

(difference in wealth levels) and the flow measure (income minus consumption) of discretionary saving may lead to different conclusions: this is due to the existence of capital gains and/or to measurement error.[18]

In contrast to what is observed for discretionary saving, mean and median mandatory saving become negative after the ages 54–59. Hence, mandatory wealth is "decumulated" at older ages. It should be recalled that in Italy pension wealth represents a relevant amount of resources for most households (this is true

---

[18]While we cannot say much about capital gains, we postpone to Section 4.7 the discussion on measurement error.

TABLE 4.8   Annuitized Retirement Income: 1991, 1993, 1995, and 1998[a]

		Number of observations	Mean	Standard deviation of mean	Median
1991	Age 20–24	75	1.08	0.93	0.00
	Age 25–29	305	0.48	0.18	0.00
	Age 30–34	663	0.42	0.12	0.00
	Age 35–39	721	0.69	0.17	0.00
	Age 40–44	902	0.79	0.13	0.00
	Age 45–49	861	1.36	0.15	0.00
	Age 50–54	940	3.15	0.28	0.00
	Age 55–59	834	5.33	0.37	2.74
	Age 60–64	877	8.97	0.35	9.56
	Age 65–69	752	11.06	0.32	10.43
	Age 70–74	489	10.58	0.33	9.56
	Age 75–79	437	10.49	0.39	9.56
	Age 80+	332	9.44	0.56	8.69
1993	Age 20–24	51	1.63	0.52	0.00
	Age 25–29	304	0.93	0.21	0.00
	Age 30–34	592	0.69	0.15	0.00
	Age 35–39	725	0.71	0.13	0.00
	Age 40–44	793	0.96	0.13	0.00
	Age 45–49	858	1.68	0.17	0.00
	Age 50–54	879	3.12	0.27	0.00
	Age 55–59	828	6.84	0.34	4.82
	Age 60–64	838	9.72	0.30	9.50
	Age 65–69	798	11.44	0.35	10.03
	Age 70–74	680	10.72	0.29	9.57
	Age 75–79	360	9.92	0.39	8.74
	Age 80+	383	9.73	0.55	8.70
1995	Age 20–24	56	0.58	0.27	0.00
	Age 25–29	259	0.88	0.2	0.00
	Age 30–34	593	0.78	0.19	0.00
	Age 35–39	707	0.87	0.14	0.00
	Age 40–44	755	0.82	0.13	0.00
	Age 45–49	942	1.96	0.19	0.00

(*Continues*)

TABLE 4.8   (*Continued*)

		Number of observations	Mean	Standard deviation of mean	Median
	Age 50–54	818	3.94	0.3	0.00
	Age 55–59	903	7.04	0.33	5.02
	Age 60–64	796	10.14	0.39	9.11
	Age 65–69	825	11.16	0.3	10.12
	Age 70–74	691	10.82	0.29	9.47
	Age 75–79	344	9.65	0.32	8.74
	Age 80+	446	9.42	0.36	8.67
1998	Age 20–24	44	0.80	0.41	0.00
	Age 25–29	193	0.67	0.19	0.00
	Age 30–34	493	0.68	0.16	0.00
	Age 35–39	660	0.79	0.18	0.00
	Age 40–44	733	0.90	0.15	0.00
	Age 45–49	824	1.81	0.21	0.00
	Age 50–54	858	3.70	0.28	0.00
	Age 55–59	739	7.71	0.43	6.20
	Age 60–64	705	10.50	0.41	9.40
	Age 65–69	633	10.69	0.4	9.07
	Age 70–74	563	11.81	0.34	10.74
	Age 75–79	384	10.51	0.47	9.30
	Age 80+	318	10.03	0.45	8.73

[a]The table reports for 1991, 1993, 1995, and 1998 annuitized retirement income by age bracket; figures are in thousands of 1998 euro. Sample statistics are computed using sample weights. Households headed by individuals younger than 20 are excluded. In the first column we report the age group of the head of the household, in the second column the number of observations, in the third column the mean, in the fourth column the standard deviation of the mean, and in the last column the median.

if one computes the present value of past contributions at the retirement age of the household head, and even more so if one takes the present value at retirement of future expected benefits). Figure 4.4 displays the cross-sectional age profile of discretionary and mandatory saving. The top panel plots the cross-sectional age profile of mean and median discretionary saving, whereas the bottom panel plots mean and median mandatory saving against the age of the household head.

To allow for cross-country comparability we also measure saving rates. It is worth recalling the reasons why it may be useful in this context to focus on saving

TABLE 4.9   Earned Income: 1991, 1993, 1995, and 1998[a]

		Number of observations	Mean	Standard deviation of mean	Median
1991	Age 20–24	75	20.79	1.76	19.15
	Age 25–29	305	30.19	1.53	24.92
	Age 30–34	663	31.69	1.01	27.91
	Age 35–39	721	32.45	0.89	28.41
	Age 40–44	902	35.88	0.81	32.99
	Age 45–49	861	39.14	1.34	33.08
	Age 50–54	940	35.88	1.10	32.42
	Age 55–59	834	29.30	1.17	24.92
	Age 60–64	877	20.64	1.12	16.70
	Age 65–69	752	12.16	1.01	3.97
	Age 70–74	489	8.13	0.93	3.23
	Age 75–79	437	7.67	1.34	3.09
	Age 80		332	5.51	0.73	2.32
1993	Age 20–24	51	20.44	2.33	20.97
	Age 25–29	304	25.76	1.24	23.34
	Age 30–34	592	31.50	1.13	27.45
	Age 35–39	725	33.04	1.06	29.06
	Age 40–44	793	36.04	1.27	31.36
	Age 45–49	858	35.77	1.20	31.35
	Age 50–54	879	36.81	1.24	32.44
	Age 55–59	828	28.09	1.49	20.17
	Age 60–64	838	16.88	0.89	8.45
	Age 65–69	798	11.08	0.69	4.68
	Age 70–74	680	7.70	0.54	3.52
	Age 75–79	360	7.41	1.28	3.07
	Age 80+	383	4.44	0.47	2.23
1995	Age 20–24	56	23.47	3.72	22.05
	Age 25–29	259	27.15	1.29	24.76
	Age 30–34	593	29.35	1.15	25.28
	Age 35–39	707	30.02	0.86	27.25
	Age 40–44	755	32.82	1.16	28.69
	Age 45–49	942	35.80	0.94	32.07
	Age 50–54	818	33.25	1.17	28.64

(*Continues*)

TABLE 4.9   (*Continued*)

		Number of observations	Mean	Standard deviation of mean	Median
	Age 55–59	903	27.91	1.34	20.49
	Age 60–64	796	20.02	1.24	13.58
	Age 65–69	825	12.80	0.86	5.31
	Age 70–74	691	7.05	0.45	3.34
	Age 75–79	344	7.28	0.92	3.02
	Age 80+	446	6.21	1.05	2.63
1998	Age 20–24	44	17.62	2.23	16.03
	Age 25–29	193	26.63	1.52	24.95
	Age 30–34	493	31.80	1.38	28.18
	Age 35–39	660	34.86	1.23	30.72
	Age 40–44	733	37.11	1.06	34.42
	Age 45–49	824	42.41	1.96	36.12
	Age 50–54	858	36.71	1.01	33.84
	Age 55–59	739	30.63	1.62	25.27
	Age 60–64	705	22.98	1.62	14.93
	Age 65–69	633	14.05	1.12	5.83
	Age 70–74	563	8.90	0.81	3.90
	Age 75–79	384	8.16	1.29	3.10
	Age 80+	318	6.66	0.88	3.10

[a]The table reports for 1991, 1993, 1995, and 1998 the earned income by age bracket; figures are in thousands of 1998 euro. Sample statistics are computed using sample weights. Households headed by individuals younger than 20 are excluded. In the first column we report the age group of the head of the household, in the second column the number of observations, in the third column the mean, in the fourth column the standard deviation of the mean, and in the last column the median.

levels, even if saving rates have well-known advantages, which make them so popular in international studies.[19]

First, saving rates do not aggregate.[20] Secondly, saving rates tend to be more sensitive to extreme outliers than saving levels.[21] Finally, it is easier to track saving

[19]On this point see also the discussion in Chapter 2.

[20]Several authors approximate saving rates by the difference of the log of income and the log of consumption. This difference can be aggregated consistently. However, the log approximation is not appropriate in the presence of high saving rates.

[21]Suppose that both income and consumption are measured with error. If this error enters in an additive way, the saving rate can be very badly measured. The overall measurement error is inflated, because the measurement error of the nominator and of the denominator are correlated. The practice of taking the log approximation does not do better.

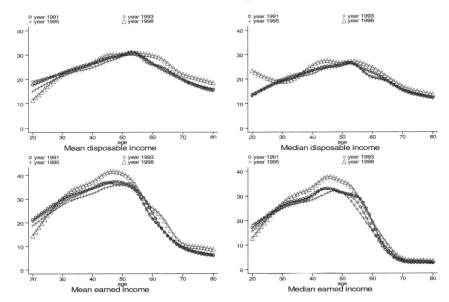

FIGURE 4.2   Cross-sectional age profile of disposable and earned income (thousands of 1998 euro). The figures plot the cross-sectional age profile of mean and median earned and disposable income for the years 1991, 1993, 1995, and 1998. Raw data are smoothed using a cubic spline with 9 knots, each corresponding to a decile.

behavior when saving is measured in levels, rather than in ratios: although saving rates may be a useful statistic in making comparisons, theoretical predictions on dynamic saving behavior over the life cycle are normally formulated in terms of saving levels. For instance, the life-cycle hypothesis predicts that saving should be negative after retirement (Modigliani, 1986), whereas predictions on saving rates by age would be more complex.

Saving rates are computed as 1 minus the ratio of consumption on disposable income; consequently, they reflect only the discretionary component of total saving. Table 4.12 shows the median saving rates by age and some features of the saving rate distribution (see also Figure 4.5 for cross-sectional profiles). In all the 4 years used in this chapter, the median is positive and it starts to decrease at the age of 65–69. Moreover, most households save more than 1% of their disposable income, and only a few exhibit a saving rate between −1% and 1%. In other words, most households still save at older ages (even if they may save less).

The results presented so far are simple summary measures of the raw data. However, it is a well-known problem that cross-sectional age profiles are the joint result of age, cohort, and time effects. Hence, for example, if cohort effects are present and sizable, the differences in saving levels observed at different ages for the same year of the survey cannot be interpreted as life-cycle patterns. For

TABLE 4.10   Consumption Expenditure: 1991, 1993, 1995, and 1998[a]

		Number of observations	Mean	Standard deviation of mean	Median
1991	Age 20–24	75	14.63	1.09	13.64
	Age 25–29	305	18.35	1.08	15.58
	Age 30–34	663	17.97	0.55	16.05
	Age 35–39	721	17.89	0.42	16.45
	Age 40–44	902	20.31	0.41	18.46
	Age 45–49	861	22.08	0.65	18.86
	Age 50–54	940	21.11	0.48	18.93
	Age 55–59	834	19.38	0.51	17.63
	Age 60–64	877	17.07	0.49	15.89
	Age 65–69	752	13.63	0.46	11.70
	Age 70–74	489	12.43	0.57	10.80
	Age 75–79	437	11.04	0.46	9.63
	Age 80+	332	9.86	0.49	8.15
1993	Age 20–24	51	12.95	1.08	11.83
	Age 25–29	304	16.16	0.56	14.43
	Age 30–34	592	18.95	0.57	16.80
	Age 35–39	725	18.52	0.46	16.43
	Age 40–44	793	19.85	0.57	17.53
	Age 45–49	858	20.90	0.62	18.81
	Age 50–54	879	21.51	0.53	18.86
	Age 55–59	828	19.35	0.62	16.80
	Age 60–64	838	16.17	0.40	13.88
	Age 65–69	798	14.83	0.42	12.80
	Age 70–74	680	12.81	0.36	11.11
	Age 75–79	360	11.37	0.51	10.62
	Age 80+	383	10.39	0.42	9.13
1995	Age 20–24	56	18.15	2.45	14.01
	Age 25–29	259	17.57	0.82	15.34
	Age 30–34	593	18.98	0.59	16.36
	Age 35–39	707	19.98	0.52	18.40
	Age 40–44	755	20.07	0.52	17.35
	Age 45–49	942	22.38	0.51	20.57
	Age 50–54	818	22.27	0.51	19.68

(*Continues*)

TABLE 4.10   (*Continued*)

		Number of observations	Mean	Standard deviation of mean	Median
	Age 55–59	903	20.89	0.67	17.99
	Age 60–64	796	18.93	0.65	15.90
	Age 65–69	825	15.93	0.5	13.34
	Age 70–74	691	12.80	0.34	11.34
	Age 75–79	344	11.83	0.46	10.01
	Age 80+	446	11.02	0.39	10.01
1998	Age 20–24	44	11.69	1.13	9.30
	Age 25–29	193	16.20	0.79	14.46
	Age 30–34	493	17.84	0.62	16.12
	Age 35–39	660	18.80	0.56	16.43
	Age 40–44	733	20.10	0.51	18.36
	Age 45–49	824	22.01	0.81	18.60
	Age 50–54	858	20.94	0.53	18.90
	Age 55–59	739	20.22	0.65	17.36
	Age 60–64	705	18.31	0.64	15.81
	Age 65–69	633	15.39	0.54	12.50
	Age 70–74	563	14.13	0.66	11.47
	Age 75–79	384	12.63	1.18	9.92
	Age 80+	318	10.42	0.48	9.30

*The table reports for 1991, 1993, 1995, and 1998 the consumption by age bracket; figures are in thousands of 1998 euro. Sample statistics are computed using sample weights. Households headed by individuals younger than 20 are excluded. In the first column we report the age group of the head of the household, in the second column the number of observations, in the third column the mean, in the fourth column the standard deviation of the mean, and in the last column the median.

this reason, we have to make assumptions on the way in which these effects jointly determine saving.

4.4 COHORT-ADJUSTED AGE PROFILES OF INCOME AND SAVING

Since individuals in various age classes belong to different generations (cohorts), which differ in mortality rates, preferences, and productivity, the use of a single cross section, where each individual is observed only once, does not allow for the identification of some of the underlying factors determining saving. In repeated cross sections a sample of individuals belonging to the same generation can be

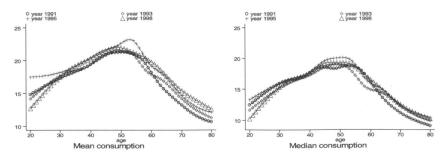

FIGURE 4.3   Cross-sectional age profile of consumption (thousands of 1998 euro). The figures plot the cross-sectional age profile of mean and median consumption for the years 1991, 1993, 1995, and 1998. Raw data are smoothed using a cubic spline with 9 knots, each corresponding to a decile of the consumption distribution.

observed at each date, so that one can track the income, consumption, and saving of a cohort of individuals. Since our aim is to purge age–saving profiles of cohort effects, repeated cross-sectional data are particularly well suited in our context.

Sorting the Italian SHIW data by the year of birth of the head of the household and by the year in which the household was interviewed results in defining 12 generations. Generation 1 includes all households whose head was born between 1910 and 1914, generation 2 those born between 1915 and 1919, and so on, up to generation 12, including those born between 1965 and 1969. For each cohort–age–year group, we then compute average (or median) income and average saving. The "age" of the household is then defined to be the median age within each cell, so that, for instance, generation 1 was 72 years old in 1984 (the year of the first survey) and 86 years old in 1998 (the year of the last available survey). Households headed by persons older than 80 or younger than 20 (regardless of year of birth) are excluded from our analysis. After excluding a few more observations with missing data for consumption, income, or wealth, our final sample covers 58,041 households.

The first four columns in Table 4.13 report the year-of-birth intervals, the range over which the median age of each cohort is observed in 1984 and in 1998, respectively, and the average cell size for each cohort. The next two columns display average disposable income and consumption, and the difference between the two is reported in the next column as discretionary saving. The gap resulting between the mean and the median of saving (final column) signals that the saving distribution is skewed, hence suggesting that means do not adequately characterize the age–saving profiles. We thus also report median income and median saving figures.

Figure 4.6 reports the cohort-adjusted age profile of financial and real wealth.[22] The numbers in the graph refer to the different generations, going from 1 (the oldest) to 12 (the youngest).

---

[22]Financial and real wealth are collected on a continuous basis from 1987. To maximize homogeneity of definitions across subsequent waves, the graph is constructed using data from 1991.

TABLE 4.11   Discretionary and Mandatory Saving: 1991, 1993, 1995, and 1998[a]

		Number of observations	Discretionary saving			Mandatory saving		
			Mean	Standard deviation of mean	Median	Mean	Standard deviation of mean	Median
1991	Age 20–24	75	2.22	1.05	1.23	3.59	1.13	4.72
	Age 25–29	305	4.84	1.12	3.41	7.00	0.44	6.56
	Age 30–34	663	5.95	0.41	5.19	7.78	0.32	7.04
	Age 35–39	721	6.82	0.41	5.36	7.74	0.35	7.54
	Age 40–44	902	7.30	0.40	5.69	8.28	0.28	7.87
	Age 45–49	861	8.68	0.62	6.15	8.37	0.36	8.20
	Age 50–54	940	9.24	0.51	6.83	5.53	0.52	6.56
	Age 55–59	834	8.48	0.49	5.74	1.44	0.59	2.84
	Age 60–64	877	8.38	0.51	5.58	−4.82	0.52	−6.47
	Age 65–69	752	7.45	0.57	4.40	−8.92	0.41	−8.69
	Age 70–74	489	4.89	0.38	3.25	−9.19	0.44	−8.78
	Age 75–79	437	5.94	0.84	3.19	−9.31	0.41	−8.69
	Age 80+	332	4.68	0.53	2.17	−9.03	0.57	−8.03
1993	Age 20–24	51	4.49	1.45	3.65	3.33	1.11	3.76
	Age 25–29	304	3.94	0.81	2.54	5.66	0.43	5.68
	Age 30–34	592	5.08	0.71	4.01	7.47	0.39	7.49
	Age 35–39	725	6.73	0.61	4.65	7.79	0.33	7.49
	Age 40–44	793	7.59	0.61	4.90	8.60	0.43	7.87
	Age 45–49	858	7.36	0.69	4.80	7.50	0.37	7.52
	Age 50–54	879	9.52	0.72	6.71	5.79	0.52	6.64
	Age 55–59	828	9.10	0.79	4.70	−0.36	0.59	−2.34
	Age 60–64	838	7.23	0.51	3.96	−6.52	0.39	−6.68
	Age 65–69	798	5.79	0.46	2.87	−9.54	0.38	−8.31
	Age 70–74	680	4.62	0.35	2.39	−9.73	0.31	−9.10
	Age 75–79	360	4.86	0.77	1.70	−8.82	0.45	−7.91
	Age 80+	383	3.44	0.44	1.40	−9.39	0.56	−8.70
1995	Age 20–24	56	−0.31	3.36	0.15	6.05	1.36	5.56
	Age 25–29	259	3.22	0.92	2.98	6.36	0.45	6.84
	Age 30–34	593	3.92	0.57	2.26	6.45	0.4	6.26
	Age 35–39	707	3.16	0.5	2.13	6.87	0.3	7.13
	Age 40–44	755	4.98	0.57	3.24	7.78	0.4	7.13

(*Continues*)

TABLE 4.11   (Continued)

			Discretionary saving			Mandatory saving		
		Number of observations	Mean	Standard deviation of mean	Median	Mean	Standard deviation of mean	Median
	Age 45–49	942	6.31	0.45	4.66	7.11	0.36	7.70
	Age 50–54	818	7.05	0.72	3.45	3.93	0.47	4.89
	Age 55–59	903	7.94	0.65	5.46	−0.92	0.5	−0.59
	Age 60–64	796	7.40	0.6	3.56	−6.31	0.51	−6.50
	Age 65–69	825	5.95	0.45	2.71	−9.07	0.34	−8.40
	Age 70–74	691	4.31	0.3	2.22	10.06	0.31	−9.03
	Age 75–79	344	4.16	0.55	1.76	−8.71	0.38	−8.38
	Age 80+	446	3.99	0.83	1.45	−8.79	0.38	−8.24
1998	Age 20–24	44	1.55	1.36	0.36	4.80	1.05	5.77
	Age 25–29	193	2.75	0.77	2.69	7.67	0.68	7.41
	Age 30–34	493	4.85	0.72	3.29	9.11	0.47	8.57
	Age 35–39	660	6.50	0.61	4.25	9.56	0.42	8.92
	Age 40–44	733	6.45	0.54	4.53	10.57	0.41	10.29
	Age 45–49	824	9.34	1.24	6.92	11.05	0.56	10.46
	Age 50–54	858	8.56	0.53	6.36	7.21	0.51	8.57
	Age 55–59	739	10.13	1.16	6.65	0.28	0.67	0.00
	Age 60–64	705	10.00	1.06	5.89	−5.33	0.59	−6.51
	Age 65–69	633	6.75	0.71	3.20	−8.09	0.47	−7.41
	Age 70–74	563	5.42	0.42	3.12	−10.65	0.37	−9.54
	Age 75–79	384	5.39	0.63	2.74	−9.86	0.49	−9.07
	Age 80+	318	5.61	0.7	2.96	−9.37	0.46	−8.39

[a]The table reports for 1991, 1993, 1995, and 1998 the discretionary and mandatory saving by age bracket; figures are in thousands of 1998 euro. Sample statistics are computed using sample weights. Households headed by individuals younger than 20 are excluded. In the first column we report the age group of the head of the household, in the second column the number of observations, in the third and sixth columns the mean, in the fourth and seventh columns the standard deviation of the mean, and in the fifth and final columns the median.

The smoothed lines presented in Figure 4.6 are the estimated age profile of a representative household. They are obtained from the fitted values of a regression of financial (real) wealth on a third-order polynomial in age, a full set of cohort dummies, and a set of restricted time dummies. Since age, cohort, and time are perfectly collinear variables, normalization is needed to estimate their separate effect on consumption. Here we follow Deaton and Paxson (1994) and estimate the

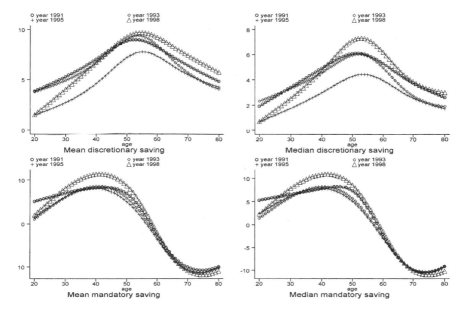

FIGURE 4.4   Cross-sectional age profile of discretionary and mandatory saving (thousands of 1998 euro). The figures plot the cross-sectional age profile of mean and median discretionary and mandatory saving for the years 1991, 1993, 1995, and 1998. Raw data are smoothed using a cubic spline with 9 knots, each corresponding to a decile.

regression by constraining the year dummies to be orthogonal to a time trend and to sum to zero. This normalization of time effects is useful, but it is important to keep in mind that it is arbitrary and it rules out time–age or time–cohort interaction terms. In all other figures the age profiles are constructed in similar fashion.

The adjusted profile of mean financial wealth is slightly increasing with age. This is due to the steep age profile of cohorts 3, 5, and 7. On the other hand, the adjusted profile of median financial wealth is hump shaped, thus providing some evidence for wealth decumulation. The bottom panel of Figure 4.6 hosts the mean and median real wealth. The age profile of mean real wealth is also slightly increasing; however, this seems to be mostly due to the fact that older cohorts – i.e. cohorts 1, 2, and 3 – do not decumulate at the end of their life cycle. A more robust measure, such as the median, is displayed in the bottom-right panel: this statistic suggests that some decumulation actually takes place. Figure 4.7 shows the cohort-adjusted age profile of disposable and earned income. After adjusting for cohort effects, average disposable income is much flatter than earned income. Overall, the smoothed data support the hypothesis that cohort effects may strongly affect the shape of the unadjusted saving profiles.

TABLE 4.12   Saving Rates: 1991, 1993, 1995, and 1998[a]

		Number of observations	Median	Percent of households with saving rate <−1%	Percent of households with saving rate between −1% and 1%	Percent of households with saving rate >1%
1991	Age 20–24	75	0.06	0.24	0.05	0.71
	Age 25–29	305	0.20	0.13	0.03	0.84
	Age 30–34	663	0.23	0.13	0.02	0.85
	Age 35–39	721	0.24	0.10	0.02	0.88
	Age 40–44	902	0.23	0.11	0.02	0.88
	Age 45–49	861	0.23	0.08	0.01	0.91
	Age 50–54	940	0.25	0.07	0.01	0.92
	Age 55–59	834	0.25	0.07	0.01	0.92
	Age 60–64	877	0.28	0.05	0.02	0.93
	Age 65–69	752	0.27	0.03	0.01	0.95
	Age 70–74	489	0.24	0.03	0.02	0.95
	Age 75–79	437	0.26	0.02	0.02	0.96
	Age 80+	332	0.23	0.03	0.02	0.95
1993	Age 20–24	51	0.23	0.24	0.04	0.73
	Age 25–29	304	0.16	0.29	0.01	0.69
	Age 30–34	592	0.20	0.31	0.02	0.67
	Age 35–39	725	0.21	0.24	0.02	0.74
	Age 40–44	793	0.22	0.21	0.02	0.77
	Age 45–49	858	0.20	0.22	0.02	0.76
	Age 50–54	879	0.27	0.16	0.01	0.82
	Age 55–59	828	0.22	0.18	0.02	0.80
	Age 60–64	838	0.22	0.15	0.02	0.84
	Age 65–69	798	0.20	0.15	0.02	0.83
	Age 70–74	680	0.16	0.15	0.03	0.82
	Age 75–79	360	0.14	0.10	0.03	0.88
	Age 80+	383	0.14	0.16	0.02	0.82
1995	Age 20–24	56	0.02	0.45	0.07	0.48
	Age 25–29	259	0.18	0.32	0.02	0.66
	Age 30–34	593	0.11	0.33	0.02	0.65
	Age 35–39	707	0.11	0.32	0.04	0.65
	Age 40–44	755	0.14	0.27	0.03	0.71
	Age 45–49	942	0.19	0.24	0.03	0.74

(*Continues*)

TABLE 4.12   (*Continued*)

		Number of observations	Median	Percent of households with saving rate <−1%	Percent of households with saving rate between −1% and 1%	Percent of households with saving rate >1%
	Age 50–54	818	0.16	0.22	0.02	0.76
	Age 55–59	903	0.21	0.21	0.03	0.77
	Age 60–64	796	0.20	0.16	0.02	0.82
	Age 65–69	825	0.19	0.16	0.02	0.82
	Age 70–74	691	0.17	0.12	0.01	0.86
	Age 75–79	344	0.15	0.12	0.03	0.85
	Age 80+	446	0.15	0.14	0.03	0.83
1998	Age 20–24	44	0.04	0.45	0.00	0.55
	Age 25–29	193	0.16	0.33	0.02	0.65
	Age 30–34	493	0.19	0.28	0.02	0.70
	Age 35–39	660	0.22	0.26	0.01	0.72
	Age 40–44	733	0.20	0.24	0.02	0.75
	Age 45–49	824	0.27	0.20	0.02	0.78
	Age 50–54	858	0.26	0.17	0.02	0.81
	Age 55–59	739	0.28	0.18	0.01	0.81
	Age 60–64	705	0.27	0.15	0.01	0.84
	Age 65–69	633	0.22	0.18	0.02	0.80
	Age 70–74	563	0.23	0.14	0.02	0.84
	Age 75–79	384	0.22	0.16	0.02	0.83
	Age 80+	318	0.24	0.13	0.01	0.86

[a]The table reports for 1991, 1993, 1995, and 1998 the saving rates by age bracket. Sample statistics are computed using sample weights. Households headed by individuals younger than 20 are excluded.

In the left bottom corner of Figure 4.7 we plot earned income: the sum of after-tax earnings and capital income. The unadjusted profile peaks around the age of 50, and rapidly declines after age 55, a reflection of the increasing number of retirees in the older age groups. Cohort effects are again very clearly seen affecting the resources of each generation, as the broken segments for successive older generations lie below the ones of younger generations. In Figure 4.8 we plot the cohort-adjusted age profiles of our two definitions of saving. The top panels plot the mean and the median of discretionary saving (disposable income minus consumption). The age–saving profile is rather flat and does not fall below zero until very old ages. Similar flat age–saving profiles of discretionary saving have been found by several studies. To take just a few recent examples, Poterba (1994) summarizes the evidence for

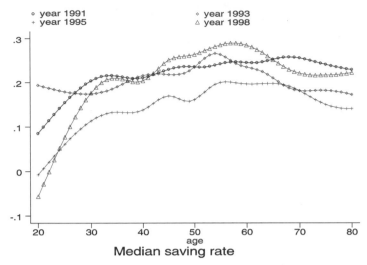

FIGURE 4.5   Cross-sectional age profile of median saving rate. The figures plot the cross-sectional age profile of median saving rate for the years 1991, 1993, 1995, and 1998. Raw data are smoothed using a cubic spline with 9 knots, each corresponding to a decile.

TABLE 4.13   Cell Size, Income, Consumption, and Saving by Year of Birth of the Household Head[a]

Year of birth	Median age in 1984	Median age in 1998	Average cell size	Disposable income	Total consumption	Private saving (mean)	Private saving (median)
1910–14	72	86	390	15.09	10.89	4.20	2.48
1915–19	67	81	416	17.57	12.96	5.31	2.88
1920–24	62	76	669	20.02	14.18	5.84	2.99
1925–29	57	71	754	23.83	16.71	7.12	4.10
1930–34	52	66	794	27.38	19.35	8.03	4.85
1935–39	47	61	880	29.41	20.90	8.51	5.40
1940–44	42	56	813	29.87	22.05	7.82	5.05
1945–49	37	51	895	28.32	21.13	7.20	5.06
1950–54	32	46	739	26.72	20.25	6.47	4.36
1955–59	27	41	669	24.03	18.97	5.06	3.49
1960–64	22	36	518	23.46	18.95	4.51	3.29
1965–69	17	31	310	21.26	17.28	3.98	2.48

[a]Income, consumption, and saving in thousands of 1998 euro. Sample statistics are computed using sample weights.

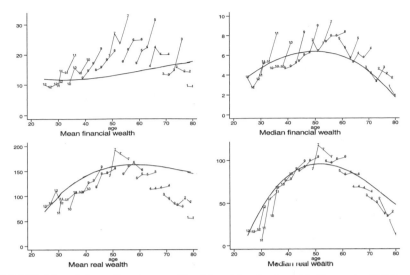

FIGURE 4.6   Cohort-adjusted age profile of financial and real wealth (thousands of 1998 euro). The figures plot the cohort-adjusted profile of mean and median financial and real wealth. The smoothed line in the figure is the fitted line of a regression on a third-order age polynomial, a full set of cohort dummies, and a set of restricted time dummies.

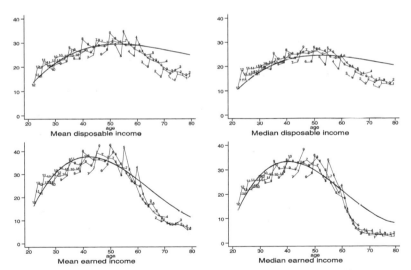

FIGURE 4.7   Cohort-adjusted age profile of disposable and earned income (thousands of 1998 euro). The figures plot the cohort-adjusted age profile of mean and median disposable income and earned income. Earned income is labor income plus capital income. Disposable income is earned income minus social security contributions and severance pay, plus social security benefits. The smoothed line in the figure is the fitted line of a regression on a third-order age polynomial, a full set of cohort dummies, and a set of restricted time dummies.

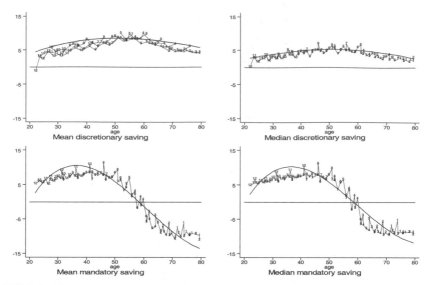

FIGURE 4.8   Cohort-adjusted age profile of discretionary and mandatory saving (thousands of 1998 euro). The figures plot the cohort-adjusted profile of mean and median discretionary and mandatory saving. Discretionary saving is disposable income minus total consumption. Mandatory saving is social security benefits, plus severance pay, minus social security benefits. The smoothed line in the figure is the fitted line of a regression on a third-order age polynomial, a full set of cohort dummies, and a set of restricted time dummies.

the group of most industrialized countries, Alessie *et al.* (1997) for the Netherlands, and Paxson (1996) for the United States and the UK. As we argued, one of the reasons for the existence of a flat age–saving profile might be a sizable level of mandatory saving in the form of social security and, more generally, the importance of welfare arrangements.

The bottom panels of Figure 4.8 show that mandatory saving is very substantial in the Italian economy: up to retirement, contributions average between €3000 and €3500 and are matched by generous pension provisions (about €7000). The mean and the median of mandatory saving peak before age 40 and decline after age 60. This latter result is an obvious implication of the social security arrangements, as Italian workers tend to retire at a relatively early age (around age 60 for men) and benefit from generous early retirement provisions.[23] Indirectly, this shows that social security wealth, the area under the curve of mandatory saving, has a concave shape with its maximum at the retirement age. As a first approximation, the social security wealth at the retirement age can be computed as the integral of the mandatory saving curve evaluated at the retirement age. However, this

[23]See Brugiavini (1999) for evidence on early retirement.

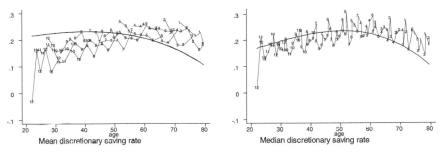

FIGURE 4.9   Cohort-adjusted age profile of discretionary saving rate. The figures plot the cohort-adjusted profile of the mean and median discretionary saving rate. Discretionary saving rate is computed as 1 minus the ratio of total consumption and disposable income. The smoothed line in the figure is the fitted line of a regression on a third-order age polynomial, a full set of cohort dummies, and a set of restricted time dummies.

computation is a valid approximation only when the rate of return from social security wealth and the mortality rates at all ages are small.

Saving rates, presented in Figure 4.9, convey the same main message obtained for the level of saving. However, when looking at the actual cohort profiles, saving rates are obviously more volatile than saving levels. They also seem to remain relatively high in old age, presumably as a result of diminishing disposable income levels in old age.

4.5   ANALYZING SAVING ACCORDING TO DEMOGRAPHIC GROUPS

So far, we have studied the age profile of saving and income for a representative individual of a given cohort. In this section we explore further the saving distribution to assess if saving varies systematically with other household characteristics. For brevity, we report only the adjusted median profiles, which are computed along the lines suggested by Deaton and Paxson (1994): the curves come from a regression on a third-order age polynomial, a full set of cohort dummies, and a set of restricted time dummies.

Whereas the choice of demographic and economic characteristics used in grouping households is arbitrary, it can be easily justified without resorting to a fully developed behavioral model. We focus here on four breakdowns, based on education, employment status, family type, and homeownership. We define as "low education" a schooling level of "up to 8 years of schooling" (compulsory education) and "high education" as "more than 8 years". We define households with more than two adults (aged at least 18) as composite households. There are several reasons for conditioning on education. First, education can be safely considered an exogenous variable after a certain age. Secondly, it is one of the major determinants in explaining permanent income of individuals. Finally, it may easily affect saving preference and the ability to acquire information on financial products. It is important to distinguish composite households because these households might have different needs if compared to nuclear households, and because they may produce internally a number of goods and services that nuclear households buy in the market. Saving and decision making within composite households may involve more generations, hence biasing the results of the age–saving profile according to the age composition of the extended household. Employees and self-employed differ because they may easily face different borrowing constraints and income risk; furthermore, the Italian tax system applies different marginal tax rates to the two groups of workers. If individuals must save for a down payment or for an outright home purchase, conditioning on homeownership is crucial in explaining the level of wealth as well as wealth accumulation.

Figure 4.10 refers to the split in education groups and employment-status groups. The age profiles of discretionary and mandatory saving are similar to the general picture (see Figure 4.8). Notice, however, that the lower education group exhibits slightly more dissaving in retirement. This is more apparent when the

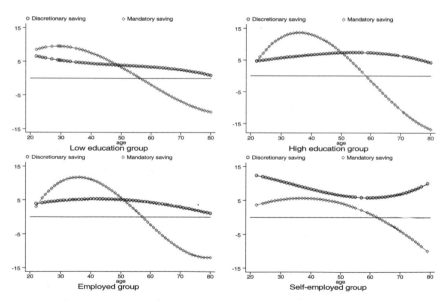

FIGURE 4.10 Cohort-adjusted age profiles of saving by education and employment status (thousands of 1998 euro). The figure reports the cohort-adjusted age profile of discretionary saving and mandatory saving by education and employment status of the household head. Low and high education are defined as less (or more) than high school degree. Each line in the figure is the fitted line of a regression on a third-order age polynomial, a full set of cohort dummies, and a set of restricted dummies.

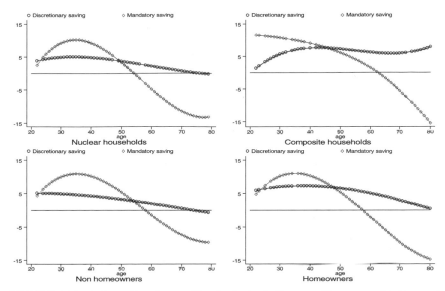

FIGURE 4.11   Cohort-adjusted age profiles of saving by family type and homeownership (thousands of 1998 euro). The figure reports the cohort-adjusted age profile of discretionary saving and mandatory saving by family type and homeownership. Each line in the figure represents a fitted line of a saving regression on a third-order age polynomial, a full set of cohort dummies, and a set of restricted dummies.

discretionary saving component is considered. For the self-employed we find an increasing discretionary saving profile in old age. This might be a mere statistical effect because there are few observations in the upper-tail age distribution for the self-employed.[24]

Figure 4.11 (top part) shows that nuclear households start dissaving at a much earlier age than composite households do (the first group at age 59, the second at age 69). This might be due to the fact that in the composite households there are family members still in education and in any case may result from a complex decision making within the household.

The bottom part of Figure 4.11 reports the breakdown by homeownership. The pattern of saving is similar in the two groups. Note, however, that the comparison between the two groups is also affected by the changing composition of the household and by the fact that homeownership itself varies considerably by age.

In Table 4.14 we summarize the main features of the data by carrying out regression analysis for saving. The main purpose of this regression is to illustrate

---

[24]This is a general problem. Conditioning can make the size of the cell very small. This is particularly true for old ages, when the *unconditional* cell size is already small.

TABLE 4.14   Saving Regressions[a]

Variable	Coefficient	t-Ratio
Dependent variable: discretionary saving		
More than two adults	2.24	45.13
High school or college	2.25	46.06
Homeowner	1.68	36.87
Self-employed	0.98	17.26
Dependent variable: ratio of discretionary saving on consumption		
More than two adults	9.05	19.80
Education	10.43	23.23
Homeowner	11.17	26.60
Self-employed	2.03	3.87

[a]In the top table, the dependent variable is the level of discretionary saving. In the bottom table the dependent variable is the ratio of discretionary saving to total consumption. The regressions also include a third-order age polynomial, a full set of cohort dummies, and a set of restricted time dummies (not reported in the table). Each regression is estimated by least absolute deviations (LAD).

how savings relate to a parsimonious set of characteristics. The estimates are obtained by pooling all the data together and by making use of dummy variables as indicators of each specific attribute. Since when carrying out estimates by ordinary least squares the estimated coefficients might be affected by a few influential values, we prefer to make use of least absolute deviations. In the top part of the table the dependent variable is the level of saving, whereas in the bottom part we address potential heteroscedasticity[25] problems by taking the ratio of saving over total consumption. The explanatory variables are a third-order age polynomial, a full set of cohort dummies, a set of restricted time dummies (constrained to sum to zero and to be orthogonal to a trend), and a set of dummies controlling for educational attainment, employment status, family type, and homeownership. The top part of Table 4.14 indicates that homeownership, education, self-employment, and the existence of composite households correlate with saving, regardless of the saving definition. The results are confirmed in the bottom part of the table.

[25]It is clear that heteroscedasticity is an issue in our data, but in order to provide prima facie evidence based on least absolute deviation (LAD) regression analysis we do not engage in adjustment procedures for the standard errors. Also, we have reasons to believe that even in the present form the results are informative as (1) the use of sample weights should mitigate the heteroscedasticity problem and (2) if it is true that the presence of a panel component in the sample makes the autocorrelation of residuals a likely issue, this autocorrelation should cause an upward bias in the standard errors; hence, a correction would probably make our results more precise.

4.6 THE IMPORTANCE OF PENSION ARRANGEMENTS FOR SAVING CHOICES

To shed some light on the methodological issues involved in the computation of social security wealth and to assess the importance of the underlying assumptions, we present the results from a simple simulation. This simulation computes the accrual of social security wealth (SSW) based on a number of extreme assumptions.

We look at a "typical" household characterized by a given age–earnings profile. We assume a certain lifetime, up to a maximum life of 75 years. The exercise can be easily extended to include age-specific survival probabilities, but the results do not differ substantially. We also assume that the household pays a constant fraction of its earnings to the social security administration and receives a constant benefit in old age. The benefit is assumed to be 65% of last wage (at the fixed retirement age of 60); hence, the replacement rate (65%) is somewhat close to what we observe in reality.[26] We impose that the present expected value of benefits is equal to the present expected value of contributions, and this is achieved by determining the payroll tax rate endogenously; in other words, we assume that the pension is actuarially fair. We also assume that the household pays a constant fraction of its earnings into the severance pay (TFR) fund (6.91%) and that it receives a lump sum payment based on the actual legislation. In particular, we assume a zero growth in the TFR funds in real terms. Results are presented in Figure 4.12.

The simplest case (top panel) assumes an interest rate equal to zero and a zero growth rate for earnings. We calibrate the simulation on our survey data and assume an initial earnings level equal to €15,000. Under the zero growth assumption, we have a flat age–earnings profile at, approximately, household median earnings. The resulting contribution rate is around 23% and it guarantees a constant household pension benefit of around €9,800, a figure which is close to what we observe in reality. In the bottom panel, we show results for a case where real earnings grow at 1.5%/year. The latter case describes a more realistic situation where earnings grow (as we observe in the data), while maintaining the same median value of approximately €15,000. This is achieved by assuming a starting value of €10,000, growing to a maximum value of €18,000 at age 60. However, the assumption of constant earnings growth is, once again, a gross simplification. In this case the implied contribution rate grows to 31%, while the benefit emerging is approximately €11,000.

Both pictures show TFR wealth and SSW, plus the sum of these two components, referred to as "mandatory wealth," over the life cycle. It is interesting to note how pension wealth (and pension wealth plus TFR wealth) has a typical

[26]Replacement rates computed at the individual level are often higher (in the range of 75–80% of last wage, see for example Brugiavini, 1999). But the evidence available from micro data typically looks at workers characterized by stable earnings histories, whereas the overall average replacement rate may actually reflect different work experiences. Hence, 65% is probably a more realistic figure.

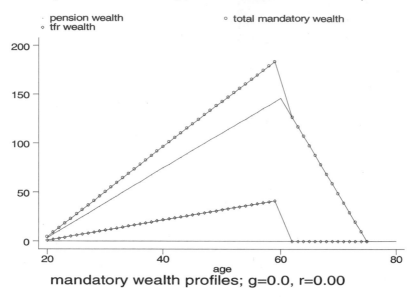

mandatory wealth profiles; g=0.0, r=0.00

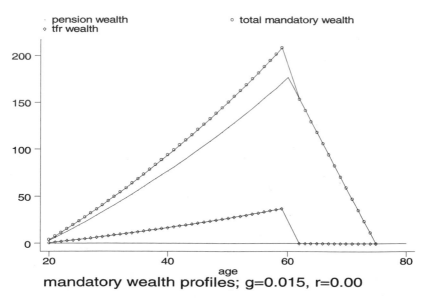

mandatory wealth profiles; g=0.015, r=0.00

FIGURE 4.12 Social security wealth age profiles (thousands of 1998 euro). The upper panel hosts the social security wealth and TFR wealth under the assumption of a flat age–earnings profile. The bottom panel looks at the same variables with earnings growing at a constant rate.

triangular shape: the maximum SSW is around €140,000 (approximately 10 times earnings) in the top panel and €175,000 in the bottom panel. This is an obvious consequence of the accounting procedure we impose, but it describes in more detail what we speculated about the data in Section 4.3. The blip at age 60 is produced by the TFR fund: TFR wealth increases gradually and then drops to zero as the lump sum payment is cashed in by the household.

The purpose of this simulation is to show, for a typical household, the importance of public pension provision for life-cycle savings. Although we present an oversimplification of reality, the magnitudes of the variables involved are not unrealistic. The exercise suggests that for Italian households, on average, a very large fraction of resources is mandated for protecting retirement, hence reducing the need for further wealth accumulation for old age.

4.7 MEASUREMENT ERROR

It is a common problem for survey data to be affected by measurement error. We are concerned that measurement error may be present in the income and consumption variables of the SHIW and bias the results systematically when carrying out summary statistics of the data. The comparison of microeconomic data with national accounts data given in Table 4.1 might be a prima facie indication of the presence of noisy measures. Since the survey saving rate overestimates substantially the national account aggregate, it must be the case that either consumption is underestimated, or income is overestimated, or some combination of the two takes place. Our presumption is that both income and consumption are underestimated, but consumption is systematically underreported to a larger extent than income. This was already pointed out by Cannari and D'Alessio (1993), who argue that in comparison with national account data, the SHIW consumption is underestimated by 30%, while income is underestimated by 25%. However, we are not only interested in understanding if average income or average consumption are biased in the SHIW, but if the age profile of saving is biased. For this purpose we cannot use macroeconomic data, and must turn to the only other Italian survey that contains data on both income and consumption.

Hence, this comparison makes use of the 1991 ISTAT Survey of Household Budgets, a large cross-sectional survey containing detailed information on consumption but limited information on income.[27] Since we rely on cross-sectional

---

[27]This is a nationwide survey carried out by the Italian Statistical Office (ISTAT–Istituto Nazionale di Statistica) in order to construct consumer price indexes. The ISTAT survey reports household disposable income and the information is elicited by making use of income brackets, rather than by asking for actual income levels. Hence, the income data in the ISTAT survey is "more noisy" than in the SHIW. Further, since in the ISTAT survey there is no information on labor income and on income components in general, we cannot use the ISTAT survey to estimate mandatory saving, for example. Other important covariates used in our analysis are also missing in the ISTAT survey.

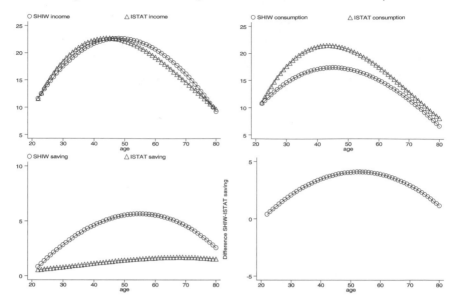

FIGURE 4.13   Comparing ISTAT and SHIW mean expenditures, income, and saving (thousands of 1998 euro). The figures plot income, consumption and discretionary saving in the 1991 ISTAT survey and in the 1991 SHIW survey. The fitted lines are obtained by a regression on a third-order age polynomial. All values are expressed in thousands of euro.

data, the profiles we use in the comparison below should not be interpreted as individual profiles. The top-left panel in Figure 4.13 plots the average age–income profile in the two surveys, while average consumption is displayed in the top-right panel. It is apparent that there is a large difference between the two consumption profiles, particularly for middle-age households, whereas average disposable income is similar in the two surveys, both in levels and over age. Battistin *et al.* (2000) discuss this issue extensively and explain the nature of underreporting of consumption in the SHIW.

The bottom panels of Figure 4.13 refer to saving and show a large difference in the two saving profiles, especially between age 40 and age 60. To assess whether in the ISTAT survey the age profile of saving substantially differs from the SHIW survey, we plot in the bottom-right panel the difference between the two age-profiles. While there is no marked difference throughout the life cycle, the gap is certainly significant at peak ages. Figure 4.14 replicates the previous analysis for median consumption, income, and saving. The results indicate that some of the large differences found for average consumption and saving are reduced when looking at median values.

Our preliminary conclusion is that both the SHIW and ISTAT survey data indicate that private saving is rather flat over the life cycle, and that saving stays positive even in old age. This conclusion holds for both the average and the median

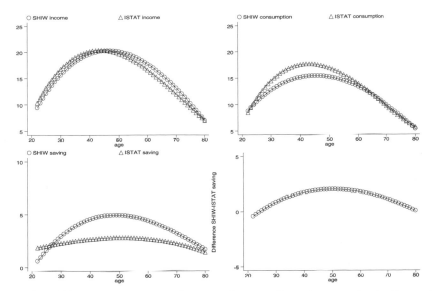

FIGURE 4.14   Comparing ISTAT and SHIW median expenditures, income, and saving (thousands of 1998 euro). The figures plot consumption, income, and discretionary saving in the 1991 ISTAT survey and in the 1991 SHIW survey. The fitted lines are obtained by a regression on a third-order age polynomial. All values are expressed in thousands of euro.

saving. In this sense, the two surveys are mutually consistent. It is well possible that the SHIW understates "true" consumption and therefore overstates savings at some ages. This bias is likely to be more severe for the upper tail of the saving distribution. Whether the difference between the two survey measures of saving depends on sample composition, survey design, or other effects is the topic for future research.

4.8 CONCLUSIONS

We use Italian micro-level data to construct several measures of saving: the relevant measures are based on a "residual" definition (income minus consumption), whereas in some cases we look at saving as the difference in wealth levels at two different points in time. We have available a large cross-sectional sample of Italian households for a number of years; this sample also contains a small panel component, which we exploit to look at financial saving and real saving. We also propose a non-standard definition of saving based on the notion of "earned income" and we refer to this as "mandatory saving" to accompany the traditional definition of saving based on disposable income (called discretionary saving). In our study the former is a definition of saving that takes account of both social security contributions and contributions to a severance pay fund and it stresses the importance of "saving for retirement" through mandated arrangements. In line with the work of Jappelli and Modigliani (1998), the novelty of this approach is that when using earned income we also account for the benefits paid out to retirees from these retirement provisions and treat them as a form of "mandatory dissaving". The reason for resorting to this non-standard measure of saving, which we present along with the traditional measure of private savings, is simply to stress the importance of the institutional setting for old-age insurance in measuring saving. We argue that in Italy a large fraction of household resources is mandated to public pensions. Thus, whatever the potential substitutability between the two forms of wealth, the desire to accumulate resources for consumption in old age must be reduced for Italian consumers. For the same reason also, the life-cycle pattern of mandatory saving is crucial to the understanding of the dynamic of discretionary saving.

By making assumptions on the relationship between age effects, cohort effects, and time effects, which typically affect saving choices, we are able to estimate cohort-adjusted age profiles for the two definitions of saving. The cohort adjustment proved very important in our data, particularly for older generations, hence suggesting that differences in cohorts cannot be neglected when explaining saving behavior.

We show that discretionary saving is positive at all ages. Similar patterns arise when we consider a number of household characteristics, such as education and employment of the head of the household, family composition, and homeowner-ship. For all these groups, discretionary saving does not fall below zero, except for non-homeowners at very old ages. This means that families hold a positive amount of private wealth until the end of the life cycle and there might be a combination of different motives for private wealth holdings. For example, private wealth is be-queathable and the fact that non-homeowners decumulate more than homeowners suggests that bequest motives may play a role. Other potential explanations are related to risk exposure or transaction costs. Whereas pension arrangements insure against longevity risk and the national health system (essentially based on universal coverage) partially insures against health risks, there might be other risks late in life or transaction costs may be more severe. For example, elderly people may be particularly concerned with permanent illness and disability and long-term care.

Hence, for Italian households, there seems to emerge some substitutability between private wealth and pension wealth, but also different degrees of fungibility: whereas pension wealth finances consumption during retirement, private wealth may be used for intergenerational transfers and to cover other contingencies at very old ages.

ACKNOWLEDGMENT

This paper is part of a research project on "Structural Analysis of Household Savings and Wealth Positions over the Life Cycle." The Training and Mobility of Researchers Network Program (TMR) of the European Commission DGXII and the Italian Ministry of Universities and Scientific Research (MURST) provided financial support. We thank Tullio Jappelli for valuable discussions and an anonymous referee for helpful comments.

REFERENCES

Alessie, R., A. Kapteyn, and F. Klijn (1997). Mandatory pensions and personal savings in the Netherlands. CentER, Tilburg University, mimeo.

Battistin, E., R. Miniaci, and G. Weber (2000). What do we learn from recall consumption data?. University of Padova, mimeo.

Brandolini, A. and L. Cannari (1994). Methodological appendix: the Bank of Italy's Survey of Household Income and Wealth. In: A. Ando, L. Guiso, and I. Visco (eds), *Saving and the Accumulation of Wealth. Essays on Italian Household and Government Saving Behavior.* Cambridge: Cambridge University Press.

Brugiavini A. (1999). Social security and retirement in Italy. In: J. Gruber and D. Wise (eds), *Social Security and Retirement around the World.* Chicago: NBER, The University of Chicago Press.

Cannari, L. and G. D'Alessio (1993). Non-reporting and under-reporting behavior in the Bank of Italy's survey of household income and wealth, *Bulletin of the International Statistical Institute – Proceedings of the ISI 49th Session,* tome LV, four books, ISI, n. 3, August–September, 395–412.

Deaton, A. and C. Paxson (1994). Saving, aging and growth in Taiwan. In: D. Wise (ed.), *Studies in the Economics of Aging.* Chicago: University of Chicago Press.

Jappelli, T. and F. Modigliani (1998). The age-saving profile and the life-cycle hypothesis. University of Salerno, CSEF Working Paper No. 4.

Modigliani, F. (1986). Life cycle, individual thrift, and the wealth of nations. *American Economic Review* 76, 297–312.

Paxson, C. (1996). Saving and growth: evidence from micro data. *European Economic Review* 40, 255–288.

Poterba, J. (1994). *International comparison of personal saving.* Chicago: University of Chicago Press.

TABLE A.4.1   Contributions to Pay-as-You-Go-System: 1991, 1993, 1995, and 1998[a]

		Number of observations	Mean	Standard deviation of mean	Median
1991	Age 20–24	75	15.18	1.85	15.74
	Age 25–29	305	24.34	0.89	22.14
	Age 30–34	663	25.89	0.60	23.61
	Age 35–39	721	26.42	0.58	22.60
	Age 40–44	902	28.97	0.52	27.11
	Age 45–49	861	31.06	0.53	27.11
	Age 50–54	940	28.14	0.51	25.70
	Age 55–59	834	21.95	0.54	18.98
	Age 60–64	877	14.09	0.52	11.72
	Age 65–69	752	7.47	0.57	0.00
	Age 70–74	489	4.18	0.70	0.00
	Age 75–79	437	3.56	0.74	0.00
	Age 80+	332	1.67	0.85	0.00
1993	Age 20–24	51	15.52	2.29	15.01
	Age 25–29	304	20.42	0.93	19.18
	Age 30–34	592	25.03	0.66	21.48
	Age 35–39	725	25.63	0.60	22.67
	Age 40–44	793	28.47	0.57	24.53
	Age 45–49	858	27.46	0.55	24.18
	Age 50–54	879	27.58	0.54	24.45
	Age 55–59	828	20.47	0.56	15.16
	Age 60–64	838	10.24	0.56	0.00
	Age 65–69	798	5.77	0.57	0.00
	Age 70–74	680	2.95	0.62	0.00
	Age 75–79	360	3.10	0.85	0.00
	Age 80+	383	1.01	0.82	0.00

(*Continues*)

TABLE A.4.1 *(Continued)*

		Number of observations	Mean	Standard deviation of mean	Median
1995	Age 20–24	56	18.84	2.38	15.99
	Age 25–29	259	21.74	1.08	20.79
	Age 30–34	593	22.52	0.71	19.62
	Age 35–39	707	23.09	0.65	20.56
	Age 40–44	755	25.27	0.63	21.79
	Age 45–49	942	27.08	0.56	24.37
	Age 50–54	818	24.55	0.61	20.93
	Age 55–59	903	19.24	0.58	14.85
	Age 60–64	796	12.31	0.61	5.33
	Age 65–69	825	6.69	0.60	0.00
	Age 70–74	691	2.39	0.66	0.00
	Age 75–79	344	2.82	0.93	0.00
	Age 80+	446	2.26	0.82	0.00
1998	Age 20–24	44	13.72	3.17	13.88
	Age 25–29	193	20.65	1.42	19.27
	Age 30–34	493	25.22	0.89	21.59
	Age 35–39	660	27.34	0.77	23.13
	Age 40–44	733	28.53	0.73	26.98
	Age 45–49	824	32.96	0.69	27.75
	Age 50–54	858	27.69	0.67	24.82
	Age 55–59	739	21.01	0.73	16.96
	Age 60–64	705	14.46	0.74	7.32
	Age 65–69	633	7.04	0.79	0.00
	Age 70–74	563	3.13	0.83	0.00
	Age 75–79	384	1.77	1.01	0.00
	Age 80+	318	1.76	1.11	0.00

[a]The table reports for 1991, 1993, 1995, and 1998 contributions to pay-as-you-go-system by age bracket; figures are expressed in thousands of 1998 euro. Sample statistics are computed using sample weights. Households headed by individuals younger than 20 are excluded. In the first column we report the age group of the head of the household, in the second column the number of observations, in the third column the mean, in the fourth column the standard deviation of the mean, and in the last column the median.

CHAPTER 5

Household Savings and Wealth Distribution in Japan

Yukinobu Kitamura

Hitotsubashi University, Institute of Economic Research, Tokyo, Japan

Noriyuki Takayama

Hitotsubashi University, Institute of Economic Research, Tokyo, Japan

Fumiko Arita

*Toyo Eiwa Women's University, Department of
International Social Science, Yokohama, Japan*

5.1 INTRODUCTION

It has been 7 years since our publication on household savings in Japan. Our previous publication made use of the large micro data, the National Survey of Family Income and Expenditure (NSFIE), over the period of 1979–89: see Takayama and Kitamura (1994). Now that the micro data from the 1994 NSFIE has become available among academic users, we would like to add new information to our previous work and uncover new facts that have emerged after the burst of the bubble economy in Japan.

Life Cycle Savings and Public Policy

The main objectives of this chapter are to update the data provided in Takayama and Kitamura (1994) and to present descriptive information rather than testing particular models of household saving behavior, so that future researchers can examine the household saving behavior in Japan.

Before presenting our results, it is worthwhile reviewing the recent literature on the household saving behavior in Japan. First of all, Hayashi (1997) provided a landmark for this literature. Chapter 10 of Hayashi (1997) provides an excellent account of recent literature and evidences on Japanese saving. He identifies key factors:

1. Japan's saving rate is not as high as commonly thought;
2. the accumulation of wealth by Japanese households starts very early and lasts until very late in life, with unconsumed wealth transferred to the next generation in the form of bequests.

As to the second point, Hayashi *et al.* (1988a) argue that the bulk of intergenerational transfers take place in the form of bequests and that bequests come not only from the independent (nuclear) old but also from the pool of extended families that seem to accumulate wealth regardless of the parents' age. Barthold and Ito (1992), using bequest tax filing information, show that about one-third to one-half of household assets are obtained by bequests in Japan, which implies that the old households do not dissave enough and leave sizable bequests, intended or not. Takayama and Kitamura (1994) also find some evidence of substantial intergenerational transfers from the NSFIEs. Ohtake (1991) argues that bequests are motivated by selfishness rather than by altruism. From these studies, we conclude that intergenerational transfers occur at a substantial magnitude, no matter what motivation lies behind them.

Horioka (1990, 1993) provides another good survey of the literature from the viewpoint of different motives for saving. The author has identified more than 30 factors. Horioka and Watanabe (1997) also conducted empirical investigation of saving motives using micro data from a Japanese government survey. Horioka finds that net saving for retirement and precautionary motives are of dominant importance. Using a different data set, Ohtake and Horioka (2002) discover that retirement and housing motivations are of importance. Motivation for the acquisition of owner-occupied housing remains strong and it promotes high saving, especially because of limited mortgage markets and high down-payment requirements (i.e., the presence of liquidity constraints). Hayashi *et al.* (1988b) investigate the effects of tax incentives and down-payment requirements on a household's tenure choice and on saving behavior in the United States and Japan by simulation methods. The result is that these factors do not offer a complete explanation of the large gap between the saving rates of the two countries, largely because of institutional differences in the typical down-payment ratio and tax incentives.

5.2 THE DATA

Several large-sample micro-surveys concerning Japanese household behavior are conducted regularly by the government.[1] Detailed comparisons of the NSFIE with other data sources in Takayama et al. (1989, Chapter 3) indicate that the NSFIE captures a fairly accurate and unbiased picture of the household behavior in Japan and thus the NSFIE is one of the most reliable sources of information (though we admit that it contains possible reporting errors). For this reason, throughout this paper, the NSFIE is used to identify household behavior in Japan. In addition, fortunately, we are able to use four different NSFIE data points in time, i.e., the 1979, 1984, 1989, and 1994 surveys. Although these are not panel data, intertemporal comparisons among four data points in time can be made to approximate actual life-cycle behavior.[2]

Since 1959, the NSFIE has been conducted every 5 years to reveal levels of income, consumption, and household assets, their structure and distribution, as well as the differences among regions. All these analyses are performed through the investigation of two key areas: family income and expenditure, and assets and liabilities in Japanese households. This survey is designed to sample over 50,000 households (53,000 in 1979, 54,000 in 1984, 59,100 in 1989, and 56,000 in 1994). Survey items include (1) family income and expenditure; (2) annual income, financial assets, and liabilities; (3) major durable goods; and (4) attributes of households and their members, including housing conditions.

With a large sample size and wide coverage in items, the NSFIE is a treasure trove of information. It enables researchers to make detailed analyses according to various household characteristics.[3]

We need to explain briefly how we construct our final data set.

First, we eliminate two large categories from the original sample over 50,000: agricultural households and a single member household (about 4900).

Secondly, if some relevant data such as yearly income, savings, financial assets, housing assets, homeownership, or durable assets are missing, these households are eliminated from the sample.

---

[1]For details, see Takayama and Kitamura (1994, Section 3.2). The major surveys include the Family Income and Expenditure Survey (Designated Statistics No. 56), the Family Saving Survey (Approved Statistical Report), the National Survey of Family Income and Expenditure (Designated Statistics No. 97), the Basic Survey of Japanese Living Conditions (Designated Statistics, No. 116), and the Survey on Time Use and Leisure Activities (Designated Statistics, No. 114).

[2]The statistical surveys by the government are published regularly in highly summarized forms. Although these summaries contain valuable information and are accessible to everyone, detailed data analysis cannot be made without using the original micro data tapes. According to laws governing the use of these statistics, researchers must apply to use these original tapes and give sound reasons. Only after obtaining permission from the government can researchers use the data tapes in which individual identities are carefully disguised.

[3]For details of the NSFIE, see Hayashi et al. (1988a).

Thirdly, we also drop the households whose yearly incomes exceed four times of standard deviation of the income distribution of the whole sample from its mean.

Fourthly, if information on debt outstanding and golf club membership certificates are missing, we put zero value on such items.

Fifthly, employee's households include (1) regular laborers, (2) private office workers, (3) public office workers, and (4) corporate administrators. The rest are considered as self-employed households.

Finally, the definitions of disposable income and consumption in the system of national accounts differ from those of the NSFIE in the treatment of imputed rents from housing and depreciation of housing structures. It is useful to list characteristic features and shortfalls of the disposable income concept used in this chapter. These are as follows:

1. On the one hand, remittances to other family members or relatives are treated as part of "other consumption expenditures." On the other hand, remittances from relatives are counted as a source of yearly income of receiving households. Intergenerational transfers within extended families are not reported separately and counted in consumption expenditures.
2. Medical benefits in kind are excluded.
3. Imputed rent from housing is excluded from income.
4. The flow of services from consumer durables is not reported. Expenditure on consumer durables is counted as consumption.
5. Capital gains or losses on stocks, equity in one's own home, and equity in consumer durables are not included.
6. The annual tax burden is not reported. Income and resident taxes are to be estimated. Annual social security contributions are also not reported in the NSFIE, while annual social security benefits are reported.
7. Interest on loans is included in income and is also treated as part of non-consumption expenditures.
8. Interest and dividends are underreported.[4]

The most discussed data problem with the NSFIE is the sample selection bias with old households. One problem is the prevalence of the extended family: for example, in 1994, 17.5% of all households were extended family (i.e., the heads of households are the younger members of the families) and 30.6% of all households have household members aged above 65.[5] The existence of extended families implies that there are two categories of older people: those still maintaining an independent household (i.e., the independent old) and those living with children

---

[4]Around 70% of households in the NSFIE don't report any amount of interest or dividends. With such a low awareness of capital income, the value of real interest income seems to be hardly recognized by households.

[5]This implies that 13.1% of the elderly live on their own and this trend has been increasing over time. Sooner or later, of all people aged above 65, more than half of them will live independently from their children, given the rapid urbanization and generous social security benefits.

(i.e., the dependent old). Wealth and flow of savings for the dependent old cannot be observed directly because of no breakdown among family members in the NSFIE. When the true age profile of saving behavior is to be identified, we have to extract savings and wealth of dependent old from the extended families and add them to those of the independent old. As the economic status of the independent old is substantially better than that of the dependent old, the old–age saving behavior would have a self-selection bias if we do not make such adjustments. Hayashi *et al.* (1988a) suggest a method of removing this bias by comparing nuclear families and extended families whose younger generation is similarly aged. We find, however, that this method needs to be refined due to insufficient control of household characteristics to carry out statistical matching between nuclear and extended families.[6] Takayama and Kitamura (1994) provide a complementary estimation method of intergenerational transfers to Hayashi *et al.* (1988a).

It is quite important to adjust this sample selection bias if the main research issues are concerned with the saving and wealth accumulation behavior of the old households or intergenerational transfers from the old to the young households.

We decide not to adjust our data for two reasons. First, we find ample evidence of a rapidly decreasing number of extended families; thus, it may be quite misleading to excessively stress the importance of extended family in Japan. Secondly, this chapter is not directly concerned with the old households as it were, but with the entire household saving behavior in Japan.

In the following subsections, we explain our definitions of variables in the NSFIE data.[7]

Disposable Income

In the NSFIE, gross yearly income (all household members) includes wages and salaries, income through business and work at home, returns from assets, social security benefits, donations, and consumption in kind. The amount left over after deducting non-consumption expenditures such as taxes and social security contributions is disposable income. After subtracting consumption expenditures from disposable income, we obtain savings on the flow base.

Taxes and social security contribution on annual base are not available in the NSFIE. We need to estimate these items for individual households by adjusting

[6]For example, the extended families are prevalent in self-employed households living in the rural areas, whereas the nuclear families are prevalent in employees' households living in the big cities. A simple comparison between the two, only adjusting age cohorts, is quite misleading, because this comparison may reflect differences in region, occupation, and social values.

[7]For those who want to convert yen into euro values, the following two steps can be used. (1) To convert nominal values into the 1998 real values in yen, use consumer price index (CPI) by setting $1998 = 100$, $1979 = 69.96$, $1984 = 83.72$, $1989 = 88.57$, $1994 = 97.38$, and $2000 = 98.35$. (2) To exchange yen into euros, use the market exchange rate in 1998 of €$1 = $¥$159.57$.

with household characteristics such as yearly income, family composition, age, and employment status. We consider only two types of taxes – income tax and inhabitant tax – and two types of social security contributions – public pension contribution and social health insurance contribution (employment insurance tax is negligible, as it is lower than 0.4%).

The definition of disposable income is given as follows (see Table 5.1):

$$\text{Disposable Income} = \text{Yearly Income}$$
$$- \text{Tax and Social Security Contribution} \qquad (5.1)$$

Consumption Expenditure

The NSFIE definition of consumption expenditure includes medical expenditures in cash and purchases of consumer durables. Remittances to other family members and intergenerational transfers in the form of gifts are also included.

In the NSFIE, monthly average household income and expenditure are obtained only for 3 months, i.e., September through November. It is necessary to convert monthly data to yearly data. In so doing, seasonal adjustment ratios for 10 major expenditure items are calculated to obtain an annual conversion factor (see Tables 5.2 and 5.3). For example, yearly consumption for 1994 is calculated as follows:

$$
\begin{aligned}
\text{Yearly Consumption} \\
= {}& 12.288947 \times (\text{Foods}) + 11.994339 \times (\text{Housing}) \\
& + 12.97166261 \times (\text{Fuel, Light \& Water Charges}) \\
& + 12.34859801 \times (\text{Housing Furniture \& Household Appliances}) \\
& + 13.46894251 \times (\text{Clothes and Footwear}) \\
& + 12.311852 \times (\text{Medical Care}) \\
& + 11.847619 \times (\text{Transportation \& Communication}) \\
& + 12.192596 \times (\text{Education}) \\
& + 13.340823 \times (\text{Recreation}) + 12.973387 \times (\text{Others}) \qquad (5.2)
\end{aligned}
$$

Saving Flows

After subtracting consumption expenditures from disposable income, we obtain savings on the flow base (see Tables 5.4 and 5.5):

$$\text{Saving Flows} = \text{Disposable Income} - \text{Yearly Consumption} \qquad (5.3)$$

TABLE 5.1   Disposable Income (Euro 1998 constant)

Year	Age	All households Mean	Median	Employees households Mean	Median	Self-employed households Mean	Median
1979	−24	21,767	19,976	21,588	19,797	24,455	23,021
	25−	25,350	23,021	25,440	23,111	24,007	21,140
	30−	27,500	25,709	27,500	25,977	27,232	24,007
	35−	31,083	28,934	31,263	29,561	30,456	25,709
	40−	33,950	31,621	34,398	32,517	32,785	27,769
	45−	36,727	34,398	37,623	35,652	34,666	30,098
	50−	40,131	37,623	40,668	38,966	38,877	33,860
	55−	38,250	35,025	40,758	38,429	35,383	30,277
	60−	32,785	28,575	36,368	33,771	31,173	25,798
	65−	32,158	26,425	37,712	34,577	30,456	23,201
	70−	31,352	23,559	36,816	31,083	30,636	22,574
	75−	24,455	19,170	28,754	23,290	24,276	18,722
	80+	24,544	15,766	33,592	37,085	24,455	15,586
	Average	32,875	29,650	33,144	30,546	32,337	26,873
1984	−24	20,585	19,163	20,884	19,462	18,115	16,543
	25−	25,151	23,579	25,525	23,729	22,007	20,585
	30−	28,669	26,873	29,044	27,247	27,097	23,954
	35−	32,262	30,466	33,236	31,439	29,343	25,600
	40−	35,556	33,909	36,829	35,257	32,188	27,696
	45−	38,026	36,379	39,823	38,475	34,658	30,092
	50−	40,047	38,026	42,967	41,544	36,155	31,589
	55−	39,523	36,754	43,940	41,844	37,128	31,813
	60−	34,957	30,166	37,577	34,134	38,101	33,011
	65−	30,915	25,376	34,882	32,412	36,080	30,092
	70−	28,295	23,504	38,251	30,466	32,936	28,520
	75−	27,397	22,232	36,379	29,418	35,107	27,846
	80+	22,456	17,142	13,698	13,698	34,433	28,894
	Average	34,283	31,364	35,631	33,086	34,134	28,969
1989	−24	22,642	21,368	22,500	21,085	29,151	29,788
	25−	27,170	24,765	26,958	24,694	30,637	26,463
	30−	31,557	28,939	31,274	28,939	34,175	29,081
	35−	35,944	33,326	35,802	33,538	37,218	32,194
	40−	39,765	37,288	39,836	37,713	39,623	34,458
	45−	44,647	42,524	44,505	43,303	45,496	39,552

(*Continues*)

TABLE 5.1   (*Continued*)

Year	Age	All households		Employees households		Self-employed households	
		Mean	Median	Mean	Median	Mean	Median
	50–	48,468	45,708	49,034	47,619	48,114	42,241
	55–	46,557	43,727	48,397	46,204	46,699	41,675
	60–	38,067	33,043	40,897	37,501	43,444	38,067
	65–	34,104	27,878	42,100	35,944	40,826	34,104
	70–	32,760	25,189	38,137	35,590	42,737	36,227
	75–	30,283	21,864	34,741	29,788	46,204	36,298
	80+	27,241	20,448	36,227	26,887	40,119	35,307
	Average	39,482	35,802	39,906	36,935	43,161	37,076
1994	–24	22,653	22,074	22,910	22,460	18,792	17,118
	25–	28,573	26,707	28,445	26,707	30,311	26,707
	30–	32,821	30,826	33,078	31,148	29,925	26,578
	35–	38,034	35,845	38,291	36,103	35,717	32,113
	40–	42,474	40,286	42,989	40,865	39,063	35,845
	45–	47,301	45,177	48,395	46,335	41,380	38,227
	50–	51,548	49,489	53,414	51,097	43,375	40,157
	55–	50,003	46,979	52,964	50,454	39,964	35,395
	60–	38,934	33,464	44,919	39,578	33,722	28,059
	65–	33,657	27,479	44,533	38,227	29,796	24,648
	70–	30,182	24,583	47,494	41,573	27,737	23,489
	75–	27,866	23,039	49,424	38,291	26,128	22,202
	80+	31,276	22,588	54,186	38,291	29,667	21,881
	Average	41,316	37,776	43,954	40,415	34,108	28,831

Note: Figures for jobless households are included in those for self-employed households only for 1979.

Saving rate is defined as the ratio between saving flows and disposable income (see Table 5.6):

$$\text{Saving Rate} = \text{Saving Flows/Disposable Income} \qquad (5.4)$$

When we calculate the saving rates for different age group, income class, home-ownership (see Table 5.7), and employment status, we use the following definition for the mean saving rate (see Tables 5.8–5.13):

$$\text{Mean Saving Rate for Group } i = S_i(\text{Saving Flow})/S_i(\text{Disposable Income}) \qquad (5.5)$$

TABLE 5.2 Month-to-Year Consumption Conversion Ratio Items

Items	1979/1984	1989	1994
1. Foods	12.240	12.028	12.289
2. Housing	12.252	11.845	11.994
3. Fuel, light, and water charges	13.476	12.790	12.972
4. Housing furniture and household appliances	11.952	11.328	12.349
5. Clothes and footwear	12.960	12.361	13.469
6. Medical care	11.808	11.948	12.312
7. Transportation and communications	12.120	12.173	11.848
8. Education	12.900	11.942	12.193
9. Recreation	13.008	12.914	13.341
10. Others	13.092	13.511	12.973

Note: For the 1979 and 1984 adjustments, the conversion ratios are calculated from the 1984 FIES.
Source: The 1984, 1989, and 1994 FIES.

If the distributions of disposable income and saving flow are skewed, the mean and median saving rates would differ. We use the following definition for the median saving rate:

Median Saving Rate for Group i

$$= (\text{Median Saving in } i)/(\text{Median Disposable Income in } i) \quad (5.6)$$

Net Worth

Net worth is calculated as a sum of net financial assets, net housing assets, and consumer durables (i.e., total durables minus golf club membership certificates) (see Tables 5.14–5.16):

Net Financial Assets = Financial Assets

$$- (\text{Total Debt} - \text{Debt for Housing Assets}) \quad (5.7)$$

Net Housing Assets = Housing Assets − Debt for Housing Assets $\quad (5.8)$

Where housing assets include only the primary house, excluding the other houses such as summerhouses:

Net Worth = Financial Assets − Total Debt + Housing Assets

$$+ (\text{Durables} - \text{Golf Club Membership Certificates}) \quad (5.9)$$

It is worth noting that the NSFIE reports much lower per-household financial assets than do the Flow of Funds Accounts (FFA) and the Annual Report on

TABLE 5.3   Consumption Expenditure (Euro 1998 constant)

Year	Age	All households		Employees households		Self-employed households	
		Mean	Median	Mean	Median	Mean	Median
1979	−24	18,901	16,661	18,632	16,661	22,305	17,468
	25−	20,424	18,722	20,424	18,901	20,334	17,736
	30−	21,588	19,617	21,588	19,797	21,588	18,990
	35−	23,380	21,767	23,290	21,857	23,917	21,051
	40−	25,709	23,738	25,440	23,828	26,515	23,380
	45−	29,023	26,067	29,023	26,425	28,754	24,992
	50−	30,367	26,784	30,904	27,679	29,292	24,634
	55−	27,411	23,738	28,306	25,082	26,425	21,499
	60−	23,738	19,617	24,992	20,961	23,111	18,990
	65−	21,409	18,005	22,574	19,349	21,140	17,647
	70−	20,961	16,841	22,215	19,617	20,782	16,393
	75−	17,109	15,049	19,976	13,705	17,020	15,049
	80+	16,034	12,272	22,126	14,870	15,945	11,914
	Average	24,992	22,215	24,992	22,484	24,903	21,140
1984	−24	17,666	15,794	17,666	16,094	19,537	13,025
	25−	19,986	18,639	20,061	18,714	19,837	17,516
	30−	21,408	19,911	21,483	20,286	20,959	18,639
	35−	23,205	21,633	23,579	21,932	22,082	20,286
	40−	25,675	24,028	25,900	24,328	25,001	22,831
	45−	28,520	25,900	29,493	27,023	26,873	23,430
	50−	29,493	26,199	31,514	28,445	26,723	22,606
	55−	27,996	23,504	30,616	26,873	25,900	20,361
	60−	24,178	20,061	26,948	22,232	24,328	20,061
	65−	21,184	18,040	23,205	19,986	22,831	19,163
	70−	20,061	16,618	23,729	21,259	22,157	18,339
	75−	17,890	15,420	24,103	17,965	21,109	18,639
	80+	16,693	12,950	45,512	45,512	22,906	18,639
	Average	24,927	22,232	25,750	23,205	24,552	20,959
1989	−24	19,599	16,911	19,599	16,698	20,873	19,387
	25−	21,156	18,821	21,156	18,821	20,944	18,963
	30−	22,925	20,802	23,066	21,014	21,793	18,750
	35−	24,482	22,783	24,765	23,137	23,420	20,944
	40−	27,099	25,048	27,382	25,401	26,321	23,279
	45−	31,911	28,798	32,477	29,647	30,779	26,533

(*Continues*)

TABLE 5.3   (*Continued*)

Year	Age	All households		Employees households		Self-employed households	
		Mean	Median	Mean	Median	Mean	Median
	50–	33,184	28,656	34,458	30,425	30,991	24,835
	55–	30,496	25,826	32,265	27,453	28,656	23,420
	60–	26,038	21,934	28,090	23,703	26,180	21,651
	65–	23,208	19,529	27,241	22,925	23,562	19,812
	70–	21,722	17,972	24,694	20,448	24,057	20,378
	75–	20,873	21,934	19,599	15,496	28,302	21,297
	80+	18,538	13,727	13,585	16,415	25,048	17,760
	Average	27,241	23,703	28,090	24,765	27,170	22,642
1994	–24	18,148	16,603	18,341	16,603	15,445	14,544
	25–	21,301	19,306	21,301	19,306	21,881	19,435
	30–	23,039	21,301	23,168	21,430	21,237	19,049
	35–	24,905	23,168	25,163	23,425	22,588	21,173
	40–	27,866	25,742	28,123	25,999	26,450	24,133
	45–	33,271	29,796	33,915	30,247	29,989	26,514
	50–	34,237	30,504	35,459	31,662	29,024	24,841
	55–	32,177	27,222	34,172	29,024	25,549	20,787
	60–	27,415	22,846	30,375	25,484	24,905	21,044
	65–	23,682	20,851	28,638	24,776	21,945	19,564
	70–	21,945	18,598	28,638	24,004	21,044	17,955
	75–	19,242	16,153	27,801	20,207	18,598	15,767
	80+	18,727	15,316	25,291	22,653	18,277	15,123
	Average	28,059	24,519	29,539	25,871	24,069	20,658

Note: Figures of jobless households are included in those of self-employed households only for 1979. Consumer durables are included.

National Accounts (SNA). In 1984, the FFA estimated ¥10.35 million on average, and the SNA ¥8.8 million, whereas the NSFIE reported ¥6.2 million. In 1989, the FFA reported ¥16.45 million, the SNA ¥16.90 million, and the NSFIE ¥10.30 million. The gap between the FFA and the SNA is relatively small (i.e., SNA/FFA was 0.850 in 1984 and 1.027 in 1989), compared with that between the NSFIE and the FFA (or between the NSFIE and the SNA) (i.e., NSFIE/FFA was 0.600 in 1984 and 0.626 in 1989; NSFIE/SNA was 0.705 in 1984 and 0.609 in 1989). These facts imply that, although the gap between the SNA and the FFA (less than 15%) can be explained in terms of differences in statistical coverage (e.g., private non-profit institutions and health insurance funds are included in the FFA but not in the SNA), the approximately 40% difference between the NSFIE and the FFA

TABLE 5.4   Savings (I) (Euro 1998 constant)

Year	Age	All households		Employees households		Self-employed households	
		Mean	Median	Mean	Median	Mean	Median
1979	−24	2,866	2,956	2,956	2,956	2,060	2,239
	25−	4,927	4,748	5,016	4,837	3,673	3,494
	30−	5,912	5,912	6,002	6,091	5,733	3,852
	35−	7,614	7,077	7,972	7,525	6,539	4,031
	40−	8,241	7,614	8,958	8,331	6,270	3,852
	45−	7,793	7,704	8,510	8,510	5,912	4,300
	50−	9,764	9,406	9,854	10,391	9,585	7,077
	55−	10,839	9,316	12,451	11,018	8,958	6,808
	60−	9,047	6,897	11,376	9,137	8,062	5,643
	65−	10,660	6,539	15,139	14,780	9,406	5,106
	70−	10,391	6,091	14,601	11,645	9,764	5,464
	75−	7,345	3,225	8,779	4,837	7,256	2,956
	80+	8,510	2,866	11,376	22,305	8,510	2,866
	Average	7,972	6,897	8,152	7,525	7,435	4,837
1984	−24	2,844	2,770	3,219	2,919	−1,422	−2,470
	25−	5,165	4,940	5,539	5,240	2,171	1,722
	30−	7,261	6,662	7,560	6,961	6,138	4,416
	35−	9,132	8,533	9,656	9,132	7,261	5,464
	40−	9,881	9,507	10,929	10,629	7,186	5,090
	45−	9,507	9,132	10,405	10,255	7,785	6,138
	50−	10,480	10,405	11,453	11,677	9,507	8,234
	55−	11,528	10,779	13,324	13,249	11,228	9,282
	60−	10,779	8,384	10,629	9,581	13,773	10,779
	65−	9,731	6,587	11,677	10,929	13,249	9,656
	70−	8,234	5,539	14,522	9,656	10,779	7,860
	75−	9,507	5,539	12,276	12,576	13,998	8,758
	80+	5,764	2,545	9,132	9,132	11,602	7,785
	Average	9,357	8,309	9,881	9,207	9,581	7,261
1989	−24	3,042	4,104	2,830	4,033	8,278	8,349
	25−	6,014	6,085	5,802	6,085	9,694	5,802
	30−	8,632	7,925	8,208	7,854	12,382	9,623
	35−	11,462	10,401	11,038	10,401	13,727	10,330
	40−	12,665	12,028	12,453	12,241	13,302	10,826
	45−	12,736	12,170	12,099	12,453	14,717	10,967

(*Continues*)

TABLE 5.4 (*Continued*)

Year	Age	All households		Employees households		Self-employed households	
		Mean	Median	Mean	Median	Mean	Median
	50–	15,283	14,576	14,576	14,646	17,123	15,071
	55–	16,062	15,000	16,132	15,920	17,972	15,637
	60–	12,028	9,340	12,807	11,462	17,264	14,151
	65–	10,896	7,571	14,859	12,170	17,264	11,887
	70–	11,038	7,005	13,444	15,142	18,680	13,514
	75–	9,411	4,670	15,142	18,609	17,972	14,505
	80+	8,703	6,368	22,642	10,472	15,071	13,939
	Average	12,241	10,613	11,816	11,109	15,991	12,524
1994	–24	4,505	4,891	4,569	5,277	3,346	193
	25–	7,208	7,015	7,143	7,079	8,430	6,886
	30–	9,782	9,138	9,911	9,331	8,688	5,728
	35–	13,128	12,163	13,128	12,356	13,128	9,267
	40–	14,544	14,029	14,866	14,351	12,613	11,906
	45–	14,029	13,901	14,480	14,351	11,326	9,782
	50–	17,311	16,475	17,955	17,183	14,351	12,485
	55–	17,826	16,539	18,856	17,955	14,415	12,292
	60–	11,455	8,945	14,544	12,356	8,817	6,049
	65–	9,975	7,015	15,896	13,000	7,916	5,534
	70–	8,237	5,728	18,920	15,059	6,693	5,020
	75–	8,559	6,693	21,623	13,000	7,529	6,114
	80+	12,485	6,371	28,895	20,722	11,326	5,921
	Average	13,257	11,777	14,480	13,193	10,104	7,272

Note: Figures of jobless households are included in those of self-employed households only for 1979.

(or between the NSFIE and the SNA) must go beyond the usual explanations of differences in statistical coverage and reporting months. Three explanations can be made:

1. As was discussed above, there is a sample selection bias due to refusals among wealthier households to participate in the survey. Consequently, the mean asset holdings in the NSFIE are lower than in the SNA or the FFA.
2. The difference may be affected by underreporting by self-employed households. Although both the NSFIE and the FFA (and the SNA) include self-employed households, those in the NSFIE seem to report financial assets only for personal use and exclude those for business purposes.

TABLE 5.5   Savings (II) (Euro 1998 constant)

Year	Age	Home owning Mean	Home owning Median	Tenant Mean	Tenant Median	Household head working Mean	Household head working Median	Household head nonworking Mean	Household head nonworking Median
1979	−24	5,554	5,643	2,150	2,239	2,866	2,956	11,735	11,735
	25−	8,152	7,077	3,314	3,762	4,927	4,748	90	2,598
	30−	8,062	7,614	4,031	4,479	5,912	5,912	3,135	2,687
	35−	9,047	8,420	5,106	5,106	7,704	7,077	3,404	1,612
	40−	9,316	8,599	5,554	5,106	8,241	7,614	−627	−448
	45−	8,420	8,510	5,285	4,927	7,883	7,793	−1,075	−358
	50−	10,391	10,391	6,539	6,181	9,943	9,674	−806	985
	55−	11,376	9,943	7,345	7,166	11,914	10,391	−1,075	−179
	60−	9,585	7,793	6,002	3,314	11,466	9,406	1,612	1,792
	65−	11,555	7,972	5,643	2,508	15,497	11,914	2,239	1,881
	70−	11,376	6,718	2,508	2,060	15,855	11,018	3,583	2,419
	75−	8,062	4,121	1,971	2,239	9,943	6,270	5,016	2,866
	80+	10,122	4,837	2,239	1,344	16,572	6,629	2,598	1,344
	Average	9,406	8,420	4,748	4,479	8,241	7,166	1,881	1,702
1984	−24	6,512	5,839	1,871	2,246	2,919	2,844	299	−1,647
	25−	8,159	8,009	3,892	3,967	5,240	5,015	−1,797	−2,021
	30−	9,731	9,207	4,940	4,866	7,336	6,737	−1,048	−898
	35−	10,854	10,330	5,614	5,539	9,132	8,608	−1,722	−2,320
	40−	11,079	10,779	5,839	5,839	9,956	9,581	−4,192	−2,994
	45−	10,255	10,031	5,764	5,165	9,581	9,207	−973	−1,422
	50−	11,228	11,228	6,213	5,914	10,629	10,480	−2,545	−2,395
	55−	12,052	11,453	6,512	6,063	12,351	11,602	1,273	1,497
	60−	11,528	9,282	4,342	3,368	12,725	10,105	3,593	3,443
	65−	10,480	7,485	4,042	2,844	12,950	9,956	3,069	2,695
	70−	8,833	5,988	2,246	2,246	11,228	8,234	3,294	2,994
	75−	10,255	6,438	3,219	973	13,923	9,282	4,940	2,470
	80+	6,363	3,294	1,123	599	11,528	8,384	1,946	1,123
	Average	10,779	9,956	5,165	4,940	9,806	8,758	2,844	2,395
1989	−24	2,759	7,712	3,113	3,538	3,042	4,104	2,335	−2,123
	25−	9,764	9,552	4,670	5,165	6,085	6,085	2,972	3,326
	30−	12,028	10,755	5,873	5,802	8,632	7,925	2,193	5,094
	35−	13,514	12,524	7,642	7,359	11,462	10,401	6,651	2,901
	40−	14,151	13,444	7,854	7,642	12,665	12,028	14,859	17,052

(Continues)

TABLE 5.5 *(Continued)*

Year	Age	Home owning		Tenant		Household head working		Household head nonworking	
		Mean	Median	Mean	Median	Mean	Median	Mean	Median
	45–	13,868	13,373	7,005	6,722	12,736	12,241	9,552	3,396
	50–	16,062	15,779	10,472	8,491	15,354	14,717	8,420	6,934
	55–	16,769	15,920	9,906	8,420	16,840	15,779	3,679	2,830
	60–	12,595	9,977	6,227	4,741	15,425	12,878	3,750	3,538
	65–	11,321	7,995	6,934	3,679	16,628	12,028	3,042	3,042
	70–	11,392	7,288	7,500	3,326	17,830	13,939	4,175	3,326
	75–	10,189	5,660	4,175	708	17,760	14,505	3,679	2,547
	80+	9,057	7,217	5,943	4,528	15,212	13,939	5,165	4,528
	Average	13,868	12,524	7,005	6,439	13,019	11,392	4,104	3,326
1994	–24	8,237	7,208	3,733	4,698	4,569	5,148	386	–708
	25–	10,683	10,297	6,242	6,435	7,208	7,015	5,534	5,277
	30–	13,128	12,227	7,723	7,851	9,846	9,138	6,950	4,569
	35–	15,896	15,059	9,074	8,752	13,128	12,163	12,549	10,876
	40–	16,282	15,638	9,718	8,945	14,673	14,029	5,534	12,935
	45–	15,316	15,252	7,980	7,594	14,029	13,965	9,911	8,881
	50–	15,381	17,376	12,163	10,618	17,504	16,668	4,634	1,609
	55–	18,212	17,891	10,876	9,589	18,598	17,247	1,673	2,896
	60–	18,920	9,589	5,470	3,282	15,445	12,420	2,767	2,896
	65–	12,163	7,465	6,242	3,668	16,153	12,678	4,955	4,440
	70–	10,425	5,985	4,634	3,346	16,861	12,356	4,247	4,247
	75–	8,624	7,015	4,827	3,218	17,891	13,772	5,406	4,827
	80+	9,138	7,529	1,802	1,094	24,648	20,722	8,173	4,312
	Average	15,059	13,772	8,302	7,723	14,544	13,000	4,569	4,183

3. It should be noted that the SNA data are constructed from value added in the production sector and, that, with the commodity flow method, the household sector is treated as a residual.

Thus, in general, household sector accounts (e.g., savings) are subject to statistical (measurement) errors.[8]

---

[8]A statistical error could occur when inventories of consumer goods pile up or when these are increasingly consumed by other sectors of the economy (e.g., the corporate sector).

TABLE 5.6   Saving Rates of All Households by Income Class

Year	Age	Income class (%)				
		I	II	III	IV	Mean
1979	−24	−14.0	5.0	15.3	26.1	13.2
	25−	−5.8	13.4	17.8	33.5	19.4
	30−	−1.4	15.7	22.5	33.4	21.6
	35−	2.2	17.2	25.2	36.6	24.6
	40−	−0.8	17.7	24.3	36.7	24.2
	45−	−2.4	14.5	21.8	31.9	21.1
	50−	−1.0	17.6	23.8	35.8	24.3
	55−	−8.7	18.3	27.2	41.7	28.3
	60−	−16.9	12.6	26.4	44.0	27.7
	65−	−18.6	10.3	30.6	41.1	33.2
	70−	−32.8	12.2	23.2	53.0	33.0
	75−	7.0	11.4	16.8	47.1	30.0
	80+	−4.6	−1.3	29.4	49.6	34.7
	Average	−2.7	16.3	23.5	36.6	24.1
1984	−24	−13.8	12.3	15.8	23.6	13.9
	25−	−1.2	14.4	22.0	31.8	20.5
	30−	2.7	18.3	25.6	38.0	25.4
	35−	5.9	21.6	29.3	39.7	28.2
	40−	1.6	23.1	29.6	38.7	27.8
	45−	−1.7	19.7	26.3	35.5	24.9
	50−	−2.0	21.5	27.1	36.3	26.3
	55−	−3.3	21.5	30.8	39.3	29.1
	60−	−3.6	17.7	30.7	43.7	30.8
	65−	−5.8	12.6	28.6	47.1	31.4
	70−	−1.4	12.1	25.5	42.6	29.1
	75−	−2.3	20.1	27.7	48.8	34.7
	80+	−6.9	−3.6	19.4	41.1	25.8
	Average	−0.6	19.4	28.5	38.1	27.2
1989	−24	−14.2	1.6	16.1	30.4	13.5
	25−	1.7	12.7	22.8	37.1	22.3
	30−	7.9	18.1	26.5	41.0	27.4
	35−	10.2	25.3	31.3	44.4	31.8
	40−	11.5	25.7	32.5	42.6	31.8
	45−	9.3	23.0	27.5	39.3	28.5

(*Continues*)

TABLE 5.6   (*Continued*)

Year	Age	Income class (%)				
		I	II	III	IV	Mean
	50–	11.0	26.9	32.3	39.9	31.5
	55–	1.4	29.6	37.9	43.3	34.5
	60–	−3.5	14.9	32.1	46.2	31.7
	65–	−8.3	15.5	29.1	48.5	32.0
	70–	−4.3	10.1	30.2	50.8	33.8
	75–	−15.2	13.7	18.4	49.4	31.1
	80+	−23.4	23.2	34.8	42.3	31.9
	Average	4.6	22.9	31.5	42.1	31.0
1994	–24	4.2	14.8	16.2	31.7	19.8
	25–	6.8	18.7	26.3	36.7	25.3
	30–	11.1	26.3	28.5	41.1	29.9
	35–	18.8	29.7	33.4	44.6	34.4
	40–	14.8	29.8	35.9	43.4	34.3
	45–	10.7	25.2	30.0	38.8	29.6
	50–	16.5	26.9	31.7	44.4	33.6
	55–	11.7	30.4	37.3	44.0	35.6
	60–	−7.7	14.6	27.5	45.7	29.5
	65–	0.5	12.0	27.6	45.4	29.7
	70–	−4.1	13.3	18.7	45.4	27.2
	75–	−8.0	20.0	25.7	47.0	30.8
	80+	6.5	18.6	34.5	54.7	40.0
	Average	8.1	25.7	32.3	45.1	32.1

Note: Income classes I–IV are yearly income quartile groups.

5.3   AGE PROFILE OF SAVINGS

The age–income, the age–consumption, and the age–saving profiles are shown in Figures 5.1, 5.2, and 5.3 respectively. Disposable income, consumption expenditure, and saving increase its nominal values in all age profiles over time. As before, the age–income, the age–consumption, and the age–saving profiles are hump-shaped, reaching their peaks at ages 50–54.

To put these data together, the age–saving rate profile is shown in Figure 5.4. The saving rates over a life cycle follow, more or less, the same pattern over time, i.e., the saving rate as a whole keeps rising over the age profile. Figure 5.5 shows an alternative age–saving rate profile for the median household. Compared with

TABLE 5.7   Age Profile of Homeownership Rate

Age	1979	1984	1989	1994
−24	20.8	20.6	15.9	17.0
25–29	33.0	29.5	27.1	21.7
30–34	47.5	48.9	45.0	38.3
35–39	64.1	66.1	64.6	59.1
40–44	71.4	76.7	76.5	73.5
45–49	79.1	82.9	83.2	81.4
50–54	83.9	85.3	85.6	85.3
55–59	85.5	90.4	89.1	86.1
60–64	85.7	89.0	91.3	89.9
65–69	85.2	88.1	90.4	89.9
70–74	88.2	90.3	90.4	90.3
75–79	87.3	89.2	86.9	87.6
80+	80.0	88.5	88.0	87.0
Average	68.3	74.2	75.6	73.8

Source: The 1979, 1984, 1989, and 1994 NSFIE.

Figure 5.4, the pattern is almost identical until age 55–59. After age 60, the saving rates of the median household go down steadily.

As far as flow data in Figures 5.1–5.4 are concerned, no strong signs of behavioral change after the burst of Japan's bubble economy in the early 1990s are found. In retrospect, the economic recession did not penetrate enough into the daily life of the households in 1994. The worse came later, in 1997–98, when a series of large bankruptcies occurred in various industries. We have to wait until the 1999 NSFIE to examine the impacts of the economic recession in 1997–98.

5.4 SAVING RATES BY INCOME CLASS

The average saving rates in all households by quartile income class are shown in Table 5.6 and Figures 5.6–5.9. Throughout the sample period, the poorest quarter of the households (I) experiences negative saving rates usually in their sixties and after, while the other quarters of the households (II–IV) keep positive saving rates steadily over the life cycle.

To be more precise, for the second and third quarters of households (II–III), the age profiles of saving rates are, more or less, hump shape over the age profile. For the richest quarter (IV), the age profile of saving rates is somewhat different from those of the other quarters. It keeps rising and ends with a very high rate (easily above 40%) over age 80.

TABLE 5.8   Saving Rates of Homeowning Households by Income Class

Year	Age	Income class (%)				
		I	II	III	IV	Mean
1979	–24	5.5	3.3	22.7	29.2	19.4
	25–	3.7	20.6	28.6	39.7	28
	30–	5.1	20.8	26	38.3	26.6
	35–	6.4	21.8	28.3	38.5	27.6
	40–	2.7	20.5	25.9	37.9	26.1
	45–	–2.7	16.5	24	32.1	22
	50–	0.4	17.9	25.3	36.2	24.9
	55–	–6	20.3	27.1	42.3	28.8
	60–	–15.5	14.5	26.5	44.5	28.2
	65–	–21.5	11.5	33.7	52.1	34.1
	70–	–26.9	12.8	23.5	54.5	34.5
	75–	7.2	7.8	23.5	47.1	31.2
	80+	–8.5	–5.3	29.2	54.9	37.7
	Average	0.1	19.5	25.8	38.2	26.4
1984	–24	5.4	13	19.4	44.2	26.8
	25–	5.1	22.9	31	39.6	29
	30–	11	23.4	31.3	42.2	31
	35–	11.6	25.3	33.2	42	31.7
	40–	6.5	25	31.4	40.2	29.9
	45–	1.9	21.3	27.4	36.1	26.1
	50–	0	22.9	28.5	36.6	27.3
	55–	–4.2	22.4	31.5	40.1	29.7
	60–	–3.1	19.8	32.4	44.4	31.9
	65–	–2.7	13.4	31.7	47.3	32.6
	70–	0.6	14	26.2	44.5	30.5
	75–	0.4	21.3	29.2	49.6	35.7
	80+	–13.9	7.2	19.1	41.6	27.1
	Average	3.2	23.3	30.5	39.5	29.5
1989	–24	20.9	–58.6	13	37.1	10.3
	25–	3.6	26.2	35.3	41.4	31.2
	30–	14.9	30.2	35.7	44.1	34.7
	35–	15.8	28.4	34.8	47.1	35.2
	40–	16	28.5	34.5	43.8	34
	45–	12.5	24.6	29.3	40	30

(*Continues*)

TABLE 5.8 (*Continued*)

Year	Age	Income class (%)				
		I	II	III	IV	Mean
	50–	11.9	28.6	33.4	39.8	32.2
	55–	2.6	31.1	38.2	43.8	35.2
	60–	−3.6	15.7	34.1	46.3	32.2
	65–	−7.7	15.7	29.6	48.9	32.3
	70–	−4.9	11.5	29.7	51.2	33.9
	75–	−13.1	19	21.1	48.4	32
	80+	−21	27.7	32.3	42.3	31.9
	Average	7.9	26.3	33.8	43.1	33
1994	−24	−10.3	15	38.2	46.9	32.5
	25–	13.4	27	36	46.1	34.5
	30–	20.7	33.2	35.1	47	36.9
	35–	26.5	34.7	37.9	48.4	39.3
	40–	20.2	33.7	37.6	44.1	36.6
	45–	14.5	26.6	30.6	40.7	31.2
	50–	16.9	28.2	33.5	44.5	34.3
	55–	16	31.3	37.8	44.3	36.5
	60–	−6.9	15.8	29.4	46.3	30.5
	65–	2.5	11.9	27.3	46.3	30.1
	70–	2.9	12.9	18.9	45.7	27.8
	75–	−4.8	17.4	27.8	47.9	31.7
	80+	14.2	22.1	35.6	56.8	42.5
	Average	10.3	28.5	34.2	43.9	34.1

Note: Income classes I–IV are yearly income quartile groups.

The acquisition of a house is probably the most significant consumption decision each household makes over the life cycle. Therefore, saving behavior is quite likely to be affected by the housing purchase decision (see Hayashi *et al.* 1988b). Table 5.7 presents the age profile of the homeownership rate. Regardless of the survey years, the rate starts rising at around ages 30–34 and reaches a steady-state level (i.e., about 90%) at ages 55–59, just before retirement. This steady-state level seems quite high by international standards.

Table 5.8 presents the saving rates of households that own their homes. This table shows that it is income class that mainly differentiates saving rates. Homeowning households with little, if any, saving motivation for housing purchase keep high savings, except for the very poor elderly households.

TABLE 5.9   Saving Rates of Tenant Households by Income Class

Year	Age	Income class (%)				
		I	II	III	IV	Mean
1979	–24	–18.6	2.3	16.8	23.6	10.9
	25–	–6.8	8.5	14.8	26.2	14.2
	30–	–7.0	10.5	18.3	27.3	16.1
	35–	–2.9	12.2	18.9	31.0	18.4
	40–	–5.6	11.8	19.3	31.6	18.6
	45–	–8.5	13.1	16.1	28.5	16.9
	50–	–9.1	12.9	24.1	30.3	20.2
	55–	–17.0	17.5	20.5	38.7	24.2
	60–	–22.3	1.1	22.2	43.5	23.6
	65–	–18.2	–1.2	21.4	44.0	25.3
	70–	–39.6	0.7	5.7	29.0	13.6
	75–	–23.4	19.2	5.0	28.6	14.4
	80+	–0.5	21.6	n.a.	13.1	14.2
	Average	–8.9	11.0	17.9	30.3	15.6
1984	–24	–17.3	9.5	19.3	13.1	9.7
	25–	–7.5	12.4	18.8	26.6	16.3
	30–	–4.4	15.1	19.6	30.4	19.0
	35–	–1.6	14.2	20.1	31.4	19.8
	40–	–9.9	14.6	22.5	30.3	19.4
	45–	–16.3	10.2	19.1	31.0	18.0
	50–	–7.4	8.9	21.8	29.5	19.0
	55–	–5.5	12.7	18.0	34.4	21.4
	60–	–10.9	7.1	16.7	30.9	17.9
	65–	–34.9	6.7	19.9	33.3	18.3
	70–	–29.4	10.0	19.9	13.6	10.9
	75–	–27.5	16.5	1.5	38.4	19.8
	80+	–50.6	–2.0	10.9	23.4	8.0
	Average	–7.3	11.7	19.4	29.9	18.7
1989	–24	–16.2	4.9	17.3	30.2	14.2
	25–	–2.9	11.8	18.8	31.2	18.2
	30–	3.6	12.3	18.5	34.5	20.2
	35–	3.4	18.4	26.7	36.2	24.3
	40–	–0.7	16.7	26.6	33.9	23.1
	45–	–3.4	15.4	18.4	29.1	19.1

(*Continues*)

TABLE 5.9   (*Continued*)

Year	Age	Income class (%)				
		I	II	III	IV	Mean
	50–	10.0	16.7	24.8	37.8	26.6
	55–	−12.3	23.4	29.0	37.7	27.3
	60–	−9.0	16.0	19.9	35.9	22.7
	65–	−4.6	8.9	28.3	43.4	27.4
	70–	−12.5	8.9	29.4	51.6	32.2
	75–	−37.4	−11.9	17.8	48.1	22.1
	80+	−90.5	12.8	28.9	55.1	31.7
	Average	0.0	15.0	22.5	33.9	22.4
1994	–24	8.3	12.6	14.4	25.3	16.8
	25–	5.3	19.7	21.0	33.1	22.5
	30–	7.1	21.8	26.0	34.1	24.9
	35–	10.7	21.9	27.4	34.8	26.3
	40–	6.8	19.2	27.4	38.4	26.7
	45–	−2.0	16.1	24.3	28.7	20.7
	50–	7.3	23.3	25.9	39.2	28.4
	55–	−7.1	21.7	30.5	40.4	28.5
	60–	−21.1	13.0	14.1	30.9	17.7
	65–	−10.6	7.0	20.8	41.9	24.1
	70–	−46.0	4.2	25.1	40.3	19.9
	75–	−25.5	9.8	33.7	35.3	22.8
	80+	−58.3	20.2	27.1	25.6	9.8
	Average	3.3	19.6	25.6	34.6	24.8

Note: Income classes I–IV are yearly income quartile groups.

Table 5.9 shows that the saving rates of tenant households are, in general, lower than those of homeowning households. It is the poorest quarter (I) that dissaves throughout the age profile.

The general pictures in Table 5.10 of households with a working head overlap with those in Table 5.6. Table 5.11 shows that the saving rate goes down substantially when the household head is not working. Only the richest quarter (IV) has positive saving rates throughout the age profile.

Tables 5.12 and 5.13 compare the saving rates between employee and self-employed households. In general, the saving rates of poorer quarters (I–III) are higher in the employee households, whereas those of the richest quarter (IV) are higher in the self-employed households. Income flows of the employee households

TABLE 5.10   Saving Rates of Households with Working Head by Income Class

Year	Age	Income class (%)				
		I	II	III	IV	Mean
1979	−24	−14.2	5.0	15.3	26.0	13.2
	25−	−5.9	13.5	17.9	33.5	19.5
	30−	−1.2	15.6	22.6	33.4	21.6
	35−	2.3	17.2	25.2	36.5	24.7
	40−	−0.4	18.1	24.3	36.6	24.3
	45−	−1.6	14.6	21.9	32.0	21.3
	50−	0.3	18.3	24.6	35.8	24.6
	55−	−1.8	21.6	28.6	42.6	29.9
	60−	−6.2	20.4	29.1	46.7	31.8
	65−	−1.4	25.8	40.2	52.9	39.8
	70−	−39.4	28.1	28.1	58.7	39.6
	75−	4.9	9.1	12.1	54.8	31.6
	80+	−7.1	27.1	22.0	66.3	46.5
	Average	−0.1	16.9	24.0	36.7	24.6
1984	−24	−11.1	11.4	15.8	23.6	14.1
	25−	0.2	14.4	22.1	31.8	20.8
	30−	2.9	18.3	25.7	38.1	25.5
	35−	6.7	21.5	29.2	39.9	28.3
	40−	2.3	23.4	29.6	38.7	28.0
	45−	−1.0	19.4	26.6	35.5	25.0
	50−	−1.1	21.9	27.3	36.3	26.5
	55−	2.8	22.2	32.3	39.8	30.3
	60−	3.5	22.0	34.5	45.0	33.6
	65−	−0.5	23.8	36.3	48.4	36.1
	70−	11.9	14.9	31.5	45.3	33.4
	75−	20.4	20.6	37.1	51.1	39.5
	80+	3.7	21.8	21.8	49.3	33.7
	Average	2.7	20.7	28.8	38.3	27.8
1989	−24	−13.9	1.6	15.8	30.4	13.5
	25−	0.1	12.7	22.8	37.1	22.3
	30−	8.3	18.2	26.5	41.0	27.4
	35−	10.6	25.3	31.2	44.4	31.9
	40−	11.9	25.6	32.4	42.4	31.8
	45−	9.8	22.9	27.4	39.2	28.5

(*Continues*)

TABLE 5.10   (*Continued*)

Year	Age	Income class (%)				
		I	II	III	IV	Mean
	50–	11.7	26.9	32.3	39.8	31.6
	55–	6.4	31.1	38.0	43.5	35.3
	60–	6.5	25.1	36.0	48.7	36.4
	65–	13.9	28.3	38.2	52.6	40.5
	70–	9.7	29.4	40.4	55.4	42.5
	75–	0.1	11.5	40.5	54.4	39.1
	80+	−11.0	31.8	32.3	50.7	38.0
	Average	8.5	24.6	32.3	42.3	31.9
1994	–24	5.9	14.9	16.1	31.8	19.9
	25–	7.1	18.6	26.3	36.7	25.3
	30–	11.0	26.4	28.7	41.1	29.9
	35–	19.0	29.6	33.4	44.4	34.4
	40–	16.8	29.7	35.9	43.4	34.6
	45–	11.5	25.0	30.1	38.8	29.7
	50–	17.7	27.3	31.9	44.5	33.8
	55–	16.5	31.8	37.5	44.1	36.4
	60–	11.4	22.4	33.9	47.8	35.3
	65–	14.2	24.0	35.2	51.9	38.1
	70–	12.0	22.7	44.3	51.3	40.3
	75–	8.8	33.5	42.4	56.6	43.9
	80+	38.4	38.3	35.2	66.7	51.0
	Average	14.2	27.7	32.9	43.0	33.5

Note: Income classes I–IV are yearly income quartile groups.

remain stable over the age profile, and thus income distribution among them is more equal than that among the self-employed households.

5.5 COHORT ANALYSIS

The mean saving rates by cohort are shown in Figure 5.10, constructed from Table 5.6. A general pattern of the saving rates remains the same as in Figure 5.4; i.e., even the elderly households keep saving at a substantial margin.

Figure 5.11 shows the median saving rates by cohort. A general pattern of the saving rates remains the same as in Figure 5.5; i.e., the households after age 60 reduce their saving rates steadily.

TABLE 5.11 Saving Rates of Households with Nonworking Head by Income Class

Year	Age	Income class (%)				
		I	II	III	IV	Mean
1979	−24	37.3	n.a.	n.a.	n.a.	37.3
	25−	−104.2	−0.3	22.7	9.8	1.1
	30−	−48.6	15.7	24.1	24.2	16.2
	35−	−13.2	8.8	9.4	34.1	18.4
	40−	−160.8	−22.3	16.2	21.5	−3.9
	45−	−73.9	−3.5	11.9	−4.0	−5.6
	50−	−55.5	−14.6	−24.4	21.6	−4.3
	55−	−52.2	−31.9	7.6	8.0	−5.0
	60−	−35.2	−2.6	1.3	25.6	7.3
	65−	−25.7	−13.8	3.7	33.0	11.0
	70−	−22.4	4.4	15.0	32.4	17.3
	75−	−2.8	12.6	17.8	44.9	27.5
	80+	−3.6	−7.6	22.5	25.4	16.0
	Average	−26.7	−10.5	5.6	27.1	9.2
1984	−24	n.a.	n.a.	−15.4	22.1	2.7
	25−	−0.4	−74.1	−38.4	−10.2	−22.9
	30−	−100.9	−11.9	−21.1	11.8	−9.3
	35−	−103.6	−28.9	−3.0	4.6	−16.8
	40−	−135.3	−56.3	−46.1	5.2	−31.3
	45−	−92.1	−6.7	−17.0	19.4	−6.2
	50−	−46.1	−52.1	−10.0	5.6	−14.4
	55−	−63.7	−15.1	4.9	28.5	5.5
	60−	−10.9	0.6	11.0	29.3	14.8
	65−	−13.8	8.9	8.2	28.5	14.6
	70−	−9.2	7.3	11.2	32.1	16.9
	75−	−20.9	11.1	19.8	43.3	25.4
	80+	−5.1	−31.7	25.2	28.3	13.5
	Average	−21.5	2.7	9.7	28.1	13.4
1989	−24	−101.0	−33.7	41.1	n.a.	16.9
	25−	19.0	−45.6	20.0	62.4	18.7
	30−	−288.8	20.4	25.0	60.7	9.6
	35−	−120.9	−2.3	43.7	48.6	25.3
	40−	−116.4	16.1	55.8	50.3	39.2
	45−	−80.4	−17.8	28.9	51.2	28.4

(*Continues*)

TABLE 5.11   (*Continued*)

Year	Age	Income class (%)				
		I	II	III	IV	Mean
	50–	−74.1	16.8	20.0	47.5	27.1
	55–	−50.3	−9.2	4.3	39.4	13.4
	60–	−11.1	−4.5	10.1	30.9	13.7
	65–	−27.9	1.3	10.9	30.9	12.5
	70–	−7.0	9.5	2.5	36.7	18.0
	75–	−12.8	5.0	17.6	34.2	18.6
	80+	−26.2	18.9	36.4	34.5	25.5
	Average	−22.0	3.0	9.7	34.9	16.2
1994	–24	−340.1	0.4	1.4	18.6	3.8
	25–	−73.0	−50.0	38.8	37.4	22.6
	30–	−34.2	−3.3	37.6	45.8	28.6
	35–	−0.9	19.3	43.1	53.9	38.1
	40–	−111.2	−28.6	42.2	40.1	14.4
	45–	−71.4	13.2	20.4	44.5	25.2
	50–	−60.0	−10.7	4.4	37.8	12.5
	55–	−47.3	−13.1	3.9	27.8	5.9
	60–	−32.8	−5.6	5.3	31.5	10.0
	65–	−1.9	4.8	14.2	34.7	18.6
	70–	−9.2	13.6	13.1	30.6	17.1
	75–	−8.6	16.3	20.0	37.3	23.0
	80+	4.4	13.2	24.9	47.4	32.5
	Average	−15.1	5.4	11.4	34.5	17.0

Note: Income classes I–IV are yearly income quartile groups.

Among many cohorts, the baby-boomer cohort (birth year 1945–49)[9] deserves a special attention because it comprises the largest demographic cohort. As Figure 5.10 shows, the baby-boomer cohort in their forties reduces their saving rates from 1989 to 1994, whereas most neighboring cohorts raised their saving rates in 1994. Kitamura *et al.* (2001) conducted analysis of variance (ANOVA) for this cohort data and found a statistical evidence that the baby-boomer generation indeed started behaving differently as early as in their forties in 1989.

[9]We have to be careful about the conceptual differences of the baby-boomer generations in the United States and in Japan. In the United States the baby boomer includes those who were born from 1946 to 1961, whereas in Japan, it usually includes only those who were born from 1946 to 1949.

TABLE 5.12   Saving Rates of Employee Households by Income Class

Year	Age	I	II	III	IV	Mean
				Income class (%)		
1979	−24	−14.1	4.3	17.4	26.6	13.6
	25−	−2.1	14.1	18.5	33.1	19.9
	30−	2.9	15.9	22.9	32.5	21.7
	35−	9.4	20.2	26.3	35.3	25.5
	40−	9.9	20.8	25.8	36.0	26.0
	45−	7.4	17.9	23.1	31.3	22.7
	50−	9.0	19.2	24.1	32.6	24.1
	55−	9.7	25.6	30.0	39.8	30.5
	60−	3.6	27.7	28.0	42.6	31.3
	65−	17.6	35.9	42.1	46.5	40.1
	70−	−9.1	25.6	34.6	54.2	39.6
	75−	24.9	30.8	31.4	30.9	30.5
	80+	n.a.	−3.7	n.a.	60.0	34.0
	Average	6.0	19.9	24.8	33.9	24.6
1984	−24	−9.2	11.7	17.3	25.2	15.4
	25−	1.2	14.9	22.2	33.1	21.6
	30−	7.3	19.6	25.4	37.8	25.9
	35−	13.4	23.3	29.8	38.7	29.1
	40−	13.8	26.4	31.0	37.6	29.7
	45−	10.7	23.9	26.5	33.2	26.1
	50−	13.3	23.6	27.7	32.4	26.6
	55−	17.8	22.4	31.5	38.1	30.3
	60−	14.1	19.7	27.0	37.5	28.3
	65−	16.6	31.6	33.9	39.4	33.5
	70−	36.3	18.1	39.1	45.0	38.0
	75−	34.5	−2.8	49.2	37.3	33.7
	80+	n.a.	n.a.	n.a.	66.8	66.8
	Average	11.4	23.1	29.0	35.2	27.7
1989	−24	−13.6	1.6	16.2	28.7	12.7
	25−	0.5	12.8	23.6	35.1	21.6
	30−	9.2	17.6	26.6	38.9	26.3
	35−	14.0	26.1	30.3	41.7	30.8
	40−	16.8	26.4	32.4	39.8	31.3
	45−	15.3	23.4	26.3	35.3	27.2
	50−	15.6	26.6	30.5	36.4	29.8

(*Continues*)

TABLE 5.12   (*Continued*)

Year	Age	I	II	III	IV	Mean
				Income class (%)		
	55–	14.4	31.1	36.8	38.2	33.3
	60–	9.6	21.5	33.6	41.1	31.4
	65–	21.1	32.3	31.4	43.2	35.4
	70–	31.0	37.3	33.3	37.7	35.3
	75–	1.8	54.3	42.3	49.9	43.5
	80+	38.9	n.a.	83.2	n.a.	62.5
	Average	12.1	24.9	30.8	37.4	29.6
1994	–24	6.5	16.8	15.9	30.5	19.9
	25–	6.8	18.9	27.1	35.9	25.1
	30–	12.5	26.7	28.6	40.7	29.9
	35–	20.6	30.3	33.0	43.5	34.2
	40–	19.7	30.1	35.8	42.6	34.6
	45–	16.1	25.5	29.9	38.1	30.0
	50–	21.3	26.3	32.5	43.4	33.7
	55–	19.7	31.3	36.4	42.4	35.6
	60–	12.1	20.6	33.5	42.7	32.3
	65–	7.9	27.2	30.9	49.6	35.7
	70–	8.7	28.4	42.4	50.9	39.8
	75–	20.4	16.0	50.1	54.5	43.7
	80+	8.0	64.8	50.1	65.6	53.4
	Average	16.9	28.0	32.3	41.2	32.9

Note: Income classes I–IV are yearly income quartile groups.

Why did this happen? As the hump shapes show in Figures 5.1 and 5.2, both the disposable income and consumption reach their peaks around the mid-fifties, with accelerating increases in consumption expenditure in the forties. The baby-boomer cohort happened to be in their forties in 1994. As discussed before, consumption expenditure increases steadily from 1989 to 1994, and especially so for the baby-boomer cohort. That results in a drop in saving rates. It is noteworthy that in the United States the unprecedented economic boom in the 1990s has enabled the baby-boomer generation to accumulate their wealth (see Sterling and Waite, 1998) in the forms of real estate, pension funds, and stocks. Conversely, the protracted Japanese economic recession in the 1990s has made very little room for the baby boomers to accumulate their wealth for after retirement by themselves and through firms' retirement severance pay funds.

TABLE 5.13   Saving Rates of Self-Employed Households by Income Class

Year	Age	Income class (%)				
		I	II	III	IV	Mean
1979	−24	−17.2	14.3	3.6	17.0	8.6
	25−	−28.8	2.0	11.4	35.8	15.2
	30−	−27.2	6.1	16.6	42.6	20.9
	35−	−24.3	4.2	17.9	41.4	21.4
	40−	−24.8	3.0	15.8	38.7	19.1
	45−	−29.5	0.3	18.5	33.3	17.0
	50−	−24.3	8.0	23.1	42.0	24.6
	55−	−30.8	8.1	24.4	42.7	25.3
	60−	−23.0	1.8	24.8	44.9	25.7
	65−	−25.3	2.3	23.9	51.3	30.7
	70−	−33.1	10.1	24.0	51.0	32.0
	75−	5.5	11.5	16.1	47.7	30.0
	80+	−6.8	−0.1	26.8	50.6	34.7
	Average	−25.1	5.1	19.3	41.7	23.0
1984	−24	−26.3	−15.4	−12.3	1.8	−7.7
	25−	−26.2	7.7	13.5	18.0	9.8
	30−	−21.4	7.4	23.9	40.2	22.6
	35−	−19.7	9.8	23.9	44.2	24.8
	40−	−26.7	7.2	22.0	41.6	22.3
	45−	−28.5	9.6	22.3	40.1	22.4
	50−	−19.8	13.4	26.6	41.8	26.2
	55−	−16.1	18.9	34.6	41.3	30.3
	60−	−4.5	24.9	37.3	48.6	36.2
	65−	−7.0	21.1	36.6	50.9	36.8
	70−	9.3	13.6	32.8	43.9	32.6
	75−	19.5	22.1	36.0	52.2	39.9
	80+	0.5	21.8	21.8	49.3	33.6
	Average	−16.7	12.8	28.6	43.6	28.0
1989	−24	−23.0	8.9	43.0	56.3	28.4
	25−	−8.3	13.8	20.2	60.4	31.6
	30−	1.6	23.7	33.2	53.5	36.3
	35−	−7.3	20.2	37.5	54.9	37.0
	40−	−5.6	21.0	32.1	50.6	33.5
	45−	−8.8	20.4	30.6	48.4	32.3

(*Continues*)

TABLE 5.13   (*Continued*)

Year	Age	Income class (%)				
		I	II	III	IV	Mean
	50–	1.0	25.9	39.5	45.7	35.6
	55–	−6.4	29.1	40.5	51.4	38.6
	60–	3.6	27.8	39.3	52.3	39.7
	65–	12.6	25.8	41.3	55.3	42.3
	70–	5.5	27.0	42.2	57.6	43.7
	75–	2.0	7.9	40.3	54.9	38.8
	80+	−11.0	31.5	32.3	50.1	37.6
	Average	−0.7	22.9	37.5	51.1	37.1
1994	−24	−16.8	−15.0	−4.6	50.9	17.9
	25–	−19.3	29.0	24.5	40.3	27.9
	30–	−15.0	18.5	29.4	45.6	29.0
	35–	0.1	22.0	37.1	53.7	36.8
	40–	−13.6	18.0	35.9	49.1	32.2
	45–	−20.0	16.0	30.7	43.2	27.5
	50–	−10.5	18.9	33.4	50.6	33.1
	55–	−11.8	20.4	35.3	53.3	36.0
	60–	−21.1	4.3	20.8	48.8	26.2
	65–	0.6	9.4	20.1	44.7	26.5
	70–	−5.8	12.4	14.7	43.2	24.2
	75–	−9.4	18.3	23.5	46.2	28.9
	80+	4.6	17.4	36.7	51.4	38.3
	Average	−9.8	12.0	26.5	47.7	29.5

Note: Income classes I–IV are yearly income quartile groups. Figures for jobless households are included in 1979.

Generational accounting results from Japan (see Takayama *et al.*, 1999; Takayama and Kitamura, 1999) also indicate that we cannot afford to provide generous public pension benefits to the baby-boomer cohort and that further public pension reforms would be inevitable, if the public pension scheme were to be kept running.

5.6 AGE–WEALTH PROFILE

Net worth (financial and housing assets) increases over all the age profile without a substantial decrease after retirement (see Figures 5.12–5.14). With a closer scrutiny,

TABLE 5.14   Net Worth by Homeownership (Euro 1998 constant)

Year	Age	Total		Homeowning		Tenant	
		Mean	Median	Mean	Median	Mean	Median
1979	−24	39,235	18,005	123,527	104	17,020	14,870
	25−	56,971	31,800	122,990	108,658	24,455	21,230
	30−	80,530	50,074	137,770	120,303	28,665	25,619
	35−	105,433	86,084	145,563	127,827	33,592	28,754
	40−	125,319	103,193	160,344	134,366	37,802	31,531
	45−	151,117	122,542	180,678	147,355	38,877	33,054
	50−	178,707	143,951	203,878	164,375	47,118	37,533
	55−	196,354	155,148	220,182	178,080	55,896	42,012
	60−	203,251	161,598	227,796	177,901	56,523	37,175
	65−	206,924	166,256	235,589	191,517	42,370	29,919
	70−	223,496	158,463	247,144	181,842	46,222	26,157
	75−	211,851	153,625	237,739	179,513	34,129	21,678
	80+	188,381	145,922	229,229	193,040	25,530	20,334
	Average	132,843	102,298	178,618	144,220	33,860	27,142
1984	−24	46,784	18,190	162,734	135,188	16,693	14,672
	25−	63,252	30,466	153,827	136,685	25,376	22,756
	30−	101,204	59,734	173,588	150,009	32,038	27,547
	35−	135,038	101,877	186,838	157,345	33,909	30,316
	40−	165,504	137,134	204,428	171,118	36,978	31,589
	45−	190,356	156,970	220,522	181,897	44,314	35,406
	50−	214,833	178,080	243,503	201,734	48,581	36,829
	55−	260,345	210,566	282,577	227,109	51,725	35,406
	60−	284,972	227,633	313,791	254,132	50,976	37,727
	65−	282,352	231,676	313,267	257,500	54,120	40,646
	70−	267,157	220,372	290,586	243,802	49,254	34,209
	75−	273,669	221,046	302,713	237,514	34,358	28,744
	80+	275,690	207,872	304,734	227,633	52,773	24,702
	Average	183,843	143,422	235,119	189,907	36,155	29,044
1989	−24	51,369	17,123	221,324	146,677	19,175	14,363
	25−	90,780	31,274	266,113	167,550	25,543	23,208
	30−	138,964	56,888	267,881	172,715	34,317	29,647
	35−	194,366	109,247	278,707	181,489	40,897	33,680
	40−	242,763	152,054	303,401	200,310	45,991	35,095
	45−	287,976	186,866	335,878	227,338	51,156	35,661

(Continues)

TABLE 5.14   (*Continued*)

Year	Age	Total		Homeowning		Tenant	
		Mean	Median	Mean	Median	Mean	Median
	50–	323,283	206,112	368,142	244,461	58,657	36,793
	55–	379,676	233,919	417,035	264,627	67,501	42,029
	60–	412,436	265,051	444,842	289,604	70,261	45,850
	65–	410,313	252,881	447,601	284,580	64,600	40,048
	70–	435,007	254,084	476,187	277,787	54,057	45,496
	75–	500,880	268,094	569,301	342,953	55,331	35,732
	80+	463,309	295,122	521,046	344,439	48,892	23,632
	Average	284,792	166,205	362,907	230,805	43,232	31,416
1994	–24	44,791	14,029	185,856	150,075	15,767	11,777
	25–	71,047	30,182	224,211	167,322	28,702	24,776
	30–	115,516	51,226	240,943	160,050	37,583	32,499
	35–	159,213	94,859	236,760	170,539	47,108	41,444
	40–	218,677	142,545	277,690	191,841	55,345	44,018
	45–	261,858	186,113	308,580	224,211	57,082	43,311
	50–	302,402	218,097	342,688	249,116	67,894	48,974
	55–	358,133	251,176	403,889	292,105	74,394	46,786
	60–	431,497	293,135	470,818	323,896	80,121	49,424
	65–	424,418	311,283	463,739	343,524	74,394	47,815
	70–	439,091	322,609	476,223	344,876	95,052	57,983
	75–	451,318	300,986	503,445	337,926	81,988	48,845
	80+	589,938	313,857	663,431	371,390	100,136	57,983
	Average	276,145	175,881	356,074	243,904	50,518	37,133

however, net housing assets in 1994 became slightly lower for the younger households than in 1989. It means that the younger households could not purchase the housing assets in 1994 as much as those in 1989. Net financial assets, on the other hand, are higher than those in the previous period. As housing assets accounted for 66% of total net worth in 1994 (see Tables 5.14–5.16), overall net worth in 1994 remains the same as in 1989. It should be noted, therefore, that as far as the household worth is concerned, net worth does not drop even after the burst of the Japanese bubble economy in the early 1990s.[10]

[10]This is partly because the officially evaluated land prices (koji-chi-ka) in 1994 do not reflect fully a sharp drop in market land prices after the burst of the bubble economy.

TABLE 5.15   Net Financial Assets by Homeownership (Euro 1998 constant)

Year	Age	Total		Homeowning		Tenant	
		Mean	Median	Mean	Median	Mean	Median
1979	–24	12,272	6,270	26,515	13,437	8,510	5,554
	25–	18,184	11,914	23,290	14,243	15,676	11,287
	30–	24,365	17,468	27,321	18,990	21,767	15,945
	35–	30,456	22,305	31,979	23,290	27,590	20,155
	40–	38,070	26,873	40,220	28,665	32,606	22,753
	45–	47,207	32,248	50,701	34,039	33,860	24,186
	50–	57,330	38,787	60,375	40,758	41,743	29,740
	55–	69,691	45,416	73,095	47,028	49,716	35,921
	60–	69,154	44,072	72,558	46,759	49,178	28,306
	65–	67,989	42,908	73,722	46,670	34,935	22,394
	70–	78,022	43,445	83,218	47,476	39,593	19,707
	75	68,168	37,712	73,901	42,101	29,023	18,005
	80+	60,644	27,769	70,318	33,771	21,946	17,916
	Average	42,101	26,067	48,909	30,636	27,321	18,274
1984	–24	11,752	6,138	29,642	12,501	7,111	5,240
	25–	16,917	11,902	21,483	14,971	14,971	10,704
	30–	26,424	18,489	29,717	20,585	23,280	16,693
	35–	33,460	23,579	36,155	25,376	28,071	20,735
	40–	40,721	28,445	43,041	30,017	33,086	23,055
	45–	47,907	32,188	49,928	33,310	38,101	26,948
	50–	55,917	36,305	58,387	37,427	41,470	29,044
	55–	73,283	45,587	76,202	47,682	45,437	29,418
	60–	79,795	50,976	84,137	54,419	44,913	30,316
	65–	73,882	48,132	77,475	50,153	47,383	32,188
	70–	69,765	44,763	72,534	45,437	44,164	28,445
	75–	68,342	38,101	73,208	44,164	28,445	22,456
	80+	65,573	37,427	68,118	43,266	46,410	20,136
	Average	46,410	29,193	54,494	33,610	29,044	18,863
1989	–24	13,727	4,953	32,406	11,533	10,189	4,245
	25–	23,066	14,222	36,227	20,024	18,184	12,028
	30–	32,831	23,279	37,642	25,189	28,939	21,934
	35–	44,293	30,991	47,123	32,265	39,128	28,444
	40–	55,048	37,784	58,020	39,623	45,354	31,133
	45–	68,987	44,930	72,808	47,477	50,166	32,194

(*Continues*)

TABLE 5.15   (*Continued*)

Year	Age	Total		Homeowning		Tenant	
		Mean	Median	Mean	Median	Mean	Median
	50–	77,195	47,760	80,308	50,449	59,010	31,982
	55–	96,157	58,657	99,907	62,973	65,095	38,633
	60–	117,455	73,586	122,054	77,619	68,492	41,604
	65–	117,384	70,756	123,327	77,124	62,407	37,501
	70–	115,403	64,388	122,266	68,421	51,581	42,029
	75–	103,728	58,727	111,370	66,440	53,704	34,670
	80+	110,450	59,435	119,365	68,350	46,840	22,288
	Average	70,685	41,038	80,591	47,406	40,189	25,472
1994	–24	11,005	5,084	24,004	9,653	8,366	4,312
	25–	25,291	15,767	38,291	19,306	21,687	15,123
	30–	35,588	25,098	42,281	27,029	31,405	23,682
	35–	48,395	35,395	51,162	36,167	44,276	34,108
	40–	61,523	43,118	64,483	45,048	53,221	38,291
	45–	75,295	50,840	80,121	54,701	54,058	36,360
	50–	84,691	57,919	87,844	61,780	66,285	44,405
	55–	108,244	70,661	113,907	76,067	73,042	40,029
	60–	131,412	92,027	137,590	97,819	75,810	45,370
	65–	139,585	92,670	147,243	102,195	71,047	48,330
	70–	141,387	93,314	146,793	98,784	91,062	56,181
	75–	122,081	80,443	128,259	89,581	78,126	44,276
	80+	151,748	80,443	159,921	95,953	97,240	55,667
	Average	82,309	49,231	94,987	58,563	46,593	29,989

Wealth distribution became unequal in the 1990s. In particular, net worth holdings became increasingly distorted between home owners and tenants (see Table 5.14).

Figures 5.15 and 5.16 indicate net worth and net financial assets held by cohorts over the period of 1979–94. Net worth increases substantially in the bubble period (i.e., 1984–89). It is surprising to find that net financial assets increase even after the collapse of the stock market in Japan. Net financial assets reach its peak at ages 60–64 because of lump-sum retirement severance payments at around age 60. As Takayama and Kitamura (1994) show, intergenerational transfers might be made from the elderly cohorts to the younger cohorts. However, from the net worth and financial assets holding by cohorts in Figures 5.15 and 5.16, no strong evidence of transfers can be observed, in particular, for the baby-boomer cohorts to receive.

TABLE 5.16   Net Housing assets (Euro 1998 constant)

Year	Age	Total		Homeowning	
		Mean	Median	Mean	Median
1979	−24	20,120	0	99,423	82,621
	25−	32,428	0	102,099	90,112
	30−	52,120	0	114,406	97,604
	35−	73,631	56,507	118,045	100,279
	40−	87,758	70,420	125,537	102,313
	45−	106,915	84,547	136,881	107,236
	50−	126,928	99,423	152,399	118,045
	55−	133,777	105,095	157,108	122,861
	60−	144,158	107,878	168,452	127,891
	65−	152,078	113,657	178,619	135,490
	70−	160,747	113,015	182,151	131,316
	75−	159,784	112,159	183,007	129,924
	80+	142,874	114,085	178,726	139,449
	Average	92,253	68,280	137,202	108,306
1984	−24	25,995	0	127,336	104,940
	25−	35,593	0	123,736	103,260
	30−	65,188	0	136,614	115,738
	35−	93,022	64,548	143,653	116,538
	40−	117,338	95,502	155,250	126,056
	45−	135,254	109,659	164,289	132,615
	50−	152,131	123,496	179,086	144,052
	55−	181,885	142,613	201,721	156,450
	60−	203,481	156,050	228,916	175,406
	65−	209,080	168,448	237,475	188,124
	70−	198,522	155,490	220,038	175,486
	75−	208,280	163,009	233,635	181,885
	80+	213,799	158,370	241,554	175,406
	Average	129,255	98,781	175,726	137,974
1989	−24	11,702	0	75,590	51,640
	25−	24,346	0	92,915	50,363
	30−	41,306	0	93,979	53,433
	35−	60,393	25,653	94,951	54,314
	40−	76,563	40,151	101,000	58,509
	45−	89,663	50,697	108,325	64,527

(*Continues*)

TABLE 5.16   (*Continued*)

Year	Age	Total		Homeowning	
		Mean	Median	Mean	Median
	50–	101,091	55,135	118,750	69,208
	55–	117,291	60,241	131,516	69,937
	60–	122,944	63,919	134,737	72,521
	65–	122,823	65,651	136,166	73,858
	70–	134,585	66,320	149,144	77,840
	75–	168,323	71,761	194,249	93,796
	80+	149,509	71,882	170,329	96,258
	Average	87,839	42,765	116,896	64,557
1994	–24	20,386	0	123,006	103,361
	25–	28,541	0	140,957	100,873
	30–	56,605	0	151,971	90,706
	35–	81,175	22,346	141,063	89,329
	40–	119,141	62,271	163,991	98,172
	45–	143,022	89,700	176,752	113,210
	50–	167,856	107,333	197,721	129,308
	55–	194,915	119,141	227,215	142,387
	60–	237,594	132,697	264,387	150,753
	65–	226,527	140,375	252,155	157,107
	70–	238,494	146,993	264,228	164,467
	75–	265,764	137,409	303,201	166,268
	80+	355,358	146,570	408,627	183,318
	Average	149,747	80,063	204,181	124,065

5.7 WEALTH DISTRIBUTION

So far, we have observed household savings and wealth holdings over the age profile. In this section, we add another dimension of income and wealth distribution over the age profile.

Table 5.17 shows the percentage of negative savers by income class over the age profile in 1994. This table confirms our earlier finding that within-variation of percentage of negative savers in the same income class is smaller than between-variation of different income classes and that variation of negative savers in the same age profile is much larger than that in the same income class. In short, it is income distribution that mostly determines the saving behavior. Tables 5.18 and 5.19 examine the same aspect from a slightly different perspective: i.e., the number of households holding financial assets less than ¥3 million in 1994.

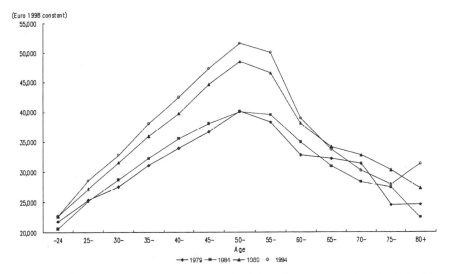

FIGURE 5.1 Age profile of disposable income (for all households). *Source*: NSFIE for 1979, 1984, 1989, and 1994.

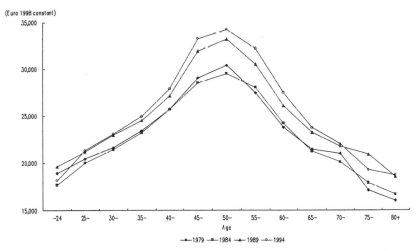

FIGURE 5.2 Age profile of consumption (for all households). *Source*: NSFIE for 1979, 1984, 1989, and 1994.

Tables 5.20–5.22 indicate wealth distribution over its own decile or over the income decile. Table 5.20 reveals that distributions of net worth and financial assets are equally skewed. Comparing Tables 5.21 and 5.22, wealth distribution over its own decile is much more skewed than that over the income decile; wealth is much more unevenly distributed than income. To confirm this conjecture,

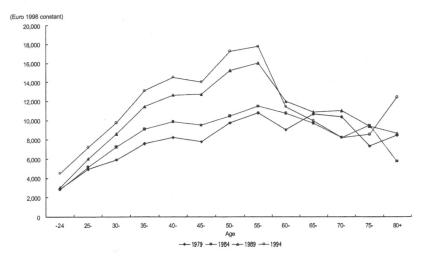

FIGURE 5.3   Age profile of saving (for all households). *Source*: NSFIE for 1979, 1984, 1989, and 1994.

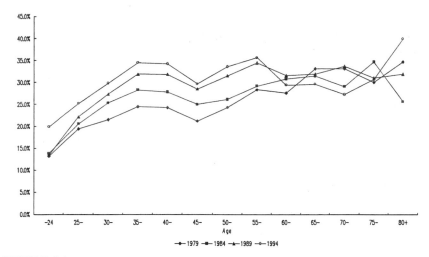

FIGURE 5.4   Age profile of mean saving rates (for all households). *Source*: NSFIE for 1979, 1984, 1989, and 1994.

the Gini coefficient of *income* distribution in Japan has been in the range of 0.3–0.4 in 1979–94, whereas the Gini coefficcient of *net worth* was 0.519 in 1984 and 0.562 in 1994.

Table 5.23 and its graphical expressions (Figures 5.17 and 5.18) reveal a three-dimensional picture of wealth distribution. These pictures show that variance of wealth distribution within the same income decile is larger than that within the same wealth decile. This implies those who belong to a lower income decile might

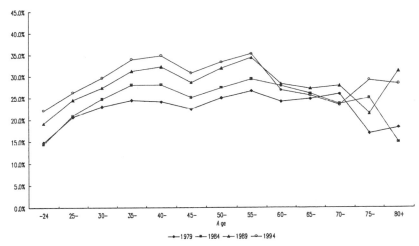

FIGURE 5.5   Age profile of median saving rates (for all households). *Source*: NSFIE for 1979, 1984, 1989, and 1994.

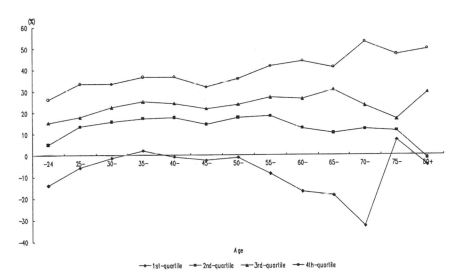

FIGURE 5.6   Age profile of saving rates by income class in 1979. *Source*: NSFIE for 1979.

have a substantially large amount of wealth, whereas those who belong to a lower wealth decile are less likely to earn a substantially high income. In other words, it may be misleading to observe wealth distribution over income decile, because income is not a good indicator of wealth holding.

Takayama (1992a) reports the decomposition of net worth distribution by means of a decomposable measure of inequality for the 1984 NSFIE. He uses the so-called

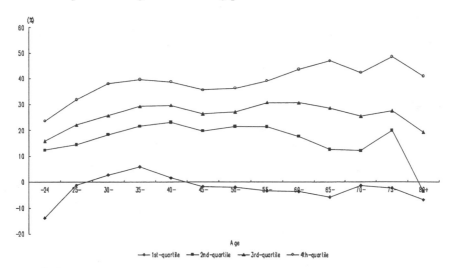

FIGURE 5.7   Age profile of saving rates by income class in 1984. *Source*: NSFIE for 1984.

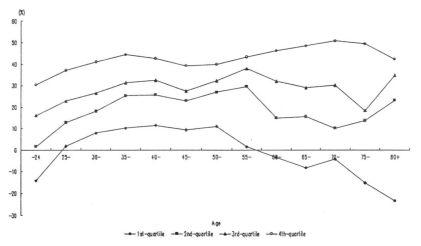

FIGURE 5.8   Age profile of saving rates by income class in 1989. *Source*: NSFIE for 1989.

Toyoda Measure of Inequality (see Toyoda, 1980), which is essentially based on the analysis of variance (ANOVA).[11] By construction, the Toyoda measure T is decomposable, such that

$$T = T_{\mathrm{b}} + \sum w_j T_{\mathrm{w}}(j) \tag{5.10}$$

[11]More precisely, the Toyoda measure T is defined as $T = (s/\mu)^2/2 = s^2/(2\mu^2)$, where s = standard deviation of the sample, μ = mean of the sample, s/μ is the coefficient of variation, and s^2 = variance of the sample.

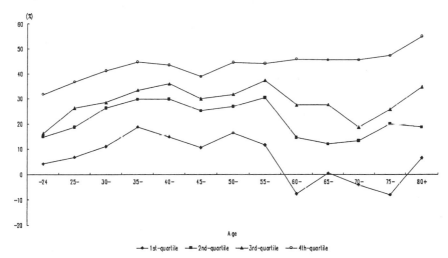

FIGURE 5.9   Age profile of saving rates by income class in 1994. *Source*: NSFIE for 1994.

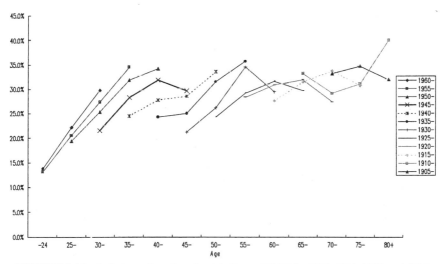

FIGURE 5.10   Saving rates by cohort (mean). *Source*: NSFIE for 1979, 1984, 1989, and 1994.

where T_b is the Toyoda measure between the groups; $T_w(j)$ is the Toyoda measure within the group, and $w(j)$, a weight, is the net worth share of each group in total net worth.

Table 5.24 reports the results. Takayama decomposes net worth distribution over homeownership, age profile, region, employment status, and income class for the 1984 NSFIE. Homeownership explains 12.2% of overall wealth inequality. Age profile, region, and employment status explain as little as 2–8%. Income class,

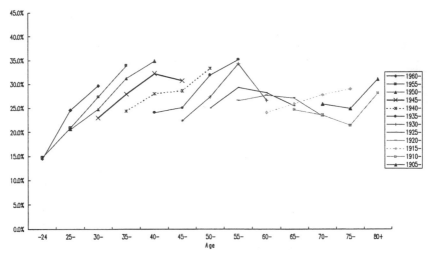

FIGURE 5.11   Saving rates by cohort (median). *Source*: NSFIE for 1979, 1984, 1989, and 1994.

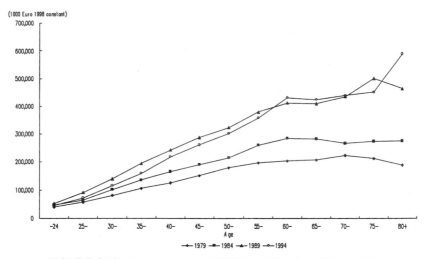

FIGURE 5.12   Net worth. *Source*: NSFIE for 1979, 1984, 1989, and 1994.

here again, plays the major role in explaining the wealth inequality by 15.9%. Nevertheless, the Toyoda measure shows that within-group variance easily exceeds between-group variance.

Table 5.25 replicates the same approach to the 1994 NSFIE. The general pattern remains the same as that in 1984: namely, homeownership, age profile, region, employment status, and income class explain as little as 1.5–8.4% of overall inequality. In other words, the Toyoda measure shows that within-group variance

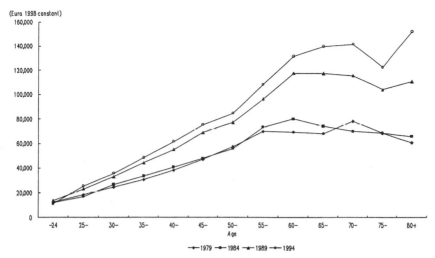

FIGURE 5.13 Net financial assets. *Source*: NSFIE for 1979, 1984, 1989, and 1994.

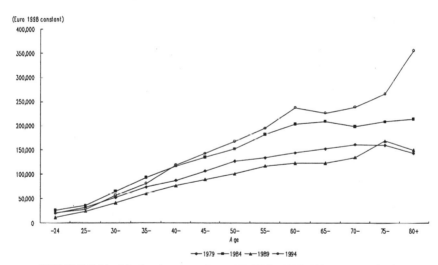

FIGURE 5.14 Net housing assets. *Source*: NSFIE for 1979, 1984, 1989, and 1994.

exceeds between-group variance. However, note that, in 1994, within-group variances became larger than those in 1984.

Taking age profile, within-group variances for the younger cohorts became two to three times larger than before. Intragenerational inequality becomes more relevant than intergenerational inequality. It is noteworthy that within-group variance for the baby-boomer cohort was much smaller than that for the neighbor cohorts in 1994.

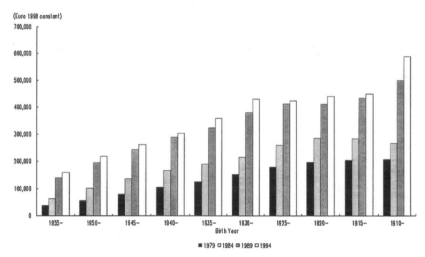

FIGURE 5.15 Net worth by birth year (for all households). *Source*: NSFIE for 1979, 1984, 1989, and 1994.

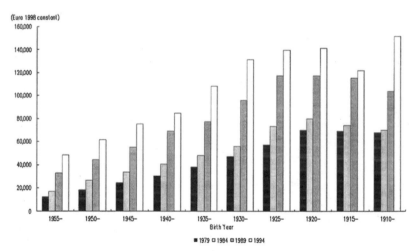

FIGURE 5.16 Net financial assets by birth year (for all households). *Source*: NSFIE for 1979, 1984, 1989, and 1994.

5.8. CONSTRUCTION OF SOCIAL SECURITY WEALTH

Another important issue in household saving is to identify whether or not the social security system affects household saving. This question was originally raised by Feldstein (1974) and extended by many authors. In the case of Japan, Takayama (1992a,b) conducted an econometric estimation of consumption expenditure,

TABLE 5.17   Share of Dissavers (Negative Savers) by Income Class

Age in 1994	Income class (%)				
	I	II	III	IV	Mean
–24	38.3	27.8	21.2	13.6	25.2
25–	34.4	15.4	10.8	6.2	16.7
30–	29.2	10.5	7.3	5.6	13.1
35–	20.8	7.3	5.7	3.8	9.4
40–	24.5	8.1	5.1	4.2	10.5
45–	30.2	14.3	11.6	7.3	15.8
50–	26.9	15.2	12.4	5.0	14.9
55–	29.7	12.5	8.2	6.3	14.2
60–	43.5	25.0	16.1	5.8	22.6
65–	38.1	29.1	14.0	6.7	22.0
70–	38.5	24.1	18.3	10.4	22.8
75–	46.6	16.3	18.6	7.7	22.3
80+	34.7	17.0	8.3	9.9	17.4
Average	31.9	12.9	9.7	6.6	15.1

TABLE 5.18   Share of Small Savers

Income decile	Financial assets less than ¥3 million (%)
I	41.5
II	32.2
III	26.2
IV	21.6
V	16.9
VI	13.1
VII	10.6
VIII	8.5
IX	4.6
X	3.0

using the present value of public pension benefits (GSSW) as one of the explanatory variables in the 1979 and 1984 NSFIE. Estimated values of the parameter for GSSW are significantly positive. For workers' households, the figures are about 1.2% in 1979 and 2.4% in 1984, implying that the presence of social

TABLE 5.19   Share of Small Savers

Age	Financial assets less than ¥3 million (%)
−24	82.1
25−	52.9
30−	34.6
35−	23.2
40−	17.5
45−	13.9
50−	12.3
55−	9.9
60−	10.1
65−	8.5
70−	9.8
75−	12.9
80+	12.7

TABLE 5.20   Distribution of Wealth (1994) (Euro 1998 constant)

	Net worth	Net financial assets
Top 1%	1,745,680	520,950
5%	839,118	274,536
50%	175,881	49,231

Source: 1994 NSFIE.

security wealth caused annual consumption expenditure to increase 1.2 and 2.4% of GSSW in 1979 and 1984, respectively.

The model can be refined by allowing the effect of human capital variables to vary by age. The presence of social security wealth is estimated to increase 1984 consumption expenditures of workers' households by about 1.5% of GSSW. This increase in consumption expenditure would be equivalent to 13.9% and 12.0% of disposable income in 1979 and 1984, respectively.

The Japanese public pension program increases working households' propensity to consume: namely, the evidence confirms the hypothesis that social security wealth discourages personal savings in Japan.

Note, however, that the public pension system has been changed many times and will be reformed again and again in the future. Benefits and contributions will be more closely balanced; the social security wealth of each individual will also be reduced in the near future by raising the normal retirement age to 65 or more and

TABLE 5.21 Distribution of Net Worth in Decile Group (1994) (Euro 1998 constant)

Net worth decile	Net worth mean
I	15,909
II	41,117
III	73,802
IV	113,715
V	157,535
VI	206,708
VII	266,049
VIII	348,524
IX	486,604
X	1,126,809

Source: 1994 NSFIE.

TABLE 5.22   Distribution of Wealth over Income Decile (1994) (Euro 1998 constant)

Income decile	Net worth		Net financial assets	
	Mean	Median	Mean	Median
I	181,713	93,012	48,702	23,489
II	192,784	106,597	54,253	29,860
III	189,976	109,287	57,716	33,722
IV	226,348	125,150	63,629	39,900
V	230,538	144,392	72,186	43,375
VI	246,285	162,978	73,675	49,746
VII	279,539	195,612	82,020	55,602
VIII	327,965	216,797	93,826	64,355
IX	378,677	267,843	115,879	81,988
X	507,554	366,750	161,210	115,130

Source: 1994 NSFIE.

by decreasing real levels of monthly benefits. The future prospects of these reforms might have encouraged household savings.[12]

According to our framework, the following identity is defined:

$$\text{Income} - (\text{Tax and Social Security Contributions})$$
$$= \text{Disposable Income} = \text{Consumption and Savings} \qquad (5.11)$$

---

[12]Although we have not conducted a similar econometric analysis using the 1989 and 1994 NSFIE, high saving rates among those aged above 55 might be evidence of precautionary savings due to uncertainty in the public pension system. See Takayama (2001) for the latest public pension reform.

TABLE 5.23   Percentiles of Wealth Distribution by Income Decile (Euro 1998 constant)

					Income in Decile Group					
All	I	II	III	IV	V	VI	VII	VIII	IX	X

Percentile point of net worth

	All	I	II	III	IV	V	VI	VII	VIII	IX	X
10	23,605	8,707	14,023	16,835	22,041	27,022	33,188	44,218	51,644	79,806	117,254
20	50,074	18,457	24,628	31,070	38,104	47,352	60,969	79,034	96,841	133,606	187,330
30	87,168	32,242	39,089	47,661	57,327	72,965	91,789	116,141	136,071	174,394	241,909
40	129,797	58,402	65,693	72,894	86,100	106,166	122,769	153,910	176,087	221,495	299,963
50	175,855	93,012	106,597	109,287	125,150	144,392	162,978	195,612	216,797	267,843	366,750
60	228,851	133,761	154,135	154,483	173,995	195,261	209,107	241,992	268,242	325,248	446,331
70	298,257	187,658	215,954	209,661	232,024	249,560	268,905	307,370	327,449	394,538	544,220
80	396,411	258,647	294,074	287,851	321,856	342,984	357,830	390,580	424,701	507,957	704,405
90	592,950	423,993	468,887	452,637	475,889	503,535	509,939	560,727	622,919	726,530	1,033,997

Percentile point of net financial assets

	All	I	II	III	IV	V	VI	VII	VIII	IX	X
10	8,044	1,673	3,733	5,470	7,723	9,138	12,871	13,128	16,089	22,781	30,247
20	17,826	5,921	9,975	12,807	15,445	18,598	21,881	25,098	27,866	37,647	50,840
30	27,286	10,618	15,960	19,306	22,524	26,385	30,890	34,944	38,613	50,840	70,146
40	37,583	16,217	22,524	26,064	30,890	34,237	39,707	44,405	50,969	65,899	89,710
50	49,231	23,489	29,860	33,722	39,900	43,375	49,746	55,602	64,355	81,988	115,130
60	64,355	32,821	39,771	43,375	48,909	54,380	61,780	68,344	78,255	101,809	141,580
70	85,978	47,108	55,023	57,919	63,067	70,404	79,156	86,943	100,908	127,551	182,960
80	122,274	67,830	83,275	82,760	87,393	99,749	106,185	119,056	137,075	170,604	243,646
90	192,677	111,977	137,075	141,065	143,768	165,455	157,669	175,044	205,934	250,854	352,148

Source: 1994 NSFIE.

Social security contributions are further divided into public pension contributions and health insurance. Let us define discretionary savings as savings in the RHS of Eq. (5.11) and mandatory savings as public pension contributions−public pension benefits + contributions to the severance pay fund + interests from social security wealth + interests from accumulated severance pay. For statistical simplicity, here we take mandatory savings simply as public pension contributions−public pension benefits (i.e., net public pension contributions), and ignore contributions to the severance pay fund, interests from social security wealth, and interests from accumulated severance pay. Then, it is obvious from the construction of Eq. (5.11) that discretionary savings are negatively correlated with mandatory savings. In addition, we calculate the crude ratio between mandatory savings and discretionary savings for different age groups. The results are given in Table 5.26.

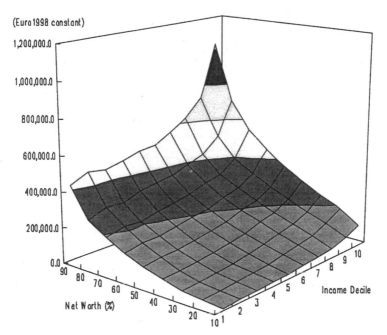

FIGURE 5.17   Distribution of net worth (for all households).

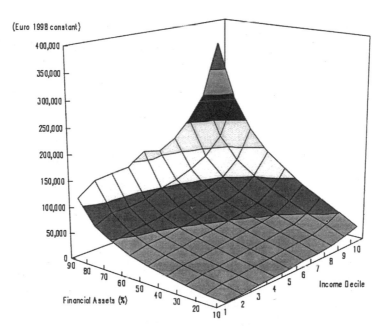

FIGURE 5.18   Distribution of financial assets (for all households).

TABLE 5.24   Decomposition of Net Worth Distribution in 1984

Household characteristics		Household share(%)	Wealth share(%)	T_w	$w_j \times T_w(j)$	T_b
All		100.0	100.0	0.923	—	—
Homeowner		74.2	95.0	0.656	0.798	0.113
Tenants		25.8	5.0	1.256	0.013	(12.2)
Age	−24	0.7	0.2	1.400	0.000	
	25−	4.7	1.5	0.890	0.004	
	30−	11.9	6.0	0.704	0.021	
	35−	16.2	11.4	0.771	0.062	
	40−	15.4	13.5	0.642	0.076	
	45−	13.4	13.9	0.643	0.093	0.077
	50−	12.0	14.1	0.587	0.097	(8.3)
	55−	10.4	15.1	0.701	0.154	
	60−	6.7	10.6	0.592	0.099	
	65−	4.5	7.5	0.513	0.189	
	70−	2.6	4.0	0.528	0.033	
	75+	1.5	2.4	0.558	0.021	
Region	Keihin area	24.5	32.3	0.933	0.397	
	(Tokyo area)					0.021
	Chukyo–Kinki area	21.6	23.1	1.189	0.294	(2.3)
	(Nagoya–Osaka area)					
	Other area	53.9	44.6	0.574	0.212	
Employers		63.2	48.9	0.611	0.231	0.047
Self-employee		30.9	44.7	0.953	0.616	(5.1)
Nonworking		5.9	6.4	0.424	0.029	
Income	−2	5.1	2.9	0.580	0.009	
(million yen)	2−	27.8	17.7	0.659	0.074	
	4−	33.5	27.1	0.488	0.107	0.147
	6−	18.1	20.3	0.424	0.097	(15.9)
	8−	8.5	12.8	0.392	0.076	
	10+	7.0	19.2	0.788	0.414	

Note: ( ) is the ratio T_b/T (%).

    It is apparent that the ratio becomes significantly negative for those aged above 60, i.e., cohorts 1–3. Cohort 1 in 1994 shows a substantially high positive value, which is because saving itself is negative, so that the ratio becomes positive. There is no surprise in the fact that cohort 1 in 1994 receives rather large net benefits; i.e., mandatory savings do matter with the old households. The ratio becomes negative

TABLE 5.25   Decomposition of Net Worth Distribution in 1994

Household characteristics		Household share(%)	Wealth share(%)	T_w	$w_j \times T_w(j)$	T_b
All		100.0	100.0	1.412		
Homeowner		73.8	95.2	1.047	1.286	0.118
Tenants		26.2	4.8	0.868	0.008	(8.4)
Age	−24	0.7	0.1	2.286	0.000	
	25−	3.9	1.0	2.244	0.006	
	30−	9.0	3.8	3.516	0.055	
	35−	11.8	6.8	2.125	0.083	
	40−	14.4	11.4	1.376	0.124	
	45−	14.4	13.6	0.860	0.111	0.086
	50−	13.1	14.3	0.971	0.152	(6.1)
	55−	10.7	13.8	1.419	0.254	
	60−	8.8	13.8	1.236	0.266	
	65−	7.3	11.2	0.928	0.160	
	70−	3.5	5.5	0.552	0.048	
	75+	2.6	4.7	0.760	0.065	
Region	Keihin area	27.0	35.9	1.368	0.653	
	(Tokyo area)					0.028
	Chukyo−Kinki area	22.3	24.6	1.568	0.426	(2.0)
	(Nagoya−Osaka area)					
	Other area	50.7	39.5	0.990	0.304	
Employers		73.2	64.1	1.430	0.802	0.022
Self-employee		14.4	18.5	1.818	0.434	(1.5)
Nonworking		12.4	17.4	0.631	0.154	
Income	−2	2.1	1.4	1.520	0.015	
(million yen)	2−	13.2	10.7	0.978	0.085	
	4−	23.6	17.3	1.905	0.242	0.046
	6−	22.0	18.1	1.121	0.167	(3.3)
	8−	15.9	17.2	2.327	0.435	
	10+	23.2	35.2	0.790	0.421	

Note: ( ) is the ratio T_b/T (%).

in overall average in 1989 and 1994, which implies that the balance of the public pension system as a whole becomes negative.

In the near future, generous public pension benefits in Japan are to be reduced, whereas the contribution rate may be permanently frozen at the current level or be reduced through a partial shift of funding to a consumption-based tax. At the same

TABLE 5.26   The Crude Ratio between Mandatory and Discretionary Savings (%)

		1984	1989	1994	1984–94
Cohort 1	(1920–24)	−315.55	−434.00	6,510.88	−779.95
Cohort 2	(1925–29)	−30.14	−277.11	−1,646.01	−264.71
Cohort 3	(1930–34)	25.82	−7.42	−270.87	−48.25
Cohort 4	(1935–39)	32.34	24.55	14.92	21.34
Cohort 5	(1940–44)	26.96	31.95	27.34	28.48
Cohort 6	(1945–49)	25.24	22.81	32.68	27.36
Cohort 7	(1950–54)	25.57	21.81	24.12	23.56
Cohort 8	(1955–59)	32.54	26.57	23.37	24.88
Cohort 9	(1960–64)	11.79	31.98	28.09	28.38
Average		8.66	−9.20	−14.36	−7.79

Note: The mandatory savings are defined as a difference between public pension contributions and its benefits, i.e., net public pension contributions. Those aged above 60 receive public pension benefits so that mandatory savings become negative.

Source: National Survey of Family Income and Expenditure, 1984, 1989, and 1994.

time, we should encourage private initiatives, including a private, personal saving account for retirement, through the use of powerful tax incentives.[13]

To construct social security wealth (SSW) as a measure for mandatory savings, we need to use the baseline equation as follows:

$$SSW_{t+1} = (1 + \rho)SSW_t + \tau_t - b_t \qquad (5.12)$$

where SSW is the social security wealth, ρ is the internal rate of return, τ_t is the public pension contribution, and b_t are public pension benefits.

First, the stream of public pension contributions can be calculated from the age–income profile multiplied by historical public pension contribution rates over the period of 1960–99. Secondly, the stream of public pension benefits is to be adjusted annually with inflation and is added up to the average life expectancy (from 2000 to 2022). Thirdly, we have to set $SSW_{t+R} = 0$ such that the internal rate of return equates two streams: public pension contributions and benefits under the pay-as-you-go system. At the age of retirement, 60 in the year 2000, SSW in Japan is estimated to equal ¥34.21 million (€218,000 [1998 constant] as €1 = ¥159.57 in 1998) and the nominal internal rate of return is 8.7% per year.

Given the average net financial assets (excluding SSW) for age 60–64 in 1994 was ¥20.42 million (€131,000 [1998 constant]), the estimated SSW ¥34.21 million (€218,000 [1998 constant]) is very large indeed, although the actual SSW is expected to be even larger than the estimated SSW.

---

[13]A Japanese version of the 401 k plan started in October 2001 (see Takayama, 2001).

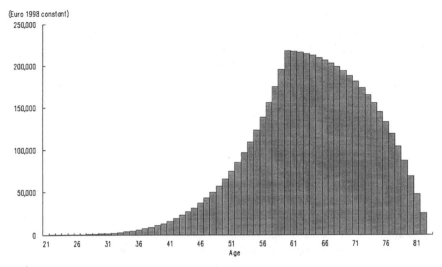

FIGURE 5.19 Social security wealth over life cycle.

As is obvious, the SSW includes a component of intergenerational transfers. If we assume that the market rate of return from investment was 5.5% in nominal terms per annum, and that the discount rate for the future SSW will be 4.0%, then, the estimated SSW will go up to ¥50.92 million (€324,000 [1998 constant]). This figure is rather common to the Japanese. Consequently, the component of intergenerational transfers in the SSW will turn out to be as much as ¥29.13 million (€185,600 [1998 constant]), in this case (see Figure 5.19).

5.9 CONCLUSION

This chapter confirms that most findings in Takayama and Kitamura (1994) are still valid. These include (1) variations in saving behavior across different income classes are much wider than those over the age profile within the same income class; (2) as income grows and wealth accumulation increases, richer households save at increasingly high rates over the age profile; and (3) diversity of saving behavior among elderly households is much greater than among younger households, as their employment status, homeownership, and financial asset holdings differ substantially. The richer elderly households keep saving at significantly positive rates.

In this sense, the bottom line of the household saving behavior remains the same after the burst of the bubble economy in the early 1990s.

Our new findings are as follows:

1. The cohort analysis indicates that the saving behavior follows, more or less, the same pattern of that of cross-sectional observations in respective years. The saving

rates of younger cohorts are stable, but this does not imply homogeneity of younger cohorts, but the degree of heterogeneity is more or less the same amongst the younger cohorts.

2. However, according to the 1989 and 1994 NSFIE, the baby-boomer cohort (age 40–44 in 1989 and 45–49 in 1994) has deviated from other younger cohorts. This phenomenon did not exist in the 1984 NSFIE when the baby-boomer cohort was age 35–39.

3. Estimated social security wealth (SSW) under the Japanese environment, is as much as ¥50.92 million (€324,000) at the age of retirement. The share of intergenerational transfers in the SSW is also very large.

The first point may be explained by the fact that increase in heterogeneity after age 55 (especially after 60) is mostly due to differences in lump-sum retirement severance payments or social security wealth. Variability of these benefits is much wider than that of regular monthly salaries, as the firms' economic performances, welfare plans for retirement severance pay funds, and unions' bargaining powers differ substantially among firms and organizations.

The second point is important because the baby-boomer cohort comprises the largest demographic group: hence, the behavior of this group significantly affects macroeconomic variables such as aggregate consumption, investment, and income distribution.

This leads to the third point. When the baby-boomer generation reaches their late fifties and early sixties, variability of retirement severance payments, of social security wealth, and of intergenerational transfers will be much wider than now. Intergenerational equity issues will inevitably be focused on the baby-boomer generation. It is quite crucial to set up institutional arrangements concerning intergenerational equity (e.g. public and private pension schemes) before the baby-boomer generation reaches their retirement age. This task is left to our future research project.

ACKNOWLEDGMENT

We are grateful to Dr Axel Börsch-Supan and to Richard Blundell, Fumio Hayashi, and Charles Yuji Horioka for their constructive comments on the early draft. We are also grateful to Michiko Baba for her efficient and skillful data processing. This research is partially financed by the grants from the Ministry of Education, Science and Culture, given to the Project on Intergenerational Equity (Director General, Professor Noriyuki Takayama) as one of the Scientific Researches Priority Areas.

REFERENCES

Barthold, T. and T. Ito (1991). Bequest taxes and accumulation of household wealth: U.S.–Japan comparison. In: T. Ito, and A. Kruger (eds), *The Political Economy of Tax Reform*. Chicago: The University of Chicago Press, 235–290.

Feldstein, M. (1974). Social security, induced retirement and aggregate capital accumulation. *Journal of Political Economy* 82(5), 905–926.

Hayashi, F. (1997). *Understanding Saving*. Cambridge: MIT Press.

Hayashi, F., A. Ando, and R. Ferris (1988a). Life cycle and bequest savings: A study of Japanese and U.S. households based on data from the 1984 NSFIE and the 1983 Survey of Consumer Finance. *Journal of the Japanese and International Economies* 2, 450–491.

Hayashi, F., T. Ito, and J. Slemrod (1988b). Housing finance imperfections, taxation, and private saving: A comparative simulation analysis of the United States and Japan. *Journal of the Japanese and International Economies* 2, 215–238.

Horioka, C.Y. (1990). Why is Japan's saving so high? A literature survey. *Journal of the Japanese and International Economies* 4, 49–92.

Horioka, C.Y. (1993). Savings in Japan. In: A. Heertje (ed.), *World Savings: An International Survey*. Oxford: Blackwell.

Horioka, C.Y. and W. Watanabe (1997). Why do people save? A micro-analysis of motives for household saving in Japan. *Economic Journal* 107, 537–552.

Kitamura, Y., N. Takayama, and F. Arita (2001). Household savings in Japan revisited. *Research in Economics* 55(2), 135–153.

Ohtake, F. (1991). Bequest motives of aged households in Japan. *Ricerche Economiche* 45(2/3), 283–306.

Ohtake, F. and C.Y. Horioka (2002). Saving motives in Japan. In: T. Ishikawa (ed.), *The Distribution of Income and Wealth in Japan*. Oxford: Oxford University Press.

Sterling, W. and S. Waite (1998). *Boomernomics*. New York: Balantine Books.

Takayama, N. (ed.) (1992a). *The Stock Economy* (in Japanese). Tokyo: Toyo-Keizai.

Takayama, N. (1992b). *The Greying of Japan; An Economic Perspective on Public Pensions*. Tokyo: Kinokuniya and Oxford: Oxford University Press.

Takayama, N. (2001). Pension reform in Japan at turn of the century. *Geneva Papers on Risk and Insurance* October.

Takayama, N. and Y. Kitamura (1994). Household saving behavior in Japan. In: J.M. Poterba (ed.), *International Comparisons of Household Saving*. Chicago: University of Chicago Press, 125–167.

Takayama, N. and Y. Kitamura (1999). Lessons from generational accounting in Japan. *American Economic Review* 89(2), 171–175.

Takayama, N., F. Funaoka, F. Ohtake, M. Sekiguchi, and T. Shibuya (1989). Household assets and the saving rate in Japan. *Keizai Bunseki* No.116 (in Japanese).

Takayama, N., Y. Kitamura, and H. Yoshida (1999). Generational accounting in Japan. In A.J. Auerbach, L.J. Kotlikoff, and W. Leibfritz (eds), *Generational Accounting around the World*. Chicago: University of Chicago Press, 447–469.

Toyoda, K. (1980). Decomposability of inequality measures. *Economic Studies Quarterly* 31(3), 207–216.

CHAPTER 6

Savings and Pensions in the Netherlands

Rob Alessie

Utrecht School of Economics (USE), Utrecht University, the Netherlands and Department of Economics, Vrije Universiteit Amsterdam, the Netherlands and Tinbergen Institute, the Netherlands

Arie Kapteyn

RAND Corporation, Santa Monica, California

6.1 INTRODUCTION

Much recent work on saving and consumption behavior has emphasized the importance of examining household data to study the predictions of the life cycle–permanent income model (LCH–PIH model). Simple versions of the LCH–PIH model predict, among other things, that (1) there is full displacement between discretionary saving and mandatory (contractual) saving and (2) that the elderly exhaust their wealth holdings. In this study we try to answer the question whether or not the two predictions above characterize (in part) the saving behavior of Dutch households.

To estimate the level of displacement between several forms of saving, it is useful to make a distinction between (1) mandatory saving, (2) notional saving, and (3) discretionary saving. Discretionary saving is defined as the changes in financial and real wealth of which magnitude and composition are under the control of the household. Mandatory saving is defined as changes in wealth through mandatory contributions to funded pension plans. Notional savings are contributions to pay-as-you-go (PAYG) systems such as public pensions and social insurance schemes. The displacement of discretionary saving by mandatory saving is of considerable policy interest. If there is full displacement, mandatory schemes are essentially superfluous and it can be left to private households to accumulate wealth to live off in old age. On the other hand, if there is (considerably) less than full displacement, mandatory schemes may be necessary to make sure that households save enough to be comfortable in old age.[1]

As we said before, according to the simple version of the LCH model, retired households dissave. This prediction cannot be tested by using cross-sectional data because cohort and age effects cannot be disentangled. However, we have longitudinal data at our disposal which permits us to construct cohort corrected age–saving profiles. This allows us to investigate whether or not people dissave during retirement.

This chapter is organized as follows. After a description of the data used (Section 6.2), the chapter describes, in Section 6.3, the distribution of income, notional and mandatory saving in the Netherlands. In Section 6.4 we present the distribution of discretionary saving and wealth across age and cohort. In the second part of the chapter (Section 6.5), we provide a short description of the Dutch pension and tax system. Moreover, we try to answer the question of whether the existence of an extensive pension and social insurance system displaces discretionary saving. The aggregate data provide some suggestive evidence in favor of this hypothesis: the so-called "free saving rate" (which excludes "contractual saving" through pension funds and life insurance companies) is very low in the Netherlands. Alessie *et al.* (2000) report that in the period 1985–97 (with the exception of 1989 and 1990) the total household saving rate was fairly constant and equal to about 12%. In the 1990s the contractual saving rate gradually increased from 10% to 12%. As a result, the free saving rate was low, with a decreasing trend towards zero. Although this decreasing trend in the free saving rate concomitant with an increase in contractual saving is suggestive of displacement, the low free saving rate can also be attributed to other factors such as the substantial capital gains households received in the 1990s due to the developments in the housing and stock markets. Therefore, we review in Section 6.5 somewhat more convincing evidence on the displacement issue based on longitudinal data. Inevitably, even this evidence is not that strong because during the 1980s and 1990s the Dutch pension system has not been restructured in a dramatic way and because the data sets do not contain that much information on the details of the respondents' occupational pension schemes. Therefore, comparing saving patterns across countries using micro data might help to identify more precisely the impact of notional and mandatory saving on discretionary saving.

---

[1]This argument leaves out the insurance aspect of mandatory schemes. To leave old-age provisions entirely to individual household decisions, there also have to exist well-functioning annuity markets, so that households can convert accumulated wealth into annuities upon retirement, for instance.

6.2 DATA

We mainly use data from the Socio-Economic Panel (SEP). The SEP is a longitudinal survey administered by Statistics Netherlands (CBS) consisting of approximately 5000 households. The purpose of the SEP, as summarized in CBS publications (see, for example, CBS, 1991), is to provide a description of the most important elements of individual and household welfare and to monitor changes in these elements. The SEP was launched in April 1984. The same households were interviewed in October 1984 and then twice a year (in April and October) until 1989. Since 1990, the survey has been conducted once a year in May. The survey is representative of the Dutch population, excluding those living in special institutions such as nursing homes. To arrive at a representative sample, Statistics Netherlands applied a two-stage sampling procedure to collect the initial April 1984 sample. In the first stage, municipalities were drawn with probabilities depending on the number of inhabitants (big cities were drawn with certainty). In the second stage, addresses were selected randomly. All households present at the selected address were interviewed, up to a maximum of three households. The initial rate of unit-nonresponse (i.e. the percentage of households, who refused to participate in the SEP) was equal to 50%. To address the problem of sample attrition, from 1986 onwards Statistics Netherlands regularly added new households to the SEP. The yearly attrition rate is equal to about 10%. To keep the sample as representative as possible, Statistics Netherlands refreshes the sample by replacing those households who have left the sample by "similar" households. In the case of refreshment samples, the rate of unit-nonresponse is equal to about 65%.

By contrast with the American Survey of Consumer Finances (SCF), wealthy households are not oversampled (see, for example, Avery *et al.*, 1988, for more information about the SCF). The SEP also does not have a low income supplement as is the case with the Panel Study of Income Dynamics (PSID).

In the October interviews, information has been collected at the respondent level[2] on socioeconomic characteristics, income, and labor market participation. The April interviews also contain information about socioeconomic characteristics, but rather than gathering data about income, since 1987 the April questionnaires have included questions on a wide range of assets and liabilities. More details about the income and wealth data of the SEP can be found in Appendix 1. In this chapter, we present summary statistics on net worth, financial wealth, and real wealth. Net worth is obtained by subtracting total liabilities from total assets. We also analyze financial wealth holdings. Financial wealth has been defined as the difference between net worth, on the one hand, and housing equity (value of the primary residence plus life insurance mortgage minus remaining mortgage debt), other real estate, and the value of the cars, on the other hand. Real wealth is defined to be the difference between net worth and financial wealth.

---

[2]A respondent is a member of the household who is at least 16 years old.

The SEP does not contain direct information on the following asset components:

1. cash holdings;
2. the cash value of whole life insurances (except the life insurance mortgage[3]) and of privately purchased annuity insurances;
3. social security wealth;
4. occupational pension wealth (see Appendix 1 for more details).

For this study we have made the following sample selections:

1. composite households and households of which the head is younger than 20 years[4] are excluded from the analysis;
2. the self-employed are removed altogether from the sample because no wealth data have been collected for this group.

Sleijpe and Dirven (1999) have compared the income data of the SEP with those of the Income Panel Survey (IPS). This is a large survey (75,000 households), based on administrative records from the income and wealth tax register, supplemented with some information from the SEP. Sleijpe and Dirven (1999) have found that the distribution of disposable household income does not differ much across the two samples.

The income data are measured more precisely than the stock data (wealth). Alessie and Kapteyn (1999) have compared the wealth data of the SEP with those of the IPS. If one takes the IPS figures as the reference point, the SEP underestimates average net worth by 20%. A part of this underestimation has been caused by the fact that the SEP does not observe the wealth holding of the self-employed. However, the study of Alessie and Kapteyn (1999) also suggests that stock and bond holdings are severely underreported in the SEP.[5] One should keep in mind that the IPS figure on stock and bond holdings includes stocks from a substantial holding.[6]

---

[3]See Appendix 1 for more details about life insurance mortgages.

[4]In the SEP the head of the household is in principle defined to be the husband in the case of married couples.

[5]Just recently, Statistics Netherlands published the National Accounts for the year 1998. For the first time, the National Accounts include the Flows of Funds Statement for the sector "households." Comparison of the NA data with the IPS suggests that even in the IPS the average value of stock holdings might be underestimated (see Alessie et al., 2000, for more details about this comparison).

[6]In the note "Taxation in the Netherlands" of the Ministry of Finance (see http://www.minfin.nl) the term income from a substantial holding in a corporation is described as follows: a taxpayer is regarded as having a substantial holding in a corporation if he or she, either alone or with his or her spouse, holds directly or indirectly 5% of the issued capital. If the corporation has issued different classes of shares, a substantial holding also exists if the taxpayer, either alone or with his or her spouse, holds more than 5% of the issued capital of a particular class of shares. If the taxpayer holds a substantial interest in a corporation, jouissance rights and debt–claims issued by that corporation and held directly or indirectly by the taxpayer, either alone or with his or her spouse, are regarded as forming part of the substantial holding.

Typically, these stocks are not listed on the Dutch exchange. Given the way the SEP question on stock holdings has been phrased, we suspect that, in particular the stocks from a substantial holding are severely underreported by the SEP respondents. A comparison with another Dutch dataset, the CentER Savings Survey (CSS), also suggests that the ownership rate of stocks and mutual funds is substantially underestimated in the SEP.[7] Finally, the underestimation of average net worth is also partly due to the fact that in the SEP checking and saving accounts balances are underreported.

The SEP does not contain information on consumption expenditures. Consequently, the SEP can only measure saving by taking the first difference of net worth. This saving measure therefore includes (unrealized) capital gains. We will also use data from the Dutch Consumer Expenditure Survey (CES) in order to obtain a "residual" saving measure, defined as the difference between income and consumption. Appendix 1 provides some information about the CES.

6.3 THE DISTRIBUTION OF INCOME AND WEALTH

Although the pension and tax system will be described more fully in Section 6.5, it is useful to note that old-age provisions in the Netherlands essentially consist of three tiers: the first tier is social security (SS); the second tier consists of mandatory occupational pensions; and the third tier consists of private savings.

In this section we pay attention to the distribution of the gross income and private wealth of households and to the definition and distribution of mandatory and notional saving. The private wealth measure does not include social security wealth (SSW) and occupational pension wealth (PW). To investigate the displacement between private (discretionary) wealth and SSW and PW, it would have been nice to have measures for PW and SSW. However, given the scarce information in the SEP on pensions and the heterogeneity of the occupational pension schemes, it is difficult to construct a variable which could serve as a proxy for PW: see Alessie *et al.* (1997b) and Euwals (1999) for an effort to compute PW. Therefore, in this chapter we abstain from such an exercise.

In this section, we mainly perform a cross-sectional analysis for which we have used the 1996 wave of the SEP. However, it is well known that in a cross section one cannot disentangle cohort from age effects. Therefore, we also perform a cohort analysis, similar to, for example, Attanasio (1998), on disposable income and (financial) wealth.

---

[7] According to the SEP the 1996 ownership rate of stocks and mutual funds is equal to 13.2% and according to the CSS 23.7% (see Alessie *et al.*, 2000).

TABLE 6.1   Total Gross Income (in euros) by Age in 1995[a]

Age class	No. observations	Mean	Standard error	q1	q2	q3
20–24	208	16,545	1,492	6,036	9,415	21,359
25–29	366	35,075	1,012	20,779	33,894	47,772
30–34	434	46,374	1,175	32,090	44,726	57,858
35–39	508	51,200	1,533	34,460	45,782	62,257
40–44	505	51,782	1,313	34,980	48,740	64,484
45–49	436	52,630	1,526	32,669	47,935	66,596
50–54	334	53,503	1,764	33,100	48,114	66,358
55–59	265	45,928	1,677	25,790	41,593	59,283
60–64	256	35,672	2,061	18,688	28,159	41,964
65–69	316	23,344	785	13,417	18,786	30,542
70–74	253	23,202	1,515	12,755	17,588	24,412
75–79	192	18,213	872	10,891	14,496	19,709
80+	161	18,348	1,110	11,096	13,562	20,341
Total	4,234	40,241	461	18,133	35,979	53,978

Source: own calculations on the SEP.
[a]q1 = first quartile, q2 = median, q3 = third quartile.

Gross Household Income

In Table 6.1 we present the distribution of gross household income by age for the year 1995.[8] The variable "gross income" includes the following components: wages, asset income, benefits of PAYG and funded pensions, public non-transfer income, and net private transfers. More details about the construction of the variable "gross household income" and its components can be found in Appendix 1. Capital gains are not included in asset income. From Table 6.1 the following conclusions can be drawn:

- Average gross income is equal to €40,240.[9] Not surprisingly, median income is somewhat lower (€35,980), indicating that the distribution of gross income is rightly skewed.
- Average and median income rise sharply with age until about age 35. Between ages 35 and 54 average income is fairly constant; it drops considerably between ages 55 and 64 and even more after the mandatory retirement age of 65. We will explain these phenomena later when we look at the breakdown of

[8]The 1996 wave of the SEP has been used to construct this table.
[9]All amounts reported in the chapter (including the tables and graphs) are expressed in 1998 euros (€). We have converted the "1998" Dutch guilder to 1998 euro via the 1998 dollar ppp.

gross income. In any case, it should be realized that cohort and age effects are not disentangled in Table 6.1 (or in any other table presented in this section). After age 75 average and median gross income decrease even further, because household size becomes smaller after that age and consequently one receives less pension.

A breakdown of gross income into a number of components is presented in Table 6.2. The component shares sum to 100% by row. From Table 6.2 it can be seen that until 55 wages are the most important component of gross income: between ages 25 and 50 the average wage share varies between about 80 and 95%. Due to the generous (pay-as-you-go) early retirement schemes (introduced at the beginning of the 1980s) and disability schemes, it is rather attractive to stop working after about age 60: see, for example, Kapteyn and de Vos (1998). Therefore, average gross income and the average wage share drop dramatically after age 55 and especially after age 60. The wage share is virtually equal to zero after the mandatory retirement age of 65. On average, asset income does not seem to be an important income component for most age groups.

After age 65, gross income basically consists only of pensions (including social security). Asset income is on average a rather small income component for the

TABLE 6.2   Distribution of Total Gross Income (in euros) by Age in 1995[a]

Age class	totinc	wage	assetinc	SS-inc	pension	priv. transf.	pub. trans.
20–24	16,545	78	0	0	0	7	15
25–29	35,075	91	1	0	0	2	6
30–34	46,374	93	1	0	0	1	5
35–39	51,200	90	1	0	0	2	7
40–44	51,782	90	1	0	0	2	8
45–49	52,630	89	1	1	0	1	8
50–54	53,503	86	1	2	0	1	10
55–59	45,928	71	2	6	3	2	15
60–64	35,672	18	5	40	7	4	26
65–69	23,344	9	4	46	35	1	4
70–74	23,202	4	4	48	41	1	2
75–79	18,213	3	3	59	34	0	1
80+	18,348	3	8	56	32	0	1
Total	40,241	75	2	9	5	2	8

Source: own calculations on the SEP.

[a]This table reports the share (%) of each income component in total gross income: totinc = gross income (average amount); wage = gross earnings; assetinc = capital income; SS-inc = annuitized pay-as-you-go pensions; pension = annuitized pension income; priv. transf. = net private transfers; pub. trans. = public non-pension transfer income.

retired (about 5% of gross income). From Table 6.2 it becomes clear that, for the retired, SS is on average a more important income component than the annuitized funded pensions. Its share in gross income is on average equal to 47% for those retired who are younger than 75 and even 59% for those between 75 and 79.

Mandatory Saving

In the Netherlands mandatory saving consists of employers' and employees' contribution to (mandatory) occupational funded pension plans.[10] It should be stressed that in this chapter annuitized pension income is treated as income and not as dissaving. In this respect we adopt the definitions put forward by Brugiavini and Weber (see Chapter 2) and, consequently, we do not follow the convention of the National Accounts.

Pension premiums are not directly observed in the SEP. Therefore we have imputed these premiums. There is considerable variety in occupational pension schemes. Hence, the imputation of pension premiums is a rather tricky exercise. The SEP contains enough information to identify (former) civil servants. For civil servants and former civil servants who currently receive a UI benefit or an early retirement benefit, it is possible to impute the pension premiums rather precisely.

The imputation exercise is much more difficult for the majority of employees who are not civil servants or former civil servants (about 70%), i.e., those working in the private sector (and former private sector employees who currently receive an early retirement benefit). Basically, we have adopted a crude imputation formula used by the Netherlands Bureau for Economic Policy Analysis (CPB) in its microtax simulation model (see www.cpb.nl). The CPB has estimated two premium percentages (12.47% for the employer part and 4.59% for the employee part) from data of the National Accounts. CPB assumes that pension premiums are only levied on wage income above a threshold of €12,722 (= gross minimum wage in 1995). Most pension funds apply such a threshold in determining the premiums. Although the CPB assumptions are reasonable, their procedure does not take into account the variation in premium percentages and thresholds in the private sector. Therefore, our figures for mandatory pension premiums should be interpreted with care.

Table 6.3 summarizes the distribution of mandatory saving by age. Average (median) mandatory saving is equal to €2066 (€1292). Average mandatory saving appears to be highest in the age range 35–55 (around €3400). Obviously, for the retired (>65) households mandatory saving is virtually equal to zero. Since most households in the age range 20–24 do not earn very much, they do not need to pay pension premiums because of the existence of the threshold.

---

[10]Most pension funds do not allow their clients to make a lump sum withdrawal.

TABLE 6.3   Mandatory Saving by Age in 1995[a]

Age class	No. observations	Mean	Standard error	q1	q2	q3
20–24	208	519	167	0	0	264
25–29	366	1,540	77	121	1,368	2,318
30–34	434	2,663	116	1,434	2,321	3,457
35–39	508	3,345	186	1,555	2,643	4,280
40–44	505	3,412	160	1,590	2,759	4,361
45–49	436	3,351	183	1,296	2,664	4,424
50–54	334	3,455	220	639	2,761	4,791
55–59	265	2,428	177	0	1,559	3,963
60–64	256	679	91	0	0	669
65–69	316	119	31	0	0	0
70–74	253	58	25	0	0	0
75–79	192	26	21	0	0	0
80+	161	39	31	0	0	0
Total	4,234	2,066	49	0	1,292	3,179

Source: own calculations on the SEP.
[a]q1 = first quartile, q2 = median, q3 = third quartile.

Notional Saving (Contributions to PAYG Systems)

Notional saving is equal to the contribution to all pay-as-you-go systems, or the sum of:

1. Employees' mandatory contributions to unfunded pension plans:
   a. SS [AOW], tax in 1995: 14.55% of taxable personal income up to a maximum of €20,125 (see Appendix 1 for an explanation of "taxable personal income").
   b. General widows' and orphans' pensions [AWW], tax in 1995: 1.80% of taxable personal income up to a maximum of €20,125.
2. Employees' mandatory contributions to other unfunded schemes (e.g., health and LTC insurance):
   a. General disability pension [AAW], tax in 1995: 6.30% of taxable personal income up to a maximum of €20,125.
   b. Special health cost act [AWBZ], tax in 1995: 8.55% of taxable personal income up to a maximum of €20,125 (plus a small nominal premium).
   c. Sick fund insurance (employee part).[11]

[11]Employees with an income below a certain threshold have a mandatory health insurance, the so-called sick fund.

       d. Payroll tax (employee part), consisting of short-term unemployment bene-
         fits [WW]; UI benefits for the civil servants; disability benefits [WAO];
         invalidity pension for ex-civil servants; and sickness benefits [ZW].
   3. Employers' mandatory contributions to other unfunded schemes:
       a. Sick fund insurance (employers' part).
       b. Social insurance premiums (employers' part).
   4. Employees' voluntary contributions to other unfunded schemes:
       a. Premium for private health insurance.

Concerning the definition of notional saving, we follow the convention adopted in this book: income from pay-as-you-go schemes is treated as income and not as dissaving.[12] None of the components mentioned above are directly observed in the SEP. However, given the rich income information in the SEP and given the relevant premium and payroll tax percentages, it is possible to impute most components of notional saving rather precisely. This is not true for the premium for private health insurance (or for possible employer's contribution to an employee's private health insurance). Persons with a "gross" personal income (net of occupational pension premiums) below €26,750 are compulsory insured through the sick fund. This implies that private health insurances are only relevant for persons with an income above €26,750. Data from the SEP suggest that basically everyone of this group is covered by a private health insurance policy. We have adopted the CPB procedure of imputing the premium of a so-called "standard health insurance policy," including the employer's contribution. As with the imputation of pension premiums, this procedure does not take into account the considerable variation in the employers' contributions and in the private health insurance policies.

Table 6.4 shows that the average level of notional saving (€9765) is similar to its median (€10,647). Between ages 25 and 60 the average share of notional saving in gross household income is fairly constant at 27% (see Table 6.7). The notional saving rate drops precipitously after age 65. This is largely due to the fact that the retired do not pay taxes for most social insurances – SS, disability, unemployment – and the insurance for earnings loss as a result of illness. Since mean or median gross income do not vary much in the age range 35–55 (see Table 6.1) and given the fairly constant notional saving rate, the average level of notional saving is also fairly constant in this age range (around €13,000, see Table 6.4). It drops considerably after age 65 to around €2500.

If we look at the breakdown of notional saving (see Table 6.5), it appears that "employees' mandatory contributions to other unfunded schemes" is the most important component, followed by "employees' mandatory contributions to unfunded pension systems" and "employers' mandatory contributions to other

---

[12]If one treats income from PAYG schemes, like SS and UI, as dissaving, notional saving should be effectively equal to zero in the aggregate. We have checked in our (imputed) data set whether the average SS (UI) contributions are equal to the average income from SS and UI. The average contributions appear to be slightly higher (approximately 10%).

TABLE 6.4 Notional Saving (Contribution to PAYG Systems) by Age in 1995[a]

Age class	No. observations	Mean	Standard error	q1	q2	q3
20–24	208	4,095	327	1,196	1,411	6,574
25–29	366	10,656	317	6,292	10,916	14,870
30–34	434	13,432	262	10,380	12,640	17,520
35–39	508	13,096	234	10,556	12,855	15,941
40–44	505	13,044	233	10,880	13,152	15,942
45–49	436	13,319	277	10,423	13,152	16,391
50–54	334	13,271	306	10,638	13,082	16,245
55–59	265	11,501	330	7,423	12,076	13,918
60–64	256	8,403	287	5,127	8,008	9,997
65–69	316	2,731	154	1,150	1,842	3,504
70–74	253	2,277	136	1,027	1,642	2,888
75–79	192	1,844	124	935	1,282	2,373
80+	161	1,805	137	856	1,220	2,448
Total	4,234	9,765	103	3,160	10,647	13,822

Source: own calculations on the SEP.

[a]q1 = first quartile, q2 = median, q3 = third quartile.

unfunded schemes." Voluntary contributions to unfunded schemes (= premium private health insurance) are small. This is the direct consequence of the fact that most persons are covered by the mandatory sick fund scheme. As we have said before, only persons with higher incomes (above €26,750) have to buy a private health insurance. It appears that 33% of the households have at least one private health insurance policy. Consequently, the distributions of the employees' and employers' contributions to private health insurance are rightly skewed and the averages are rather low.

Disposable Income, Notional and Mandatory Saving Rates

Disposable household income is obtained by subtracting taxes, notional and mandatory saving from gross household income. Table 6.6 presents the distribution of disposable household income by age. Average disposable income is equal to €24,000 and somewhat higher than the median (€22,000). The shape of the age profile of disposable income is similar to that of gross household income. Its average level rises quickly until age 35, to a level of about €27,000, remains fairly constant until age 55, drops somewhat after age 60 (early retirement), age 65 (mandatory retirement age), and after age 75 (due to a decrease in average family size).

TABLE 6.5   Distribution (%) of Notional Saving (in euros) by Age in 1995[a]

Age class	notsav	SS–tax	social ins. tax	employer's cont.	vol. soc. ins.
20–24	4,095	29	44	15	11
25–29	10,656	32	49	17	2
30–34	13,432	31	51	16	2
35–39	13,096	31	51	14	4
40–44	13,044	31	52	14	4
45–49	13,319	31	51	14	4
50–54	13,271	31	51	13	4
55–59	11,501	33	50	13	4
60–64	8,403	39	47	10	4
65–69	2,731	18	64	5	13
70–74	2,277	16	67	3	14
75–79	1,844	15	70	1	14
80+	1,805	15	68	1	16
Total	9,765	31	51	14	4

Source: own calculations on the SEP.

[a]notsav = notional saving (average amount); SS-tax = employee's mandatory contribution to unfunded pension systems; social ins. tax = employee's mandatory contributions to other unfunded schemes; employer's cont. = employer's mandatory contributions to other unfunded schemes; vol. soc. ins. = employee's voluntary contribution to other unfunded schemes.

Again, we wish to point out that on the basis of a cross section no conclusions can be drawn concerning the life-cycle profile of disposable income. The hump-shaped profile may be caused by cohort effects, e.g. stemming from productivity growth. Therefore we exploit in Figures 6.1a and 6.1b the longitudinal nature of the SEP. In these figures, we plot median and mean disposable income (expressed in 1990 prices) from 1985 to 1996 for each 5-year-of-birth-cohort.[13] For clarity, the graphs only indicate the average year when the head of the household was born (e. g., "38" refers to heads of households born between 1936 and 1940). The vertical difference

[13]In 1990, Statistics Netherlands revised the income part of the SEP questionnaire considerably. Before the 1990 wave, the SEP questionnaire contained for each component questions about net income, earned last month. From the 1990 wave onwards, the SEP collected for most income components information on "gross income" of the previous calendar year. For instance, the 1990 wave of the SEP contains information on income of the calendar year 1989. See Appendix 1 for more details. Obviously, the revision of the SEP questionnaire hampers the comparability over time of the income figures considerably. However, notice that we effectively have two observations on disposable income in 1989. This allows us to assess the effect of the revision of the income questionnaire. From Figures 6.1a and 6.1b it becomes apparent that the revision of the questionnaire has only a small effect on median disposable income. However, for the young and middle-aged cohorts the revision of the questionnaire has a sizable impact on average disposable income.

TABLE 6.6   Total Disposable Income (in euros) by Age in 1995[a]

Age class	No. observations	Mean	Standard error	q1	q2	q3
20–24	208	10,747	681	5,123	8,048	13,231
25–29	366	20,828	557	12,737	20,028	28,140
30–34	434	26,524	584	18,470	25,946	32,273
35–39	508	28,905	693	20,110	27,161	34,562
40–44	505	29,536	645	20,295	28,191	36,024
45–49	436	29,420	721	19,378	27,510	36,308
50–54	334	29,214	831	18,973	26,650	37,105
55–59	265	25,806	868	16,259	23,901	32,165
60–64	256	21,940	1,538	12,224	17,721	25,625
65–69	316	18,455	508	11,614	15,729	23,657
70–74	253	18,001	789	11,113	15,197	20,242
75–79	192	14,758	552	9,347	12,720	17,108
80+	161	14,520	634	9,455	11,999	16,390
Total	4,234	23,988	232	13,735	21,867	31,140

Source: own calculations on the SEP.
[a]q1 = first quartile, q2 = median, q3 = third quartile.

between lines measures the "cohort–time" effect. The difference along a line measures the "age–time" effect.[14] Figures 6.1a and 6.1b suggest that (except for the old generations) a cohort–time effect is present. The study of Kapteyn *et al.* (1999) suggests that this cohort–time effect can be partly attributed to productivity growth. Figures 6.1a and 6.1b also suggest that (after a cohort correction) the age–income profile is still hump shaped, with a top around age 57.

Table 6.7 presents the average notional and mandatory saving rates and the average tax rate by age. From Table 6.7 it can be inferred that the wedge between gross household income and disposable income is fairly constant at a level of 45% in the age range 30–55. The wedge decreases considerably after age 65, mainly because the retired do not pay any occupational pension premiums (which falls under mandatory saving) and any SS and social insurance premiums (part of notional saving). In the age range 30–55 the mandatory saving rate is equal to about 5%.

Financial Wealth, Real Wealth, Net Worth

Tables 6.8, 6.9, and 6.10 summarize for the year 1996 the age gradient of the distribution of net worth, financial wealth, and real wealth, respectively. According to

[14]We use this terminology to emphasize that it is not possible to disentangle age from cohort and time effects in these figures. See also below.

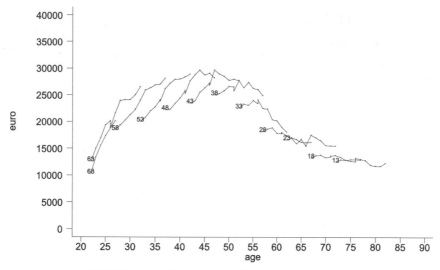

FIGURE 6.1a   Median disposable income by age and cohort.

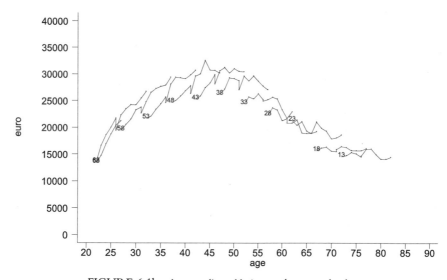

FIGURE 6.1b   Average disposable income by age and cohort.

Table 6.8, the distribution of net worth is rightly skewed and very dispersed: average net worth (€63,095) is clearly greater than median net worth (€27,135). Alessie and Kapteyn (1999) have shown that, in contrast with the United States, wealth inequality decreased in the Netherlands between 1987 and 1996. They suggest that the positive trend in the homeownership rate and the increasing house

TABLE 6.7   Notional and Mandatory Saving Rates (%) by Age[a]

Age class	totinc	mandsav	notsav	inctax	dispinc
20–24	16,545	3	25	7	65
25–29	35,075	4	30	6	59
30–34	46,374	6	29	8	57
35–39	51,200	7	26	11	56
40–44	51,782	7	25	11	57
45–49	52,630	6	25	12	56
50–54	53,503	6	25	14	55
55–59	45,928	5	25	13	56
60–64	35,672	2	24	13	62
65–69	23,344	1	12	9	79
70–74	23,202	0	10	12	78
75–79	18,213	0	10	9	81
80+	18,348	0	10	11	79
Total	40,241	5	24	11	60

Source: own calculations on the SEP.

[a]totinc = gross income (average amount) in euros; notsav = notional saving; mandsav = mandatory saving; inctax = income tax; dispinc = disposable income.

prices may explain why median net worth has increased so much between 1987 and 1996.[15] For the median household the share of housing equity in total net worth is considerably larger (especially in 1996) than for households in the top decile in the wealth distribution. Thus, the increase in the house prices is relatively less important for the rich than for the median household, which in turn might explain the decreasing tendency in wealth inequality between 1987 and 1996. To back up their claim, Alessie and Kapteyn (1999) have also investigated the distribution of financial wealth. The figures do not show a negative trend in financial wealth inequality.

From Table 6.9 one can infer that the value of median financial wealth (€4600 in 1998 prices) is low. Jappelli and Pistafferri (1999) also report a rather low, though somewhat higher, number for median financial wealth (€7350) in Italy. In contrast to our financial wealth measure, they include the cash values of life insurances and of defined contribution pension plans and "foreign assets." Moreover, in contradistinction to our procedure, Jappelli and Pistafferri (1999) do not subtract consumer credit from their financial wealth measure. Finally, they have included the self-employed (compared with the Netherlands relatively many

[15]Between 1987 and 1996 the homeownership rate rose considerably from 42.7% to 50.5%. According to data of the Society of Real Estate Agents the average price of houses sold rose from €69,500 in 1987 to €119,000 in 1996.

TABLE 6.8   Net Worth (in euros) by Age in 1996[a]

Age class	No. observations	Mean	Standard error	q1	q2	q3
20–24	210	3,421	568	−248	1,439	5,469
25–29	370	19,172	1,689	36	8,124	29,389
30–34	440	45,707	3,092	5,475	29,270	69,734
35–39	509	63,735	3,540	6,678	47,213	92,674
40–44	516	68,438	3,275	9,611	52,481	99,156
45–49	438	70,161	3,951	7,962	48,154	112,399
50–54	348	94,632	8,233	13,227	73,067	132,877
55–59	270	102,819	9,435	7,544	60,470	136,123
60–64	262	83,009	7,396	4,471	35,213	123,661
65–69	313	72,848	6,214	3,269	20,902	108,277
70–74	245	71,698	7,142	4,946	14,345	109,811
75–79	184	50,045	7,404	2,448	8,143	50,279
80+	151	66,941	10,654	2,057	6,925	70,734
Total	4,256	63,095	1,551	3,463	27,135	92,186

Source: own calculations on the SEP.
[a]q1 = first quartile, q2 = median, q3 = third quartile.

more people are self-employed in Italy). On balance, therefore the differences between Italy and the Netherlands may not be that large.

Table 6.8 shows that there exists a clear hump-shaped age profile for median net worth, with a peak in the age range 50–54. In comparison with households in their middle ages, median net worth is rather low for the young and old households. One can also observe a hump-shaped pattern in the age profile of average net worth with a peak around age 55. After age 60, average net worth decreases at a much slower pace than median net worth. From Table 6.8, one can compute the interquartile distance $((p75-p25)/p50)$. This inequality measure suggests that, among the old, wealth inequality is much greater than among the young. In contrast to net worth, we do not observe a clear hump-shaped age pattern in median and average financial wealth.

From Table 6.8 one could be tempted to conclude that people dissave after retirement as the standard life-cycle model predicts. To verify this, we plot in Figures 6.2a and 6.2b median and mean net worth (expressed in 1987 prices) from 1987 to 1996 for each 5-year-of-birth-cohort. The figures show that there are substantial cohort–time effects as well as age–time effects in total net worth. Within the same cohort, both mean and median net worth are steadily increasing over time. This is particularly true for the young cohorts but, even for some elderly cohorts, mean net worth, mean and median financial wealth (see Figures 6.3a and 6.3b) continue to increase over time (median net worth remains fairly constant for

TABLE 6.9 Financial Wealth (in euros) by Age in 1996[a]

Age class	No. observations	Mean	Standard error	q1	q2	q3
20–24	210	1,084	445	−1,484	693	2,572
25–29	370	4,558	1,028	−1,875	1,532	8,205
30–34	440	8,351	1,122	205	3,215	11,741
35–39	509	12,809	1,726	247	4,514	12,881
40–44	516	11,647	1,315	212	4,487	13,929
45–49	438	13,538	1,709	290	4,686	15,482
50–54	348	16,820	1,770	481	6,923	21,956
55–59	270	29,475	5,212	619	7,573	25,524
60–64	262	19,868	2,472	1,325	7,163	25,425
65–69	313	21,226	2,705	1,376	6,276	21,248
70–74	245	27,828	3,549	2,895	8,805	21,764
75–79	184	17,861	3,197	1,484	5,290	20,157
80+	151	30,492	5,586	1,980	5,936	22,062
Total	4,256	15,136	653	495	4,600	15,152

[a]q1 = first quartile, q2 = median, q3 = third quartile.

TABLE 6.10 Real Wealth (in euros) by Age in 1996[a]

Age class	No. observations	Mean	Standard error	q1	q2	q3
20–24	210	2,336	31	0	0	989
25–29	370	14,615	67	0	2,968	17,313
30 34	440	37,355	120	2,162	19,792	57,323
35–39	509	50,926	125	3,957	38,834	76,958
40–44	516	56,791	120	3,463	45,855	84,957
45–49	438	56,623	149	3,957	40,493	90,319
50–54	348	77,812	415	4,946	58,522	110,404
55–59	270	73,344	351	3,957	53,221	108,920
60–64	262	63,141	394	742	12,366	98,861
65–69	313	51,621	263	0	6,925	88,541
70–74	245	43,870	296	0	2,968	86,563
75–79	184	32,183	375	0	0	10,017
80+	151	36,449	568	0	0	7,420
Total	4,256	47,960	19	76	12,861	76,546

[a]q1 = first quartile, q2 = median, q3 = third quartile.

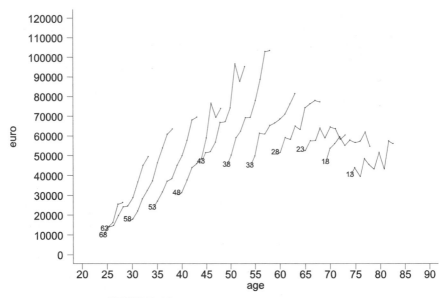

FIGURE 6.2a   Mean net worth by age and cohort.

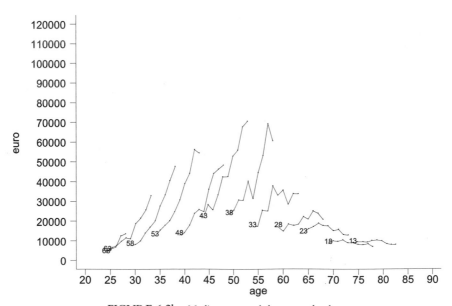

FIGURE 6.2b   Median net worth by age and cohort.

old cohorts).[16] The increase in mean total net worth over the 10-year period is as big as €60,000 for the 1936–40 cohort. Altogether we see little evidence for a hump-shaped life-cycle pattern of net worth. The fact that mean and median net worth increase for most cohorts (except the old ones) in a "parallel" way suggests that time effects may be important. Such a time effect may be due, for example, to common macro shocks, changes in housing prices, and the increase in homeownership rates.[17] Figures 6.4a, 6.4b, and Figure 6.5a suggest that there are some strong cohort–time effects in the homeownership rates and average and median real wealth, even between the young cohorts (the difference in the homeownership rates between the 1963 and 1958 generations). Obviously, the strong cohort effects are the main cause for the very hump-shaped cross-sectional age–homeownership profile (Table 6.11).[18]

Although important, homeownership is, however, not solely responsible for the existence of cohort–time effects in total net worth. In Figures 6.3a and 6.3b we report financial wealth and show that cohort–time effects are also present in the mean and median of this more restrictive measure of wealth.

Figures 6.2a and 6.2b clearly illustrate that on the basis of cross-sectional evidence (e.g. Tables 6.8, 6.9, and 6.10) one cannot answer the question whether or not people dissave after retirement. In contrast with Table 6.8, the figures suggest that the elderly do not dissave; see, however, footnote 16.

6.4 FINANCIAL, REAL, AND DISCRETIONARY SAVING

So far, we have exploited mainly the cross-sectional variation in the data. Let us now have a more in-depth look at longitudinal patterns. By looking at changes in net worth, financial, and real wealth, we can calculate savings, as in Avery and Kennickell (1991). After having calculated such (discretionary) saving measures, we can relate them to the notional and mandatory saving measures presented in the previous section.

There are some problems with such saving measures. The first problem is related to the way the different SEP waves have been merged. The second problem is measurement error.

[16]The age–time effects of the old cohorts (especially the cohort 1910–15) should be interpreted with care because the estimate of the age–time could be biased for reasons of differential mortality: survival probabilities are known to be positively correlated with wealth, implying that rich households are overrepresented in the oldest cohorts (see, e.g., Smith, 1999). This correlation implies that one may find a low rate of decumulation after retirement simply because the poor tend to disappear from the sample earlier than the rich.

[17]There is another potential cause for the existence of these time effects. It is possible that the amount of measurement error, and particularly underreporting of wealth, is decreasing over time.

[18]Figures 6.5b and 6.5c and Table 6.11 give some information about some other relevant background variables: employment status of the head of household and family size.

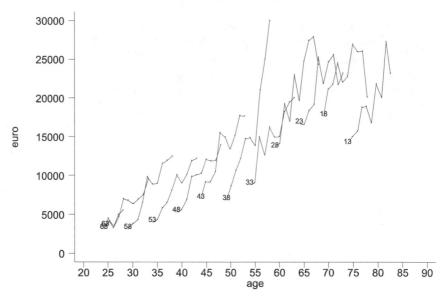

FIGURE 6.3a   Mean financial wealth by age and cohort.

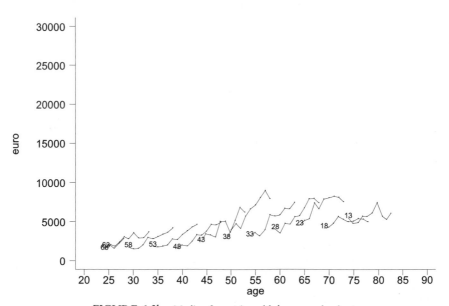

FIGURE 6.3b   Median financial wealth by age and cohort.

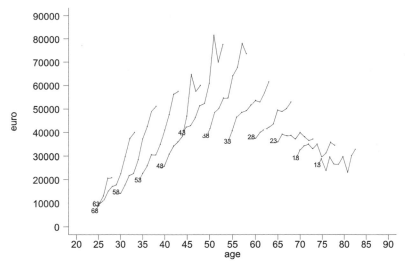

FIGURE 6.4a   Mean real wealth by age and cohort.

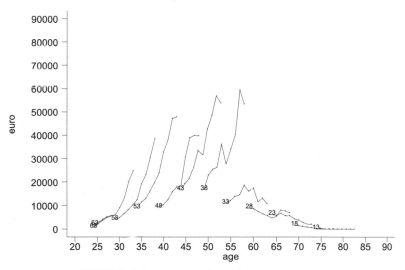

FIGURE 6.4b   Median real wealth by age and cohort.

The data were merged by means of the variable *khnr*, which is in principle the identification number of the head of the household.[19] If a household breaks up, the SEP follows both new households. The household to which the (former) head belongs continues to retain the original identification number. The other household

---

[19]For married or cohabiting couples, the head of the household is the male. For single-parent households, the head is the parent.

TABLE 6.11   Covariates by Age in 1996

Age class	Family size	Head employed (%)	Home owner (%)
20–24	1.27	72.4	10.0
25–29	1.93	87.0	34.6
30–34	2.61	93.2	60.5
35–39	3.31	91.2	65.8
40–44	3.45	90.5	68.4
45–49	3.08	86.3	63.9
50–54	2.57	79.9	66.1
55–59	2.16	57.8	57.8
60–64	1.81	5.7	45.8
65–69	1.71	2.6	39.9
70–74	1.58	1.6	30.2
75–79	1.49	0.0	22.8
80+	1.35	0.0	22.5
Total	2.42	62.4	50.8

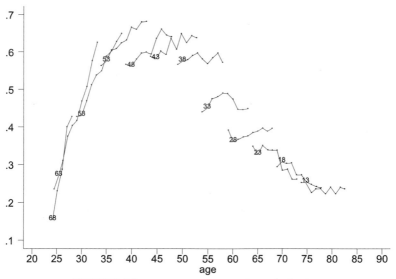

FIGURE 6.5a   Homeownership rate by age and cohort.

gets a new identification number. There is one exception to this rule: the household remains in the data set (and its identification number does not change) in the case of the death of the head of the household unless it concerns a single-person household (e.g. death of an elderly individual living alone). Measuring

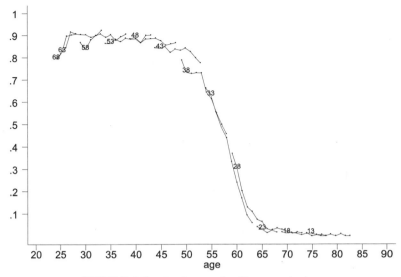

FIGURE 6.5b   Employment head by age and cohort.

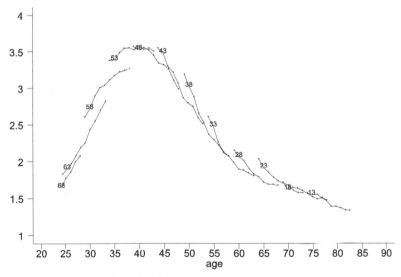

FIGURE 6.5c   Family size by age and cohort.

saving of those households who experienced a change in family composition (e.g. divorce, marriage) is difficult. In this chapter we assume, due to the way *khnr* is constructed, that in cases of divorce the total amount of wealth will not be divided between the partners, but remains with the head of the household. We admit that this is a questionable assumption. Alternatively, Avery and Kennickell (1989) assume that in such cases net worth will be divided in two equal parts. This is a reasonable assumption if the couple is married under common property law. Not everyone (especially the wealthy) in the Netherlands is married under such a contract and in such cases our assumption may be more reasonable than that of Avery and Kennickell (1989).

Another problem is the treatment of those persons who "married into" the sample. While calculating saving, we implicitly assume (due to our choice of identification variable) that these new household members did not own any wealth when entering the sample. Avery and Kennickell (1989) make the alternative assumption that the new household member owned the same amount of wealth as the original household members together. It is clear that both kinds of assumption are arbitrary. Given the discussion above, it seems worthwhile to also consider an alternative saving measure: e.g., the difference between income and consumption. As mentioned in Section 6.2, the SEP does not observe consumption expenditures. Therefore, we will also use the Dutch Consumer Expenditure Survey (CES) to obtain a residual saving measure.

Given the problem with measuring saving of non-intact families, one would also be tempted to remove non-intact families altogether from the data set. However, this could lead to considerable sample selection bias especially if one wants to analyze the saving behavior of the elderly. If one of the members of an elderly household dies, it is conceivable that bequests to children cause the household to lose a substantial portion of its wealth.[20] Such changes in wealth are of interest if one wants to investigate whether households dissave during retirement. Presumably, the problem of mismeasuring savings due to changes in wealth related to the death of a spouse is less severe if one considers the residual saving measure (income minus consumption).[21]

As other studies have pointed out, both savings derived from differencing wealth and from income minus consumption show extreme variability (Avery and Kennickell, 1991; Bosworth et al., 1991; Browning and Lusardi, 1996). As Avery and Kennickell (1991, p. 432) mention in their conclusions: "either the measurement error in these data is quite large, or idiosyncratic factors are very important, or both." With these considerations in mind, the characteristics of the savings data require that appropriate econometric techniques be used. After some experimentation, it appeared that the saving data was so noisy that we decided to pool the saving data in the following way: 1988–90, 1991–93, and 1994–96. Although this had the disadvantage of reducing the data points to three per cohort, we at least cover the time period by three "stable" points.

In Figure 6.6 we present for different years the age profile of median change in net worth. This age profile has been estimated non-parametrically by using a

---

[20]The elderly household also loses a considerable amount of wealth in the case of death of one of the spouses if the survivor holds a part of the wealth in usufruct.

[21]Neither the income nor the consumption measure of the Dutch CES contain information about bequests and gifts.

kernel-smoothed quantile estimator. For details on the non-parametric estimation and the algorithm used, see Magee *et al.* (1991). Given the noisiness of the saving measure, a rather large bandwidth (15) has been used to construct Figure 6.6. For all years we observe a hump-shaped age–saving profile. Median saving of very young and retired households is about equal to zero. Thus, about 50% of the households do not dissave during retirement. This should be related to the fact that according to Figure 6.3b, the median level of financial wealth of the retired is on the order of €5000. This level of financial wealth is too low to have any appreciable use as a source of consumption financing. Rather, these funds are probably held for precautionary purposes (e.g., to replace durables that break down). Figure 6.6 also suggests that, especially at middle ages, median saving is relatively high in 1993 and 1994. Although the age–saving profile is hump shaped for all years, their shapes differ considerably across years.

In Figure 6.7 we plot median saving from 1988 through 1996 for different cohorts (1963, 1958,..., 1913). Figure 6.7 has been derived from Figure 6.6, meaning that Figure 6.7 is based on kernel estimates of the age–saving profiles. We can draw some tentative conclusions from Figure 6.7. First, the figure suggests that the "true" age–saving profile is hump shaped. In order to check this claim, we have followed the approach of Deaton and Paxson (1994) by assuming that time effects are orthogonal to a trend. Given these assumptions, we have performed a median regression of the change in net worth on a second-degree age polynomial, a second-degree year of birth polynomial, and a set of time dummies (on which

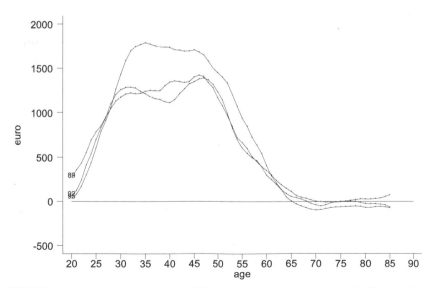

FIGURE 6.6   Median saving across age: 1988–96 (saving=change in net worth): 89 = pooled data 1988–90; 92 = pooled data 1991–93; 95 = pooled data 1994–96.

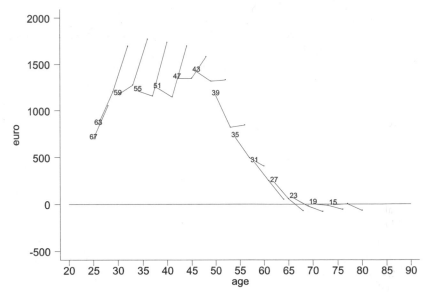

FIGURE 6.7 Median saving by age and cohort (saving = change in net worth).

we have imposed the "Deaton–Paxson" restrictions). The results of this regression corroborate the claim that the age profile is hump shaped.[22] Secondly, from Figure 6.7 one can observe some cohort–time effects at middle ages. Finally, Figure 6.7 indicates that median saving changes for most cohorts (except the old ones) in a "parallel" way, which in turn suggests that time effects (e.g., the evolution of housing prices) may also be important. Figures 6.8 and 6.9 are similar to Figures 6.6 and 6.7. The only difference is that in Figures 6.8 and 6.9 median saving rates have been analyzed and not median saving (in levels).

The cross-sectional age–homeownership profile which can be inferred from Figure 6.5a may explain the fact that the cross-sectional age–median saving profiles have an inverted U shape. Moreover, the cohort–time effects observed in Figure 6.7 may be attributed to the evidence presented in Figure 6.5a and the evolution of housing prices. To investigate this issue further, we also analyze in Figures 6.10 and 6.11 median changes in financial wealth. These figures suggest that median financial saving is low in the Netherlands: it varies between −€500 and €1500 (at middle ages the median saving rate varies between 1 and 3%). One can observe only a slight hump shape in the age profile of financial saving. From this result it follows that the age profile of homeownership rate and capital gains on housing mainly explains the inverted U shape observed in Figures 6.6 and 6.8.

---

[22]For the saving rates (change in net worth over disposable income) we obtain a similar result.

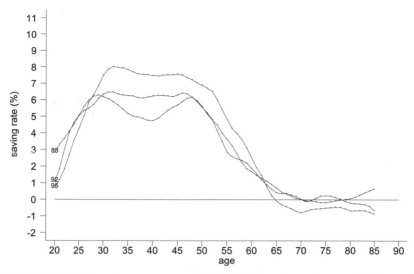

FIGURE 6.8   Median saving rate across age: 1988–96 (saving = change in net worth). 89 = pooled data 1988–90; 92 = pooled data 1991–93; 95 = pooled data 1994–96.

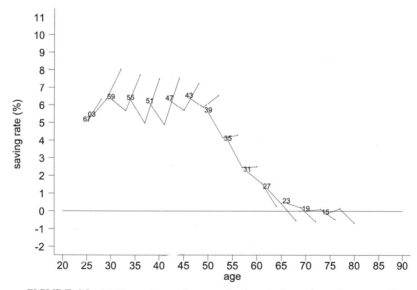

FIGURE 6.9   Median saving rate by age and cohort (saving = change in net worth).

In view of the noisiness of saving measures obtained by first differencing wealth, we have also analyzed in Figures 6.12 and 6.13 the age pattern of a residual saving measure (income minus consumption). The residual saving measure differs in several respects from the "change in wealth" measure. First, the net worth measure

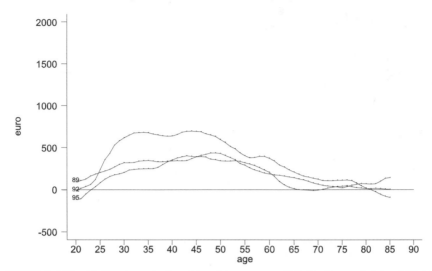

FIGURE 6.10   Median change in financial wealth across age: 1988–96. 89 = pooled data 1988–90;
92 = pooled data 1991–93; 95 = pooled data 1994–96.

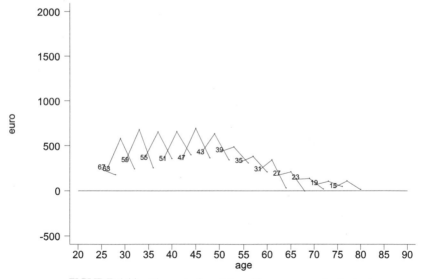

FIGURE 6.11   Change in financial wealth across age and cohort.

based on the SEP does not include (1) cash holdings and (2) the cash value of
whole life insurances (except the life insurance mortgage) and of privately
purchased annuity insurances. Savings through these asset items are implicitly
included in the residual saving measure. Secondly, the residual saving measure

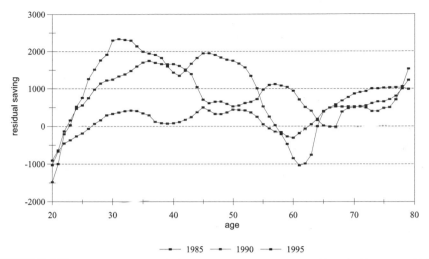

FIGURE 6.12 Median saving (residual measure) across age in 1985, 1990, and 1995. *Source*: CES.

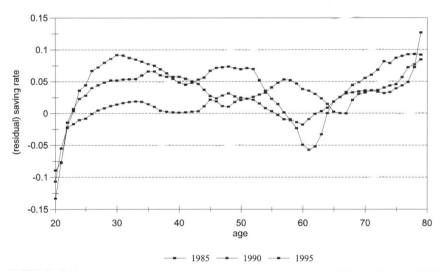

FIGURE 6.13 Median saving rate (residual measure) across age in 1985, 1990, and 1995. *Source*: CES.

does not include capital gains because they are not observed in the Dutch CES. Thirdly, the residual saving measure does not measure bequests or inter-vivos transfers.

In contrast to the "change in wealth" measure (see Figure 6.6), the age profile of residual saving (see Figure 6.12) does not appear to be hump shaped.[23] Moreover, it appears that according to the residual saving measure, saving increases with age after age 65. According to Figure 6.13, the residual saving rate increases to more than 5% after age 65. A similar result based on a residual saving measure has been found by Börsch-Supan and Stahl (1991). They have suggested that the elderly do not dissave because they are physically constrained by health, in particular when very old, and cannot consume as much as they had anticipated. However, we have to reconcile the big differences between the agemedian saving profiles of the two saving measures before drawing such conclusions. One possibility would be the prevalence of *inter-vivos* transfers, which appear not to be recorded correctly in the Dutch CES. Another explanation here appears to be a data problem with the consumption or wealth data: certain expenditure items or (the change in) net worth may simply not be measured appropriately by the CES or the SEP. At this moment we can only speculate about the nature of the mismeasurement.

6.5 POLICIES AFFECTING SAVINGS

Description of the Pension System

To better understand the low discretionary saving rates presented in the previous section, it is important to know more about the pension system in the Netherlands: see also Bovenberg and Meijdam (1999) for an extensive description of the Dutch pension system. The pension system consists of three tiers. The first tier is social security (SS): everyone in the Netherlands is covered by a general old-age pension starting at the age of 65. The second tier of the pension system consists of funded occupational pension plans. Finally, some retired (e.g., the ex-self-employed) have privately bought a pension insurance in the past (this is the third tier of the pension system). As a result, they receive an annuity income from this insurance policy.

The level of the SS benefits is independent of other income but does depend on household composition. In principle, every individual older than 65 receives an SS benefit equal to 50% of the minimum wage. This rule implies that a couple of which both head and spouse are older than 65 receives an SS benefit equal to the minimum wage. A single person household is entitled to a supplement of 20% of the minimum wage so that such a household receives 70% of the minimum wage. There are special rules for couples of which only one of the household members is older than 65. In any case, they are entitled to an SS benefit of a single individual. Moreover, such a household may receive a supplementary SS benefit, which is

---

[23]Figures 6.12 and 6.13 suggest that in 1995 there is a considerable dip in saving around age 60. It should be realized that this result might be an artifact of the high variability in the data due to measurement error.

negatively related to the earnings of the younger (<65) spouse: if the earnings of the younger spouse are high, the household is not entitled to a supplementary benefit. The maximum supplementary SS benefit is equal to 50% of the minimum wage.[24]

The SS benefit level is indexed by the minimum wage. Normally, the government yearly adjusts the minimum wage by the "general wage index" ("index regelingsloon"). During the 1980s and early 1990s, however, the government did not correct the minimum wage for changes in the general wage level, leading to a loss in purchasing power of those retired households who only live on social security. For retired individuals with an occupational Definal Benefit Pension benefit, most pension funds have mitigated the effect of the non-indexing of the SS benefit by raising the pension benefits. By reducing the generosity of the public pension scheme, the government has effectively privatized part of the pension system (see Bovenberg and Meijdam (1999)).

The SS benefits are financed on the basis of pay-as-you-go (PAYG): part of the tax rate over the first income bracket (in 2000: 0–€22,256) is earmarked to finance the SS benefits (in 2000 the SS premium percentage was equal to 17.9%). The SS tax is paid only by those younger than 65 years of age. Due to the aging of the population, the SS tax has crept up during the 1990s from 14.05% in 1991 to 17.9% in 2000. However, in 1997 the government modified the financing of the public pension system. As a first modification, it intends to fix the SS tax in the first bracket of the personal income tax at its 1997 level. As the population ages, a fixed SS tax rate implies that revenues from SS taxes fall short of expenditures on SS benefits (Bovenberg and Meijdam, 1999). Since this deficit will be financed out of general tax revenues, the elderly will implicitly start contributing to the financing of the SS benefits. The second modification to the PAYG system is the accumulation of a so-called SS fund to deal with temporarily high spending on public pensions when the baby-boom generation retires. As Bovenberg and Meijdam (1999) point out, the build up of the AOW fund counts as a reduction of the fiscal deficit.

In order to get an impression of the (relative) importance of SS, we have computed social security wealth in 1995 for three household types.[25] The first household consists of a couple whose head and partner are 65 years old in 1995.

---

[24]Between 1988 and 1999 the Dutch government has gradually tightened the rules on the supplementary SS benefit leading to (considerable) reductions of social security wealth of future retirees. Before 1988, every individual older than 65 who lived with a partner younger than 65 was entitled to an SS benefit equal to 100% of the minimum wage, irrespective of the earnings level of the partner. In 1999 the government decided that individuals with a younger partner who qualify for SS only after 2015 will not receive any supplementary SS benefit. Alessie et al. (1997) have effectively used these changes in the SS regulations to identify the displacement between social security wealth and private wealth.

[25]For these types of households SSW is equal to the actuarially discounted value of current and future social security benefits. In this calculation we have assumed that the discount rate (real market interest rate) is equal to 4%.

The second (third) household consists of a single male (female) who is 65 years old in 1995. Our calculations show that SSW of the first household type is equal to €177,197. Social security wealth of the single males and females are equal to €97,508 and €125,677, respectively.[26] Alessie *et al.* (1995) have found that median SSW is considerably higher than the median value of occupational pension wealth.

The second tier of the pension system consists of funded occupational pension plans. In general, if the employer offers a pension scheme, participation in such a scheme is compulsory. Occupational pensions are, therefore, quite important in the Netherlands. The vast majority of the occupational pensions are of the defined benefit type. In most cases benefits are determined on the basis of final pay. Such schemes aim at a benefit level such that the sum of before-tax SS benefits and before-tax occupational pension benefits is equal to 70% of final earnings. This replacement rate is reached if one works for 40 years with the same employer (implying an annual accrual rate of 1.75%). In this system, pension premiums are usually related to earnings above a certain threshold. The motivation of the threshold lies in the fact that the lower part of earnings is taxed to finance SS benefits. In practice, many workers do not achieve the 70% final wage aspiration level because of incomplete careers. Furthermore, even in the case of full careers, two-earner families and single-person households get less than 70% because the threshold is based on an SS benefit of a couple (= 100% of the minimum wage). However, members of two-earner families or single-person households receive only a SS benefit of, respectively, 50% and 70% of the minimum wage.

Contributions to the funded occupational pension schemes are typically shared between employers and employees. Premiums are usually levied on earnings above the threshold mentioned in the previous paragraph. Occupational pension saving is tax-preferred in comparison with most other forms of discretionary saving (see also Kremers, 2000):[27] pension contributions are tax-exempt, capital income from pension funds are tax-exempt, and benefits are taxed. This regime is especially advantageous because the retirees (65+) benefit from a low tax rate in the first tax bracket as they are exempted from paying SS and several other social insurance contributions (see preceding comments).

Given the institutional background considered earlier, it is not surprising that the vast majority of employees, about 90% (van der Werf and Smidt, 1997) is covered by an occupational pension scheme. In *Pensioenkaart van Nederland* (1987), *Pension Map of the Netherlands* or PN (1987), it is estimated that 99.4% of the pension schemes are of the defined benefit type, whereas the remaining 0.6% are of

---

[26]SSW of single females is greater than that of single males because females are expected to live longer than males.

[27]Alessie *et al.* (2000) give a short overview of the Dutch tax system.

the defined contribution type. More than 72% of the pension benefits are defined on the basis of final pay. Combining the effects of SS and the occupational pension schemes leads to the following before-tax replacement rates for those individuals who contributed for a sufficient number of years: 34% receives less than 60% of the final pay; 27% receives between 60 and 69%; 20% receives between 70 and 79%; and 19% receives at least 80% of final pay (PN, 1987). One should keep in mind that because of the (favorable) tax treatment of occupational pensions (see above), after-tax replacement rates are usually substantially higher. For instance, if the before-tax replacement rate is 70%, then the after-tax replacement rate exceeds 85%.

The numbers reported above are not current; however, recent figures still indicate that most pension plans are of the defined benefit type although, between 1995 and 1999, more pension funds have shifted towards a defined contribution scheme (Insurance Board, 2000). The Insurance Board also observes a shift from DB schemes based on final pay toward DB schemes based on average earnings.

Apart from the old-age (65+) pension schemes introduced above, a vast array of early retirement schemes (VUT) were introduced during the 1980 recession, with the aim of reducing the number of unemployed. These early retirement schemes are quite different from the occupational pensions discussed above. They are not funded, there is no state provision (no first tier), and early retirees (<65 years) receive gross benefits which are usually 80% of final pay, irrespective of years of service (apart from a common vesting period of 10 years). Kapteyn and De Vos (1998) document that these early retirement schemes are highly actuarially unfair and that most employees retire early once they are given the opportunity. In an aging society like the Netherlands, these very generous early retirement schemes cannot be sustained in the future. Therefore, increasingly, pension funds replace the very generous PAYG early retirement schemes by less-generous funded schemes (Insurance Board, 2000). Next to the very extensive occupational pension system, most employees are covered by reasonably generous (earnings related) disability and unemployment insurance schemes.

The government has decided to overhaul the tax system. In the new tax system, in effect from January 1, 2001, annuity insurances are treated in a different way. Under the previous tax law, the premiums of (single-premium) annuity insurance policies were tax-deductible under certain restrictions and up to an upper limit (€2703 for singles or €5406 for couples); the limit is higher for some groups such as the self-employed, who are not covered by an occupational pension plan. Under the new tax law, the deductibility of annuity insurance contributions is curtailed to a ceiling of €1022. However, this ceiling will be increased for persons who have accrued "inadequate" occupational pension wealth.[28] Such persons can choose

---

[28]Self-employed and employees who regularly changed jobs and faced pension vesting rules, have presumably no "adequate" pension wealth (i.e., the sum of the SS benefit and the occupational pension benefit will be less than 70% of final earnings).

between contributing more to their occupational DB pension scheme[29] or buying an extra annuity based on a defined contribution insurance from a private life insurance company.

The old-age pension scheme also provides for a survivor pension even if the employee has no spouse. From 1999 onwards, pension funds had to give their participants the opportunity to abstain from a survivor's pension. In return for this, the employee gets a higher pension.

Discretionary Saving versus Notional and Pension Saving

In this section we pay some attention to the question of how the social insurance system, SS, and occupational pension schemes may crowd out discretionary saving. Since the seminal paper of Feldstein (1974), this question has been addressed many times in the literature. There are not many empirical papers on Dutch survey data that investigate the issue of displacement between private wealth on the one hand and SS and pension wealth on the other hand: we are aware of only three papers (Alessie et al. 1997b; Euwals, 1999; Kapteyn et al., 1999). In this section, we also briefly review these papers.

In the previous section we pointed out that the Netherlands has an extensive social insurance system. This is one of the reasons for the high notional saving rate (see Section 6.3). Compared with the United States, for instance, there is less reason to save in order to have a buffer in the event that a member of the household becomes unemployed or disabled. Studies (e.g., Hochgürtel, 1998) do not find much evidence for a precautionary saving motive in the Netherlands. Consequently, the large safety net may be one of the reasons why the discretionary saving rate is low in the Netherlands (see Section 6.4).

This evidence can be backed up with data on saving motives. The questionnaire of the 1987 and 1988 waves of the SEP asked whether or not people were planning to put money aside and if so, for what purpose. Several possibilities for the motives were given in the questionnaire and the respondent could choose one or several combinations of the motives listed. The main possibilities were: to buy a house, to buy a car, to buy other durables, for unforeseen events, for children, for old age, for no specific purpose, and all possible combinations of the above motives. Examining the motives to save in more detail, it is interesting to note that the households who indicated unforeseen events alone or in combination with other motives accounted for 22% of the total sample. A very small proportion of households, only 2%, indicated that they were saving for old age. The percentage of people who indicated buying a house as a motive to save was 13%, the

---

[29]In return for the higher contribution to the DB plan, the yearly accrual rate increases from 1.75% to, say, 2%.

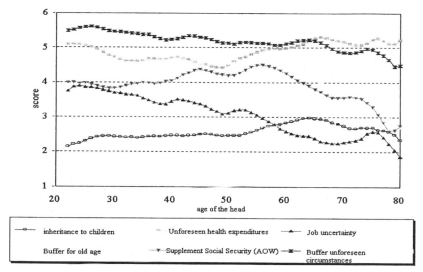

FIGURE 6.14   Saving motives across age. *Source*: CSS (1993).

percentage indicating car purchase as a motive was 12%; whereas 15% indicated the purchase of other durables. Although the 22% mentioning a precautionary motive was more than for most other motives, it is still a relatively small minority of respondents.

The CentER Saving Survey (CSS) also contains some questions on saving attitudes. The respondents are asked the following questions:

> We would like to ask you some questions on your personal opinion about savings. People have many different reasons for saving money for a short or for a long time. Please indicate your opinion about each statement mentioned on the screen below. Is it to you personally of much or little importance?

Several motives to save have been considered in the questionnaire, where answers could be given on a scale from 1 (very unimportant) to 7 (very important).

In Figure 6.14 we present the average response to six such questions by age. The graphs presented in Figure 6.14 are based on the first wave of the CSS (1993). It appears that on average, people do not find it important to save in order to create a buffer for job losses. Given the extensive safety net existing in the Netherlands, this is not surprising. Still, some precautionary saving seems to be going on, in view of the fact that, in particular, saving for unforeseen health expenditures and to have a buffer for unforeseen circumstances are given considerable weight. Supplementing (expected) future SS and pension benefits is not the most important saving motive. On the basis of the CSS data, Euwals (1999) has computed SS wealth (SSW) and pension wealth (PW) and has investigated by means of a multivariate ordered probit model the relationship between SSW and PW and the answers to the two saving motive questions presented above. He finds that households with high SSW and pension wealth find it less important to save in order to supplement (in the future) possibly lower SS and/or pension benefits. Again, this result can be interpreted as evidence for substitution between discretionary saving and mandatory saving.

By using the SEP data on private wealth and (constructed) data on SS wealth and pension wealth, Alessie *et al.* (1997b) and Kapteyn *et al.* (1999) have investigated the question whether or not there is displacement between discretionary wealth on the one hand and SS and pension wealth on the other hand.[30] For pension wealth they do not find displacement at all and for SS wealth they find (more than) full displacement.

6.6 SUMMARY AND CONCLUSIONS

This chapter consists of two parts. In the first part we have presented summary statistics on the composition of gross income and wealth. Due to the extent of the social safety net, there is a considerable wedge between gross and net household income. Discretionary saving appears to be rather small in the Netherlands, although between 1995 and 1998 private wealth changed considerably due to capital gains (Alessie *et al.*, 2000). We have not obtained a clear picture of the saving behavior of the elderly. From the two types of saving measures considered in this study – change in net worth or financial wealth and income minus consumption – one can draw rather different conclusions. It appears that differences in measurement are a serious issue that warrants more research.

In the second part of the chapter, we have paid some attention to the question of how the social insurance system, SS, and occupational pension schemes may crowd out discretionary saving. We find that the amount of notional and mandatory saving is considerable for most (non-retired) households. Discretionary saving rates are low for the median household. Combining these two results, provides us with (preliminary) prima facie evidence for substitution between discretionary and mandatory (notional) saving of households. We also review other empirical studies on Dutch data, which indicate that there exists displacement between private and SS wealth.

---

[30]Euwals (1999) has done a similar study on the CSS data. He did not find any evidence for displacement. However, the wealth data of the CSS survey were not fully cleaned and imputed yet when Euwals conducted his study. By not imputing missing values, Euwals has underestimated the wealth holdings of households considerably. His results, therefore, should be viewed with care. On the other hand, the most recent waves of the CSS contain detailed data on pension rights so that the computation of, especially, pension wealth does not have to rely on many assumptions (these data were not available when Euwals carried out his study). In this respect, the CSS is more suitable to investigate the displacement issue than the SEP, especially with "cleaned" and imputed wealth data.

ACKNOWLEDGMENT

This research is part of the Savings, Pensions and Portfolio Choice: International Savings Comparison Project, supervised by Axel Börsch-Supan (University of Mannheim, Germany). Comments from Orazio Attanasio, Axel Börsch-Supan, Stefan Höderlein, and an anonymous referee are gratefully acknowledged. We should like to thank Adriaan Hoogendoorn and Klaas De Vos for providing SPSS programs for the computation of mandatory and notional saving rates.

REFERENCES

Alessie, R. and C. Zandvliet (1993). An exploratory analysis of the socio-economic panel data with regard to the financial position of households. VSB Progress Report No. 14, CentER, Tilburg University.

Alessie, R., A. Lusardi, and T. Aldershof (1997a). Income and wealth over the life cycle: Evidence from panel data. *Review of Income and Wealth* 43, 1–32.

Alessie, R., A. Kapteyn, and F. Klijn (1997b). Mandatory pensions and personal savings in the Netherlands. *De Economist* 145, 291–324.

Alessie, R. and A. Kapteyn (1999). Wealth and Savings: data and trends in the Netherlands. Research memorandum 1999–46, Free University Amsterdam.

Alessie, R., A. Lusardi, and A. Kapteyn (1999). Saving after retirement: evidence based on three different savings measures. *Labour Economics* 6, 277–310.

Alessie, R., M. Pradhan and C. Zandvliet (1993). An exploratory analysis of the socio-economic panel data with regard to the financial position of households. VSB progress report No. 14, CentER, Tilburg University.

Alessie, R., S. Hochgürtel, and A. Van Soest (2000). Household portfolios in the Netherlands. Mimeo, Free University Amsterdam.

Attanasio, O. (1998). A cohort analysis of saving behavior by US households. *Journal of Human Resources* 33, 575–609.

Avery, R. B. and A. B. Kennickell (1991). Household saving in the U.S. *The Review of Income and Wealth* 37, 409–432.

Avery, R. B., G. E. Elliehausen, and A. B. Kennickell (1988). Measuring wealth with survey data: An evaluation of the 1983 survey of consumer finances. *The Review of Income and Wealth* 34, 339–369.

Börsch-Supan, A. and K. Stahl (1991). Life cycle saving and consumption constraints. Theory, empirical evidence and fiscal implications. *Journal of Population Economics* 4, 233–255.

Bosworth, B., G. Burtless, and J. Sabelhaus (1991). The decline in saving: Evidence from household data. *Brookings Papers on Economic Activity* 1, 183–256.

Bovenberg, A.L. and L. Meijdam (1999). The Dutch pension system. Mimeo, Tilburg University.

Browning, M. and A. Lusardi (1996). Household saving: Micro theories and micro facts. *Journal of Economic Literature* 34, 1797–1855.

Camphuis, H. (1993). Checking, editing and imputation of wealth data in the Dutch Socio-Economic Panel for the period 1987–1989. VSB progress reports No. 10. CentER, Tilburg University.

CBS (1991). *Sociaal-Economisch Panelonderzoek: Inhoud, Opzet en Organisatie*. The Hague: SDU.

Deaton, A. and C. Paxson (1994). Saving, growth and aging in Taiwan. In: D. Wise (ed.), *Studies in the Economics of Aging*. Chicago: University of Chicago Press, 331–357.

Euwals, R. (1999). Do mandatory pensions decrease household savings? Evidence for the Netherlands. Mimeo, University of Mannheim.

Feldstein, M. (1974). Social security, induced retirement, and aggregate capital accumulation. *Journal of Political Economy* 82, 905–925.

Insurance Board (2002) *Pensioenmonitor, niet-financiële gegevens pensioenfondsen, stand van zaken 1 januari 2001 (in Dutch.*, Insurance Board, Apeldoorn: The Netherlands.

Jappelli, T. and L. Pistafferri (1999). The dynamics of household wealth accumulation in Italy: Measurement and distributional issues. Mimeo, University of Salerno.

Kapteyn, A. and K. de Vos (1998). Social security and labor-force participation in the Netherlands. *The American Economic Review* 88, 164–167.

Kapteyn, A., R. Alessie, and A. Lusardi (1999). Explaining the wealth holdings of different cohorts: Productivity growth and social security. Mimeo, Tinbergen Institute.

Kremers, J. (2002). Pension reform: issues in the Netherlands. In M. Feldstein and H. Sibert (eds), *Social Security Pension Reform in Europe*. Chicago: University of Chicago Press.

Magee, L., J. B. Burbidge, and L. A. Robb (1991). Computing kernel-smoothed conditional quantiles from many observations. *Journal of the American Statistical Association* 86, 673–677.

PN (1987). *Pensioenkaart van Nederland (Pension Map of the Netherlands)*.

PN (1987). *Pensioenkaart van Nederland*, Staatsuitgeverij. The Hague: The Netherlands.

Sleijpe, G. and H.J. Dirven (1999). The Validation of income in the Dutch ECHP. Mimeo, CBS Heerlen.

Smith, J.P. (1999). Healthy bodies and thick wallets: The dual relationship between health and economic status. *Journal of Economic Perspectives* 13, 145–166.

Van der Werf, C. and E. Smidt (1997). *Witte vlekken op pensioengebied: stand van zaken in 1996 en vergelijking met 1997* (in Dutch). The Hague: VUGA.

Socioeconomic Panel

The SEP is a survey administered by Statistics Netherlands for a panel of approximately 5000 households. The SEP is representative of the Dutch population, excluding those living in special institutions such as nursing homes. The first survey was conducted in April 1984. The same households were interviewed in October 1984 and then twice a year (in April and October) until 1989. Since 1990 the survey has been conducted once a year in May. In the October interview, information is collected on socioeconomic characteristics, income, and labor market participation. The April interviews contain information about socioeconomic characteristics, as in the October interview, but rather than gathering data about income, the April questionnaire includes questions on a wide range of assets and liabilities from 1987 onwards.

INCOME, MANDATORY SAVING, AND NOTIONAL SAVING

From the 1990 wave onwards, the SEP has collected for most income components information on "gross income" of the previous calendar year. For instance, the 1990 wave of the SEP contains information on income for the calendar year 1989. Each employer (or social insurance institution) is obliged to give their employees (social insurance recipients) at the end of the calendar year a so-called "annual statement." Among other things this annual statement provides information on the "gross" salary (or social insurance benefit). The word "gross" in this context means income before taxes, SS contributions, and health insurance premiums (both the employer and employee part). However, this gross income excludes social insurance premiums (both the employer and employee part), the premiums associated with the occupational pension (again, both the employer and employee part), and the (employers') contributions to dedicated saving plans (see below).

To construct the variable "disposable income of the household," five construction steps have to be taken consecutively. First, the "annual statement income" of all respondents is determined. This "annual statement income" consists of the sum of a number of recorded sources of "gross" income (see Table 6.A1). On the basis of these annual statement incomes it is established which of the persons in the core of the household (head of the household or spouse/partner) has the highest "annual statement income." This person is considered to be the "fiscal

TABLE 6.A1   Steps and the (Coordinated) Calculation Diagram for the Spendable Income of the Household

Income components	Step 1 Annual statement income[a]	Step 2 Gross pers. income[b]	Step 3 Tax pers. income	Step 4 Disp. pers. income
A. Income from work				
Wage	+	+	+	+
(Employer) contr. to dedicated saving plans	0	+	0	+
Fiscal profit	+	+	+	+
B. Asset income				
Dividends	+	+	+	+
Interests	+	+	+	+
Real estate income (rents, etc.)	+	+	+	+
Rateable value of own accommodation	0	0	0	0
Mortgage interest paid	0	0	0	0
Capital gains	0	0	0	0
Government contribution to home owners	+	+	+	+
C. Annuitized PAYG pensions (private and public pensions)				
Early retirement pension [VUT]	+	+	+	+
General old-age pension [AOW]	+	+	+	+
[AWW] and other widows' pensions	+	+	+	+
D. Annuitized funded pensions				
Annuity	+	+	+	+
Other occupational old-age pensions	+	+	+	+
E. Public non-pension transfer income				
Short-term unemployment benefits [WW]	+	+	+	+
Long-term unemployment benefits [RWW]	+	+	+	+
UI benefit for ex-civil servants	+	+	+	+
Disability pension [WAO]	+	+	+	+
General disability pension [AAW]	+	+	+	+
Invalidity pension of ex-civil servants	+	+	+	+

(*Continues*)

TABLE 6.A1   (*Continued*)

Income components	Step 1 Annual statement income[a]	Step 2 Gross pers. income[b]	Step 3 Tax pers. income	Step 4 Disp. pers. income
Welfare [ABW, BZ]	+	+	+	+
Sickness benefits	+	+	+	+
Individual rent allowance	+	+	0	+
Public student grant	+	+	+	+
Child allowance	0	0	0	+
F. Net private transfers				
Alimony received	+	+	+	+
Alimony received on behalf of children	+	+	0	+
Support from family	+	+	0	+
Other income	+	+	0	+
Inheritances, gifts	0	+	0	+
Alimony paid	−	−	−	−
Alimony paid on behalf of children	−	−	0	−
Support for relatives paid	−	−	0	−
Components relevant for fiscal calculations				
Work-related expenses (5% arrangement)	0	0	−	0
Deduction for self-employed	0	0	−	0
Car provided by employer	0	0	+	0
Income tax + SS premiums	0	0	0	−
Health insurance premiums (mandatory)	0	0	0	−
Health insurance premiums (voluntary)	0	0	0	−
Premiums occupational pensions	0	0	0	−
Premiums social insurance	0	0	0	−

Calculation: + = plus; − = minus; 0 = not included in the income calculation.
[a] Income items are net of social insurance and pension premiums.
[b] Income items are gross of social insurance and pension premiums.

main wage earner of the household." This information is relevant to compute taxes and SS contributions.

In step 2, we calculate for each relevant income component the occupational (funded) pension premiums (employer and employee part), the social insurance premiums (UI insurance, disability insurance, etc.) (employer and employee part), and the mandatory and voluntary health insurance premiums (employer and employee part). Pension premiums are calculated for the following income components: (1) wages (separate calculations for civil servants and private sector employees); (2) early retirement benefits (VUT); and (3) UI benefits of civil servants. For the other income components pension premiums are equal to zero. Mandatory and voluntary health insurance premiums are calculated for wages and all wage-replacing transfers (all social insurance and SS benefits). For those who are not obliged to pay mandatory health insurance premiums (basically individuals with a high income), a private health insurance premium has been imputed. Social insurance premiums have been calculated for the following income components: wage, UI benefits, disability benefits, and sickness benefits. For the other income components, the social insurance premiums are equal to zero.

For each income component (wages, UI benefits, etc.) we have added the pension and social insurance taxes in step 2 to the annual statement figures. For instance, gross wage (before taxes, SS contributions, social insurance contributions, and pension premiums) is basically the sum of the wage according to annual statement (directly observed in the SEP), and the social insurance and pension premiums paid by the employer and the employee. Moreover, in comparison with the income concept "annual statement income" the following income components have been added in order to calculate the income "gross personal income": (1) (employer) contributions to dedicated saving plans (see later), (2) gifts and inheritances, and (3) child allowances. Notice that strictly speaking the income component "child allowances" is not individual-specific but household-specific. We have assigned these income items to the "fiscal main wage earner of the household."

Some of these calculations are based on rough approximations. For employees in the private sector, the determination of the pension premiums and the private (voluntary) health insurance premiums is based on an approximation adopted by the Netherlands Bureau of Economic Analysis (CPB) in their so-called *microtax model*. Step 2 is necessary because we want to calculate the mandatory and notional saving rates.

In step 3, a number of additions to or deductions from "annual statement income" are combined in order to calculate the final taxable personal income of the main wage earner and of other persons in the household. On the basis of this result and the information about the income tax coding, the amount of withheld income tax and SS premiums paid can be determined on the basis of the taxable sum (i.e., the taxable income minus the exemption level).

In step 4, the disposable personal income is determined by subtracting the amount of income tax, SS premiums, social insurance premiums, pension premiums, and health insurance premiums paid from the gross personal income (as calculated in step 2). In step 5, gross income and disposable income of the household are calculated. This is done by adding up the gross and disposable incomes of all household members.

The way in which steps 1 through 4 are carried out is indicated in Table 6.A1.

EXPLANATION OF SOME INCOME COMPONENTS

Income from Work

- Wages/salaries
- (Employer) contributions to dedicated saving plans.

As per January 1, 1994, new employee savings and profit sharing schemes have been introduced for employees in the Netherlands. Two main facilities can be distinguished:

1. The "employee saving scheme"
2. The "premium saving scheme."

These two saving schemes are somewhat similar to IRAs. The contributions to these schemes are withheld by the employer. The contribution to the "employee saving scheme" is directly observed in the SEP. Under the following conditions one does not need to pay income and social insurance taxes on the contributions to the "employee saving scheme":[31]

- There is an annual contribution limit: €699 in 1994 and €774 in 1999.
- The contribution is placed in a separate account. In principle, this money cannot be withdrawn for a period of 4 years. The money can be withdrawn earlier if it is used for: (1) buying a house; (2) buying bonds, shares, mutual funds, and options;[32] and (3) paying a life insurance premium (no pension insurance). This life insurance could be either an annuity insurance or a whole life insurance. If one uses the contribution to the employee saving scheme to buy an annuity insurance, one can deduct under some conditions the annuity insurance premium from taxable income. Notice that in this case, one can deduct the contribution to the employee saving scheme twice: this contribution in itself is already tax deductible and the annuity insurance premium is tax deductible.

The "premium saving scheme," which has also been observed in the SEP, is very similar to the employee saving scheme. However, the contribution to the premium saving scheme is not tax deductible and therefore included in the "annual statement income wage," which has been observed in the SEP. The employer can match the employees' contribution up to 100%. The amount added by the employer is tax-free as long as it does not exceed €516 (in 1999). In our

---

[31]Moreover, there are separate exemptions of amounts on the interest and dividend income from employee saving (premium saving) schemes.

[32]The employer can offer the possibility of using the contribution to the employee saving scheme to buy stock options of the company. In that case, the contribution limit is equal to €1548 instead of €774.

calculations we assume that the employers' contribution to the premium saving scheme is exactly equal to the employees' contribution. Notice that the variable "gross personal income" (column "step 2" in Table 6.A1) should include the employers' contribution to the "premium saving scheme."

Fiscal Profit (of Own Business)

First, respondents were asked to provide the fiscal profit for the previous calendar year, and *not* to include compulsory pension premiums, paid at the expense of the profit. If the fiscal profit for the previous calendar year was not yet known, respondents were asked to provide an estimate of it. If they could not give an estimate, respondents were asked to provide (an estimate of) the fiscal profit of 2 years ago. Obviously, the fiscal profit may be negative and is also included in the calculation as such.

Asset Income

This category includes the following sources of income:

- Dividends from shares, stocks, investment accounts, or investment funds
- Interest from savings, loans, stocks, bonds, mortgage bonds, investment accounts
- Real estate income (including the letting of rooms)
- Government contribution to homeowners (assigned to the "fiscal main wage earner of the household").

Annuitized PAYE Pensions

This category includes the following sources of income (all components directly observed):

- Early (occupational) retirement pension [VUT]
- SS [AOW]
- General widows' and orphans' pensions [AWW] (flat rate public pension, like SS).

Annuitized Funded Pensions

This includes (all components directly observed):

- Private annuities
- Other occupational pensions.

Public Non-Pension Transfer Income

This category includes the following sources of income (all components directly observed):

a. Social insurance benefits

- Short-term unemployment benefits [WW]
- UI benefits for the civil servants ("wachtgeld")
- Disability benefits [WAO]
- Invalidity pension for former civil servants
- Sickness benefits [ZW].

b. Other social benefits

- General disability pension [AAW]
- Welfare [ABW, BZ]
- Long-term unemployment benefits [RWW]
- Individual rent subsidy
- Child allowances, assigned to the "fiscal main wage earner of the household" (we have imputed this income component. The SEP contains enough information to perform a proper imputation)
- Scholarship or additional support through a government scholarship scheme.

Net Private Transfers

- Alimony received from former spouse
- Child support
- Parental support received by students
- Support from family
- Inheritances, gifts
- Alimony paid to former spouse
- Child support
- Other support to relatives
- Other income.

Components Relevant for Fiscal Calculations

- Work-related expenses (5%). We have used the maximum deduction for work-related expenses (for current or past jobs).
- Deduction for self-employed. This concerns an amount that can be deducted from the income from business/enterprise.

- Rateable value of owner-occupied accommodation (see above for an explanation).
- Mortgage interest paid.
- Company car. Where the employee has a car provided by his or her employer, a part (20%) of the list value of the car is added to the taxable income.
- Income and social insurance tax withheld. The amount tax of withheld in 1993 is based on the taxable amount. The taxable amount is calculated by subtracting the exemption (according to the income tax schedule) from the taxable income. The exemption level depends on socioeconomic and demographic characteristics of the household. Since 1990 the tax schedule has not changed dramatically. The tax schedule in 1995 is as follows:

Tax bracket	Marginal tax rate
taxable sum < €44,349	6.35% (excl. payroll taxes)
€44,349 ≤ taxable sum ≤ €86,696	50%
taxable sum > €86,696	60%

Payroll taxes are levied over the lowest tax bracket. Payroll taxes include the following components:[33]

a. SS [AOW], tax in 1995: 14.55%
b. General widows' and orphans' pensions [AWW], tax in 1995: 1.80%
c. General disability pension [AAW], tax in 1995: 6.30%
d. Special health cost act [AWBZ], tax in 1995: 8.55% (plus a small nominal premium).

The purpose of the AWBZ is to cover risks which are not covered by the sick fund insurance and the standard private health insurance policies. It is basically a long-term care and a preventive health care (vaccinations, etc.) insurance.

- Mandatory health insurance premiums. This concerns, in particular, the premiums of the compulsory sick fund insurance. Basically, only those persons with sufficiently high income (about €27,000) are not compulsory insured through the sick fund. They have to buy a private health insurance. The sick fund premiums (employer and employee part) are imputed on the basis of (annual statement) income information in the SEP.
- Private health insurance. Like the Netherlands Bureau for Economic Policy Analysis (CPB) we have imputed the premium of a so-called standard health insurance and the employer contribution to the private health insurance.
- Social insurance taxes (employer and employee part). Apart from the sick fund insurance (see preceding comments) it concerns the premiums of the following insurances:

a. Short-term unemployment insurance [WW]
b. Disability insurance [WAO]

[33]Individuals who are at least 65 years old do not pay SS and (most) social insurance taxes.

    c. Sickness benefits (this insurance replaces earnings in case of sickness) [ZW].

The social insurance taxes (employer and employee part) are imputed on the basis of (annual statement) income information in the SEP.

- Occupational pension premiums. The SEP contains enough information to identify (former) civil servants. For civil servants and former civil servants who currently receive a UI benefit ("wachtgeld") or an early retirement benefit, the SEP contains enough information to impute the pension premiums rather precisely. The imputation exercise is much more difficult for private sector employees and ex-private sector employees who currently receive an early retirement benefit. Basically, we have adopted the imputation formula proposed by the Netherlands Bureau for Economic Policy Analysis (CPB).

The calculations performed in steps 1 through 5 (Table 6.A1) provide us with sufficient information to calculate the notional and mandatory saving rates at the household level. Disposable household income can be obtained by subtracting taxes and notional and mandatory saving from gross household income.

Assets and Liabilities

Every respondent (i.e, a person who is at least 16 years old) in the household has to complete a short questionnaire on assets and liabilities.[34] In the SEP questionnaire, a distinction is made between the ownership of a particular asset or liability on the one hand, and the value of the asset and liability on the other. Information is collected for the following assets:[35] (1) checking accounts; (2) savings and deposit

---

[34]From 1990 onwards, only one household member (the head of the household) reports the value of housing-related assets and liabilities (i.e., the value of the primary residence, remaining mortgage debt, and life insurance mortgage). In most other wealth surveys only one household member has to fill in the questionnaire. There are pros and cons of the approach adopted in the SEP. It is rather unlikely that the main respondent (head of household) has a full knowledge of all asset items held by the members of the household. This problem is especially relevant for those households whose head and spouse keep their financial administration separate. Therefore, Statistics Netherlands has decided to interview all respondents. A disadvantage of the "SEP approach" is that for instance the balance of joint checking and saving accounts can be reported both by the head of the household and/or his spouse. In that case, there is a potential problem of double counting, although the SEP questionnaire explicitly indicates that in case of joint ownership of some asset and liability items, only one respondent should report it, preferably the head of the household.

[35]The April 1987 and 1988 questionnaires also contain questions concerning the asset category "Claims against private persons" (friends, acquaintances). In all waves information has been collected on tangibles (paintings, jewelry, etc.). However, Alessie and Zandvliet (1993) find that this information is of doubtful quality. They have analyzed changes in ownership status over time of this asset category. Their analysis shows that far more changes in ownership are reported than appear plausible. For instance, it appears that from the 1277 households that do report ownership of tangibles for 1987 and/or 1988, only 781 households have some tangibles in both years. Given these implausible results we have decided not to use the information on tangibles.

accounts;[36] (3) saving certificates (certificates of deposit); (4) bonds, mortgage bonds; (5) shares, mutual funds, options, and other securities; (6) value of the primary residence; (7) other real estate (not used for own residence); (8) value of the car(s); (9) net worth of own company (for the self-employed); (10) life insurance mortgage;[37] (11) other life insurances with a saving element[38] (starting date of the insurance, insurance premium); and (12) other assets. These assets are reported at the current market value. From the 1990 wave onwards, no information has been collected on "other life insurances with a saving element" and "net worth of the own company" (as of 1990, self-employed respondents do not have to report their assets and liabilities). Notice also that the SEP does not contain information on cash holdings and on occupational pension wealth.

The surveys collect information on the liabilities of every respondent. Unfortunately, Statistics Netherlands has revised the questions on liabilities regularly. This potentially limits the comparability of the liability data between years. In the SEP questionnaire of April 1987 and April 1988, the following categories are listed: (1) personal loans and revolving credit; (2) purchase on credit, hire purchase; (3) remaining mortgage debt; (4) other loans; and (5) other debt. In 1989, 10 liability categories have been distinguished: (1) personal loans; (2) revolving credit; (3) debt with mail orders, retail debt; (4) other purchases on credit; (5) hire purchase; (6) remaining mortgage debt; (7) collateral-based loans; (8) debt with relatives and friends; (9) other outstanding debt, unpaid bills; and (10) other debt.

In 1990 and 1991, the SEP distinguishes the following liability categories: (1) personal loans and revolving credit; (2) debt with mail order firms, retail debt; (3) hire purchase, other purchases on credit, collateral-based loans; (4) debt with relatives and friends; (5) remaining mortgage debt; and (6) other loans.

---

[36] We assume that the respondents include the balance of their dedicated saving accounts when they answer the question on the total balance of all their saving accounts. Notice that we cannot distinguish the balance of the dedicated saving accounts from the balance of the other saving accounts. However, we know whether the household has dedicated saving accounts and we know the annual contribution to these saving accounts. Unfortunately we do not observe the annual withdrawal from the saving accounts.

[37] A special type of mortgage is possible in the Netherlands when buying a house. With this contract, the mortgage debt remains constant during the contract period. The mortgage holder pays life insurance premiums and, at the end of the contract period, the value of the life insurance policy is used to redeem the mortgage. The cash value of the life insurance mortgage is not directly observed. However, we have imputed its value using the information provided in the survey (the starting date of the insurance, the balance of the mortgage, and assuming an interest rate of 3% on a 30-year maturity). The 1990 wave does not contain enough information to impute the cash value of the life insurance mortgage. We have attempted to remedy this problem by merging into the 1990 dataset some relevant information from the 1991 wave.

[38] As already noted by Alessie and Zandvliet (1993), the questions about the other life insurances are rather messy. Only information on the annual premium and the year when the insurance policy was purchased has been collected. Moreover, no clear distinction has been made between whole life insurance policies and (single premium) annuity insurance policies. Given the information at hand, it is impossible to come up with a reasonable estimate for the cash value of the other life insurance policies (see also Alessie et al., 1993). Therefore we have not included this asset item in our measure of net worth.

In 1992, Statistics Netherlands has used the following liability categories: (1) personal loans and revolving credit; (2) debt with mail order firms, retail debt; (3) hire purchase; (4) other purchases on credit; (5) collateral-based loans; (6) debt with relatives and friends; (7) remaining mortgage debt; and (8) other loans.

Since 1993, Statistics Netherlands has used the following liability categories: (1) personal loans and revolving credit; (2) debt with mail order firms, retail debt; (3) hire purchase, other purchases on credit; (4) collateral-based loans; (5) (interest bearing) student loans (WSF18+); (6) debt with relatives and friends; (7) remaining mortgage debt; and (8) other loans.

As of the May 1990 wave, the questions on assets and liabilities have not been asked anymore to those respondents who are self-employed. It appeared that the data on business equity, which have been collected in the April 1987, 1988, and 1989 waves of the SEP, are rather unreliable (Alessie et al., 1997a; Alessie and Zandvliet, 1993). Therefore we have deleted the self-employed from our sample. Household assets and liabilities are obtained by summing all the assets (except the asset items "business equity" and "other life insurances with a saving element") and liabilities, respectively, of each respondent in the household. Net worth is obtained by subtracting total liabilities from total assets. In this study we also analyze financial wealth holdings. Financial wealth has been defined as the difference between net worth on the one hand and housing equity (value of the primary residence plus life insurance mortgage minus remaining mortgage debt), other real estate, and the value of the cars on the other hand.

For confidentiality reasons, the values of all asset and liability items have been top coded for each category and set at the value of Dfl. 999,997 if the values exceed that amount.[39] Note, however, that very few households are affected by top coding, which is concentrated among the self-employed. In our sample, we exclude the self-employed, and top coding is barely a problem.

We have examined the relevance of nonresponses at the respondent level regarding both the size and ownership of assets and liabilities. Nonresponses are of two types: "refuse to answer" and "do not know." Most respondents were prepared to answer the question concerning ownership properly. Alessie et al. (1997a) report that a sizable fraction of respondents refused to report or did not know the amount held in certain assets, such as (mortgage) bonds, savings certificates, other real estate and shares, options, and other securities.[40] In the 1996 wave these fractions are smaller for most asset categories (this remark especially applies to the categories "shares, options, and other securities" and "other real estate"). The panel feature of the SEP has been exploited to impute some of the missing values (for example, in the case of a missing value in the house value in period t, a value equal to the average of

[39]As of 1990, the wealth items "value of the primary residence" and "remaining mortgage debt" have been top coded at a value of Dfl.9,999,997. In 1995, the US dollar–Dutch guilder (Dutch florin: Dfl.) exchange rate was equal to: US$1 = Dfl.1.61.

[40]Unlike the SCF, PSID, and the Health and Retirement Study (HRS), the SEP does not include bracket questions in order to alleviate the problem of item nonresponse.

period $t-1$ and $t+1$ has been imputed, if the household lived in the same house in periods, $t-1$, t, and $t+1$). See Camphuis (1993) for details.

To calculate net worth at the household level, we have chosen the following criteria (this refers to the data after imputation): we exclude observations for which (i) the head of the household or the spouse "refuses to answer" one or more questions about their assets or debts; or (ii) at least one respondent answers with "do not know" to one or more questions about his/her assets and debt. After removing the self-employed from the sample, it is possible to calculate net worth for approximately 90% of the households in 1987 (4154 out of 4531 households) and for about 95% of the households in 1988 and 1989 (4287 out of 4538 in 1988, and 4410 out of 4712 in 1989). These samples show some evidence of selectivity (Alessie et al., 1997a). Since 1990, item nonresponse seems to be less of a problem: net worth cannot be measured for less than 5% of the households. It appears that item nonresponse is especially relevant for saving and checking accounts. No attempts have been made to impute the missing values.

THE CONSUMER EXPENDITURE SURVEY (CES)

The CES is administered by Statistics Netherlands for a sample ranging from 2000 to 3000 households per year. Only in one specific year, 1991, the sample contained approximately 1000 households. The CES is a time series of cross sections. The survey started in 1978 and is repeated annually. Households in the survey keep a daily record of all expenses over 25 guilders (per item) during 1 year. For a limited time period all expenses are recorded, from which yearly expenses on goods with a price below 25 guilders are deduced. In addition to reporting detailed information on the expenditure items of Dutch households, the survey contains information on income, family composition, and background information on all members of the household (age, education, etc.).

The CES is not a random sample of the Dutch population. Every 5 years Statistics Netherlands constructs a weighting scheme based on the CES surveys, which is used for the calculation of price indices for the employed. Thus, households whose head is employed are overrepresented in the years 1980, 1985, and 1990. In addition, the non-employed are overrepresented in 1981, and the self-employed are overrepresented in 1982 for specific research purposes. Furthermore, since 1985 the method of "optimal allocation" is used in sampling the households (see Statistics Netherlands, 1992). This means that households with a well-defined spending behavior are underrepresented compared to those with a larger variability in their spending behavior.

We have aggregated consumption expenditure reported in the CES into eleven major groups: (1) food (at home and outside home, including alcoholic beverages); (2) clothing (which includes footwear); (3) housing (rent or the imputed rental value of the house for homeowners, housing maintenance, and expenses for the garden);

(4) furniture (so-called white durables, oven and kitchen utensils [cups, plates, pans, etc.]); (5) utilities (electricity, telephone, water, heating, and maintenance of central heating); (6) health insurance; (7) health expenditure (out of pocket); (8) personal care; (9) travel and leisure (education, sport, entertainment, durables such as sailing boats, smoking, holidays expenditure); (10) transportation (cars, motorbikes, bikes, public and private transportation, communication excluding telephone costs); and (11) miscellaneous.

CHAPTER 7

Pensions and Life-Cycle Savings Profiles in the UK

James Banks

Institute for Fiscal Studies and University College London

Susann Rohwedder

Institute for Fiscal Studies and University College London

7.1 INTRODUCTION

Many issues related to household saving behavior are still little understood, at least empirically. Despite a vast literature this also remains true for the particular relationship between savings in pension schemes and other household savings. This chapter, along with the other contributions in this volume, seeks to further explore this relationship by gathering extensive data related to this issue. In studying household savings, and paying special attention to the impact of pension arrangements, it is important to bear in mind the main features of the economic and demographic environment in the UK. Partly this is because household saving is the outcome of complex economic choices which will depend on a variety of household factors, both past, current, and expected, which means that it is not always straightforward to look at household saving without detailed analysis of micro data. More importantly perhaps, there are many determinants of savings choices that differ across European countries, and these must be borne in mind in a comparative study such as this.

Whereas in many other industrialized countries the debate on pension reforms has been forced onto the policy agenda by severe sustainability problems in domestic social security schemes, the situation is very different in the UK. None of the factors at the root of the problem elsewhere are particularly extreme in the UK, whether these are demographic trends, labor market trends, or the generosity of current or projected pension provisions by the state. Of course, the British population is still aging, driven by the life cycles of the baby-boom generation, general trends to low fertility rates, and ever-increasing longevity. However, this development is less pronounced in the UK than in other comparable countries. Organization of Economic Cooperation and Development (OECD) projections of the dependency ratio, i.e., the number of people aged 65 and above divided by the number of people of working age (20–64), suggest it might rise to 38.7% by the year 2030. Another trend usually causing strain on the public pension scheme is rapidly increasing early retirement. Again, this phenomenon is also observed in the UK, but not to the same extent as in France and Germany, for example. With a decline in labor market participation of older men from roughly 80% in the 1970s to about 50% in the late 1990s, the UK is placed in the middle of the extremes observed elsewhere.[1] Thirdly, financial burden on public spending entailed by early retirement is obviously proportional to the generosity of public pension provision. Yet again, replacement rates of state pensions in the UK rank at the lower end when considered from an international perspective. A final important feature has prevented the UK public pension scheme from running into sustainability problems – private (employer) pension coverage has been an integral part of pension provision ever since the 1950s, and has been available on a personal defined contribution basis since 1988. As a result, a substantial fraction of wealth is now held in private pensions. Hence, the state plays a reduced role in the provision of pensions and government spending on this item is well contained, quite opposite to the situation found in many other industrialized countries.

As with the chapters from other countries in this volume, the goal of this chapter is to provide comparable evidence, based on microeconomic data sources, regarding the lifetime savings profiles of households in the UK. Following households over their life cycle is important not only because savings choices naturally change with age (according to current resources, needs, and even changing horizons or expectations about the future) but also because the construction of such age profiles allows us to compare the levels of such profiles across cohorts or to use the information from older cohorts to predict the future experiences of younger cohorts. The estimation of lifetime profiles is aided by as long a time series of data as possible,[2] and hence the evidence in this chapter is based on the Family Expenditure Survey, which provides us with a valuable long time series of cross sections. Using data spanning the 22-year period from 1974 to 1995 we are able to follow groups of the population with the same date of birth over a long period of time – for some cohorts we have data on the majority of their working life, for others we see the transition

---

[1]See Gruber and Wise (1999).

[2]The issues involved in synthetic cohort techniques are discussed in Brugiavini and Weber (2001).

from work to retirement, for example. We present age profiles both of cross-sectional data as well as of date-of-birth cohorts for measures of savings and other related key variables for comparison with the evidence from other countries. Care has been taken to retain a comparable treatment of both concepts and data across countries, although as will be seen this raises issues in the UK, given the available data and policy environment. In particular, at the time of writing there is no available repeated household survey that collects either stocks of wealth or flows of saving, let alone a panel data set with such information.[3] Therefore, the only reliable way of measuring saving in the UK is to take the residual of income minus consumption expenditure. In the interpretation of the observed patterns we focus on the impact of the institutional framework, concentrating mainly on the pension scheme in particular, given its importance as a method of saving, but also given the amount of reform that has taken place over the period of our sample. Some of the trends in pension policy have been mirrored in policies relating to non-pension saving, and these are also discussed.

The structure of this chapter is as follows. In Section 7.2, we describe the data set we use in our analysis, and discuss briefly the definitional issues that arise in what follows. Following the pattern of the other chapters in this volume, in Section 7.3 we present cross-sectional age profiles for particular components of "contributions" to saving of different forms in 4 years spread evenly over the last two decades – 1978, 1983, 1988, and 1993. In particular, we focus on mandatory saving payments (pensions) and contributions to pay-as-you-go (PAYG) systems such as the basic state pension and the state earnings-related pension scheme (SERPS).[4] Furthermore, we present cross-sectional age profiles of the variables used to construct the residual measure of saving: i.e., total disposable household income and expenditure, followed by age profiles for annuitized retirement income, total savings, and saving rates. We use means for all the cross-sectional profiles to facilitate comparison with later sections. Full tables of means and medians for each of the cross sections in this section are reported in the Appendix.

In Section 7.4 we look at how the main cross-sectional profiles presented in the previous section may be affected by the presence of cohort or time effects. As is well known, cross-sectional age profiles are not reliable predictors of the experiences of single households, or groups of households. Differences that are observed across age groups in a cross section could be a result of newer generations being wealthier than their predecessors due to economic growth, or a result of different generations having lived through different business cycles, as well as pure differences related to age.

---

[3]As discussed, below, the British Household Panel Study will provide some information on wealth profiles once the second wealth measurement (taken in wave 10) becomes publicly available.

[4]In our discussions along the way with the presented age and cohort profiles we repeatedly refer to some features of the UK pension system. For the reader who is not entirely familiar with its structure and how it works we provide a brief exposition in Appendix II.

Section 7.5 presents some brief analysis of three further issues. First, we give an overview of pension policies and other institutional issues that allows us to put the patterns observed both in the cross-sectional and the cohort profiles from the previous sections into context. Secondly, we investigate the importance of the particular identification strategy for age and cohort effects in the life-cycle profiles – when presenting the empirical evidence for various date-of-birth cohorts we adopt the same identification strategy as the other chapters in this volume and assume time effects to be equal to zero. However, the UK data situation is particularly good for evaluating this approach, since the length of our time series of cross sections allows us to also experiment with other identification strategies. Therefore, we add estimates of age, time, and cohort effects for some key variables following the methodology suggested by Deaton and Paxson (1994). Finally in this section, we discuss issues arising for the estimation of age profiles as a result of considering the nature of household composition and formation at younger ages of the life cycle. Section 7.6 concludes.

7.2 DATA

This study uses data from the Family Expenditure Survey (FES) that provides detailed information on characteristics, expenditures, and incomes on all members of participating households. It is a repeated cross-sectional household survey that has been collected on an annual basis since 1961. We use the years spanning the period from 1974 until 1995 throughout which the information collected has been broadly consistent. Information on approximately 7000 households is recorded every year, representing a response rate of about 70% of those initially contacted and roughly a 1 in 3000 sample of the population. Demographic information and income data are collected in a face-to-face interview, as well as some further information on usual earnings, last monthly earnings, tax payments, and benefit levels. Information on expenditures is collected in a 2-week diary kept by each adult household member covering all purchases. To capture less-frequent purchases the FES records recall information on large items, such as furniture and holidays, purchased over a longer period. Spending on certain items, such as fuel expenditures, is collected from the most recent bill over whichever is the relevant period for the household's method of payment.

The FES sample frame does not include all consumers. Groups such as the institutional population (people in old-aged people's homes, students' hall of residence, military barracks, and residents of hostels or temporary homes) and the homeless are not captured. However, the survey captures the aggregate consumption and income of the household sector well. In terms of how well the FES matches estimates from the National Accounts, we discuss income and expenditure figures in turn.[5] The FES keeps track of about £9 in every £10 of income

---

[5] A detailed analysis of this issue is provided in Banks and Johnson (1998).

recorded in the National Accounts. Looking into different income categories separately one finds that the largest components of income – earnings[6] and social security benefits – follow the National Accounts quite closely; self-employment and investment income are, however, seriously underrecorded, which might be in part due to their underrepresentation in the sample.[7] Some of these problems can be alleviated by using an improved income definition based on the FES data. The Department of Social Security established a carefully revised income measure based on the FES raw data with the initial goal of studying low-income households – hence the name "household below average income" method (HBAI) – and we use this throughout what follows. However, this does not improve the measurement of self-employment income, which is commonly thought to be extremely poor in the FES. Hence we follow all other similar studies that use this data set and drop from our sample those households whose primary source of income is self-employment income.

On the expenditure side, Attanasio and Weber (1994) and Tanner (1998) show that spending information in the FES matches well the main patterns – booms and busts – for the respective periods of their studies, covering the 1970s to mid-1990s. In addition, the large majority of consumption expenditures are captured: grossed-up FES spending as a proportion of the National Account totals averages 86% between 1974 and 1992 (and some underreporting is to be expected given the exclusion of certain groups, including the institutional population, armed forces, students, and tourists from the FES sample) and this proportion is reasonably stable over time.

In view of potential problems entailed by nonrandom survey nonresponse there is a case for applying weights to the data to ensure that they are representative of the population in a consistent way over time. The survey weights we use in our analysis reweight each year of sample data to take account of annual population frequencies across age, marital status, and household composition cells. Whilst ensuring a consistent basis across years, these weights will not therefore alleviate potential problems due to unreliable information on high-earners, or on particular components of income such as self-employment or benefit income.

Finally, as will be clear from the preceding, the information in the FES does not allow us to construct flow measures of savings: i.e., from measures of deposits and withdrawals into or out of households' financial accounts. Nor does the survey collect information on the level of wealth holdings of sample respondents, so we cannot take differences from one year to the next (which would be prohibited anyway because the FES is a cross section not a panel design). As a result we are

---

[6]Over the period 1985–92 the proportion of earnings recorded in the FES to those contained in the National Accounts varies between 93.3 and 98.6%.

[7]Recorded investment income deviates quite heavily from the figures in the National Accounts (41.3% in 1985, 60.3% in 1992) and the proportion changes over the years. Total benefit income is relatively close to that in the NAs; certain benefits, however (family credit and housing benefit for private tenants), exhibit some serious underrecording.

forced to rely on the residual between income and consumption as a measure of household saving. Unfortunately, there is no other appropriate household survey which we can use to supplement our analysis. Other official household surveys do not contain the relevant information, and the one detailed specialist survey that is available to us (the Financial Research Survey, collected privately by National Opinion Polls) is a cross section only available in the most recent years. In the future, the British Household Panel Study (BHPS) promises to be a useful source of information on changes in wealth, having collected a brief module of questions on the value of household assets in both the 1995 and the 2000 waves. The second wave of this data is not yet available at the time of writing, and the first wave contains too few disaggregate wealth categories to be useful for what follows.

When it comes to specific components of income or contributions to particular forms of saving, the FES offers a fairly complete picture. The one exception is with respect to contributions into pension plans (public or private) that are made by employers on behalf of their employees, about which there is no information recorded in the FES questionnaire. For what follows we compute employer contributions to public pensions by applying the contribution rules and percentages in place at the time of observation to individuals' observed gross earnings.

To compute lifetime profiles for all variables we divide the FES into date-of-birth cohorts using groups comparable to the other chapters in this volume, i.e., 5-year bands, with the first cohort being born between 1896 and 1900, the second born between 1901 and 1905, and so on. Age profiles are initially estimated under the assumption of no time effects; hence, all variation in the data is attributed to either cohort or age.[8] All values are annualized and converted to 1998 euros using purchasing power parities published by the OECD (i.e., $£1 = €1.474$).

7.3 CROSS-SECTIONAL DESCRIPTIVE EVIDENCE, 1978–93

For the purposes of comparison with the other country studies in this project, we consider saving in three categories – discretionary saving, mandatory saving, and "notional" saving (i.e., contributions to pay-as-you-go systems that may crowd out private saving). Since data limitations only allow us to compute one comprehensive measure of saving – i.e., the residual between income and expenditure – the degree to which we are able to examine these disaggregate categories individually is severely limited. We provide what information we can and add some aggregate statistics from other available data sets for certain variables to give some idea of the magnitude of

---

[8]Further investigation of these issues, presented in more detail at the end of this chapter, suggests that this process yields profiles similar to those estimated using more sophisticated identifying assumptions, probably because the time series of data is long, comprising two complete business cycles, and time effects are close to averaging out in the estimation of the profiles.

various components in the UK relative to other countries. As the income information is detailed we are able to provide some information for the second, and complete information for the final of these three categories. However, since we are unable to sum the three components in our survey, for a detailed analysis of the age profiles of total saving, the interested reader should turn immediately to the analysis in the Income subsection and onwards.

Discretionary Saving

As outlined earlier, it is not possible to compute estimates of financial or real saving from flows of household funds in and out of various assets since such data are not collected in the FES data, nor to our knowledge in any other survey in the UK. The only component of discretionary information about which we have information on this basis is life insurance premiums. The FES data on life insurance premiums show a marked increase over time in the cross-sectional profile (Figure 7.1). There is also a clear jump in the profiles across years, most likely due to a more inclusive definition of this item in the data set: in 1984 the FES included further financial products that should be counted as "life insurance." Further widening of the definition occurred in 1985 and in 1994. The take-up of life insurance policies is strongest between the ages 25 and 35 where the cohort profiles show a steep increase. Such an increase is commonly associated with homeownership, since one of the common forms of mortgage in the UK entails saving in the form of life insurance in order to pay off the principal at the end of the term, while paying only the interest in the interim periods.

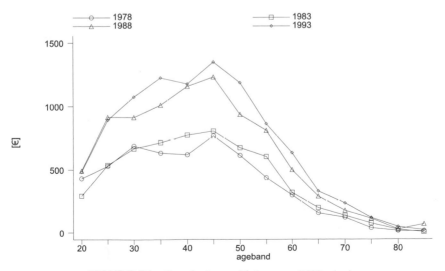

FIGURE 7.1   Contributions to life insurance (1998 prices).

We can at least get some idea of the relative importance of real and financial wealth in the household portfolio by looking at aggregate statistics on wealth holdings. Figures from the Inland Revenue (1998) show that financial wealth accounts for 55% of household wealth, with the remainder in real forms of wealth, predominantly real estate (35%). Inland Revenue data also give a good indication of the enormous concentration of wealth at the very top of the distribution – in 1995 the wealthiest 1% of individuals owned 19% of total marketable wealth in the UK, for example (Inland Revenue, 1998).

Looking within financial wealth, what is known is that life insurance and private pension wealth accounts for one-half of this financial wealth. Since these are treated as one item for the purposes of official statistics, a breakdown of this aggregate into the discretionary as opposed to the mandatory component is difficult. Banks *et al.* (2000) present some cross-sectional analysis of the 1995 British Household Panel Study, and show that, for stocks of saving, at least, there is considerable inequality in the nonpension and nonlife insurance component of wealth accumulation, and that levels are particularly low for younger households as would be expected.

Mandatory Saving

In this category we include payments to funded forms of saving to which the households are precommitted: i.e., contributions to private pension schemes. Although private occupational (DB) schemes have existed in Britain for many years, coverage of private pension schemes has increased substantially since the 1986 pension reform and the subsequent introduction of personal pensions in 1988.

Private pension schemes, and occupational pensions in particular, have been an integral element in the UK pension arrangements for more than four decades. Since the 1960s a more or less stable portion of about half the working population has been covered by an occupational pension. With the introduction of personal pensions the proportion of individuals with some form of private pension has increased further, so that by the year 1993 roughly 87% of employed men (62% of women) had been contracted-out of the second tier of the public pension scheme.

Note that the numbers replicated in the age-profile graphs that follow do not include employers' contributions to private pension plans.[9] As a guide to the potential importance of this issue, an individual who wanted to save the maximum allowed could have *total* contributions (employer and employee together) of 17.5% of their income until age 35, then rising to 25% by age 50, and 35% by age 60. But the rules for the employer component of such contributions differ widely across

---

[9]Traditionally, private pensions have been occupational schemes offered by the employer. Since 1988 so-called Approved Personal Pensions (APP) have become a further option as part of the mandatory second-tier pension schemes. Employers do, however, only match contributions for occupational schemes.

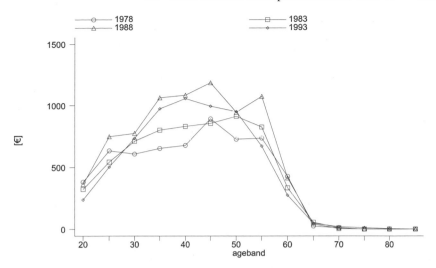

FIGURE 7.2 Mean saving in private pensions.

the various schemes and the data does not contain information on this component. Indeed it would be extremely problematic to collect, since other evidence has shown that respondents to surveys typically have a low level of awareness of the contributions being put into their schemes by third parties. The diversity of employer contribution regimes, and the lack of pension plan details in the data that would facilitate a linkage to the rules of the scheme (as has been done in the United States for the Health and Retirement Study) mean that it would be impossible to impute even a general approximation into our data.

Figure 7.2 displays the cross-sectional profiles of the mean amounts that households contributed to private pension funds in each of the 4 years we use. The figure shows an increase in this form of saving over time until 1988 across all working age groups. However, it is worth noting that the data points for 1993 lie below the 1988 line. This seems quite surprising at first sight. In fact, one would expect to see the exact opposite given that personal pensions were introduced in 1988 and invoked a strong take-up that quickly reached 30% by 1995. We will observe the same phenomenon in the case of national insurance contributions described in the next section, which suggests that some common effect is at work.

During the 1980s the UK saw an unprecedented increase in income inequality that also extended into the early 1990s. This development, which is well documented in Goodman *et al.* (1997), was in part due to a rise in inequality in earnings – the variable that determines amounts contributed to private pensions as well as those to national insurance. The cross-sectional profiles of mean total household income in Figure 7.4 below show an increase from 1988 to 1993 and hence disguise the changes in the distribution. When considering, however, the distribution of household income from earnings (included in Appendix III) the picture becomes much clearer. The lower percentiles in 1993 reach earnings levels that lie significantly below those observed 5 years earlier in 1988. The higher unemployment rate in 1993[10] certainly plays a role in this and explains the increase in the proportion of working age households in our data with zero contributions to private pensions from 55.6% in 1988 to 64.91% in 1993.[11]

Whereas the described effects of inequality and unemployment also apply to the case of national insurance contributions, there is an additional issue to be taken into account here concerning the quality of the data. The FES does not capture actual contributions to personal pensions very well: i.e., contributions to the form of private pensions that was only introduced in 1988. One particular fraction is most likely to systematically escape the FES records due to how personal pensions are administered. Even though members of personal pension schemes are entitled to the contracted-out rebate of the second tier of the state scheme, they have to pay the full national insurance contributions in the first place. It is the Department of Social Security that redirects this rebate to the individual's personal pension fund. This part of contributions will therefore systematically not show up in the FES figures, so that underreporting becomes more and more important with the increase of personal pension coverage ever since their introduction in 1988. Since personal pensions have been particularly popular among people with higher earnings, and in particular young male workers, the underreporting may be important, especially for people with high contributions – a selection process that again leads the 1993 line to appear lower.

Contributions to PAYG Systems

Payment of national insurance contributions that finance the UK PAYG system is compulsory for everybody with earnings above a certain threshold (lower earnings limit – LEL). On the difference between earnings and this threshold the individual has to pay a certain percentage (currently 10% on earnings above the LEL (+2% of the LEL, if one earns more than the LEL)). There is, however, a ceiling to the amounts contributed, as no contributions need to be paid on earnings that lie above the upper earnings limit (UEL). Remember that workers who are enrolled in an occupational or a personal pension scheme pay reduced NI contributions.[12]

Apart from paying for the government's expenditure on retirement pensions, national insurance contributions are also used to finance various other state benefits.

---

[10]The unemployment rate in 1993 lies 2.5 percentage points above the one recorded in 1988 (OECD Economic Outlook: 1988, 7.8%; 1993, 10.3%).

[11]This increase in noncontributing households does not contradict the reported increase in private pension coverage. The latter refers to the percentage of *individuals* covered in the *active workforce*, whereas the number of noncontributing *households* is taken from the entire observed population.

[12]Contracted-out NI contribution rates are currently 1.8 percentage points below the contracted-in rate.

These include unemployment benefit, statutory sick and maternity pay, incapacity benefit, maternity allowance, widow's payment, widowed mother's allowance, and widow's pension, all of which could feasibly crowd out private saving. There are no fixed percentages allocated to each program, which makes it impossible to single out specific items.

Payments to health insurance are usually also considered to be a form of notional saving in other chapters in this comparative study. A particularity of the United Kingdom is, however, that health care under the National Health Service is free of charge and its usage is noncontributory: i.e., it is paid out of the general tax income of the government. Hence, this form of notional saving can neither be identified nor be allocated in the UK. This obviously implies at the same time that health expenditure of the elderly – an important item in old-age expenditure in other countries – will be relatively low in the UK, and hence this motive for saving will also be relatively weaker.

As is the case with mandatory saving, we do not observe any information on employer national insurance contributions. Unlike mandatory saving through employer pension contributions, however, employer NI contributions can be calculated using individuals' observed earnings and applying each year's contributions schedule. National insurance contributions were subject to a number of changes over time from flat-rate to earnings-related; nowadays, 10% contributions rates exist in respect of most employees, with no upper limit for employer contributions.

The average amounts that households of different ages contributed to the state's PAYGO scheme are shown in Figure 7.3, indicating an increase over the years until 1988. Again, there are several effects explaining the observed patterns: one is economic growth, and hence higher incomes on which contributions are paid;

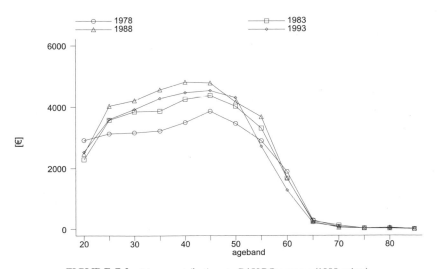

FIGURE 7.3   Mean contributions to PAYGO systems (1998 prices).

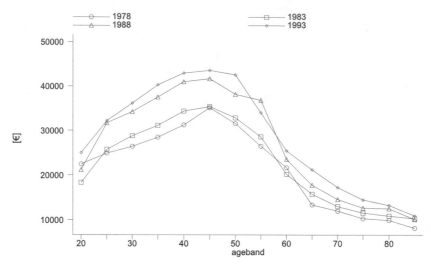

FIGURE 7.4   Mean total household gross income.

another concerns changes in the contribution system and, finally, the evolution of the earnings limits. When looking in detail at early years of our sample, the increases are due to a rise in earnings (see also the gross income profiles in Figure 7.4) as well as a widening of the range of earnings on which contributions are to be paid (i.e., the LEL dropped slightly in real terms while the UEL went up). The structure of contribution payments was changed substantially in 1978 when SERPS – the state earnings-related pension scheme – was introduced. The actual percentages for NI contributions did not change very much at first, but this was not to last very long. By 1983 the contribution rates had been raised by 2.5 percentage points. Along with the beginning of the strong earnings growth of the 1980s, especially among younger cohorts, this led to those high figures until the end of that decade (see the cross-sectional profile for 1988). In the 1990s the levels appear to be significantly lower. The same observation was already made for contributions to private pensions and the explanations based on the increase in earnings inequality and high unemployment apply here also.[13] However, the impact of the rise in inequality is amplified in this case through the interaction with the earnings limits that define the lower and the upper bound of national insurance contributions to be paid. With high levels of unemployment and a substantial fraction of the population on low earnings there are as many as 28.2% of households who do not pay any national

---

[13]Note that the systematic underreporting of contributions to personal pensions mentioned in the previous section will have the opposite effect for national insurance contributions (NICs). The contracting-out rebates are recorded as part of the NICs, since they are collected by the Department of Social Security first and only then are they redirected to the individuals' personal pension funds.

insurance contributions. This compares to 20.86% in 1988.[14] Those earners at the upper end of the distribution do, however, not pay higher contributions over time once their earnings have hit the upper threshold (UEL) above which any extra earnings are not liable to national insurance contributions. Hence this fraction of the population benefits from high increases in earnings while paying constant NICs in real terms because the earnings limits have only been uprated in line with prices ever since 1981.[15] The sum of all the effects described led to the surprisingly low average national insurance contributions in the year 1993.

Finally, note the decline in the cross-sectional profiles from age 55 onwards, reflecting an increasing portion of people retiring from the work force before statutory pension age. The official pension age for men is 65 and the profiles have clearly dropped very close to zero by that age.[16]

Income

Our definition of income is predominantly composed of the components earnings, income from self-employment, asset income, annuitized payments from PAYGO schemes and funded pension schemes, and other public nonpension transfers (i.e., social security benefits). Lump-sum payments from PAYGO schemes do not exist in the UK. The income definition we use is based on a refined definition established by the Department of Social Security for measuring income distributions (see Goodman and Webb, 1994, for a detailed description). Throughout this section we present age profiles for the mean of each variable of interest. This retains comparability in the text with the cohort adjustments that will be presented later. In the descriptive tables presented in the Appendices both means and medians are reported. In general, as in the German analysis presented in this volume, medians lie between 10 and 20% below the mean.

Total Gross Income

Figure 7.4 shows the cross-sectional age profile of household gross income for the 4 selected years of our sample period. The familiar hump-shaped profile is

---

[14]These fractions are extremely high considering the fact that *every* employee has to pay some NICs as soon as his earnings pass the threshold defined by the lower earnings limit (LEL) — even if he is contracted out.

[15]The LEL is linked to the value of the full-rate basic state pension payable to a single person. From 1981 onward the state pension benefits were legislated to only be increased in line with prices (as opposed to with the higher of earnings and prices as was the case before). Hence, the LEL has been price indexed ever since and the UEL is supposed to be a multiple of the LEL ($6\frac{1}{2}$ to 7 times the LEL).

[16]Remember that households are sorted by the age of the head of household. It is therefore normal that contributions do not fall down to zero completely since a younger household member might still be working and hence still pay into a pension scheme or make PAYG contributions.

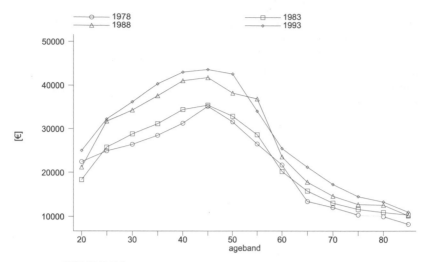

FIGURE 7.5   Mean total household disposable income (1998 prices).

immediately evident, although the cross-sectional age profiles peak in the mid- to late-forties, slightly earlier than expected given that early retirement typically only begins after age 50 (see Figure 7.13). The other striking feature of the figure is the rapid income growth observed across all working ages between the 1983 and 1988 cross sections.

In Figure 7.5 we present the cross-sectional age profile of mean disposable household income, which again displays a hump shape. The shift in the levels of incomes over time again suggests some economic growth over the observed period, and the difference between 1988 and 1993 profiles – that is greater than the one observed in Figure 7.4 for gross income – is consistent with the average reduction in national insurance contributions and direct taxes over that period.

Annuitized Retirement Income

The most important component of income for elderly households is annuitized retirement income. In Figure 7.6 we present profiles for mean annuitized retirement income, defined to include public and private pensions and income from annuities. An interesting feature of the UK experience is that pensioners' average incomes over the last 30 years have risen faster than average incomes of those in work for several reasons and this is indicated clearly by the growth in annuity income profiles across years in our sample. First, with earnings-related, i.e., second tier, coverage becoming compulsory in 1978 for everyone who earns more than a certain threshold, many more individuals now receive additional pension benefits to supplement their basic state pension when they retire. Moreover, for those who are members of a private scheme the indexation rules have significantly

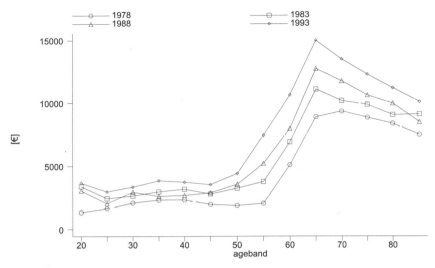

FIGURE 7.6 Annuitized retirement income, including social security (1998 prices).

improved and, with an increasing number of women earning their own entitlements to a private pension, the amounts of private pension income that households receive on average have risen markedly over time.

It is important to point out that means-tested benefits take an important role in income of the elderly in the UK: in 1996–97 they accounted for 12% of pensioner income or 1.2% of GDP. We discuss this in more detail in Section 7.5 where we link pension policies to particular features of the observed patterns.

Finally, it is worth noting that the UK provides substantial noncontributory, nonfinancial benefits for the elderly: free health care (government spending on the NHS is 4.4% of GDP[17] and around two-thirds of these resources go to pensioners), free prescriptions and dental care, and (some) free public transport. The latter benefits are not available for working-age individuals. We do not attempt to impute monetary values to these benefits in order to add them to income, but merely point out this feature to bear in mind when comparing the UK to other countries in this volume.

Of course, mean age profiles can hide inequality within age groups. In particular, there are groups of individuals or households on low income with hardly any SERPS entitlements and no occupational pensions. With the decreasing value of the basic state pension in real terms due to price indexation, future payments for these groups will be very low. On the other hand, there is an increasingly large group covered by good private pensions that are providing increasingly high levels of retirement income.

[17]Figure from HM Treasury (1997), Public Expenditure, Statistical Analyses 1997–98, London: HMSO.

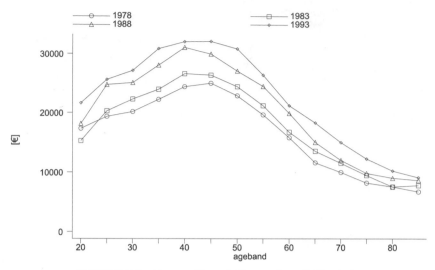

FIGURE 7.7   Mean total household expenditure (1998 prices).

Saving (Residual Definition)

Having constructed the income variable in the previous section, we still need a measure of total household expenditure to compute saving as a residual between the two. In Figure 7.7 we present cross-sectional age profiles of mean total household expenditure for the 4 years.

As with income, the expenditure age profiles are hump-shaped, as has now been pointed out in a large number of papers using FES expenditure data to analyse the dynamics of consumption growth (Blundell *et al.*, 1994; Banks and Blundell, 1994).

Typically, studies look at nondurable components of expenditure only. For the purposes of this paper, however, we define expenditure to include spending on all items, including durable purchases and housing, since this is the definition that will give us a residual definition comparable to financial saving. Two things are worth pointing out about the cross-sectional expenditure age profile at this stage. The first is that the peak of the profile is at an earlier age than the peak of the income profile. Secondly, expenditure continues to fall throughout retirement. This is consistent with the evidence of other studies on life-cycle expenditure paths for the UK (Banks *et al.*, 1998).

Saving

With both income and consumption data established we can finally present our measures of total household saving. We begin with an analysis of the level of saving, where we have computed saving defined as the residual between household disposable income and total household expenditure. This is presented in Figure 7.8. As might be expected, the profile is substantially more noisy than those for either expenditure or income. As a result, we also present profiles in Figure 7.9 for median saving, which are more robust to outliers typically caused by households

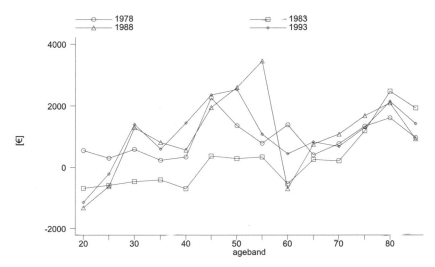

FIGURE 7.8   Mean total household saving (1998 prices).

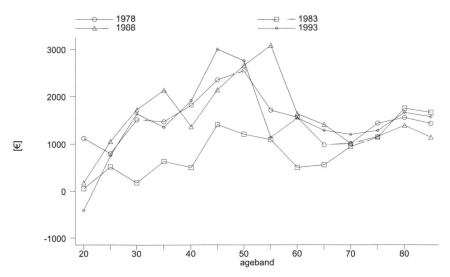

FIGURE 7.9   Median household saving (1998 prices).

having abnormally high incomes (bonuses) or expenditures (due to infrequency of purchase) in the weeks in which they were surveyed.

The cross-sectional patterns of saving in Figures 7.8 and 7.9 show positive saving for most of the working life with levels rising until age 55. What is striking about these figures, however, is the uniformly positive saving for older (retired) age groups in all years. This is further evidence that the consumption profile continues to fall below income after retirement – the phenomenon investigated in detail in Banks *et al.* (1998) – a fact that, on the surface at least, requires some investigation. We leave this until we discuss cohort-adjusted profiles below.

Saving Rates

Figure 7.10 depicts median saving rates, calculated as saving divided by disposable income. Any hump shape observed up until age 65 disappears and savings rates are observed to rise continuously until retirement age for all years. Unlike income and expenditure profiles, there are not uniform time effects separating the profiles – the level of the saving rate profile rises and falls over time, as would be expected from a cyclical variable. Finally, and perhaps unusually, saving rates increase, at least in cross section, with age, as older households save as much as their younger counterparts but have lower annuitized incomes. Again, we leave discussion of this in more detail to Section 7.4.

Finally in this section we look at the distribution within the population of the above measures by giving a cross-sectional snapshot for the year 1993 of each of the

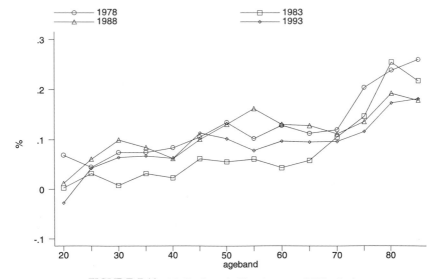

FIGURE 7.10   Median household saving rates (1998 prices).

distributions of the variables that we use to construct our residual measure of saving: i.e., "disposable household income" and "total household expenditure," and also the distribution of the resulting savings and saving rates. More precisely, Figure 7.11 presents the mean and median, along with the 25th and 75th percentiles for each of these variables.

For both income and expenditure the mean lies above the median, indicating the presence of some households with particularly high incomes and expenditures that skew the distribution. The gap between the 25th and the 75th percentile turns out to be largest around the middle of the life cycle, that is around age 45 – this is true for income, expenditure, and saving. The normalization of saving by income removes this change in distance so that the different percentiles move more or less in parallel across the age bands. Note that for saving rates the median is above the mean (for all other presented variables it is the other way round). This suggests that in 1993 there are some heavy dissavers that pull the mean down below the median, as would be expected.

Covariates

Many other factors have been changing in the household population in Britain since 1973, and these could well underpin some of the changes over time in the cross-sectional profiles for income, expenditure, and saving discussed above. Although a full structural analysis is far beyond the scope of this descriptive chapter, in this subsection we present cross-sectional profiles for the same 4 years for variables that might plausibly be considered covariates in household income, spending, and savings profiles. We focus on household size, employment rates, marginal tax rates, and homeownership rates.

Marginal Tax Rates

There have been many tax changes in Britain over the last 20 years. Broadly speaking, these can be summed up as, since 1980, a steady reduction in marginal rates of income tax, a small decrease in national insurance contributions (although not in terms of the tax rate, instead as a result of the evolution of earning limits interacted with increasing earnings inequality), and increases in indirect taxes.

Household Size

One of the most striking features of the UK household population has been the change in household structure over the last 20 years. Despite low population growth, increasing divorce rates, delayed household formation, and increased longevity have led to marked increases in the number of households in the population, and hence reductions in the average size of households. Such trends are

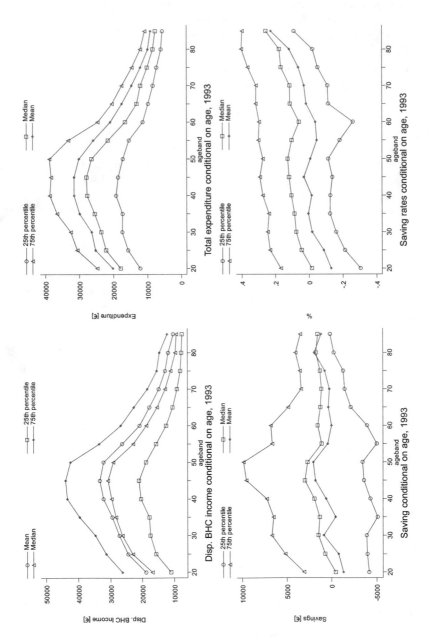

FIGURE 7.11   Snapshot for the year 1993 of saving variables.

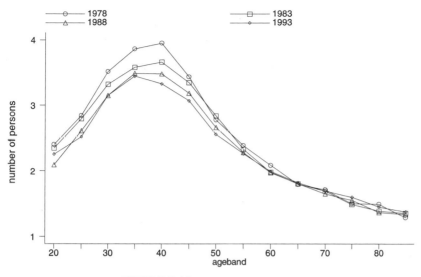

FIGURE 7.12   Average household size.

predicted to continue, or even accelerate, for the next 10 years at least. Since saving is the way of providing for expected future needs, and current needs also determine one's ability to save, such trends might be thought to have effects on saving behavior.

In Figure 7.12 we present cross-sectional age profiles for household size (counting adults and children separately). As is clear, the profile has moved steadily downward over our sample period, reflecting the fall in average household size predominantly in middle age and furthermore the peak of the household-size profile has moved slightly to the right, indicating later childbearing on average.

Male Labor Force Participation

In keeping with most other developed countries, the UK has a declining cross-sectional age profile for employment rates for men after age 50. This profile is presented in Figure 7.13. Looking within cohorts, it is clear that men with occupational pensions are more likely to retire early (i.e., from 55 onwards). What is most striking is the declining levels of the profile at all ages, and particularly at the early retirement ages. These effects have been so rapid that over 50% of men are not working by age 60, whereas 20 years ago that number would only have been around 25%.

Female Labor Force Participation

In contrast to male employment rates, the proportion of women of working age in employment has increased over time, and the increases have been concentrated at

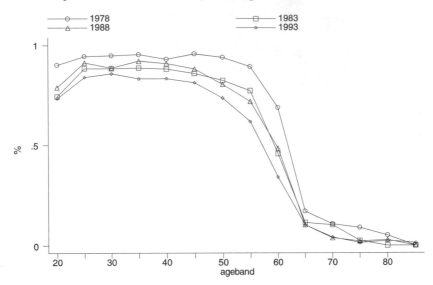

FIGURE 7.13   Labor force participation of men.

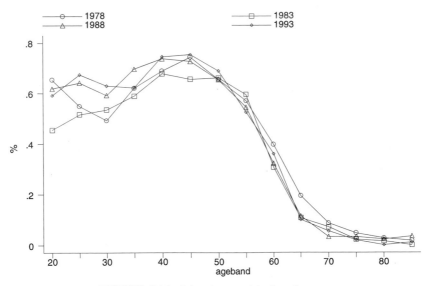

FIGURE 7.14   Labor force participation of women.

the bottom end of the age distribution (Figure 7.14). Among women aged 50–59 the proportion of those in employment and not working has remained relatively stable over the period. The result of these changes is that, while there are still differences between the employment rate profiles for men and women, these differences are far less substantial than they have been in previous years. It is worth noting, however, that the proportion of those working part-time versus full-time still differs across genders.

Homeownership

Homeownership is more prevalent in the UK than in many European countries, particularly at younger ages. In addition, homeownership rates have increased markedly over the years, possibly as a result of a number of supply-side reforms, such as the sale of public housing to tenants, and relaxations in credit and mortgage markets.

Figure 7.15 presents cross-sectional age profiles for the prevalence of home-ownership in each of the 4 years, and the differences between profiles are striking. The most substantial differences in profiles across time periods are mainly in middle age. More specifically, there is not a particularly higher incidence in ownership rates for the youngest cohorts, as is shown in Figure 7.15(b), which shows cohort profiles for the same variable. Partly, the period of expansion in homeownership over the last 30 years is over. In addition, however, this is likely to be in part due to a combination of business cycle effects (particularly the early 1990s downturn in the housing market), but also due to composition effects, since these cohorts are not getting married or having children, and less household formation typically leads to less homeownership.

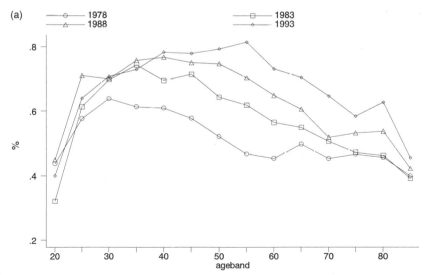

FIGURE 7.15   (a) Portion of householders owning their home. (b) Cohort age profiles of portion of householders owning their home.

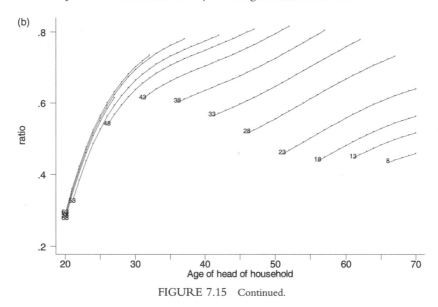

FIGURE 7.15 Continued.

7.4 COHORT EFFECTS AND LIFE-CYCLE PROFILES

This section presents the main features of the available empirical evidence for savings and related variables. Note that the residual measure of savings based on the difference between income and consumption does not allow us to recover the various components of most forms of savings. Hence, as before, the information we can provide on the subcategories discussed in other chapters of this volume – discretionary, mandatory, and "notional savings" – is limited. We therefore focus on the one where we are able to recover a complete measure: i.e., "notional savings." At the end of this section we discuss the identifying assumption of zero-time effects for the presented cohort profiles. We offer alternative ways to construct cohort profiles for selected key variables.

Notional Savings

Payment of national insurance (NI) contributions that finance the UK PAYG system is compulsory for everybody with earnings above a certain threshold (lower earnings limit – LEL). Contributions to the scheme are required to be made both by employees themselves and by employers on behalf of the employees. Employee contributions are currently 10% on earnings above the LEL plus 2% of the value of the LEL if one earns above the LEL. There is, however, a ceiling to the amounts contributed, as the employee does not pay contributions on earnings that lie above the upper earnings limit (UEL). The 1998 values of the LEL and UEL were €5658

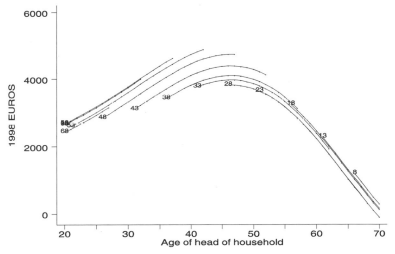

FIGURE 7.16   Cohort age profiles for total NICs.

and   €42,874   respectively.   Workers   who   are   enrolled   in   an occupational or a personal pension scheme pay reduced NI contributions.[18]

The FES does not collect any information on employers' national insurance contributions but we can recover these on the basis of recorded gross earnings applying the relevant contribution rules over time. Like employees' contributions, these were subject to a number of important changes – from flat-rate to various forms of earnings-related contribution scales. Current rates are at 10% of the employee's gross earnings. There is, however, no upper limit for employer contributions.

Figure 7.16 shows the average amounts of total national insurance contributions (NICs) in constant prices paid by the various cohorts over time.[19] Note that in the remainder of this study the indicated cohorts are denoted by the midpoint of the date-of-birth intervals contained in each of the 5-year band cohorts (e.g., 43 for the cohort where the head was born between 1941 and 1945).

With regard to the shape of the profile, contributions rise slightly through working ages (tracking increases in earnings) and then fall as more households in each group are observed as retired.[20] Positive cohort effects reflect real income

---

[18]Contracted-out NI contribution rates are currently 1.8 percentage points below the contracted-in rate.

[19]As the other chapters in this volume, we allow for linear cohort effects, but restrict time effects to be zero. We smooth the cohort age profiles by using a fifth-order polynomial in age. The methodology and assumptions involved in the construction of the presented cohort profiles are discussed in Brugiavini and Weber (2001).

[20]Remember that households are grouped by the age of the head of the household. It is therefore normal that contributions do not fall down to zero completely, since a younger household member might still be working and hence still make PAYG contributions.

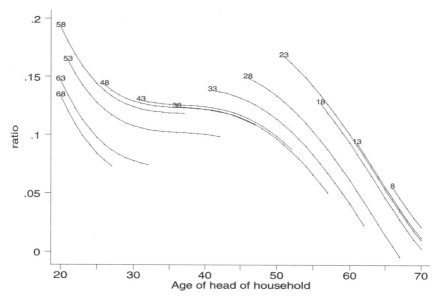

FIGURE 7.17   Cohort age profiles for total NICs over gross household income.

growth amongst cohorts going through their middle ages during our sample period.

When plotting NICs as a fraction of total household income – presented in Figure 7.17 – it becomes immediately apparent that for those younger cohorts who are currently on the upward slope of their income paths the fraction of income paid in NICs has fallen, even though there had been some increases in the percentages of NICs to be paid. This is mainly due to a combination of two effects. The most important one is the evolution of the thresholds defining the earnings bracket on which NICs are levied: since 1980 these have been linked to prices. As a result, an increasing fraction of people with high earnings are paying NICs up to the upper earnings limit, but not on earnings that lie above this threshold, especially with the rise in income inequality observed in the 1980s. This is an interesting aspect from a policy point of view, since this implies that more and more people at the upper end of the income distribution pay less NICs as a fraction of their total earnings. Another reason for less NICs paid as a percentage of total household income is that, especially among young male earners, there was a rapid take-up of personal pensions that were introduced in 1988 as a further possibility of contracting out of the public pension scheme. These individuals paid reduced NICs on condition that the rebate was contributed to a Defined Contribution (DC) personal pension.

To get an idea of the degree to which such "notional savings" contributions may crowd out other forms of saving we compute the lifetime profile for (expected) public pension wealth arising from these contributions for a male worker retiring in 2001 who did not contract out of the public scheme at any point

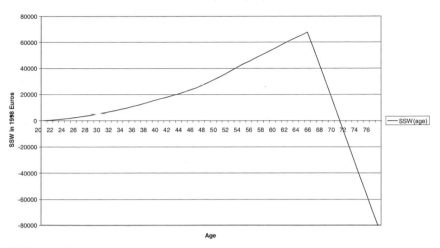

FIGURE 7.18   Social security wealth (SSW) accumulation over the life cycle for a typical worker born in 1936.

during his working life. Hence, we estimate the lifetime average earnings profile (under the same assumptions as the profiles in the following section) for a male person born in 1936 and retiring at age 65 in 2001. On this basis we calculate actual contributions paid, as well as expected receipts conditioning on given rules (either currently in place or already announced). We include all the various components of public pensions: benefits from the basic state pension, graduated pensions,[21] and the state earnings-related pension scheme (SERPS).

In line with the measures of social security wealth (SSW) used in the other chapters of this book, we define:[22]

$$\text{SSW}(t) = \text{SSW}(t-1) + c(t), \text{ for ages } t = 20, \ldots, 64$$
$$\text{SSW}(t) = \text{SSW}(t-1) - b(t), \text{ for ages } t = 65, \ldots, T \qquad (7.1)$$

where $c(t)$ and $b(t)$ denote contributions and benefits at time t, respectively, and T is the final period until which an average male person will survive in expectation. All values in the above equations are assumed to be in real terms. The resulting age profile for SSW is presented in Figure 7.18.

---

[21]Graduated pensions were in place between 1961 and 1975; it was an earnings-related scheme and, as such, the predecessor of SERPS.

[22]See the German study (Chapter 3) for more discussion of this technique.

By retirement age, cumulated social security wealth amounts to around €70,000 for an individual who remains in the public scheme for the entire working life. It is worth noting here that those contracted out of the earnings-related part of the scheme will get substantially less public pension entitlements.[23]

Apart from paying for the government's expenditure on retirement pensions, national insurance contributions are also used to finance various other state benefits.[24] Payments to health insurance are usually also considered to be a form of "notional saving." As discussed earlier, a particularity of the UK is, however, that health care under the National Health Service is free of charge and its usage is noncontributory – i.e., it is paid out of the general tax income of the government – and this form of "notional saving" can neither be identified nor be allocated in the UK. At the same time, the health expenditures of the elderly – an important item in old-age expenditure in other countries – will be relatively low in the UK.

Total Savings: Residual Measure

Our measure of total savings is constructed from the difference of total disposable household income and total household expenditure. Therefore we present cohort age profiles for the latter two variables first, before passing on to discussing total savings.

The cohort effects in the income profiles are clearly visible in Figure 7.19 and the decomposition confirms that later cohorts have higher levels of lifetime incomes, presumably due to productivity growth and higher female labor market participation. The cohort effects are strongly jointly significant in the estimation equation. The age pattern is hump shaped: the average household income profile increases steeply until age 50; thereafter it decreases. That is, despite cohort adjustment, income for all cohorts still peaks before retirement age, presumably as a result of the falling labor market activity of adults (in particular men) aged 50 and over. This does, of course, not imply that the income profiles of single workers would necessarily drop in such a strong way, but simply that the cohort's average income decreases with age as more and more people from that cohort retire.

As for expenditure, we define it to include spending on all items, including durable purchases and housing, since this is the definition that will give us a

---

[23]Also, those contracted out tend to be higher-income households, so whether mean lifetime income profiles are an appropriate measure of the resources of those contracted in for their entire working lives is another concern.

[24]These include unemployment benefit, statutory sick and maternity pay, incapacity benefit, maternity allowance, widow's payment, widowed mother's allowance, and widow's pension, all of which could feasibly crowd out private saving. There are no fixed percentages allocated to each program, which makes it impossible to single out specific items.

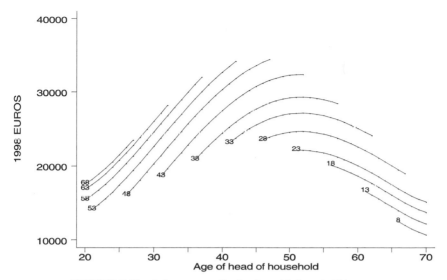

FIGURE 7.19   Cohort age profiles for disposable household income.

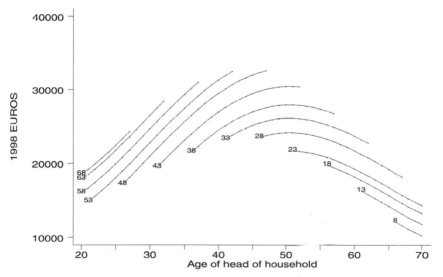

FIGURE 7.20   Cohort age profiles for household expenditure.

residual definition comparable to (mandatory and discretionary) financial saving. In Figure 7.20 we present the cohort-adjusted age profiles for total expenditure. As with income, the expenditure age profiles are hump shaped, as has now been pointed out in a large number of papers using FES expenditure data to analyse the dynamics of consumption growth (Blundell *et al.*, 1994; Banks and Blundell,

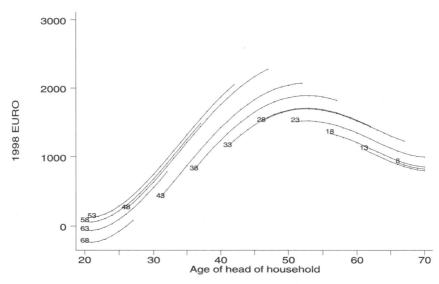

FIGURE 7.21   Cohort age profiles for total household saving (median).

1994). They peak at around ages 47–50, the age when family needs associated with the costs of children are presumably at their highest. Again, we see strong positive cohort effects.

Note that expenditure continues to fall throughout retirement. This feature of the evidence has also been pointed out in other studies on life-cycle expenditure paths for the UK (Banks *et al.*, 1998). We discuss this point in more detail when considering the empirical evidence on total savings.

In Figure 7.21 we present the cohort age profiles for median saving. We use the median rather than the mean, because the latter measure is very sensitive to outliers associated with temporarily low incomes or expenditures.

The patterns of median saving show positive saving for most of working life, with levels rising until age 52, and declining thereafter. What is striking about this figure is that saving for older (retired) age groups remains positive throughout. This is obviously linked to the observation made earlier that consumption profiles continue to fall after retirement.

Figure 7.22 depicts cohort profiles for median saving rates by age: i.e., dividing the residual measure of savings by total disposable household income. Here the story is very different to income and expenditure, since there are no real cohort effects observed in the saving-rate profiles, and also the hump shape has virtually disappeared. Unlike the income and expenditure profiles, there are not uniform time effects separating the profiles. The youngest cohorts (born between 1956 and 1970) seem to start off at significantly lower levels of savings as well as lower saving rates than their older counterparts. Also note that the saving rate does not turn

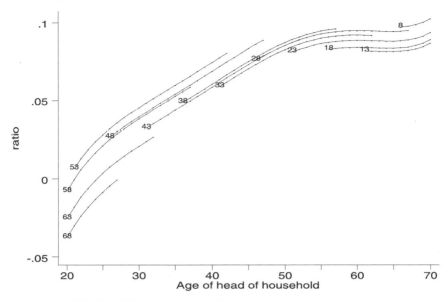

FIGURE 7.22   Cohort age profiles for household saving rate (median).

negative beyond retirement age. Quite the opposite: it basically remains as high as at times before retirement. This phenomenon is related to the "retirement savings puzzle" which has been analysed in detail by Banks *et al.* (1998). They show that controlling for the effects of mortality risk, the removal of work-related costs, and demographic variables cannot account for all of the fall in consumption growth that happens around the time of retirement.

Yet, the age profile of the saving rate during retirement is still an interesting phenomenon. One possibility is that differential mortality begins to dominate, although such an explanation would require the rich to be saving more during their retirement than the poor, which is unlikely. An alternative possibility is the previous overannuitization of wealth, possibly due to institutional reasons, which, in the presence of a bequest motive, would lead to the need for resaving to provide the bequest. Alternatively, bequest motives could become more important as households are aging. Finally, unanticipated events could explain this pattern. In particular, if pension wealth expectations are not met, or if the marginal utility of consumption falls in an unexpected way (possibly due to aging, as suggested by Börsch-Supan and Stahl, 1991), then the observed patterns of saving may be a rational response. The puzzle, as such, is why the effects are so much more marked in the UK than elsewhere. Part of this may be due to the time period over which these effects have been estimated. Under any scenario, however, it will be interesting to see if such behavior persists, as retiring generations become successively richer and retire with more wealth in both annuitized and non-annuitized forms.

7.5 FURTHER ISSUES

Pension Policies and Other Institutional Issues

Recent years have seen many reforms to the policy environment in which British households take their savings decisions. A full structural analysis of the effects of such policy change on the profiles reported earlier would be a massive modeling exercise, as well as requiring a country-specific approach not appropriate in a comparative volume such as this. However, individual country experiences with policy experiments and policy reform are a crucial determinant of differences in profiles across countries and, as such, warrant analysis. Therefore in this section we discuss the policy environment and the way it has changed over the period of our data. Due to the importance of pension saving, as well as the number of reforms that have occurred, these pension reforms are our main concern in what follows although we do discuss nonpension saving where relevant. We begin, therefore, by discussing the main features in UK pension arrangements that stand out from an international perspective, and discuss how each component contributes to the age profile for the annuity incomes of those currently retired. We go on to discuss expected pension wealth for future cohorts, and finish with some discussion of distributional issues and the relationship to nonpension saving.

Pension arrangements in the United Kingdom fall into two tiers: first, a flat-rate scheme provided by the state, and secondly, an earnings-related element that can be provided by either the state or the private sector. The role of the private sector has been relatively important ever since the 1960s, with the result that the UK – in contrast to many other countries – does not face any sustainability problems as far as the financing of the scheme is concerned. Government spending on pension payments currently amounts to 4.7% of GDP – a number that is significantly lower than in most other industrialized countries, even taking into account other social security benefits paid to pensioners (another 1.2% of GDP).[25]

Contrary to many other countries, the UK has a tradition of frequent pension reforms. Since the introduction of the current public pension scheme in 1948 there has been at least one major reform to the system in every decade: the introduction of occupational pensions in the 1950s, implementation of graduated pensions[26] in the 1960s, followed by their abolition in the 1970s, and later replacement by SERPS and the introduction of personal pensions in the 1980s. Most recently, we have seen a further major restructuring that will ultimately lead to replacement of SERPS with another flat-rate scheme, a change in the age of entitlement to receive state pension for women (from 60 to 65), and the introduction of a third form of private pension.

[25]From OECD W/P No. 168, Table 3: Australia 2.6%; Canada 5.2%; France 10.6%; Germany 11.1%; Italy 15.4% (incl. 2.1% on disability pension); Japan 6.6%; Netherlands 6.0%; New Zealand 5.9% (gross); USA 4.1% (+ 3.5% on medicare and means-tested programs).

[26]Graduated pensions were the first form of earnings-related public pension scheme in the UK.

The main result of these reforms has been that the public pension scheme no longer suffers sustainability problems of the order of magnitude of other European countries. This has been achieved by a large and rapid reduction in generosity, coupled with the introduction of a large private sector to fill some of the gap. The resulting change in the average real rate of return of the public pension scheme reflects the reduction in generosity quite clearly. Individuals retiring in the year 2000 should realize a return of 2.4% on average. This compares to an expected real return of -0.2% or -0.3% for those retiring in 2020 or 2030, respectively (Disney and Whitehouse, 1993).

These changes will only really impact on future cohorts, however. One interesting feature of the UK system is that over the last 30 years pensioners' average incomes have risen faster than the average incomes of those in work. Two main factors have driven this trend. First, with state earnings-related coverage becoming compulsory in 1978 for everyone with earnings exceeding a certain threshold, many more individuals now receive additional state pension benefits to supplement their basic state pension when they retire. Secondly, for those who are members of a private scheme, the indexation rules have significantly improved and, with an increasing number of women earning their own entitlements to a private pension, the amounts of private pension income that households receive on average have risen markedly over time.

But it is important to point out that means-tested benefits still take an important role in income of the elderly in the UK: in 1996–97 they accounted for 12% of pensioner income or 1.2% of GDP. Overall, one-third of pensioner households receive means-tested benefits of some form. In addition, the UK provides substantial noncontributory, nonfinancial benefits for the elderly: free health care (government spending on the NHS is 4.4% of GDP[27] and around two-thirds of these resources go to pensioners), free prescriptions and dental care, and (some) free public transport. The latter benefits are not available for working-age individuals. We do not attempt to impute monetary values to these benefits in order to add them to income, but merely point out this feature to bear in mind when comparing the UK to other countries in this volume. Figure 7.23 shows the levels of public pension income among the elderly population, i.e., where the head of household is aged 50 or over (hence only those cohorts who are actually observed at these ages feature in the graph).

Figure 7.23 suggests that income from public pensions increases substantially during retirement ages. Note that, to ensure comparability of methodology with other countries in this volume, these cohort age profiles are smoothed by a polynomial in age estimated across working and retirement periods. Investigation of the raw data between the ages 63 and 65 shows that the unsmoothed profiles jump discretely as cohort members retire at statutory retirement age. From this age on, profiles at most rise only slowly in real terms, possibly as a result of differential mortality.

[27]Figure from HM Treasury (1997), Public Expenditure, Statistical Analyses 1997–98, London: HMSO.

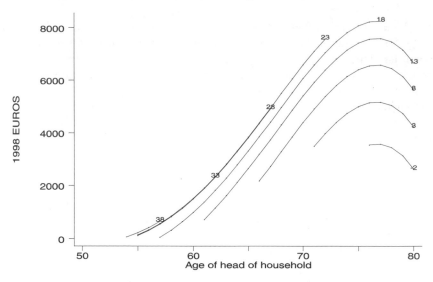

FIGURE 7.23   Income from public pensions.

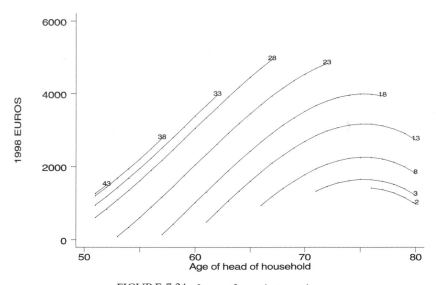

FIGURE 7.24   Income from private pensions.

In addition to state pension income, there is an increasingly large group of elderly households with substantial private pension entitlements that are providing increasingly high levels of retirement income. This is shown in Figure 7.24. For older cohorts, income from private pensions is still substantially less than their receipts from the state. Comparison of the two figures, however, shows that the relative magnitudes are much more comparable for currently retiring cohorts and, indeed in the future, private pensions will be the major source of pensioner income (at least at the mean, if not the median).

Again, Figure 7.24 indicates rising incomes from private pensions during retirement. In this case, the observation is a result of smoothing the raw data. The unsmoothed cohort profiles do not suddenly jump up close to age 65. Instead, they go up more steadily, which is observed to happen at increasingly earlier ages for later cohorts, reflecting early retirement trends. The more steady rise can be explained by the fact that people retire at different ages, so that the fraction of households of a particular cohort receiving income from a private pension increases slowly over time as more and more individuals leave the labor force. That the raw data profiles also show an increase in private pension income during retirement is likely to be due to differential mortality.

Of course, mean age profiles can hide inequality within age groups. In particular, there are groups of individuals or households on low income with hardly any SERPS entitlements and no occupational pensions. With the decreasing value of the basic state pension in real terms due to price indexation, future payments for these groups will be very low, and this leads to concerns about the incomes of those in future retired generations who did not engage in additional saving.

As mentioned above, the contraction in the size of state pension provision was accompanied by an expansion in private provision. Some idea of this can be seen in Table 7.1, which reports estimates of aggregate accrued pension rights across the various types of schemes. Private schemes are now almost as big in aggregate as the public unfunded schemes. More strikingly, perhaps, the table shows the relatively small size of the state second-tier provision, both in comparison to state first-tier provision and to private second-tier provision. The overall effect of reforms to SERPS since its introduction in 1978 has been to cut the expected annual cost

TABLE 7.1 Accrued UK Pension Rights, 1995 (in 1998 euro)

Type of pension	Value of accrued rights (€ billion)
Basic state pension	974
SERPS	242
Unfunded public sector schemes	314
Total public unfunded schemes	**1,530**
Funded occupational schemes	942
Personal pensions	266
Total private funded schemes	**1,208**
Total UK pension rights	**2,738**

Source: Pension Provision Group, 1998.

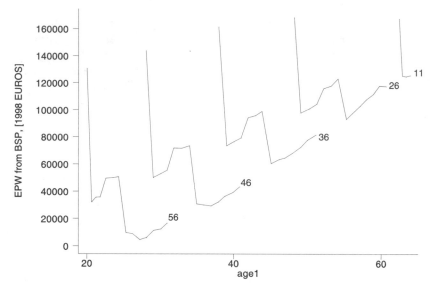

FIGURE 7.25   Present cash value of mean expected pension wealth from basic state pension (BSP) for several cohorts. *Note*: the numbers in the graph indicate the date of birth of the respective cohort profiles.

(in 2030, expressed in 1995 prices) from £41 billion to £12 billion (Government Actuary, 1995). Once again, this emphasizes that only currently retiring generations will see substantial SERPS incomes in retirement. Their predecessors would not have made enough contributions under the scheme, and their successors will either be contracted out, or will receive much less generous entitlements.

Yet even these aggregate numbers on the "stocks" of pension wealth overestimate the importance of the state second tier for current generations since the largest entitlements will only go to those currently retiring. Indeed, only a minority of employees now choose to remain in the state scheme. The response to personal pensions amongst working-aged households was quite strong: from an initial 17% of employees on their introduction in 1988, to nearly 30% in 1996. As a consequence, by the early 1990s around three-quarters of those eligible to contract out of SERPS had done so: roughly 50% into occupational pension schemes and 25% into personal pensions.[28]

Obviously the series of reforms has induced numerous (exogenous) shocks to individuals' expectations about their future pension benefits and, in principle, these shocks should have affected individuals' consumption and saving choices. To get some idea of the magnitude of such shocks, two figures (Figures 7.24 and 7.25) taken from Attanasio and Rohwedder (2001) summarize these changes for the two main state pension schemes – basic state pensions and state earnings-related

[28]Figure from Dilnot *et al.* (1994).

scheme – for the reforms occurring between the late 1970s and the mid 1990s. They display approximate public pension wealth for households observed in the FES where at least one household member is contracted into the public scheme. In Figure 7.25 we compute the discounted sum of future benefit payments in all years since 1974 in order to show how this changed over the period of our data.[29] These figures are related to Figure 7.24, but instead of computing actual pension wealth for a single cohort as they age, we compute the wealth that each cohort would expect to receive on their retirement, and show how this has varied as successive reforms altered the system. This monetary value is set in real terms and also discounted to the year in question, effectively answering the question: "What cash sum in the year in question (expressed in 1998 prices) would an individual be willing to trade for their entire pension benefits?" The discounting, as well as the effects of conditional mortality probabilities, means that these profiles slope upwards with age for each cohort even if everything else remained unchanged, since as they near their retirement date the pension is discounted less and worth more in present value terms.

The big drop in the profiles in Figure 7.25 relates to the change of indexation of pension benefits (from indexation to average earnings to indexation to average prices) for the basic state pension, by far the biggest change for this scheme during the considered time period. The real value of the basic state pension is deemed to continue to decline. At its peak in 1978 it represented roughly 20% of average male earnings, declining to just under 15% in 1998, and is projected to be worth about 8% of average male earnings by the year 2020.

Figure 7.26 features expected pension wealth profiles for SERPS and also shows several dips that are due to the cuts in generosity legislated in 1986 and 1995. For SERPS, however, we also see substantial differences *across* cohorts. Those who were closer to retirement when this second pension was introduced did not have the chance to contribute to the scheme for very long and hence did not earn comparable entitlements. Most importantly, comparing across cohorts it is clear that in the early 1980s younger cohorts should have been expecting to receive more than their predecessors. However, by the early 1990s this had reversed, and the expected wealth for the younger cohorts was substantially less than the older generations.

The above figures show considerable variation, both over the time path and over the overall level of both components of pension wealth across cohorts – certainly large enough to affect other components of wealth accumulation if individuals fully understand and act on the changes. An important and unresolved research question is that of how such changes may have affected the income, consumption, and saving profiles for existing cohorts. Equally important, perhaps, is that the experiences of today's older generations may not be good predictors of the experiences of future generations as they age, as a result of the substantial changes to the institutional system as well as to the demographic and labor market

---

[29]See Attanasio and Rohwedder (2001) for details.

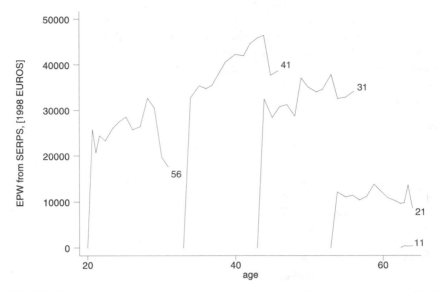

FIGURE 7.26   Present cash value of mean expected pension wealth from state earnings-related pension scheme (SERPS) for several cohorts.

conditions. Our analysis in this chapter has been descriptive, and has worked under the assumption that these effects can be summarized as changes in the levels of age profiles only. A further legitimate research question, and a crucial piece of evidence on which to base policy or policy advice, must surely be to investigate these potential differences in more detail.

Finally, with relation to policy issues, it is worth mentioning distributional or microeconomic concerns. As we pointed out, the size of the private pension system has meant that the UK is not facing quite the impending financing crisis of some of its European neighbors. However, this does not mean that the policy debate is over in the UK. Instead, focus has moved onto more microeconomic issues and, in particular, the provision for retirement incomes for those at the bottom end of the lifetime earnings distribution. The most recent reforms and debate have related to the encouragement of those remaining in SERPS to contract out. Typically, these are households with low or infrequent earnings who have been unable to afford a personal pension and who do not work for an employer offering an occupational pension.

These recent reforms raise the issue of encouraging private pensions versus other forms of financial saving. The past 20 years have seen numerous reforms to the taxation of financial assets but, broadly speaking, these have led to a more neutral taxation of saving vehicles, both with respect to consumption and with respect to other forms of savings products. Exemptions on life insurance and housing, which led to saving in these forms being taxed more favorably than consumption, have largely been abolished. Similarly, new exemptions for current-account-type savings products and certain types of equity-based saving have been introduced in a way that these forms of savings are no longer taxed less favorably than consumption, as they were in the past: see Banks and Tanner (1999) for a more detailed discussion. So it is certainly the case that individuals can now hold a broader set of savings vehicles without incurring tax disadvantages than was the case in the past. This has also meant, however, that private pensions do not stand out as such a tax-efficient way of saving as they did, apart from when individuals invest large resources over long horizons (since other vehicles offer similar tax treatments with instant access but with lower contribution limits).[30] Coupled with the growing body of evidence suggesting that a large fraction of households at the bottom end of the wealth distribution have little or no liquid financial assets, this raises the question of how far individuals should be "encouraged" into pension saving over and above other more liquid forms. Potential answers are far from clear, but it is certainly an important research question given the current movements of savings policies in the UK and given the increasing talk of private provision elsewhere in the world. At the heart of the issue is simply that pensions are only one way of deferring consumption into the future, and as such policies toward pension saving should always be thought of in conjunction with policies toward other forms of saving.

Identifying Age Profiles from a Time Series of Cross-Sectional Data

If all individuals observed at a point in time differed only by their age and a completely idiosyncratic component, a single cross-sectional survey could be used to identify the age profile of consumption, saving, and other variables by averaging these variables over individuals of the same age, along the lines of the previous section. However, if the life-cycle behavior of individuals born in different years differs systematically, the observed cross-sectional age profile does not correspond to the life-cycle profile of any individual. In a famous paper, Shorrocks (1975) has shown that the presence of strong cohort effects might introduce strong biases when one uses cross-sectional age profiles as estimates of life cycle profiles. The idea is best explained with a simple (and well-known) example. Suppose that the life-cycle profile of a variable of interest (wealth in Shorrocks' paper) increases linearly with age. Suppose also that different date-of-birth cohorts (or generations) differ in the slope of this function, in that younger cohorts accumulate wealth faster, since they are wealthier in life-cycle terms (maybe because of the presence of

---

[30]Emmerson and Tanner (2000), however, point out that if the employer makes pension contributions on behalf of the employee, then there is still a substantial advantage to pension saving over other forms such as the individual savings account.

productivity growth). If the differences in slopes are large enough, then by considering the snapshot of the age–wealth distribution at a point in time one might observe a hump-shaped age profile. The decline in the latter part of the life cycle reflects simply the fact that, in the cross section, the "older" observations come from individuals belonging to earlier and therefore "poorer" cohorts.

In this section we therefore present age profiles for key variables, adjusted for possible cohort and/or time effects, that should help to shed further light on the evolution of the age profile for household saving behavior over the past 25 years. The FES provides a valuable long time series of cross sections that enable us to construct such profiles, and we use data from all years of the FES (from 1974 onwards) in what follows.

Given aggregate evidence for the UK, there are very good reasons to expect cohort effects to appear in the data we study. To be able to control for them, we need repeated observations on individuals or groups of individuals over time. For this reason, we use the average cohort techniques developed by Browning *et al.* (1985) and Deaton (1985). The main idea is to overcome the lack of longitudinal data by constructing synthetic panels – dividing the sample on the basis of the date of birth (cohort) of the household head and averaging the variables under study for each cohort and each year of the survey. This procedure allows us to track the average of the variables under study (be it consumption, income, saving rates, or family size) for each cohort as it ages. The choice of the interval defining the cohort is somewhat arbitrary and is determined mainly by the necessity of having a sufficiently high number of households within each cohort–year cell. In Appendix II, we report the definition of cohorts used in what follows. In the table, we also report the average, and minimum number of households for each cohort across the sample.

The main problems of the synthetic panel technique are, first, that it cannot be used to study dynamic phenomena that are purely idiosyncratic and, secondly, that the assumption that the membership of the groups is fixed (or changes in a way which is unrelated to the variables under study) may be hard to maintain. For instance, if mortality and wealth are negatively related, cohort averages would reflect the fact that the population from which the samples are drawn becomes progressively "richer," as the poorer individuals die younger. This makes the interpretation of cohort profiles more controversial as the age groups grow older, particularly after age 65. Also to construct the cohort data on the basis of households as the smallest unit is a delicate compromise, as the structure of households might change over time, either through divorce and remarriage or simply due to changes in living arrangements, e.g., more single households. In this latter dimension, however, we are constrained by the fact that it is impossible to allocate FES expenditures to individual household members.

In the figures in the main analysis of this chapter we have followed the other chapters in this book and adjusted the age profiles by allowing each cohort to have its own intercept, yet restricting all cohorts to the same shape profile. Thus, in these figures, we effectively allow linear cohort effects but restrict time effects to be zero. We smooth the cohort age profiles by using a fifth-order polynomial in age. An alternative approach, as described in Chapter 2, would be to use an identification strategy that allows restricted time effects as well as cohort effects by controlling for time effects that are orthogonal to a linear trend, as in Deaton and Paxson (1994). Since we are in a good position regarding a long time series of cross-sectional data on both income and expenditure, we briefly investigate this alternative identification strategy in our data.

Figures 7.27–7.30 present this analysis for income, expenditure, saving, and saving rates, respectively. Each figure contains four panels, with the smoothed data in the top left (where smoothing is done simply by using fifth-order polynomials in age with cohort-specific intercepts). Cohort and then time and age profiles are then presented in each of the other three panels, reading clockwise from the top right. Interestingly, and importantly for our analysis elsewhere in this chapter, this technique does not yield age profiles that are significantly different (either statistically or economically) from those we present earlier that use just cohort and age effects. Presumably this is because of the very long sample period for which our cohorts are observed, making estimated profiles fairly robust to time effects (or at least those that are orthogonal to a trend).

Household Composition and Formation

So far we have been considering age profiles for income, expenditure, and saving computed by the age band of the head of the household. Within the context of the survey we use in this chapter, the head of household is defined to be the owner of the property, and in the case of joint ownership amongst a couple, the head is defined as the male. Given the higher frequency of young adults living in households with older heads in the UK, there could be serious differential bias in the age pattern of saving profiles, particularly at the earliest ages. Indeed, these biases apply to a considerably wider set of problems and relationships of interest than this one alone, with labor market outcomes and education being two particularly important cases. There are two potential biases due to household composition in looking at differences in life-cycle age profiles across countries. First, and as pointed out in Chapter 2, the very notion of a household (defined by the age of the head) results in the consideration of a selected sample. In both countries there will be young adults, at the beginning of their life cycles, who are still in the parental home, or who are in other nonspousal living arrangements, many of whom will not be picked up in our calculations in the appropriate age band. To the extent that this group is differentially sized in the two countries, the age profiles will be differentially affected.

Secondly, and related, there are substantially more single heads of household amongst the young in the UK than in many other European countries. When it

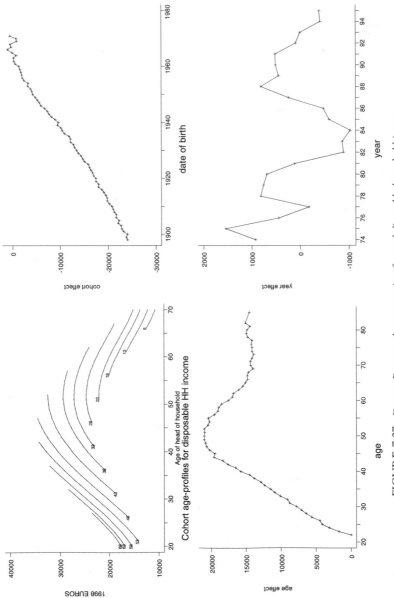

FIGURE 7.27   Deaton–Paxson cohort correction for total disposable household income.

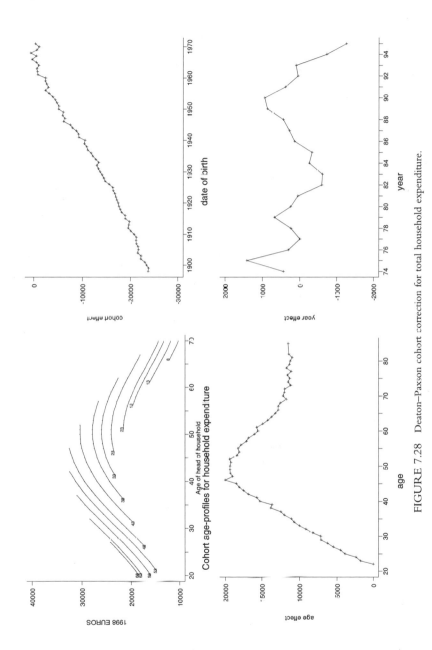

FIGURE 7.28 Deaton–Paxson cohort correction for total household expenditure.

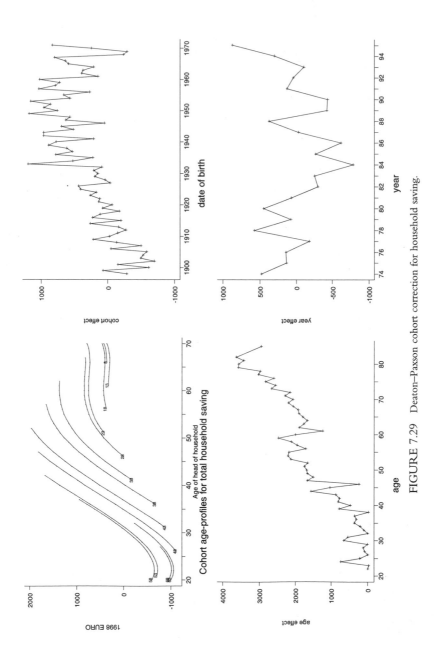

FIGURE 7.29   Deaton–Paxson cohort correction for household saving.

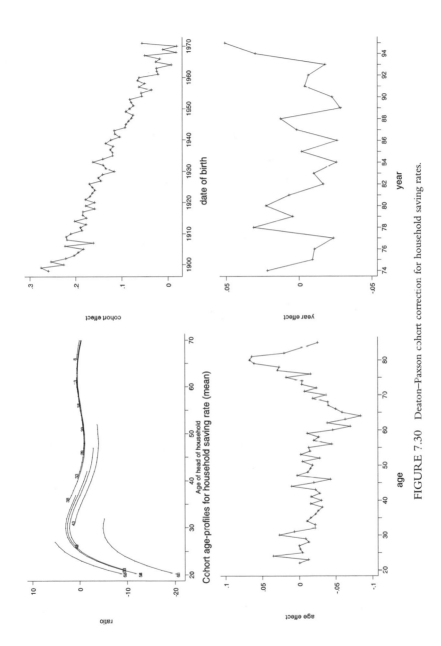

FIGURE 7.30   Deaton–Paxson cohort correction for household saving rates.

comes to analyzing saving and wealth, individuals in single and married households are treated quite differently in a household unit analysis. The combined assets of the two individuals in a married household are summed and treated as one.[31] When there are many young married households, average assets are inflated and the age gradient of wealth is affected.[32]

Banks *et al.* (2001) examine this issue when comparing US and UK age–wealth profiles. They look at (cross-sectional) wealth profiles and consider all adults in each age band (as opposed to just household heads), looking at the distribution of relationships to the head of the household in which they live. Roughly one-quarter of adults aged 20–29 are still living with their parents (i.e., they are children of the head). A high proportion of young adults in the UK are married or cohabiting with the household head, considerably less adults in the UK are actually household heads themselves, and considerably more are in "other" arrangements, where amongst the young this group is predominantly nonrelatives. Similar differences would exist between many European countries and the UK.

This means that the country-specific age profiles may well be influenced by the fact that when working at the household level we do not count many young individuals at the start of their life cycles. These children of household heads will crop up instead as members of the households aged 40–49 or 50–59. These omitted young adults from the early age bands will tend to have lower housing (in fact zero) and stock wealth so that age gradients will tend to be understated.

The magnitude of the impacts of these biases on age profiles for wealth will depend, to some extent, on the stocks of wealth (or flows of saving) within each age group identified. The discussion earlier makes it clear that there is some reason to believe that even if there were no underlying differences in wealth between young heads and other young adults we would still observe an unduly flat age profile. In fact, the situation is exacerbated because young heads (particularly when coupled with their spouses) typically have more assets than their peers. Taking data at the individual level once more from the British Household Panel Study (BHPS), the rate of stock ownership amongst young (20–29) heads and spouses is 14.7%, compared with 8.6% for young adults living in the parental home. Correspondingly, asset stocks are around 33% higher for this group also (upper-bound estimates for 1995 are around €4000 for heads, €3000 for children of heads, and €600 for nonrelatives).

Although no evidence can be obtained for saving profiles, we can form a broad understanding of the issue by using the calculations of Banks *et al.* (2001). Using data in which asset values are actually collected from individual household members, they recompute age profiles for stock wealth in the UK on a tax unit and an individual basis, as opposed to a household basis. For the tax unit breakdown they define as *separate* units all adults except spouses, as opposed to just looking at

---

[31]Individuals in married households may also individually accumulate more wealth due to marriage selection effects (being more prudent) or if marriage encourages savings.

all households. Spouses' assets are added to those of the head and the combined unit is counted only once. For the individual-based analysis the assets of a married household are divided by two and then each adult in an age band is counted as a distinct unit.

The differences in age profiles across different types of unit are not trivial. In particular, stock wealth is differentially lower for the youngest tax units, so that the resulting tax unit and individual age gradients are much steeper than household unit gradients. For example, at a household unit in the UK, the ratio of median stock wealth of the 60–69 age band is 6.4 times that of the 20–29 age band. The comparable number at the tax unit or individual unit level is about 10.6. These ratios are sufficiently different to raise questions about the sensitivity of age profiles to the widespread use of household unit analysis, particularly across countries, and suggests this as an interesting topic for future research.

7.6 CONCLUSIONS

In this chapter we have discussed what we can learn about the age profile of saving and saving rates from UK household data. As in other countries, income and expenditure profiles display strong hump shapes, both in cross section and also after adjusting for possible cohort effects. Taking the difference between these profiles to calculate a residual measure of saving we find that saving rates rise throughout working lives, as might be expected. Somewhat surprisingly, however, saving rates do not decline during retirement, although there may be a role for differential mortality in explaining some of this lack of decline amongst the very oldest ages. Of course, such a residual definition of saving is not without problems. Not least, it will fail to count as saving any (unspent) capital gains on existing funds, or any contributions into savings products that are not measured as income (such as employer pension contributions). Such effects will explain why saving rates may appear to be "low" during working life, but would not explain the positive saving and saving rates of the elderly.

We have also shown, however, that there has been substantial variation, over age cohorts and ultimately over time, in both the contributions to, and incomes from, various types of pension income. Such changes have occurred as a result of both economic factors (particularly productivity growth and cyclical factors) and reform to either the rates or structure of the UK pension system. The UK now has three groups of households, or individuals, distinguished by their experiences of the pensions and savings environment. The first group are the oldest pensioners, who are typically poor and rely almost entirely on flat-rate state pension benefits, as they were already on the verge of retirement when SERPS was introduced. The second group are those currently retiring, who have built up substantial SERPS or occupational pension benefits but who would not have had much chance to contract out into private DC schemes. These pensioners are younger than the first group and also tend to have higher resources in retirement. The final group is those currently of young- or middle-working ages who are experiencing a very different economic environment. This group will not receive large state benefits either from the flat-rate or earnings-related schemes, so the majority of retirement income is expected to come from private provision. A key future policy issue will therefore be the level and inequality in retirement incomes of this group, and in particular the potential incomes of those without substantial private provision.

Our final conclusion is more downbeat, however. Despite a series of interesting and potentially important policy reforms that would be natural focuses for those studying savings and pensions behavior, and despite having exceptionally good data on income and expenditure, the data do not exist with which to make a full assessment of potential effects in the UK. In particular, the absence of panel data on consumption, coupled with the absence of a detailed survey (either repeated cross section or panel design) on household wealth, especially for households in and approaching retirement but also for their younger counterparts, severely limits the degree to which the effects of such changes can be understood. The latter gap in empirical evidence will soon be filled, but the need for a more detailed empirical evidence base on which to base studies of savings and pension accumulation over the life cycle will remain, both in the UK and in other European countries.

ACKNOWLEDGMENT

Rohwedder's research was funded by the European Union TMR Project on the "Structural analysis of household savings and wealth positions over the life-cycle." Banks is grateful to The Leverhume Trust for funding under the research program entitled "The changing distribution of consumption and the welfare of households." Material from the Family Expenditure Survey made available by the ONS through the ESRC data archive has been used by permission of the controller of HMSO. Neither the ONS or the ESRC Data Archive bear any responsibility for the analysis or interpretation of the data reported here. Any remaining errors are entirely our own.

REFERENCES

Attanasio, O. and G. Weber (1994). The UK consumption boom of the late eighties: aggregate implications of microeconomic evidence. *Economic Journal* 104, 1269–1213.

Attanasio, O. and S. Rohwedder (2001). Pension wealth and household saving: Evidence from pension reforms in the UK. London: The Institute for Fiscal Studies, Working Paper no. W01/21.

Banks, J.W. and R.W. Blundell (1994). Household saving behaviour in the United Kingdom. In: J. Poterba (ed.), *International Comparisons of Household Saving*. Chicago: Chicago University Press, pp. 169–205.

Banks, J. and P. Johnson (1998). How Reliable is the Family Expenditure Survey? Trends in incomes and expenditures over time. London: The Institute for Fiscal Studies.

Banks, J. and S. Tanner (1999). *Household Saving in the UK*. London: The Institute for Fiscal Studies.

Banks, J., R.W. Blundell, and S. Tanner (1998). Is there a retirement savings puzzle? *American Economic Review* 88, 769–788.

Banks, J., R. Blundell, and J.P. Smith (2001). Asset portfolios over the lifecycle in the US and UK. NBER Conference on the Economics of Aging, Carefree, Arizona, May 2001. Forthcoming in accompanying conference volume (ed. David Wise), Chicago: Chicago University Press.

Blundell, R.W., M. Browning, and C. Meghir (1994). Consumer demand and the life-cycle allocation of household expenditures. *Review of Economic Studies* 61(1), 57–80.

Börsch-Supan, A.H. and K. Stahl (1991). Life cycle savings and consumption constraints: Theory, empirical evidence, and fiscal implications. *Journal of Population Economics*, 4(3), 233–255.

Browning, M. A. Deaton and M. Irish (1985). A profitable approach to labour supply and commodity demands over the life-cycle. *Econometrica* 53, 503–544.

Brugiavini, A. and G. Weber (2001). The analysis of household saving: Some methodological issues. In: A. Börsch-Supan (ed.), *Household Savings and Pension Policy*. New York: Academic Press.

Deaton, A. (1985). Panel Data from a time-series of cross-sections. *Journal of Econometrics* 30, 109–126.

Deaton, A. and C. Paxson (1994). Intertemporal choice and consumption inequality. *Journal of Political Economy* 102, 437–467.

Dilnot, A., R. Disney, P. Johnson, and E. Whitehouse (1994). Pension policy in the UK: An economic analysis. London: Institute for Fiscal Studies.

Disney, R. and E. Whitehouse (1993). Will younger cohorts obtain a worse return on their pension contributions? In: M. Casson and J. Creedy (eds.), *Industrial Concentration and Economic Inequality. Essays in Honour of Peter Hart*. Aldershot: Edward Elgar.

Disney, R., C. Emmerson, and S. Tanner (1999). Partnership in pensions: An assessment. Commentary No. 78. London: Institute for Fiscal Studies.

Emmerson, C. and S. Tanner (2000). A note on the tax treatment of private pensions and individual savings accounts. *Fiscal Studies* 21(1), 65–74.

Goodman, A. and S. Webb (1995). *For Richer for Poorer: Income Inequality in the UK, 1961–1991*, London: IFS.

Goodman, A., P. Johnson and S. Webb (1997). Inequality in the UK. Oxford: Oxford University Press.

Gruber, J. and D. Wise (1999). Introduction. In: J. Gruber and D. Wise (eds.), *Social Security and Retirement around the World*. Chicago: The University of Chicago Press.

Inland Revenue (1998). *Inland Revenue Statistics*, London: The Stationery Office.

Shorrocks, A.F. (1975). The age-wealth relationship: A cross-section and cohort analysis. *Review of Economics and Statistics*, 57, 155–163.

Tanner, S. (1998). The dynamics of male retirement behaviour. *Fiscal Studies* 19(2), 175–196.

The UK Pension System

Pension arrangements in the UK fall into two tiers: first, a flat-rate scheme provided by the state, and secondly, an earnings-related element that is provided by both the state and the private sector. The role of the private sector has been relatively important since the 1960s, with the result that the UK – in contrast to many other countries – does not face any sustainability problems as far as the financing of the scheme is concerned. Government spending on pension payments currently amounts to 4.7% of GDP,[33] a number that is significantly lower than in most other industrialized countries, even taking into account other social security benefits paid to pensioners (another 1.2% of GDP).

The flat-rate scheme, the basic state pension, was introduced in 1948 to provide a basic subsistence level of income. Anybody who has contributed nine-tenths of her working life to the scheme (men at least 44 years, women at least 39 years) receives the full flat-rate benefit. It is payable once the official retirement age is reached (age 65 for men, age 60 for women) and is set at a level that equals 15% of male average earnings. Reduced rates are paid to those with incomplete contribution records, i.e., to individuals who contributed for less than the required number of years, as long as they qualify for at least 25% of the full rate. Basically, all employed men receive the full rate (89% of men above retirement age), whereas currently only 49% of women retire on a full-rate pension on their own rights. Another 30% of women receive a full pension that they inherited from a deceased spouse; for those who remain – if they are married – the husband can usually claim a dependants' addition of 60% to his own pension. Until the early 1970s, benefits were increased on an erratic basis that was on average slightly above earnings growth. From 1974 until 1980 the benefit level rose in line with the faster growing of prices and earnings: thereafter, in line with prices. This indexation regime has been confirmed by the latest pension reform proposals in 1999, implying that the real value of the basic state pension is deemed to decline further: expressed as a percentage of average male earnings, the value of basic state pension entitlements

[33]Department of Social Security (1998). A new contract for welfare: Partnership in pensions. CM.; 4179, London: DSS.

has dwindled from its peak in 1978 of roughly 20% to just under 15% in 1998 and is projected to be worth about 8% of average male earnings by the year 2020.

Employees' contributions used to be levied as a flat rate until 1975; thereafter everyone whose earnings passed a certain threshold (the lower earnings limit – LEL) had to pay a certain percentage on the amount lying between the LEL and under the upper earnings limit – UEL. No contributions are paid on earnings above the UEL.

The major changes to the basic state pension over the period considered were the recognition of home responsibility periods introduced in 1978, which reduces the minimum required number of contribution years if a person does not work because of looking after a dependent person at home. Along with these reforms, came some improvements for widowed and divorced women. The largest change by far was, however, the change in the indexation of benefits away from earnings to price indexation from 1981 onwards. In 1993, the government announced the increase of women's retirement age to age 65, to be phased in between 2010 and 2020.

In 1978 the flat-rate provision was complemented with an earnings-related scheme[34] that was not intended to compete with the existing private occupational pensions. The motivation was to establish compulsory second-tier provision, since those without an occupational pension were retiring on extremely low incomes. Hence, the state earnings-related pension scheme (SERPS) was integrated with the private sector by providing the option to contract out of SERPS if the employer offered an occupational scheme (usually a final salary-defined benefit scheme). Until 1988, this meant that being contracted in or out was not a real choice, but was decided by the fact whether the employer provided an occupational scheme that the employee had to join in that case. From 1988 the legislation in this respect had changed in a way that the employee is not obliged to join the employer's occupational pension scheme, but can also choose to contract out into an approved personal pension, which tend to be defined by contribution schemes. The response to the new scheme among working-aged households was quite strong: from an initial 17% in 1988, when personal pensions were introduced, coverage increased to nearly 30% in 1996. This implies that in total by the early 1990s around three-quarters of those eligible to contract out of SERPS had done so, roughly 50% into occupational pension schemes and 25% into personal pensions.[35] The entitlements that people accrue from SERPS were originally set at one-quarter of their average earnings between the LEL and the UEL from their best 20 years of earnings. The 1986 reform reduced the generosity of the scheme for all those retiring after April 1999 who will only receive 20% of their average earnings between the LEL and

---

[34]In fact, there had been a previous attempt to introduce a compulsory second-tier scheme that would pay earnings-related benefits: the graduated pension scheme was introduced in 1961. However, failing to design any indexation rules, the scheme became quickly obsolete due to the periods of high inflation. Instead of reacting to this problem the government was sitting idle throughout the years and simply abolished it in 1975, by when the accrued benefits were hardly worth anything anymore.

[35]Figure from Dilnot et al. (1994).

the UEL. The average, however, is no longer based on the best 20 years of earnings, but on the average taken across the individual's entire working lifetime.[36]

In December 1998 the government announced further reforms that will, however, only start to come into effect in 2002. It will take until the middle of the 21st century to fully phase in the proposed reforms. The major changes are the replacement of SERPS with a state second pension (SSP) and the introduction of stakeholder pensions. As these changes will not be applied for a few years, they do not affect the retrospective evidence that we are analyzing here; hence, we shall not go into further detail and refer the interested reader to Disney et al. (1999).

[36]The change in the computation of the average earnings from the best 20 years to the entire working life will be phased in between 2000 and 2028.

Cohort Definition

TABLE 7.2   Definition of Cohorts

Date of birth	Cohort No.	Ages observed	Years observed	Av. cell size	Min. cell size
1886–1890	1	not used	–	–	–
1891–1895	2	81–85	74–78	158.4	103
1896–1900	-2	76–85	74–83	257.4	114
1901–1905	3	71–85	74–88	382.9	155
1906–1910	8	66–85	74–93	491.1	188
1911–1915	13	61–82	74–95	554.4	263
1916–1920	18	56–77	74–95	524.5	360
1921–1925	23	51–72	74–95	625.1	487
1926–1930	28	46–67	74–95	557.3	495
1931–1935	33	41–62	74–95	535.3	446
1936–1940	38	36–57	74–95	562.6	467
1941–1945	43	31–52	74–95	622.7	504
1946–1950	48	26–47	74–95	735.1	604
1951–1955	53	21–42	74–95	623.9	197
1956–1960	58	20–37	78–95	620.5	159
1961–1965	63	20–32	83–95	618.0	180
1966–1970	68	20–27	88–95	449.4	160
1971–1975	73	20–22	93–95	207.2	158

Distribution of Household Income from Earnings in 1988 and 1993

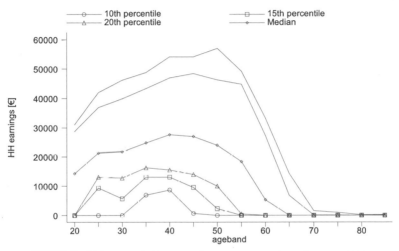

FIGURE 7.31   Household income from earnings conditional on age, 1988.

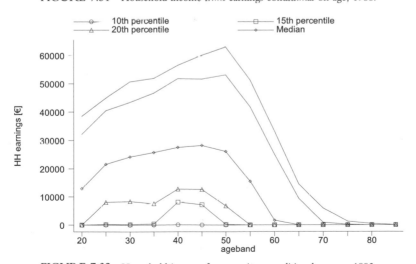

FIGURE 7.32   Household income from earnings conditional on age, 1993.

CHAPTER 8

Household Saving Behavior and Pension Policies in the United States

Orazio P. Attanasio

University College London and Institute for Fiscal Studies

Monica Paiella

Bank of Italy and Ente Einaudi

8.1 INTRODUCTION

In this paper we analyze the saving behavior of US households. In particular, we use micro data from the Consumer Expenditure Survey (CEX) from 1982 to 1995. This data set is the only micro data source in the United States that contains exhaustive and complete information on consumption at the household level. Together with the information it contains on income, it allows us to define saving and saving rates at the household level. Although far from perfect, the CEX constitutes an indispensable data source for the analysis of consumption and saving behavior. Our work extends the analysis of Attanasio (1994, 1998) and Gokhale et al. (1996) in two dimensions: first, we extend our sample to include data up to 1995; secondly, we consider explicitly the differences between mandatory and discretionary saving.

While the CEX constitutes the only available source that contains detailed data on both income and consumption, we should mention some of the problems with such a data source. First, the information on accumulated wealth and financial savings is rather scant, with financial wealth disaggregated in only four categories and the questions on the amounts held asked only once. As a consequence, it is impossible to obtain a measure of capital gains to be added to disposable income in order to compute an economically meaningful measure of the flows of saving. Secondly, there are indications that the CEX data have important measurement problems. Both consumption and income are underestimated, but the problem seems to be more serious for consumption. This is likely to be a consequence of the way the consumption questions are asked, which relies on recall. In addition, while the questions on wealth are about the market value of the stock of financial wealth, it is not clear whether they are completely understood. Therefore, the results we present should be interpreted with caution.

The United States constitutes a particularly interesting case study for at least three reasons. First, it is the largest country in the world and behavior in the United States is always seen as important because of this. Secondly, household saving rates appear to have declined significantly over the last 20 years in the United States, for reasons that are not completely obvious and about which there is less than complete consensus. The analysis of micro data can be informative about the causes of such a decline. Thirdly, partly as a consequence of the decline in personal saving rates, the United States has experimented with several pieces of fiscal legislation with the explicit aim of increasing the personal saving rates. Behind these concerns there is the widespread feeling that a large fraction of American households, and in particular those belonging to the baby-boom generation, are not saving enough to provide for a comfortable retirement. This situation is set against the background of an impending social security crisis or reform due to the fact that current demographic trends make the current pay-as-you-go social security system, with the current parameters, unsustainable in the long run.

A major issue related to the assessment of the alleged decline in personal saving is the evaluation of capital gains, whose importance has risen dramatically over the past 10 years with growing stock market prices and more and more households participating both directly and indirectly in the stock market. Accounting accurately for capital gains is not an easy task because of scant data on household asset holdings and the resulting impossibility of relating changes in asset prices to personal portfolios. The potential effect of capital gains is particularly important in the last few years of the 1990s. As pointed out by Alan Greenspan (2001), the extent of the decline of household saving rates does not appear so dramatic when allowing for the massive increase in capital values and for its influence on economic behavior. Greenspan calculates that roughly two-fifths of the 4.6 percentage-point decline in the personal saving rate that occurred between 1995 and 2000 reflects the foregoing national income and product accounts (NIPA) income-accounting conventions.[1] In addition, allowing for the likely influence of capital gains on consumption[2] might go most of the way in explaining the remainder of the measured decline. Obviously, this does not mean that if asset prices had not increased, household savings would have been unchanged. If asset prices had been flat, real income would have been different and the relationship between asset prices and savings would also have been different. Saving rates are reported to have started declining well before the dramatic increase in asset prices recorded after 1995. Nonetheless, these considerations provide important insights into the dynamics of household behavior and the relationship between asset prices, income, and consumption. The complexity of these relationships underscores the usefulness of employing alternative measures of personal savings – such as one based on the change in the stocks of assets at market value and one based on the difference between expenditure and disposable income, inclusive of capital gains – which are likely to be affected differently by changing asset prices. However, we should clarify that, while our data should, in principle, reflect any capital gains that the households in our sample experience,[3] we do not explicitly identify the effect of capital gains on savings. Our data do not distinguish between stocks and bonds and therefore the effect we are dealing with is somewhat attenuated. More importantly, our data stop in 1995, before the massive increases in the value of the stock market.

The rest of the chapter is organized as follows. Section 8.2 describes the data. Section 8.3 consists of two subsections: in the first, we carry out a cross-sectional analysis of the data and present various concepts and measures of saving, wealth, income, and expenditure. In order to explain the saving patterns by age groups, a set of covariates is also introduced. For each of the variables of interest, we report

---

[1]According to Greenspan (2001), US national income and product accounts (NIPA) accounting conventions do not account explicitly capital gains and losses and this has large effects on personal saving figures through two main channels. First, NIPA deducts taxes paid on realized capital gains from personal income, even though the capital gains that generated those taxes are excluded from income. Of the 4.6 percentage-point decline in the personal saving rate over the past 5 years, a full percentage point is attributable to the increase in federal and state capital gain taxes paid over that period. Secondly, NIPA includes employer contributions to defined benefit in disposable income, but treats benefit payments as intra-sectoral transfers. In recent years, contributions to private defined-benefit plans have declined significantly as an increasing part of these plans' accrued benefit liabilities have been met through a rise in the market value of their equity holdings. This fall in employers' contributions is estimated to account for another $\frac{3}{4}$ percentage point of the decline in the saving rate. If households viewed taxes on capital gains as a subtraction from such gains and not from income and viewed payments from defined-benefit plans as income rather than their employers' contributions, perceived disposable income would have been higher as would the personal saving rate.

[2]Although the propensities to spend out of realized and unrealized gains are likely to be different, conventional regression analysis suggests that a $1 increase in household wealth that is perceived as permanent raises the annual level of personal expenditure of approximately 3 to 5 cents, after due consideration of lags.

[3]The question asked in the Consumer Expenditure Survey that we use asks about the market value of stock and bonds.

two sets of tables in 5-year age intervals, by age of household head, for each of the years covered in the analysis. The first set of tables reports the mean, the standard deviation, and the median of the variables of interest; the second focuses on their components, which are split up into shares that add up to 100 in each row. To assess the importance of time effects, we also add some figures portraying the age profiles of the variables of interest based on some of the cross sections used. To purge the data from cohort effects and identify life-cycle changes in saving behavior, in the second subsection of Section 8.3 we combine the data from the 15 cross sections and define cohort-corrected age–saving profiles, which are displayed in a series of graphs. The tables of data generating the graphs are also included. Section 8.4 relates the observed saving patterns to the existing pension policies and, more generally, to the institutional environment, after outlining its evolution and its main features. Section 8.5 concludes.

8.2 DATA

The data we use are taken from the US Consumer Expenditure Survey (CEX), which is run on an ongoing basis by the US Bureau of Labor Statistics (BLS). The CEX is a national probability sample of households designed to be representative of the total US civilian, non-institutional population. The sampling frame is based primarily on the 1970 Census 100% detailed file until 1985 and on the 1980 Census, afterwards. The cooperation rate is above 86% in each year. The survey is a rotating panel in which consumer units are interviewed every 3 months over a 15-months period, apart from attrition. However, since the information collected in the first interview is not included in the survey and is used solely to classify the unit for the analysis, at most, four observations are available for each household. Interviews take place throughout the year and new households are introduced in the survey on a regular basis as others complete their participation. As a whole, about 4500 households are interviewed each quarter, more or less evenly spread over the 3 months: 80% are re-interviewed after 3 months, whereas the remaining 20% is dropped and a new group is added. Thus, each month approximately one-fifth of the units that are interviewed are new to the survey. This rotating procedure is designed to improve the overall efficiency of the survey and to reduce the problems of attrition.

While the sampling frame is designed to make the CEX representative of the US population, there are three important caveats to be kept in mind. First, in 1982 and 1983 the rural population was excluded from the sample. To have a consistent sample, we have therefore excluded rural households for all years. Secondly, there is some evidence that attrition during the four quarters is nonrandom.[4] Finally, Sabelhaus and Groen (2000) presents some evidence showing that the CEX does

---

[4]See Nelson (1994).

not capture the behavior of the top 2 or 3% of the income distribution, partly for its side and partly because these households tend not to respond more frequently. In what follows we have ignored these problems.[5]

Each quarterly interview collects household monthly expenditure data on a variety of goods and services for the 3 months preceding the one when the interview takes place. The expenditures covered are those that the respondents can recall for 3 months or longer. It is estimated that the survey collects detailed data on about 60–70% of total household expenditures. In addition, global estimates are obtained for food and other selected items, accounting for another 20–25% of total expenditures. The survey does not collect expenses for small household appliances and non-prescriptive drugs and, consequently, it covers about 90–95% of total expenditures. During the second and fifth interview, wage, salary, and other income and employment information is collected for each household member. In the final interview, an annual supplement is used to obtain a financial profile of the household. This profile provides information on the income of the household as a whole and on changes in assets and liabilities. In order to maintain respondent confidentiality, income and asset variables greater than the critical value of $100,000 were set to $100,000.[6] Information on household and individual attributes and characteristics is also available, together with a set of weights translating the sampled households into the universe of households.

The data are available for the period 1980 first quarter to 1996 first quarter. However, for the analysis we do not use the observations involving 1980 and 1981, since several measures indicate low data quality in this first part of the survey. In addition, we exclude composite households, households living in rural areas or in student housing, households with a head younger than 20 years old, and incomplete income respondents. Finally, we leave out those households reporting zero yearly consumption. Overall, the sample used consists of 75,283 households, for a total of 211,923 observations. Variables are deflated by using the BLS aggregate consumer price index and are in 1996 dollars. In addition, data are weighted by the available household weights to represent the universe of US households.

The CEX allows us to construct two measures of saving. The first is obtained by adding individual saving components, whereas the other measure consists of the residual of income minus consumption. As to the first measure, several issues must be mentioned. First of all, for most financial variables, the CEX provides

---

[5]An additional issue worth mentioning is that of the break of 1986 when the change in sampling frame resulted in a change in the household identification number. As a consequence of this, it is not possible to follow through 1986 those households who entered the survey at the end of 1985. Similar considerations apply to 1996, when the sampling frame was changed again.

[6]Some household-level BLS-derived income variables (e.g., total earnings, gross income, etc.) are calculated using top-coded components and exceed $100,000. In these cases, both the variable and its components are flagged as top coded.

information only on flows, which makes it impossible to compute an estimate of the stock dimension of savings. Data also on stocks are available only for some variables, namely checking and saving accounts and stocks and bonds. For these variables, the information on flows is somewhat scarce due to many invalid nonresponses or refusals to respond. Since the problem of missing data is particularly serious for the variables on flows, whenever advisable we have computed savings as first differences in the stocks. Thus, for each year we have determined mean holdings by year of birth of the household head and then we have computed the annualized difference in the mean stock for each cohort. Because of the severity of the problem of missing financial saving observations, the analysis based on the first measure of saving uses a sample of only 46,051 households. Another problem concerns the unavailability of important saving components, such as those related to cash, capital gains, consumer loans, mortgages, and real asset holdings. For all these reasons, the saving measure obtained by adding up individual components is expected to differ substantially from the residual measure. An important issue is also the unavailability of data on employers' mandatory and voluntary contributions to funded and unfunded pension schemes. The second measure of savings is determined by subtracting household total consumption, which includes expenditure on durable and nondurable goods and on services, from total disposable income. Total disposable income includes labor, business, asset, and transfer income and is computed by subtracting the total amount of personal taxes and social security contributions from household total gross yearly income as reported at the time of the last interview. Apart from total income, all the other yearly income and saving variables are determined by taking household-level averages when the respondent reports different annual values at different interviews.

8.3 HOUSEHOLD SAVINGS

The analysis that follows focuses, first, on cross-sectional saving patterns and, then, on cohort behavior to identify life-cycle changes. For the analysis, all the data are weighted by the available household weights to represent the universe of US households.

Cross-Sectional Profiles of Household Saving

In the first part of this section we focus on the individual components of household saving and classify them into two groups:

(a) *Discretionary savings*, which are defined as changes in wealth that are under the control of the household and concern both the absolute and relative composition of the asset portfolios.

(b) *Mandatory savings and contributions to pay-as-you-go systems*, which are characterized by some strong degree of pre-commitment. They include both mandatory and voluntary contributions to public or private schemes and are related to changes in wealth accumulated through funded or unfunded pension schemes. Unfortunately, since for most items only global estimates are available, the distinction between contributions to funded schemes versus pay-as-you-go systems is not always possible.

As we have mentioned in the Section 8.2, the information available does not allow us to come up with an accurate measure of total household savings by simply adding up the individual items because of lack of information on many household assets and liabilities. Despite this, studying the profiles of the items for which information is available is important for understanding the impact of demographic changes on saving aggregates and for assessing the impact of changes in pension institutions. Total household savings will be analyzed in the second part of this section.

Discretionary Savings

Discretionary savings, defined as the sum of financial and real savings, are likely to alternate with mandatory savings as the most important component of household savings at the various stages of the life cycle. Unfortunately, the CEX does not permit an accurate computation of discretionary saving since it does not allow a sensible measurement of real wealth. The same problem, however, is common to many other data sets containing information on saving behavior. Overall, although the stocks of the wealth components are definitely measured more accurately in the Survey of Consumer Finances (SCF), the CEX has two main advantages over the SCF. First, currently, it provides 17 years of data, available on a consistent basis at an annual frequency, versus five waves of the SCF. Secondly, and more importantly, it allows one to compute the flow measure of saving as the difference of income and consumption which, while excluding capital gains, is directly related to discretionary behavior.

On the basis of the CEX, *financial savings* can be defined as the sum of

- net deposits in checking, brokerage, and similar accounts and in saving accounts held at banks, savings and loans, credit unions, etc.; plus
- net purchases of US savings bonds; plus
- net purchases of stocks, bonds, mutual funds, and other similar securities; plus
- contributions to individual retirement accounts where withdrawals may be made only after retirement (BLS-derived); plus
- contributions to life insurance; plus
- contributions to health insurance.

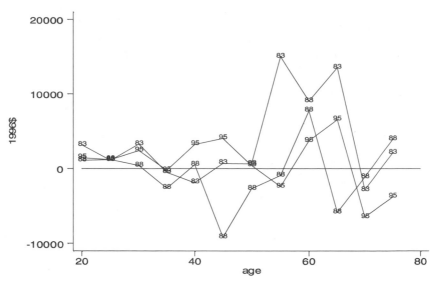

FIGURE 8.1   Mean financial savings.

For the reasons explained in Section 8.2, we have chosen to measure the first three components of financial savings as annualized difference between the stocks in 2 subsequent years for the same cohort defined on the grounds of the year of birth of the household head. This implies that the first year available for the analysis is 1983. Stock, bonds, mutual funds, and other similar securities are valued at their estimated market value. An important item for which no direct information is available is consumer loans, other than bank account overdrafts.

Figure 8.1 reports the age profile of the weighted mean, of financial savings by age of the household head, in 5-year age intervals, for the 1983, 1988, 1995 waves. The standard deviation of the weighted mean, and the median, for each of the years covered by the data set and considered in the analysis can be found in the electronic appendix on the book's website. The profiles are quite noisy, but there appears to be very little evidence of time effects as the contours for the different waves do not differ in any major respect. Overall, although the standard errors are quite large, savings appear to be low (or negative) among the young and the elderly and to peak among the middle-aged. Yet, generally speaking, interpreting these cross-sectional profiles in terms of life-cycle patterns can be quite misleading. In fact, each age category also represents a cohort, and the cross-sectional lines do not portray a life-cycle profile but the combination of age-specific and cohort-specific effects.

Turning to the distribution of financial savings across individual asset categories, reported in Table 8.1, the leading component appears to be net deposits in checking, saving, and similar accounts. Among those exhibiting positive savings, the median of the portfolio share of net investment in this type of asset is almost 30%, versus a median of 25% for the share of purchases of stocks and bonds, 20% for the contributions to health insurance, 15% for those to individual retirement accounts (IRAs) and 10% to life insurance. Net deposits in checking and saving accounts exhibit the highest variability across households, both in terms of total investment and in terms of portfolio share. Over the life cycle, this component takes on negative values, especially among those in their thirties and among the elderly. Among those exhibiting some dissaving, the median portfolio contribution of the deposits in checking and saving accounts is −96%, that of the investment in stocks and bonds is −70%; the median of the contribution to health insurance is 40%, that of the contribution to IRAs and to life insurance is below 20%, for each asset. Over the period 1983–96, the portfolio share of checking and saving accounts decreases and in the 1990s, on average, it contributes negatively to the total. Instead, the share of stocks and bonds increases steadily. Also, the share in health insurance increases more or less steadily over the period considered and exhibits a particularly pronounced rise in the mid-1990s, especially among those in their forties and older who also appear to be the age group saving relatively more through health insurance. Other important categories are life insurance and IRAs, which absorb a rather constant share of household savings over time, exhibiting a slight increase starting from the late 1980s, which is particularly pronounced for the youngest. Life insurance and IRAs represent relatively less-important saving categories for those aged 60 and older.

Information on stocks is available only for few of the items appearing in the definition of financial saving. Specifically, the CEX provides data only on the following *wealth* categories:

- amount held in checking, brokerage, and similar accounts and in saving accounts at banks, savings and loans, credit unions, etc., as of the last day of the month before that of the last interview; plus
- amount of US savings bonds as of the last day of the month before that of the last interview; plus
- estimated market value of all stocks, bonds, mutual funds, and other similar securities held on the last day of the month before that of the last interview.

Information on the amount held in dedicated saving plans, individual retirement accounts, and on the stock of consumer debt (other than bank accounts overdrafts) is not available.

Figure 8.2 reports the age profile of the weighted mean of the amounts held in checking and saving accounts and in stocks and bonds, for the 1983, 1988, and 1995 waves. For standard deviations and the median, see again the book's website. Table 8.2 reports the distribution of the stock of wealth between checking, saving, brokerage, and similar accounts and stocks, bonds, mutual funds, and similar securities. For all cross sections the stock held in financial assets increases with age up to around 65. Then, the profile levels off and some asset decumulation can be

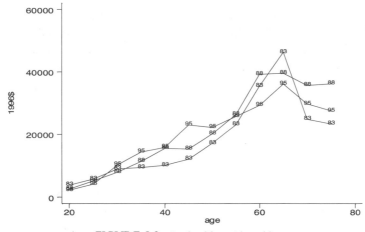

FIGURE 8.2   Stock of financial wealth.

observed, which is consistent with the evidence from Figure 8.1. Households tend to hold a relatively greater share of their assets in checking and saving accounts, especially if they are young or old, although the vertical difference between the amounts held in checking and saving accounts and the amounts held in bonds and stocks tends to shrink over the years, for all age groups. Investment in stocks and bonds peaks among households in their fifties. Finally, the cross-sectional profiles suggest that the degree of financial market participation has increased over time, especially among those aged between 40 and 60.

The measurement of *real wealth*, and in particular of real estate, is very deficient in the CEX. In the first years of the survey, only tenure information on the residence (and some general information about the type of building) was available. With this information it is possible to measure, for any group of individuals in the CEX, the proportion of renters and homeowners with a mortgage or in their own right. Since 1988, substantially richer information is available about the mortgages outstanding, including their value, the time since it was started, and so on. Unfortunately, even though a question on the value of the residence (and about its rental value) is present in the questionnaire, this information has proved to be of very low quality. We look at real assets in greater detail in the Life-cycle profiles of household savings section where the focus is shifted to cohort behavior.

Mandatory Savings

The CEX provides global estimates at the household level for pay deductions and contributions to social security, private pension, and public and private retirement schemes. The figures are derived by the BLS and, presumably, are quite accurate.

However, they do not allow us to distinguish between contributions to funded and to unfunded plans, or between voluntary and mandatory payments. Specifically, the CEX provides the following information:

- total amount of government retirement deducted from last pay annualized;
- total amount of railroad retirement deducted from last pay annualized;
- total amount of private pensions;
- total deductions for social security.

Information on employer's contributions to these and other retirement schemes is not directly available from the CEX, although it is possible to establish whether the employer is contributing to a private pension of any of the earners in the household. In this respect, the CEX is unique, as any information on employers' contributions is missing in most data sets.

Figure 8.3 reports the age profiles of the weighted mean for the 1983, 1988, and 1995 waves, of total retirement contributions, obtained by adding the items mentioned above. For standard deviations and medians, see again the book's website. Table 8.3 reports their distribution. Two of the main features of this set of age profiles are the hump shape and the pronounced shift upward of the cross-sectional profiles over time, suggesting an increase in retirement contributions, which appears to be particularly pronounced between the ages of 30 and 50. The upward shift is due primarily to the sharp increase over time in the contributions to private pension schemes and in the deductions for social security. However, once again, the interpretation of the features of these

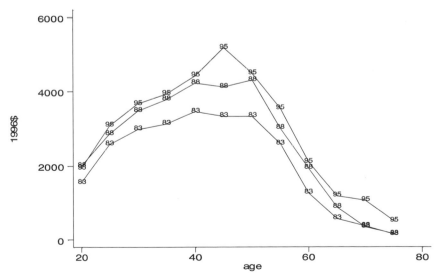

FIGURE 8.3   Total retirement contributions.

contours should be guarded, as these are cross-sectional profiles and combine the influence of both age and cohort effects. As to the distribution among the individual saving components, social security contributions are the most important item and for all years and age groups represent at least 70–80% of total contributions. The share rises above 90% for the young (less than 35 year olds) and the elderly. As to private pension contributions, they exhibit a discernible hump-shaped profile that shifts decisively upward from the late 1980s and early 1990s on. Yet, private pension contributions represent more than 10% of total contributions only for those aged between 40 and 60, and it is for this age group that the share and the actual contributions increases over time are most significant. Railroad and government retirement never represent more than 5–6% of total contributions and, if anything, their relative and absolute importance diminishes over time for all age groups.

Income

The CEX provides a measure of *total gross income*, computed by the BLS and obtained by summing family earnings income, social security and railroad benefits, supplemental security income checks, unemployment compensation, public assistance and welfare payments, interests on saving accounts and bonds, dividends, royalties, income from estates and trusts, pensions and annuities from private companies, military or government, income from roomers, boarders, and other rental units, child support, cash scholarships and fellowships or stipends not based on working, and food stamps. Information on total household income is available for all the units in the sample we have selected. In Figure 8.4 (left panel), we report its weighted mean, whereas Table 8.4 focuses on the relative shares of its components.

In each of the years considered in the cross sections the largest component of household income is earnings, whose share ranges from 68 to 73% and tends to increase slightly over the sample period considered, especially among those in their sixties or early seventies. Earnings account for more than 90% of total income among those aged less than 50; among those aged more than 50, their share decreases rapidly to around 20% for the elderly. Earnings exhibit the familiar hump shape, peaking slightly later over the life cycle in the 1990s with respect to the 1980s. The time effects appear to be small. Retirement income increases slightly over time and accounts for less than 10% of income for those aged between 40 and 60, but rises to over 60% among those over 60. Financial income, including bank accounts interests, dividends, royalties, etc., accounts for a slightly decreasing share of total income over time; it makes up for less than 5% of total income for those younger than 50, but accounts for more than 10% for those above 60. Welfare and unemployment benefits account for around 1% and exhibit a temporary, but conspicuous drop in the late 1980s, affecting mainly those under 60.

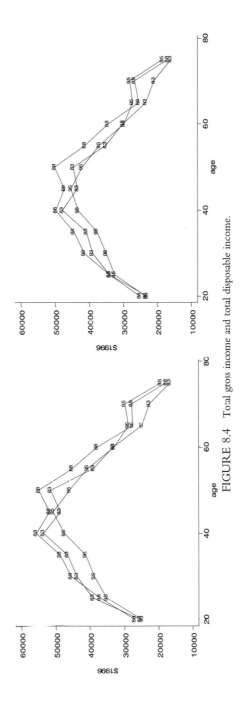

FIGURE 8.4   Total gross income and total disposable income.

Disposable income (reported in Table 8.5) is simply gross income minus the total amount of personal taxes, derived by BLS, and the contributions to social security. Personal taxes include federal, state, and local income taxes and property taxes. Disposable income is about $36,000 p.a. in 1996 dollars for the average household in the age–year cross sections and it corresponds to about 85% of average total gross income. The median is approximately 83% of the mean. As Table 8.6 suggests, the share of total income absorbed by social security increases slightly over time from 4 to about 6%. The share accounted for by income taxes diminishes slightly.

The cross-sectional weighted means of total gross income and of total disposable income are displayed in Figure 8.4. The familiar hump shape is immediately recognizable, although the cross-sectional age profiles peak in the mid-to-late forties, slightly earlier than expected given that early retirement typically begins only after age 50. Another feature of the contours is the uniform upward shift over the 1980s, followed by a downward shift in the 1990s. The corresponding profiles based on the median instead of the mean do not differ in any major respect.

Annuatized retirement income is the main source of income for elderly households. It includes social security and railroad benefits and pensions and annuities from private companies, military, or government. In the data, social security benefits cannot be disentangled from railroad benefits. However, the latter can be expected to be a small share of total retirement income, given the relatively minor weight they have in terms of contributions, as discussed earlier. Data on annuities and life insurances are very limited in the CEX. On the other hand, it is well known that the market for annuities is of very limited importance in the United States.

Total annuatized income appears to have increased over time as a result of the increase in private pension income in the late 1980s and in social security benefits in the 1990s, with the latter increase being relatively smaller. According to Table 8.7 and Figure 8.5, displaying the cross-sectional age profiles of social security benefits and of private pensions from the 1983, 1988, and 1995 waves, social security benefits are the largest source of annuatized retirement income for those households whose head is in his mid- to late-sixties. For those in their fifties, who are the ones more likely to have taken on early retirement, private pensions are relatively more important and their absolute and relative weight appears to have increased over the years. Overall, social security benefits and private pensions replace a relatively small share of working-life income, as suggested by Figure 8.6, which looks at the replacement ratio of retirement income and earnings by plotting the profiles of mean earnings and mean retirement income in 1983 and 1995. Such a low degree of replacement helps explain the fall in household savings, discussed in the next section, after households reach retirement age.

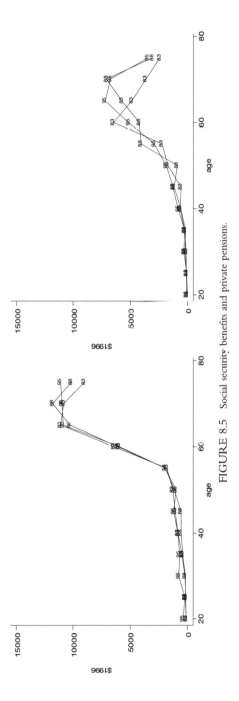

FIGURE 8.5   Social security benefits and private pensions.

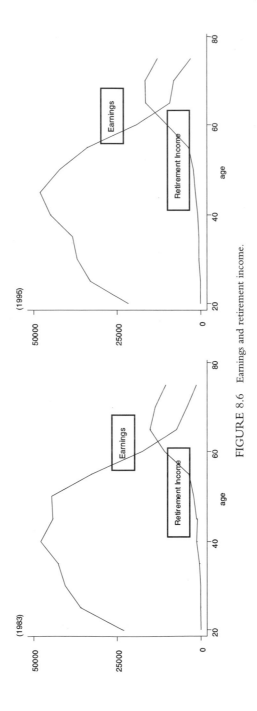

FIGURE 8.6   Earnings and retirement income.

Saving as Residual

In this section, we compute saving as a residual, subtracting all consumption expenditure from total disposable income. Total consumption includes expenditure on nondurable goods (mainly food and services), semidurables (clothing), durables (mainly cars and furniture), rent, health, and education. Its weighted mean, standard deviation, and median are reported in Table 8.8. In the age–year cross sections, total consumption is about $33,000 p.a. in 1996, for the average household. The median is approximately equal to 68% of the mean. The cross-sectional profiles of median total expenditure and of median disposable income for 1983, 1988, and 1995 are also displayed in Figure 8.7. The familiar hump-shaped profile of total expenditure is immediately detectable and it does not differ in any important way from the profile of mean expenditure. Three features of these profiles are worth pointing out. First, total expenditure tends to peak at or near the age when disposable income peaks as well. Secondly, the profiles suggest that some dissaving characterizes behavior at the ends of the age distribution, as predicted by the standard neoclassical model for consumption. Lastly, expenditure appears to fall slightly among the young in the 1990s, although, for all households aged 50 or above, it increases over the years. This pattern can be explained mainly by the decrease in family size over time (see also Sabelhaus, 1999).

Total saving, measured as difference between income and expenditure, is also reported in Table 8.8 and its median,[7] based on the 1983, 1988, and 1995 cross section, is also displayed in Figure 8.8. The cross-sectional profiles exhibit very little accumulation early in the life cycle and mean saving turns out to be generally negative among the young, despite the evidence of some, although limited, positive financial savings reported in Figure 8.1. The two sets of profiles can be reconciled by noticing that the young are likely to hold large amounts of debt, such as a mortgage, whose instalments are bound to more than offset any financial saving. However, during the working life of the household head the stock of savings increases and then becomes positive and its profile matches quite closely the profile of disposable income, peaking at approximately the same age. After retirement, savings diminish substantially. An interesting feature of this set of profiles is the slight increase in savings that, in many of the sample years, appears to characterize the behavior of the eldest. Such behavior among the elderly is common to many countries and is considered a puzzle vis-à-vis most economic theories.

---

[7]We focus on median saving, because the profile for mean savings is noisier, as it might be expected since median savings are more robust to outliers. This can be caused either by households having abnormally high incomes (due for example to bonuses) or expenditure (due for example to infrequent purchases of durable goods) in the year when they are surveyed.

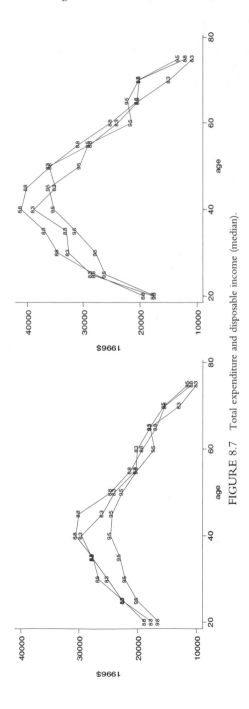

FIGURE 8.7   Total expenditure and disposable income (median).

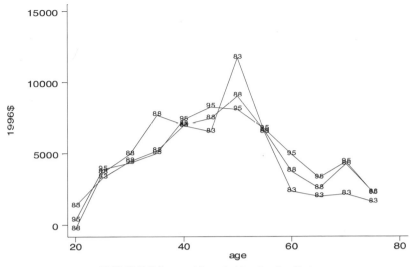

FIGURE 8.8   Total household saving (median).

Saving Rates

Finally, we compute the saving rates, by dividing our residual measure of saving by total disposable income. The ratio of mean saving to mean income is reported in the last column of Table 8.8. Instead, Table 8.9 is based on individual household saving rates and gives an account of their median and of the shares of households with a saving rate, below −1%, between −1% and +1%, and above +1%. Figure 8.9 displays the age profiles both of the ratio of mean saving to mean income, in the left-hand panel, and of the median of the individual household rates, in the right-hand panel. We prefer to focus on medians rather than means, as the saving ratios are very much affected by few observations with very low levels of income. The profiles of the ratio of means are more directly comparable to aggregate savings figures and correspond to the mean of individual saving rates weighted by the individual income share of aggregate income. This measure of the saving rate is much lower and much more volatile than the median saving rate. Both graphs suggest that saving rates have fallen during the early 1980s and the early 1990s.

The saving rates figures emerging from the analysis carried out on the CEX hardly match those from the National Accounts, which is not surprising given the difficulties in matching the CEX household consumption and income data to the aggregate figures. Moreover, to go from the age profiles to the aggregate one we would have to consider the weight (both in terms of size and of income) that each age group has on the population. For these reasons, the absolute level of saving rates is not of particular interest. The most interesting feature of the picture emerging from the analysis is the *shape* of the life-cycle profile. In Figure 8.9,

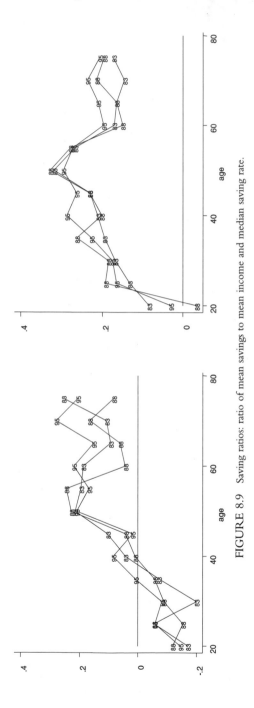

FIGURE 8.9 Saving ratios: ratio of mean savings to mean income and median saving rate.

the most apparent feature of the saving rate profile, whether measured by the median of the ratios or the ratio of means, is the hump shape. Such a shape is roughly consistent with the implications of the life-cycle model. As mentioned earlier, however, the presence of cohort effects makes the interpretation of these profiles problematic.

Covariates

The main contribution of this final paragraph is to provide some evidence on a set of household-specific variables whose evolution over time and the life cycle might explain the patterns of household consumption, income, and saving that we have documented in the previous sections. Thus, in Figure 8.10, we focus on the cross-sectional distribution of a set of variables that are usually believed to explain some of the life cycle and time variation in consumption, income, and saving behavior. Specifically, we focus on household size, employment rates, home-ownership, and ownership of life insurance.

An important feature of US household population has been the reduction in the average size of households over the years and the phenomenon appears to affect particularly those households whose head is in his forties. The cross-sectional evidence on male labor force participation rates suggests that participation has declined somewhat in the late 1980s and early 1990s, particularly among those aged 50 and above, reflecting the increase in early retirement. As to homeowner-ship rates, the age profiles do not exhibit strong time effects, but over the years tend to peak slightly later. Finally, the life insurance–ownership profiles exhibit a pronounced hump shape and a moderate downward shift over the years covered by the survey.

Life-Cycle Profiles of Household Saving

As we have pointed out several times, all the analysis carried out in the previous paragraph is cross-sectional and does not identify life-cycle changes. In fact, the cross-sectional profiles do not correspond to the life-cycle profiles unless all individuals at each point in time differ only by their age (and possibly a completely idiosyncratic component). Yet, if being born in different years causes individual behavior and attributes to differ in a systematic way, in order to identify household behavior over the life cycle we need to purge the data from cohort effect. This can be achieved by constructing synthetic panels using the available time series of cross sections,[8] overcoming the lack of a substantial longitudinal dimension in the CEX.

---

[8]See Chapter 2 for a discussion of the methodological issues related to the use of synthetic cohort techniques.

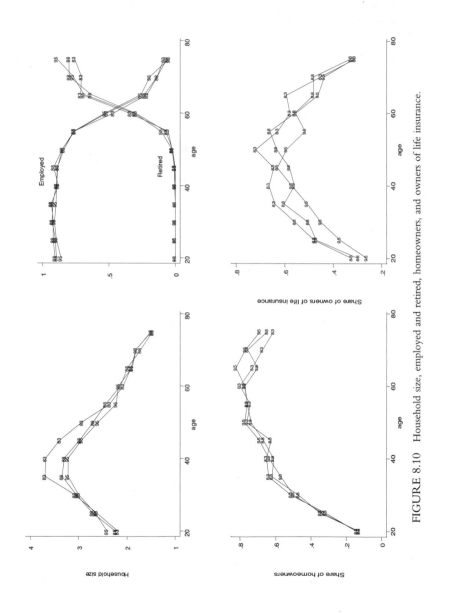

FIGURE 8.10   Household size, employed and retired, homeowners, and owners of life insurance.

The large sample size allows us to define aggregation units that are small enough to be homogeneous without loss of statistical precision. Therefore, cohorts are defined over the date of birth of the household head at 5-year ranges and the average cell size is 511 observations. For each of the 11 cohorts we define, 14 observations are available. Table 8.10 provides more details on our cohort definition and on cell size. Since the cohorts are defined by a 5-year interval and the survey covers more than 5 years, adjacent cohort profiles overlap, which implies that different cohorts are observed at the same age, but the observations correspond to different survey years. Differences between overlapping cohorts could therefore be due to either time or cohort effects. For simplicity, we will ignore the time effects (or set them to zero) and use each cohort profile to identify the "pure" age effects on the variables of interest.

This section is organized as the Cross-sectional profiles of household saving section. First, we focus on the individual saving components. As we have mentioned earlier, these items cannot be simply added up to obtain an accurate measure of total household saving because of lack of information on many household assets and liabilities. Despite this, the analysis of those saving components for which information is available is important because it provides a framework for understanding the impact of demographic changes on saving aggregates and for assessing the impact of changes in pension institutions. Then, we look at total household saving measured as the residual of income minus consumption. Finally, we turn to the cohort profiles of a set of household characteristics that can help us to understand the observed life-cycle expenditure and saving behavior. For each of the cohorts in our sample, the figures display a set of smoothed age profiles, obtained by regressing cohort data on a full set of cohort dummies and a fifth-order polynomial in age. Tables of cohort-level data, combining 14 observations, from 1982 to 1995, can be found in the electronic appendix on the book's website. Each row corresponds to a cohort, from the youngest, born between 1961 and 1965, to the oldest, born between 1911 and 1915. Each column reports the average value of the variable of interest when the cohort was aged 18–22, 19–23, . . . until 81–85. All the variables discussed in this section are defined exactly as in the Cross-sectional profiles of household saving section.

Discretionary Saving

Figure 8.11 reports the age profiles for discretionary saving, which include net deposits in bank accounts, net purchases of stocks, bonds, mutual funds, and other similar securities, and contributions to IRAs and to life and health insurance schemes.

The use of cohort techniques allows us to examine the differences between the profiles of different generations. The cohort effects are clearly visible, especially among the older groups. The profiles in the figure suggest that saving tends to be low, but increasing among the young and steadily decreasing among the elderly.

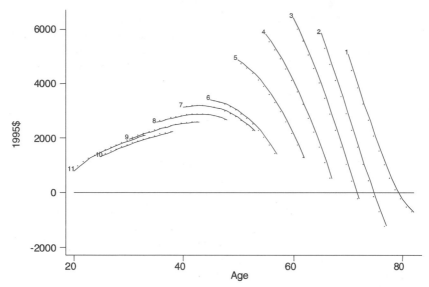

FIGURE 8.11   Financial saving by cohort. *Note*: The profiles labeled by 1, 2, . . . , 11, refer to the cohort of households whose head was born between 1911 and 1915, 1916, and 1920, . . . , 1961 and 1965, respectively.

Towards the end of the life cycle, it appears to become negative. The contours suggest also that the younger generations save somewhat less than the middle-aged and much less than the older. At the end of the life cycle, the profiles are rather steep and relatively younger cohorts appear to approach zero saving at earlier ages. For all cohorts, saving appears to peak around the age of 45, which is slightly before than expected.

Figure 8.12 displays the non-smoothed age profiles of the shares of households holding IRAs, which are an important component of discretionary financial savings. The most interesting feature of the contours is the steep increase in the shares of holders of IRAs in the mid-1980s and their subsequent drop in the 1990s. The phenomenon concerns all cohorts and is linked to the 1981 Economic Recovery Tax Act, which substantially expanded IRA eligibility. In the late 1980s, higher-income taxpayers with employer-provided pensions were excluded from making tax-deductible contributions; by the end of the 1980s total tax-deductible contributions fell by over 60% and have remained low since then.

Figure 8.13 reports the age profiles for the stock of checking and saving accounts and for that of stocks and bonds. The age profiles for checking and saving accounts are fully consistent with those for financial savings and suggest that the stocks accumulated by the younger generations are smaller than those accumulated by the elder ones at any point of the life cycle. The picture for stock and bond

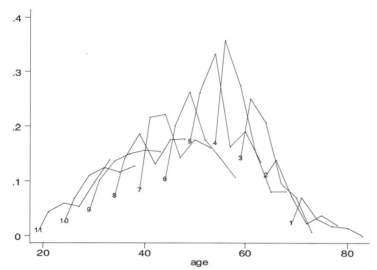

FIGURE 8.12 Share of households with individual retirement accounts (IRAs) by cohorts. *Note*: See note to Figure 8.11.

holdings is quite different. In fact, the age profiles are higher the younger the generation, with those born in the 1950s holding, at the age of forty, a stock of wealth, which is higher than the stock of those born in the late 1930s and 1940s. For all cohorts, stock and bond holdings are low and grow slowly early in the life cycle. Yet, the rate of accumulation increases fast with age and peaks around the age of 65–70. The contours suggest a dramatic increase for all cohorts in the amounts invested over the years covered by the survey. The increase appears particularly pronounced for those cohorts born after the mid-1930s. As to checking and saving accounts, the rate of accumulation is quite uniform over the whole life cycle up to the age of 60, when holdings peak. Both sets of profiles exhibit some leveling off around the age of 60–70, and thereafter they decline slightly. In addition, it is interesting to notice that the older generations hold relatively more checking and saving accounts and relatively less stocks and bonds than the younger cohorts. In fact, the vertical difference between the contours for the stocks of checking and saving accounts and for those of stocks and bonds is smaller the younger the cohort. The fact that the young hold relatively more equity, together with the rise in stock prices, might help to reconcile the profiles in the right panel of the figure, suggesting that the young have higher levels of asset stocks, with that on saving flows in Figure 8.11, suggesting that the young save relatively less.

This evidence from the CEX is consistent with that from the US Survey of Consumer Finances discussed by Bertaut and Star-McCluer (2000), who find that, between the early 1980s and the late 1990s, the composition of financial assets has changed appreciably with the relative importance of time and saving deposits

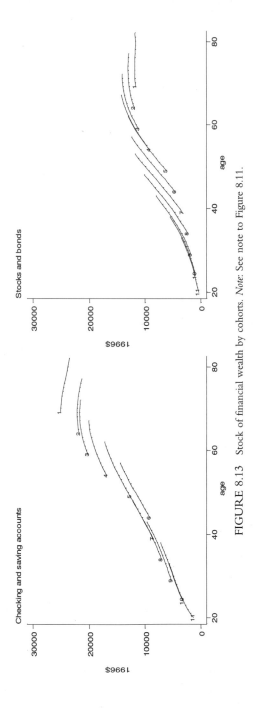

FIGURE 8.13   Stock of financial wealth by cohorts. *Note*: See note to Figure 8.11.

declining while the importance of equity, pension funds, and mutual funds has risen. Several factors appear to underline these trends. The first is the growth in stock prices over the period, with the Standard & Poor 500 stock price index rising from 165 in 1983 to 600 in 1995. Such growth, together with subdued inflation, implies an average real increase of over 10% per year. The second is the development of mutual funds, which rose from around 600 in the early 1980s to above 5000 in the 1990s. The large number of institutions offering mutual funds, the proliferation of types of funds available, and the rise of no-load funds have made it easier and less costly for households to attain a diversified portfolio of stock. Another important factor is the introduction and success of tax-deferred retirement accounts, as documented in Figure 8.12. The combination of rising stock prices and the growth of investment in equity, especially through mutual funds and retirement accounts, has been associated with a significant increase in the equity share of households' financial assets.

We have mentioned in the previous sections that the CEX provides very limited information on real asset holdings, especially in the first years covered by the survey. Yet, the information on tenure, which is accurate, allows us to measure the proportion of renters, and homeowners with a mortgage and in its own right. In Figure 8.14, we report three sets of cohort age profiles: the lowest, but increasing set refers to the fraction of homeowners without a mortgage; the hump-shaped set of contours refers to the share of homeowners with a mortgage; and the

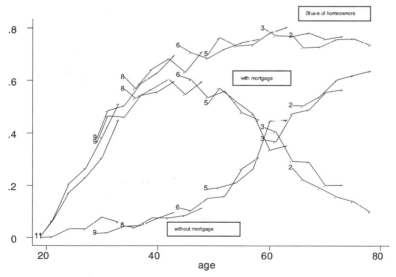

FIGURE 8.14   Share of homeowners and homeowners with and without mortgage by cohorts. *Note*: See note to Figure 8.11. The profiles of a few cohorts have not been included because they are almost undistinguishable from the contours of cohorts that come immediately before or after.

uniformly increasing and concave set refers to the overall fraction of homeowners in the population.

The three sets of profiles do not exhibit very strong cohort effects. The share of
homeowners without mortgage tends to increase with age for all cohorts and the
steepest increases occur among those households with heads in their fifties. The
share of homeowners with mortgage increases steeply early in the life cycle, peaks
around the age of 40, and then slowly declines. The cohort effects are slightly more
pronounced here, with the older generations exhibiting a relatively lower share of
households with mortgage. As to the overall shares, they increase over the life cycle
of all cohorts and tend to level off among those who enter their forties,
independently of the cohorts, which end up exhibiting similar shares of
homeownership at the peak. Yet, for the younger generations, the contours are
particularly steep early in the years and appear to be much steeper than those for
the older cohorts. Overall, the profiles in Figure 8.14 suggest that the younger
cohorts are more likely to become homeowners earlier in the life cycle, but that
they are also more likely to take on a mortgage.

Mandatory Saving and Contributions to Pay-As-You-Go Systems

Figure 8.15 displays the cohort profiles for total retirement contributions, which
include government and railroad retirement deductions, and contributions to
private pensions and to social security. As we have mentioned before, all these

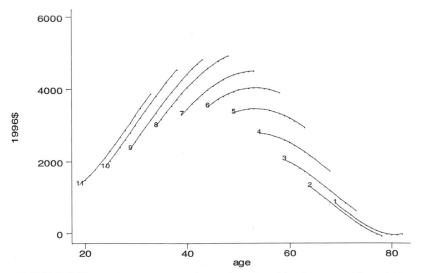

FIGURE 8.15   Total retirement contributions by cohort. *Note*: See note to Figure 8.11.

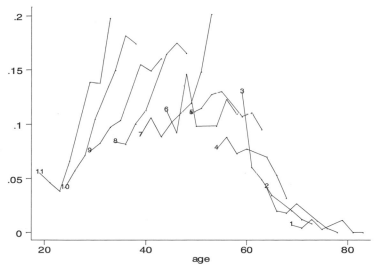

FIGURE 8.16 Share of households with private pensions by cohorts. *Note*: See note to Figure 8.11.

figures are derived by the BLS and, presumably, are quite accurate. However, they do not allow us to distinguish between contributions to funded and to unfunded plans, or between voluntary and mandatory payments. The cohort effects are strongly positive, as expected, with the younger generation contributing relatively more to social security and retirement plans. Also, the profiles for the younger cohorts are quite steep early in the life cycle. Total retirement contributions appear to peak around the age of 55–60. A comparison with Figure 8.3 (which presented three cross-sectional age profiles for the same variable) makes it clear how misleading the former can be. The cohort profiles in Figure 8.15 stress the strong increase over the last part of our sample for the youngest cohorts.

Figure 8.16 reports the age profiles of the shares of households holding a private pension. Private pensions represent a relatively small share of total retirement contributions. Yet, over the years, their importance has increased both in relative and in absolute terms. The figure also shows that the fraction of households with private pensions has increased dramatically and the increase has been particularly large among the younger cohorts, with those born after 1945 exhibiting the steepest profiles.

Income

Figure 8.17 displays the smooth cohort profiles for total gross income and for total disposable income. The familiar hump shape characterizes the two sets of contours, implying that the hump shapes observed in the cross sections are not spurious, with both sets of profiles peaking around the age of 45–50. Quite surprisingly, the

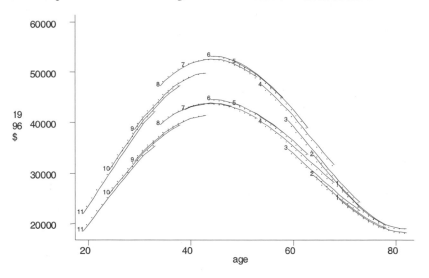

FIGURE 8.17   Total gross income and total disposable income by cohort. *Note*: See note to Figure 8.11.

cohort effects are rather small. Also, they tend to be negative among those born after 1950, with the younger generation exhibiting a profile slightly below that of the immediately preceding cohort. Those born between 1930 and 1950 exhibit the highest profile and appear to be better off than the younger and elder generations. The cohort effects are more pronounced and have a clear negative effect on the cohort profiles of household tax payments (not reported), with younger households paying less than the older ones. Finally, we have examined the cohort effects on the individual components of total income.[9]

Household earnings profiles are very similar to those of gross income until approximately the age of 60, after which they decline much more rapidly; overall, the cohort effects are extremely modest, especially among the generations born before 1930 or after 1950. The cohort effects are strong and negative on the profiles of financial income, which consists of interests on savings accounts and bonds, dividends, royalties, and income from estates and trusts. Such profiles slope upward very slightly early in the life cycle, peak around the age of 60 and, after the peak, exhibit a very modest decline. The most interesting feature of the chart is the large downward shift of the profiles of the younger generations. Among those born after 1940, the cohort differences are very small; by contrast, among those born before 1940, they are very pronounced, with each generation positioning at a significantly higher level than the generation immediately following it. The cohort effects appear to be rather large and negative also on the profiles of public assistance and unemployment benefit income, with the contours of the younger generations

[9]Charts available upon request.

positioned below those of the older ones. Such contours exhibit a rather steep decline during the first part of the life cycle, up to the age of 40; between the age of 40 and 60 they appear to be quite flat; afterwards, they start declining again at a fast rate. Finally, the profiles of retirement income are virtually flat near zero during the first part of the life cycle but slope upwards around retirement age, which appears to be lower the younger the cohort. Among the retired, the profiles of the younger cohorts are slightly higher, suggesting that these generations have or can expect to have a relatively higher income from pensions and social security.

Figure 8.18 displays the smooth cohort profiles for social security benefits and for pensions and annuities from private companies, military, or government, which add up to annuatized retirement income as defined in the Cross-sectional profiles of household saving section. The higher set of contours refers to social security benefits; the lower set refers to pensions and annuities. The figure confirms the cross-sectional results: social security appears to be the largest source of annuatized income for those aged 60 and above; for those in their fifties, who are likely to have taken early retirement, private pensions are relatively more important. The cohort effects on the social security benefits profiles are quite small and do not exhibit any clear pattern. The effects on the pensions profiles are much more pronounced, with the contours corresponding to the younger cohorts higher than those of the older ones, which helps explain the dip in the cross-sectional profiles towards the end of the age spectrum.

Saving as Residual

In this section we focus on the cohort profiles of savings, computed residually by subtracting total household expenditure from total disposable income. Figure 8.19 portrays the cohort age profiles for median total household expenditure. The profiles are similar in most respects to those of income: both are hump shaped, peak around the same age and exhibit similar, although more pronounced cohort effects. Also, the expenditure profiles of those born between 1930 and 1950 are higher than the profiles of the younger cohorts, they are slightly lower or undistinguishable from those of the older ones. The expenditure contours increase and decrease at a somewhat lower rate than income at the ends of the life cycle, suggesting that some dissaving is taking place among the young and the elderly. Starting from the age of 70, consumption levels off.

In Figure 8.20, we report the cohort age profile for median saving, computed as residual. Four features are worth noticing in this chart. First, the profiles exhibit the familiar hump shape, with savings increasing at a rather fast rate among the young, peaking in the late forties and then decreasing at a declining rate. Secondly, the cohort effects are similar to those of income and expenditure and, although modest, are such that, once again, we can divide the cohorts into three groups: the young, born after 1950; the middle-aged, born between 1930 and 1950; and the

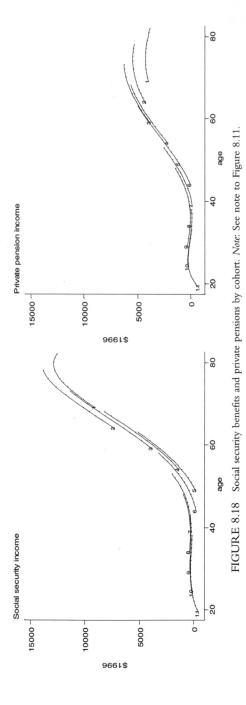

FIGURE 8.18   Social security benefits and private pensions by cohort. *Note:* See note to Figure 8.11.

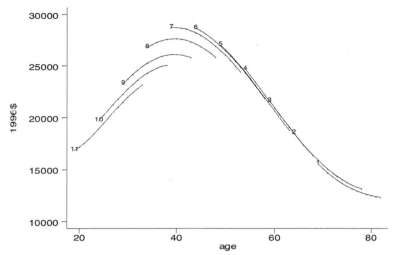

FIGURE 8.19   Total expenditure by cohort (median). *Note*: See note to Figure 8.11.

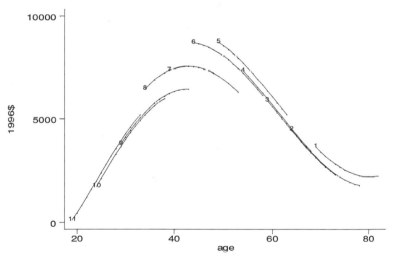

FIGURE 8.20   Total saving by cohort (median). *Note*: See note to Figure 8.11.

elderly, born before 1930. Within each group the behavior is quite similar, but there are important differences across groups. The youngest cohorts have the lowest intercept and, therefore, the lowest saving life-cycle profile. The profiles of the middle-aged, who are close to the peak of their saving contours in the years covered by the survey, are higher than those of the younger cohorts. However, the highest profiles are those for the oldest generations, who, however, are observed over a part of their life cycle where saving has already declined considerably.

Thirdly, despite the pronounced reduction, the levels of saving remain positive also in old age. Fourthly, the level of saving rates is remarkably high, given what we know about the recent performance of aggregate saving rates in the United States. Similar levels are obtained if one considers average cohort savings over average cohort income. It is obvious that such a high level of saving rates is indicative of measurement and data problems. Whereas both consumption and income are likely to be underreported in the CEX, the problem seems to be more serious for consumption, especially at the top of the income distribution, because the wealthiest households are relatively less conscious about completing the lengthy questionnaires as their opportunity cost grows high.[10] Their underestimation of expenditure tends to shift to the right the whole distribution of saving rates. However, unless there are reasons to believe that the underreporting varies systematically with age and cohorts, the figures we present are still informative about the evolution of saving over the life cycle. Having said this, nevertheless, the saving figures, and in particular their level, have to be taken with much caution, and keeping in mind the picture emerging from the balance sheet information.

Finally, Figure 8.21 reports the profiles for the cohort median saving rate, computed by dividing the residual measure of saving by disposable income at the household level. The profiles of the saving rate computed as ratio of cohort mean saving to mean income differ in only two respects: they are shifted downward and the hump shape is more pronounced with lower (negative) saving rates at the left tail of the age distribution. The profiles displayed in the figure indicate, once again, a hump shape for the saving rate, even though the decline in the latest part of the life cycle is not very strong. The saving rate seems to peak in the late forties and then slowly decline, but appears to remain positive throughout the life cycle. Cohort effects do not display a clear pattern: the youngest cohorts born after 1940 exhibit the lowest saving rates; those born between 1930 and 1935, the highest.

The evidence in Figure 8.21 somewhat contradicts that in Attanasio (1994, 1998) who only considered data up to 1992. Attanasio (1998) found negative cohort effects for the middle cohorts and had interpreted these as a possible explanation of the decline in aggregate saving rates in the United States. It seems that the addition of the last additional years reverses that finding. Cohort effects are consistently negative. Obviously, the results we have obtained should be interpreted with care. It should be remembered that the cohort effects and the age profiles are identified only under the arbitrary assumption that there are no time effects in saving rates. There are versions of the life-cycle model that predict the absence of cohort effects (rather than time effect; see Deaton and Paxson, 1994). Further investigations of this result are granted. The fact that Attanasio's result is reversed once the last few years are added seems to suggest that the last

---

[10]If one tries to reproduce National Accounts consumption using weighted CEX figures, one gets about 65% of personal consumption expenditure.

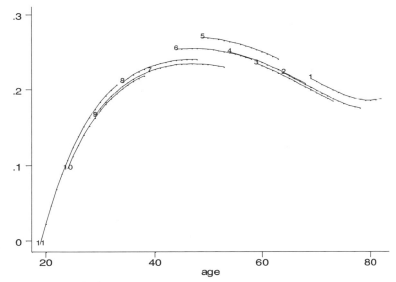

FIGURE 8.21   Median saving rate by cohort. *Note:* See note to Figure 8.11.

few years are somewhat special. A plausible hypothesis for the behavior of the last few years is that of capital gains in the stock market, which would obviously constitute an important time effect that the present identification strategy is ruling out. Once again, a comparison with the cross-sectional profiles presented in Figure 8.9 is instructive. It is clear that the age profile that emerges from Figure 8.9 does not correspond to the experience of any cohort observed during the sample.

Covariates

In this last subsection of this Life-cycle profiles of household saving section we look at the cohort profiles of a set of household characteristics that are thought to help understand life-cycle expenditure and saving behavior. Figure 8.22 displays the cohort age profiles of household size in the top-left panel; employment rates in the top-right panel; homeownership in the bottom-left panel; and ownership of life insurance in the bottom-right panel.

The profiles for family size in the top-left panel exhibit the familiar hump shape and clear negative cohort effects, with the contours for the younger cohorts being lower and peaking slightly later than those of the older generations. In the top-right panel, we report both the proportion of household heads who are employed and the proportion of household heads who are retired. The most noticeable feature of these two sets of profiles concerns the phenomenon of earlier retirement characterizing the younger cohorts. Thus, the contours for the employment rate are somewhat lower and start sloping down at lower ages for the earlier cohorts,

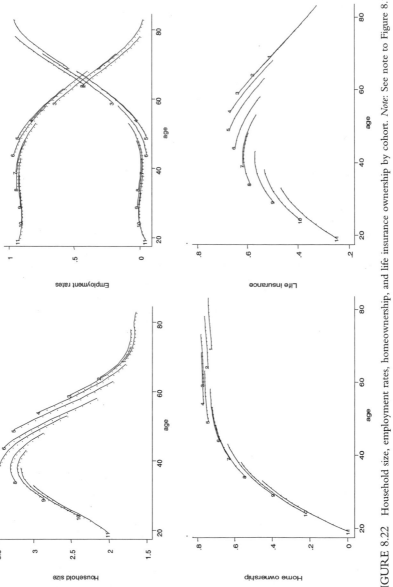

FIGURE 8.22   Household size, employment rates, homeownership, and life insurance ownership by cohort. *Note:* See note to Figure 8.11.

whereas the contours for the retirement rate are somewhat higher and start sloping upward earlier. The profile for homeownership (bottom-left panel) suggests that the proportion of homeowners is slightly smaller among the young generation, but the profiles for the young are very steep. The cohort effects are strongly negative for life insurance, with a lower proportion of younger households in the younger generations holding a life insurance. The proportion of households with a life insurance is relatively low also among the older cohorts.

8.4 PENSION POLICIES

Much of the current debate on pension policies in the United States is dominated by two important facts. The first is the decline of household saving rates, as measured in the National Income and Product Accounts as well as in the Flow of Funds figures. According to these, household saving rates went from being close to double figures at the beginning of the 1980s, to being negative last year. The other is the fact that the current pay-as-you-go social security system (OASDI) is unsustainable in the medium run, given its current parameters. Even though the system is currently enjoying a surplus because of the presence of a large generation in the labor force, it is projected to go into deficits in a few years and to exhaust the funds in less than 30 years. These two facts have stimulated a wide-ranging debate among academics and policymakers about fiscal incentives to saving, the reform of the pension system and, more generally, on the determinants of saving. The proposals for reform have varied from simple adjustments to the current formula, to the indexation of retirement age to changes in life expectancy, to the privatization of the system and the institution of individual retirement accounts. Before mentioning briefly the debate on the reform of the social security system, we review some of the evidence on the decline in household saving rates and the debate on fiscal incentives to saving.

The low saving rates of US households have induced many commentators and policymakers to advocate fiscal incentives to savings, as the perception was that US households were not saving "enough" to provide for their retirement. Many commentators seem to worry particularly about the saving behavior of the baby boomers, as it is felt that this generation will not be able to rely on the social security system currently in place, because of the problems mentioned above. The last set of results we presented, indicating negative cohort effects in the saving rates of the baby boomers seems to support this view. However, without a full understanding of the causes of the decline in household saving, it is not clear that US households are saving "too little" or "not enough." Unfortunately, a fully convincing explanation of the decline in household saving rates has not been found. Besides this study, a few other papers have analyzed household savings at the micro level. These include Bosworth et al. (1991), Attanasio (1994), Gokhale et al. (1996), and Attanasio (1998). The evidence that seems to emerge from these studies is that the baby boomers are not responsible for the decline in saving rates observed from the early 1980s to the early 1990s. As we showed in the previous paragraph, US households do exhibit a pronounced hump-shaped saving profile, so that, at each point in time, the generations that save the most are those approaching retirement at that age. Starting with the early 1980s, the generations that were in that position were the parents of the baby boomers, but there is some evidence in the literature that their saving profile was, for some reason, "shifted down" relative to that of previous and subsequent generations. One possible explanation is that these generations were about to enjoy a generous social security system and therefore did not have strong incentives to save. At least in some of the papers cited above, the baby boomers seemed to be saving more than their parents *at similar ages*. The most recent further declines in household saving rates are harder to explain, as the baby boomers are now in a phase of their life cycle when they should be saving the most. However, these trends seem to be somehow reflected in our estimates of cohort effects, which are the lowest for these cohorts, as we have documented above. Notice that this contradicts the finding in Attanasio (1998), based on data up to 1992.[11] A possible explanation, that merits serious investigation, is that the observed low saving rates are related to the recent capital gains on financial wealth and real estate that are often not included in the definition of saving. If people perceive that these capital gains are sustainable, then the incentive to save out of current earnings is not strong.

The existing studies of the recent decline in saving rates, including the present one, suffer from important limitations. The first and probably most important is data availability. Whereas the analysis of household behavior requires micro data that measure income, consumption, wealth, and so on, such data are available only since the early 1980s and have important limitations. The CEX is of very limited size and, as we saw, contains only scant information on wealth. On the other hand, the SCF is available only every 3 years and contains very limited information on the flows of saving. The second limitation is that much of the evidence on many of the hypotheses mentioned earlier is based on strong identifying assumptions. A good example is the problem of disentangling year, age, and cohort effects from the evidence on repeated cross sections. Without additional information and/or the structure provided by a theoretical model, it is not possible to disentangle, in a purely statistical way, age, cohort, and time effects. In other words, even if we observe baby boomers saving more at 35 when their parents were at the same age, we cannot say whether this is a cohort effect or a year effect. This identification problem is compounded by the fact that we have virtually no information on saving behavior at the micro level during the 1960s and 1970s. Finally, we still do not have a fully satisfactory theoretical model of saving behavior that we can use

---

[11]Because of the positive cohort effects for the cohorts that were about to enter the part of the life cycle where saving is the highest, Attanasio (1998) was predicting an increase in saving rate that obviously did not occur.

with confidence for policy analysis. There are two reasons for being unsatisfied. First, whereas the most sophisticated analyses of Euler equations for consumption that allow for the effects of demographic and labor supply variables seem to be able to fit the data, they are of limited usefulness in the analysis of saving behavior and as a guidance to policy analysis. This is because, while we can say that a flexible (and complex) version of the life-cycle model seems to fit the data, we do not know how to use in a structural fashion all but the simplest versions of the model. This situation is behind the somewhat schizophrenic approach of the profession that alternates between very descriptive analyses of saving behavior and very structural studies of consumption. Secondly, it seems that a variety of factors, but in particular education, information, and economic literacy, are important determinants of saving behavior and especially of saving for retirement[12] and yet we still do not have analytical tools sufficiently developed that account fully for these issues.

The worry about the level of household saving and its adequacy to finance the retirement of the baby boomers is probably behind the large attention to fiscal incentives to savings. One does not have to look very far to find many quotes of policymakers stating that Americans should be encouraged to save more. Regardless of whether this objective is indeed justified, a large fraction of the policy debate on saving in the United States has focused on the effectiveness of these tax incentives as provided first by the IRA legislation and then by the 401(k) legislation. It is certainly undeniable that these pieces of legislation have had a profound effect on the way Americans save, in more than one way. We have seen above the massive increase in participation to the IRA program during the years in which the tax incentives were most generous. The 401(k) programs have now grown so much that 401(k) accounts represent a substantial part of household retirement wealth. Whether these programs have had a net positive effect in stimulating national saving, however, is still hotly debated. Venti and Wise (1987) and Poterba et al. (1997) have argued in many occasions that the IRA and 401(k) fiscal incentives did create a substantial amount of new saving over and above the amount that these programs cost in lost tax revenue. On the other hand, Engen and Gale (1997) and Engen et al. (1996) have forcefully claimed that this is not the case. The main problem with this debate is that the evidence strongly rests on identification assumptions that, by their nature, are untestable. The main problem is simple to explain and typical of the evaluation of program participation. Although it is true that IRA or 401(k) participants save more than nonparticipants, the fact that they participate in a program is likely to be correlated with a high "taste for saving." Therefore, the comparison between the two groups is not informative about whether program participants would have saved less in the absence of the program.

---

[12]See for instance, Bernheim and Scholtz (1993).

The only study in the large literature on the effectiveness of the IRA legislation in stimulating saving that uses information on consumption (and therefore on saving as a residual) uses the CEX (see Attanasio and DeLeire, 1994). Attanasio and DeLeire exploit the panel dimension of the CEX and circumvent the identification problem that plagues this literature by comparing recent and "old" IRA contributors' consumption and saving behavior.[13] The idea is quite simple. Within a simple life-cycle model, the fiscal incentive can have an impact only through the substitution effect induced by the increased rate of return to saving. If such an effect is strong enough to counteract the income effect, consumers would reduce their consumption (and increase their saving) *when they start to participate in the scheme* and would remain at that (lower) level of consumption afterwards. It is therefore possible to compare those participants who joined the program recently with those who have been in the program for some time. If the scheme works, one would observe that consumption growth is significantly lower for the new participants than for the old. In the CEX, one can identify all the households at the final interview who were contributing to an IRA and compute the rate of growth of consumption for those already contributing at the first interview and those who were not. These rates of growth are not significantly different, even after controlling for income growth and a variety of other variables. This test is different from the others in the literature because it uses the structure provided by economic theory (i.e., the fact that the program can only work through the substitution effect). Attanasio and DeLeire (1998) also look at the changes in non-IRA financial assets for the two groups and find evidence that the change for the new participants is significantly lower than that of the nonparticipants, a further indication of the fact that the scheme does not generate new saving, but only a reshuffle of existing saving (or saving that would have been carried out even in the absence of the program). The identification assumption for the validity of this test is that the two groups (new and old participants) do not differ in the unobservable "taste for saving."

8.5 CONCLUSION

We have presented some evidence on the behavior of aggregate saving rates. We construct such evidence starting from data on individual households. The use of time series of cross sections and pseudo-panel techniques, together with strong identification assumptions, allows us to identify the life-cycle profiles of the variables of interest that often turn out to be substantially different from the cross-sectional age profile that emerges from a single cross section and that neglects cohort effects. Our analysis uncovers two important facts. First, the life-cycle

---

[13]The statement is not uncontroversial. As any identification assumption, the one used by Attanasio and DeLeire is not testable and therefore open to criticism.

profile for savings and saving rates is roughly hump shaped and peaks in the late forties. Secondly, there seem to be important differences in saving behavior across cohorts, with the youngest cohorts born after 1940 exhibiting the lowest saving rate and those born before 1930 the highest. These results should be interpreted with extreme care, as they are based on strong identification assumptions that, by definition, cannot be tested. However, if these assumptions hold, our results contribute to the understanding of US household saving behavior and as such are relevant for the policy debate on the incentives to savings. In fact, by identifying saving behavior over the life cycle after accounting for differences due to cohort-specific preferences, our analysis provides a framework to investigate the potential causes of the decline in saving rates and to check the desirability of specific policy interventions aimed at stimulating saving. Yet, as discussed in the last section of the chapter, determining ex post the actual effectiveness of most common incentives is not straightforward, but rests crucially on identifying assumptions that, by their nature, are untestable.

ACKNOWLEDGMENT

We would like to thank Axel Börsch-Supan and two anonymous referees for useful suggestions. We also thank the participants to the TMR conference in Deidesheim, April 2000, for their comments. The views expressed are those of the authors and do not necessarily reflect those of the Bank of Italy.

REFERENCES

Attanasio, O.P. (1994). Personal saving in the United States. In J. Poterba (ed.), *International Comparison of Household Saving*. NBER Economic Research Project Report series. Chicago: University of Chicago Press, 57–123.

Attanasio, O.P. (1998). Cohort analysis of saving behavior by U.S. households. *Journal of Human Resources* 33, 575–609.

Attanasio, O.P. and T.C. DeLeire (1994). IRA's and household saving revisited: some new evidence. NBER Working Paper, No. 4900.

Bernheim, B.D. and J.K. Scholz (1993). Private saving and public policy. In: J.M. Poterba (ed.), *Tax Policy and the Economy*, Vol. 7. Cambridge: MIT Press and NBER.

Bertaut, C. and Starr-McCluer, M. (2000). Household portfolios in the United States. In: L. Guiso, M. Haliassos and J. Tullio (eds), *Household Portfolios*. Cambridge: MIT Press and NBER.

Bosworth, B., G. Burthless, and J. Sabelhaus (1991). The decline in saving: evidence from household surveys. *Brooking Papers on Economic Activity* 183–241.

Deaton, A. and C. Paxson (1994). Intertemporal choice and inequality. *Journal of Political Economy* 102(3), 437–467.

Engen, E.M., W.G. Gale, and J.K. Scholz (1996). The effects of tax-based saving incentives on saving wealth. NBER Working Paper, No. 5759.

Engen, E.M. and W.G. Gale (1997). Effects of social security reform on private and national saving. In: S. Sass and R. Triest (eds), *Social Security Reform: Conference Proceedings: Links to Saving, Investment, and Growth*. Conference Series, No. 41, 103–142. Federal Reserve Bank of Boston.

Gokhale, J., L.J. Kotlikoff, and J. Sabelhaus (1996). Understanding the postwar decline in U.S. saving: A cohort analysis. *Brooking Papers on Economic Activity* 315–390.

Greenspan, A. (2001). Opening Remark. Federal Reserve Bank of Kansas City symposium on Economic Policy for the Information Economy, Jackson Hole, Wyoming, August 31, 2001.

Nelson, J. (1994) On testing for full insurance using consumer expenditure survey data (in comment). *Journal of Political Economy* 102(2), 384–394.

Poterba, J.M., S.F. Venti, and D.A. Wise (1997). The effects of special saving programs on saving and wealth. In: M. Hurd and N. Yashiro (eds), *The Economic Effects of Aging in the United States and Japan.* NBER Conference Report series. Chicago: University of Chicago Press, 217–240.

Sabelhaus, J. (1993). What is the distributional burden of taxing consumption. *National Tax Journal* 46(3), 331–344.

Sabelhaus, J. and J. Groen (2000). Can permanent income theory explain cross-section consumption patterns? *Review of Economics and Statistics* 82(3), 431–438.

Venti, S.F. and D.A. Wise, D.A. (1987). IRAs and saving. In: M. Feldestein (ed.), *The Effects of Taxation on Capital Accumulation.* NBER Project Report. Chicago: University of Chicago Press, 147–177.

Venti, S.F. and D.A. Wise (1995). Individual response to a retirement saving program: Result from U.S. panel data. *Ricerche Econometriche* 49(3), 235–254.

Venti, S.F. and D.A. Wise (1997). The wealth of cohorts: retirement saving and the changing assets of older Americans. In: S. Schieber and J. Shoven (eds), *Public Policy toward Pensions.* A Twentieth Century Fund Book. Cambridge: MIT Press, 85–130.

TABLE 8.1 Financial Savings (Distribution)[a]

Year	Age	Net deposits in checking, saving, brokerage and similar accounts	Net purchases of stocks, bonds, mutual funds and similar securities	Contributions to individual retirement accounts	Contributions to life insurance	Contributions to health insurance
1983	20–24	0.3468	0.5231	0.0253	0.0466	0.0582
	25–29	0.4737	−0.0786	0.1696	0.2323	0.2030
	30–34	0.2096	0.4858	0.1064	0.1169	0.0812
	35–39	−0.9346	−2.2066	0.9547	0.7762	0.4103
	40–44	−1.5482	−0.0812	0.2617	0.2555	0.1121
eee	45–49	0.7458	−1.9788	0.8920	0.7714	0.5697
	50–54	0.1559	−2.6806	1.8853	0.9328	0.7066
	55–59	0.2030	0.2334	0.5087	0.0316	0.0233
	60–64	0.7130	0.0819	0.0991	0.0482	0.0579
	65–69	0.6647	0.2233	0.0183	0.0369	0.0569
	70–74	−1.0015	−0.4867	0.0681	0.0585	0.3616
	75+	0.8726	−0.3026	0.0156	0.0511	0.3632
1984	20–24	0.4715	−0.3143	0.2469	0.2115	0.3844
	25–29	0.1338	0.3738	0.1358	0.1394	0.2172
	30–34	0.1463	−0.0363	0.3749	0.2577	0.2574
	35–39	0.8279	−0.3868	0.2439	0.1724	0.1426
	40–44	0.6246	0.0724	0.1482	0.0922	0.0627
	45–49	−0.0666	0.1043	0.3801	0.3204	0.2618
	50–54	0.4781	0.2088	0.1757	0.0667	0.0708
	55–59	0.3340	0.2683	0.1967	0.1261	0.0749
	60–64	0.1400	0.2264	0.2537	0.1743	0.2056
	65–69	1.5063	−1.2098	0.1607	0.1605	0.3824
	70–74	0.4455	0.4414	0.0064	0.0242	0.0825
	75+	0.2806	0.5248	0.0024	0.0210	0.1712

(*Continues*)

TABLE 8.1   (*Continued*)

Year	Age	Net deposits in checking, saving, brokerage and similar accounts	Net purchases of stocks, bonds, mutual funds and similar securities	Contributions to individual retirement accounts	Contributions to life insurance	Contributions to health insurance
1985	20–24	−0.4241	−5.8524	1.0646	1.3400	2.8720
	25–29	0.5420	0.1280	0.1212	0.0789	0.1300
	30–34	0.4641	0.0926	0.1567	0.1277	0.1589
	35–39	−0.1782	0.7274	0.2021	0.1338	0.1149
	40–44	−0.2262	0.5593	0.3154	0.1578	0.1937
	45–49	0.1165	0.5091	0.1553	0.1088	0.1103
	50–54	0.3298	0.3511	0.1701	0.0728	0.0762
	55–59	0.8489	−0.0717	0.1114	0.0441	0.0674
	60–64	0.4095	0.4237	0.0835	0.0294	0.0539
	65–69	−1.2253	−0.0300	0.0360	0.0547	0.1647
	70–74	−0.7249	−0.4011	0.0168	0.0229	0.0863
	75+	0.7365	0.1547	0.0060	0.0122	0.0906
1986	20–24	0.5491	0.2048	0.0375	0.0739	0.1348
	25–29	−0.9900	0.9745	0.3527	0.2443	0.4184
	30–34	0.5986	−0.1358	0.3052	0.1186	0.1134
	35–39	0.4946	0.1871	0.1613	0.0735	0.0835
	40–44	0.5105	0.0259	0.2137	0.1273	0.1226
	45–49	0.2081	0.1235	0.3254	0.1954	0.1477
	50–54	0.2282	0.4176	0.1988	0.0729	0.0826
	55–59	−1.2202	−0.4527	0.3522	0.1548	0.1659
	60–64	−50.6880	23.2137	11.5339	5.8848	9.0556
	65–69	0.4602	0.3296	0.0550	0.0481	0.1069
	70–74	0.3372	0.3787	0.0194	0.0527	0.2120
	75+	−0.5651	−0.5983	0.0064	0.0150	0.1419
1987	20–24	−1.5072	−0.7932	0.2606	0.3603	0.6795
	25–29	0.1824	−0.0178	0.2851	0.2255	0.3249
	30–34	−0.0246	0.3689	0.2273	0.1585	0.2699
	35–39	0.3218	0.0822	0.2281	0.1636	0.2042
	40–44	0.1870	0.1081	0.3452	0.1867	0.1731
	45–49	0.4208	0.4012	0.0775	0.0474	0.0529
	50–54	0.4888	0.1699	0.1882	0.0625	0.0907
	55–59	0.2447	0.3989	0.1736	0.0959	0.0870
	60–64	0.4009	0.3177	0.1123	0.0608	0.1083
	65–69	2.7011	−4.8629	0.1426	0.4509	0.5682

Year	Age				
	70–74	0.5221	0.1637	0.0268	0.0696	0.2179
	75+	−0.7204	−0.6711	0.0039	0.0538	0.3338
1988	20–24	−0.0931	0.7243	0.0780	0.0923	0.1985
	25–29	0.3187	0.0685	0.0929	0.1987	0.3212
	30–34	−1.1480	−0.7629	0.8028	0.9262	1.1820
	35–39	−0.9740	−0.5391	0.1455	0.1815	0.1861
	40–44	0.0158	−2.4481	1.0187	1.1979	1.2157
	45–49	−0.4704	−0.7220	0.0797	0.0583	0.0544
	50–54	−1.2390	−0.7620	0.4868	0.2433	0.2709
	55–59	−3.0401	−0.2079	0.9619	0.6655	0.6206
	60–64	0.5154	0.1917	0.1507	0.0481	0.0942
	65–69	−1.6901	0.2804	0.1661	0.0712	0.1725
	70–74	−0.9398	−1.3617	0.1297	0.2543	0.9175
	75+	−0.7128	1.2760	0.0091	0.1326	0.2951
1989	20–24	0.3273	0.2533	0.0570	0.0969	0.2655
	25–29	0.6507	−0.2367	0.1036	0.1545	0.3279
	30–34	0.1599	0.3870	0.1005	0.1590	0.1937
	35–39	0.1872	0.3274	0.1468	0.1435	0.1951
	40–44	0.2473	0.4563	0.1115	0.0960	0.0889
	45–49	0.2733	0.1189	0.2968	0.1458	0.1651
	50–54	0.4852	0.2199	0.1290	0.0668	0.0991
	55–59	3.3167	−9.2724	2.1651	1.8471	2.9434
	60–64	−0.3800	0.3363	0.2562	0.2294	0.5580
	65–69	−0.9248	−0.9335	0.1502	0.1836	0.5245
	70–74	1.0896	−0.3366	0.0029	0.0490	0.1951
	75+	0.6510	0.1186	0.0013	0.0203	0.2087
1990	20–24	0.7046	0.0546	0.0373	0.0573	0.1462
	25–29	−0.0941	0.0702	0.1578	0.2568	0.6093
	30–34	0.3765	0.1667	0.1542	0.1193	0.1833
	35–39	0.3578	0.3380	0.1147	0.0917	0.0978
	40–44	0.3440	−0.2859	0.2756	0.2813	0.3851
	45–49	−2.5215	−0.5548	0.6108	0.5021	0.9634

(*Continues*)

TABLE 8.1 (*Continued*)

Year	Age	Net deposits in checking, saving, brokerage and similar accounts	Net purchases of stocks, bonds, mutual funds and similar securities	Contributions to individual retirement accounts	Contributions to life insurance	Contributions to health insurance
	50–54	−41.0498	1.9805	20.1293	8.8031	11.1369

Year	Age					
	55–59	−1.8017	−2.1630	0.8887	0.7662	1.3098
	60–64	0.4042	0.3941	0.0536	0.0470	0.1012
	65–69	0.9255	−0.5983	0.1625	0.1183	0.3921
	70–74	−0.0445	0.5220	0.1290	0.0722	0.3212
	75+	−4.0028	1.9147	0.0285	0.1535	0.9061
1991	20–24	0.1227	0.5487	0.0634	0.0639	0.2013
	25–29	−0.0240	0.4908	0.1007	0.1228	0.3097
	30–34	−0.0031	0.0960	0.2268	0.2422	0.4381
	35–39	−0.9491	−0.8495	0.2624	0.2099	0.3263
	40–44	−0.6413	0.4877	0.3732	0.3310	0.4494
	45–49	0.3261	0.5014	0.0552	0.0508	0.0664
	50–54	0.1654	0.6009	0.0454	0.0952	0.0931
	55–59	−0.3481	−1.5221	0.1978	0.3103	0.3621
	60–64	0.1491	−2.0568	1.0037	0.6420	1.2620
	65–69	−1.3244	−0.2269	0.0327	0.1210	0.3976
	70–74	−0.7276	−0.4833	0.0090	0.0354	0.1665
	75+	4.4684	−5.5732	0.0036	0.2200	1.8811
1992	20–24	0.1110	−2.3326	0.2282	0.2492	0.7442
	25–29	0.3935	0.3242	0.0546	0.0744	0.1534
	30–34	0.2383	0.1553	0.1885	0.1373	0.2806
	35–39	0.0345	0.4074	0.1949	0.1305	0.2326
	40–44	0.2926	0.2825	0.1560	0.1094	0.1596
	45–49	1.0803	−1.7276	0.7113	0.4217	0.5143
	50–54	0.3052	0.1879	0.1863	0.1217	0.1990
	55–59	−0.0356	0.5274	0.1985	0.1400	0.1697
	60–64	−5.0190	1.6330	0.9908	1.0833	2.3119
	65–69	-5.1525	3.5904	0.1937	0.5807	1.7877
	70–74	−1.1481	0.8723	0.0135	0.1959	1.0663
	75+	−1.0864	−0.3828	0.0018	0.0397	0.4277
1993	20–24	−1.0458	0.5520	0.1762	0.2877	1.0299
	25–29	0.0242	0.3395	0.1414	0.1392	0.3556
	30–34	−2.6939	1.2840	0.6108	0.6369	1.1623
	35–39	0.1589	0.3425	0.1273	0.1338	0.2375

(*Continues*)

TABLE 8.1   (*Continued*)

Year	Age	Net deposits in checking, saving, brokerage and similar accounts	Net purchases of stocks, bonds, mutual funds and similar securities	Contributions to individual retirement accounts	Contributions to life insurance	Contributions to health insurance
	40–44	−0.9809	0.8245	0.3949	0.2540	0.5076

	45–49	−5.3126	−0.3502	1.6174	1.2711	1.7742
	50–54	−0.1037	0.7481	0.1710	0.0726	0.1121
	55–59	0.3346	0.3010	0.1554	0.0937	0.1153
	60–64	0.3511	0.1859	0.1112	0.0838	0.2680
	65–69	0.6263	0.2146	0.0188	0.0243	0.1160
	70–74	0.1058	0.1569	0.1327	0.0746	0.5300
	75+	0.1150	0.6433	0.0013	0.0189	0.2215
1994	20–24	0.4431	0.3294	0.0146	0.0440	0.1687
	25–29	−0.9108	−0.1781	0.4028	0.4334	1.2528
	30–34	0.4254	0.1968	0.0997	0.0786	0.1995
	35–39	0.3164	0.4782	0.0595	0.0542	0.0917
	40–44	−0.1943	−13.5050	3.6528	3.0725	5.9740
	45–49	0.2107	0.2821	0.1308	0.2024	0.1739
	50–54	2.6136	−6.6324	0.9802	0.8262	1.2125
	55–59	−0.8372	−0.9281	0.2348	0.2347	0.2959
	60–64	−1.3846	−0.8252	0.2435	0.2706	0.6958
	65–69	−1.8626	0.2527	0.0537	0.1214	0.4347
	70–74	0.4214	0.3725	0.0010	0.0656	0.1395
	75+	0.4474	0.2232	0.0073	0.0399	0.2823
1995	20–24	0.1157	0.5296	0.0576	0.0575	0.2396
	25–29	−0.0833	0.2729	0.1608	0.1361	0.5135
	30–34	0.2182	0.1873	0.1670	0.1315	0.2960
	35–39	−2.8295	−4.4411	1.9179	1.3102	3.0426
	40–44	0.1586	0.2480	0.1651	0.1634	0.2649
	45–49	0.2801	0.2063	0.1242	0.1529	0.2365
	50–54	−4.8756	1.1297	1.1113	1.3541	2.2804
	55–59	−1.9041	0.1243	0.1433	0.2608	0.3757
	60–64	−0.2556	0.5186	0.3020	0.1355	0.2995
	65–69	0.4805	0.2034	0.0243	0.0593	0.2325
	70–74	−0.7531	−0.5999	0.0146	0.0793	0.2590
	75+	−1.8058	0.3374	0.0281	0.0632	0.3771

[a]The figures in this set of tables are computed by dividing the amount of the relevant asset by total financial savings in absolute value.

TABLE 8.2   Stock of Financial Wealth (Distribution)

Year	Age	Stock of checking, saving, brokerage and similar accounts	Stock of stocks, bonds, mutual funds and similar securities
1982	20–24	0.6267	0.3733
	25–29	0.7402	0.2598
	30–34	0.7067	0.2933
	35–39	0.6583	0.3417
	40–44	0.7014	0.2986
	45–49	0.6611	0.3389
	50–54	0.5542	0.4458
	55–59	0.6247	0.3753
	60–64	0.5702	0.4298
	65–69	0.6010	0.3990
	70–74	0.7298	0.2702
	75+	0.6779	0.3221
1983	20–24	0.6031	0.3969
	25–29	0.7609	0.2391
	30–34	0.6343	0.3657
	35–39	0.7109	0.2891
	40–44	0.6170	0.3830
	45–49	0.6959	0.3041
	50–54	0.6135	0.3865
	55–59	0.6465	0.3535
	60–64	0.6456	0.3544
	65–69	0.7254	0.2746
	70–74	0.7258	0.2742
	75+	0.6683	0.3317
1984	20–24	0.7229	0.2771
	25–29	0.6836	0.3164
	30–34	0.6393	0.3607
	35–39	0.8083	0.1917
	40–44	0.6858	0.3142
	45–49	0.7008	0.2992
	50–54	0.6318	0.3682
	55–59	0.6194	0.3806
	60–64	0.6328	0.3672
	65–69	0.6973	0.3027

(*Continues*)

TABLE 8.2   (*Continued*)

Year	Age	Stock of checking, saving, brokerage and similar accounts	Stock of stocks, bonds, mutual funds and similar securities
	70–74	0.6602	0.3398
	75+	0.6484	0.3516
1985	20–24	0.9077	0.0923
	25–29	0.6437	0.3563
	30–34	0.6761	0.3239
	35–39	0.5778	0.4222
	40–44	0.6766	0.3234
	45–49	0.5926	0.4074
	50–54	0.6425	0.3575
	55–59	0.7021	0.2979
	60–64	0.6324	0.3676
	65–69	0.6144	0.3856
	70–74	0.6605	0.3395
	75+	0.7359	0.2641
1986	20–24	0.8463	0.1537
	25–29	0.6890	0.3110
	30–34	0.7577	0.2423
	35–39	0.6747	0.3253
	40–44	0.6159	0.3841
	45–49	0.5815	0.4185
	50–54	0.5726	0.4274
	55–59	0.7069	0.2931
	60–64	0.5749	0.4251
	65–69	0.6268	0.3732
	70–74	0.6153	0.3847
	75+	0.7445	0.2555
1987	20–24	0.8543	0.1457
	25–29	0.7005	0.2995
	30–34	0.7273	0.2727
	35–39	0.7000	0.3000
	40–44	0.5997	0.4003
	45–49	0.6024	0.3976
	50–54	0.5875	0.4125

(*Continues*)

TABLE 8.2 (*Continued*)

Year	Age	Stock of checking, saving, brokerage and similar accounts	Stock of stocks, bonds, mutual funds and similar securities
	55–59	0.5916	0.4084
	60–64	0.6298	0.3702
	65–69	0.6634	0.3366
	70–74	0.6371	0.3629
	75+	0.7691	0.2309
1988	20–24	0.6762	0.3238
	25–29	0.7922	0.2078
	30–34	0.6966	0.3034
	35–39	0.7000	0.3000
	40–44	0.6480	0.3520
	45–49	0.6870	0.3130
	50–54	0.6123	0.3877
	55–59	0.5471	0.4529
	60–64	0.6422	0.3578
	65–69	0.5813	0.4187
	70–74	0.6576	0.3424
	75+	0.6242	0.3758
1989	20–24	0.8163	0.1837
	25–29	0.8177	0.1823
	30–34	0.6555	0.3445
	35–39	0.6194	0.3806
	40–44	0.6497	0.3503
	45–49	0.6558	0.3442
	50–54	0.6726	0.3274
	55–59	0.6278	0.3722
	60–64	0.6066	0.3934
	65–69	0.5947	0.4053
	70–74	0.7515	0.2485
	75+	0.6850	0.3150
1990	20–24	0.8548	0.1452
	25–29	0.8219	0.1782
	30–34	0.6683	0.3317
	35–39	0.6275	0.3725

(*Continues*)

TABLE 8.2 (*Continued*)

Year	Age	Stock of checking, saving, brokerage and similar accounts	Stock of stocks, bonds, mutual funds and similar securities
	40–44	0.6685	0.3315
	45–49	0.6612	0.3388
	50–54	0.5874	0.4126
	55–59	0.6050	0.3950
	60–64	0.6525	0.3475
	65–69	0.6604	0.3396
	70–74	0.6497	0.3503
	75+	0.6224	0.3776
1991	20–24	0.7175	0.2825
	25–29	0.7599	0.2401
	30–34	0.6925	0.3075
	35–39	0.6929	0.3071
	40–44	0.5571	0.4429
	45–49	0.5226	0.4774
	50–54	0.5407	0.4593
	55–59	0.6684	0.3316
	60–64	0.6485	0.3515
	65–69	0.6430	0.3570
	70–74	0.7112	0.2888
	75+	0.6868	0.3132
1992	20–24	0.9252	0.0748
	25–29	0.6798	0.3202
	30–34	0.7030	0.2970
	35–39	0.5537	0.4463
	40–44	0.6065	0.3935
	45–49	0.6246	0.3754
	50–54	0.5650	0.4350
	55–59	0.5422	0.4578
	60–64	0.5869	0.4131
	65–69	0.5513	0.4487
	70–74	0.5529	0.4471
	75+	0.7380	0.2620
1993	20–24	0.8770	0.1230
	25–29	0.6114	0.3886

(*Continues*)

TABLE 8.2   (*Continued*)

Year	Age	Stock of checking, saving, brokerage and similar accounts	Stock of stocks, bonds, mutual funds and similar securities
	30–34	0.5172	0.4828
	35–39	0.5948	0.4052
	40–44	0.5471	0.4529
	45–49	0.6209	0.3791
	50–54	0.4362	0.5638
	55–59	0.5477	0.4523
	60–64	0.5927	0.4073
	65–69	0.6866	0.3134
	70–74	0.6485	0.3515
	75+	0.6381	0.3619
1994	20–24	0.6697	0.3303
	25–29	0.7713	0.2287
	30–34	0.5890	0.4110
	35–39	0.4964	0.5036
	40–44	0.5360	0.4640
	45–49	0.5291	0.4709
	50–54	0.6022	0.3978
	55–59	0.5220	0.4780
	60–64	0.5747	0.4253
	65–69	0.5971	0.4029
	70–74	0.5491	0.4509
	75+	0.6322	0.3678
1995	20–24	0.5320	0.4680
	25–29	0.7429	0.2571
	30–34	0.5645	0.4355
	35–39	0.5649	0.4351
	40–44	0.5141	0.4859
	45–49	0.6010	0.3990
	50–54	0.5336	0.4664
	55–59	0.4640	0.5360
	60–64	0.5201	0.4799
	65–69	0.5582	0.4418
	70–74	0.6100	0.3900
	75+	0.5981	0.4019

TABLE 8.3   Total Retirement Contributions (Distribution)

Year	Age	Deductions for social security	Contributions to private pensions	Deductions for government retirement	Deductions for railroad retirement
1982	20–24	0.9089	0.0407	0.0418	0.0086
	25–29	0.8696	0.0635	0.0528	0.0141
	30–34	0.8398	0.0868	0.0693	0.0041
	35–39	0.8148	0.1033	0.0754	0.0065
	40–44	0.8329	0.1036	0.0574	0.0062
	45–49	0.8308	0.0848	0.0773	0.0071
	50–54	0.8112	0.1087	0.0671	0.0129
	55–59	0.7807	0.1294	0.0883	0.0016
	60–64	0.8030	0.1039	0.0930	0.0000
	65–69	0.9100	0.0534	0.0366	0.0000
	70–74	0.8652	0.0425	0.0923	0.0000
	75+	0.8902	0.0825	0.0273	0.0000
1983	20–24	0.9296	0.0358	0.0333	0.0013
	25–29	0.8587	0.0889	0.0440	0.0083
	30–34	0.8449	0.0906	0.0590	0.0055
	35–39	0.8236	0.0979	0.0724	0.0062
	40–44	0.8156	0.0915	0.0812	0.0117
	45–49	0.7850	0.1371	0.0722	0.0057
	50–54	0.7795	0.1332	0.0841	0.0032
	55–59	0.7956	0.1079	0.0810	0.0156
	60–64	0.8260	0.0871	0.0869	0.0000
	65–69	0.9294	0.0263	0.0443	0.0000
	70–74	0.9058	0.0119	0.0819	0.0004
	75+	0.9484	0.0346	0.0171	0.0000
1984	20–24	0.9411	0.0385	0.0154	0.0050
	25–29	0.8794	0.0635	0.0370	0.0201
	30–34	0.8470	0.0969	0.0423	0.0138
	35–39	0.8292	0.1163	0.0435	0.0110
	40–44	0.8280	0.0992	0.0633	0.0095
	45–49	0.7246	0.1956	0.0662	0.0136
	50–54	0.7888	0.1227	0.0841	0.0044
	55–59	0.8308	0.1081	0.0594	0.0016
	60–64	0.8482	0.1029	0.0425	0.0064
	65–69	0.8400	0.0962	0.0638	0.0000

(*Continues*)

TABLE 8.3   (*Continued*)

Year	Age	Deductions for social security	Contributions to private pensions	Deductions for government retirement	Deductions for railroad retirement
	70–74	0.8897	0.0229	0.0874	0.0000
	75+	0.7312	0.2062	0.0626	0.0000
1985	20–24	0.9671	0.0194	0.0135	0.0000
	25–29	0.8967	0.0508	0.0344	0.0181
	30–34	0.8545	0.1010	0.0431	0.0014
	35–39	0.8605	0.0759	0.0511	0.0125
	40–44	0.8448	0.0903	0.0514	0.0135
	45–49	0.8379	0.0943	0.0587	0.0091
	50–54	0.8377	0.1190	0.0401	0.0032
	55–59	0.8330	0.1024	0.0520	0.0126
	60–64	0.8669	0.0767	0.0564	0.0000
	65–69	0.8581	0.0271	0.0996	0.0151
	70–74	0.8795	0.0964	0.0242	0.0000
	75+	0.8297	0.0919	0.0016	0.0769
1986	20–24	0.9129	0.0602	0.0220	0.0049
	25–29	0.8742	0.0867	0.0322	0.0069
	30–34	0.8685	0.0928	0.0338	0.0048
	35–39	0.8209	0.1126	0.0575	0.0090
	40–44	0.8385	0.0918	0.0637	0.0060
	45–49	0.8145	0.1259	0.0564	0.0032
	50–54	0.8120	0.1423	0.0441	0.0016
	55–59	0.8061	0.1154	0.0755	0.0029
	60–64	0.8017	0.1392	0.0535	0.0056
	65–69	0.8446	0.1228	0.0252	0.0074
	70–74	0.8173	0.1012	0.0815	0.0000
	75+	0.9499	0.0375	0.0127	0.0000
1987	20–24	0.9414	0.0478	0.0105	0.0003
	25–29	0.8926	0.0813	0.0209	0.0052
	30–34	0.8688	0.0874	0.0433	0.0005
	35–39	0.8680	0.0875	0.0400	0.0045
	40–44	0.7881	0.1267	0.0797	0.0055
	45–49	0.8021	0.1176	0.0755	0.0048
	50–54	0.7572	0.1557	0.0803	0.0068

(Continues)

TABLE 8.3   (*Continued*)

Year	Age	Deductions for social security	Contributions to private pensions	Deductions for government retirement	Deductions for railroad retirement
	55–59	0.7696	0.1477	0.0827	0.0000
	60–64	0.8512	0.1218	0.0219	0.0050
	65–69	0.8704	0.0956	0.0340	0.0000
	70–74	0.8790	0.0357	0.0000	0.0854
	75+	0.9109	0.0891	0.0000	0.0000
1988	20–24	0.9236	0.0607	0.0157	0.0000
	25–29	0.9060	0.0716	0.0217	0.0006
	30–34	0.8972	0.0835	0.0190	0.0003
	35–39	0.8582	0.1046	0.0342	0.0030
	40–44	0.8443	0.1030	0.0460	0.0067
	45–49	0.8337	0.1134	0.0424	0.0104
	50–54	0.8035	0.1207	0.0693	0.0064
	55–59	0.8198	0.1378	0.0320	0.0103
	60–64	0.8430	0.0966	0.0593	0.0011
	65–69	0.7806	0.1090	0.1104	0.0000
	70–74	0.8295	0.1155	0.0549	0.0000
	75+	0.9746	0.0254	0.0000	0.0000
1989	20–24	0.9381	0.0423	0.0196	0.0000
	25–29	0.8805	0.1001	0.0185	0.0009
	30–34	0.8618	0.0990	0.0355	0.0037
	35–39	0.7880	0.1890	0.0228	0.0002
	40–44	0.7654	0.2017	0.0303	0.0026
	45–49	0.8052	0.1360	0.0588	0.0000
	50–54	0.7973	0.1486	0.0541	0.0000
	55–59	0.8283	0.1170	0.0548	0.0000
	60–64	0.7899	0.1671	0.0430	0.0000
	65–69	0.8908	0.0666	0.0426	0.0000
	70–74	0.9279	0.0340	0.0380	0.0000
	75+	0.8612	0.1044	0.0345	0.0000
1990	20–24	0.9474	0.0477	0.0048	0.0001
	25–29	0.8838	0.0954	0.0197	0.0011
	30–34	0.8320	0.1356	0.0281	0.0042
	35–39	0.8525	0.1281	0.0192	0.0002

(*Continues*)

TABLE 8.3   (*Continued*)

Year	Age	Deductions for social security	Contributions to private pensions	Deductions for government retirement	Deductions for railroad retirement
	40–44	0.7671	0.1668	0.0581	0.0079
	45–49	0.8170	0.1271	0.0559	0.0000
	50–54	0.8011	0.1540	0.0446	0.0003
	55–59	0.7995	0.1494	0.0511	0.0000
	60–64	0.8034	0.1597	0.0369	0.0000
	65–69	0.9113	0.0633	0.0250	0.0004
	70–74	0.8926	0.0407	0.0667	0.0000
	75+	0.9445	0.0073	0.0482	0.0000
1991	20–24	0.9290	0.0514	0.0158	0.0037
	25–29	0.8581	0.1215	0.0190	0.0015
	30–34	0.8282	0.1362	0.0357	0.0000
	35–39	0.8339	0.1322	0.0338	0.0001
	40–44	0.7909	0.1563	0.0464	0.0063
	45–49	0.8238	0.1175	0.0584	0.0004
	50–54	0.7823	0.1764	0.0409	0.0004
	55–59	0.7570	0.1819	0.0509	0.0102
	60–64	0.7482	0.1956	0.0562	0.0000
	65–69	0.9169	0.0831	0.0000	0.0000
	70–74	0.9208	0.0792	0.0000	0.0000
	75+	0.9723	0.0277	0.0000	0.0000
1992	20–24	0.9463	0.0428	0.0109	0.0000
	25–29	0.8722	0.1109	0.0169	0.0000
	30–34	0.8395	0.1287	0.0317	0.0000
	35–39	0.7864	0.1787	0.0310	0.0039
	40–44	0.8358	0.1228	0.0404	0.0011
	45–49	0.8133	0.1352	0.0516	0.0000
	50–54	0.7657	0.1866	0.0477	0.0000
	55–59	0.7683	0.1706	0.0605	0.0006
	60–64	0.8692	0.1025	0.0283	0.0000
	65–69	0.9501	0.0262	0.0237	0.0000
	70–74	0.9126	0.0320	0.0554	0.0000
	75+	0.9067	0.0883	0.0050	0.0000
1993	20–24	0.9109	0.0616	0.0274	0.0001
	25–29	0.8702	0.1158	0.0110	0.0030

(*Continues*)

TABLE 8.3   (*Continued*)

Year	Age	Deductions for social security	Contributions to private pensions	Deductions for government retirement	Deductions for railroad retirement
	30–34	0.8033	0.1703	0.0237	0.0027
	35–39	0.7936	0.1726	0.0275	0.0064
	40–44	0.7912	0.1429	0.0612	0.0047
	45–49	0.7660	0.2000	0.0298	0.0042
	50–54	0.7963	0.1438	0.0566	0.0033
	55–59	0.8173	0.1428	0.0399	0.0000
	60–64	0.8058	0.1589	0.0350	0.0003
	65–69	0.8472	0.0992	0.0536	0.0000
	70–74	0.8654	0.0817	0.0529	0.0000
	75+	0.7146	0.1910	0.0944	0.0000
1994	20–24	0.9496	0.0464	0.0041	0.0000
	25–29	0.8587	0.1208	0.0180	0.0025
	30–34	0.8196	0.1568	0.0236	0.0000
	35–39	0.7998	0.1804	0.0175	0.0023
	40–44	0.7836	0.1732	0.0425	0.0007
	45–49	0.7353	0.1931	0.0705	0.0011
	50–54	0.7609	0.1691	0.0700	0.0000
	55–59	0.8066	0.1698	0.0180	0.0056
	60–64	0.7907	0.1798	0.0295	0.0000
	65–69	0.8287	0.1587	0.0126	0.0000
	70–74	0.9094	0.0812	0.0094	0.0000
	75+	0.8368	0.1593	0.0039	0.0000
1995	20–24	0.9071	0.0885	0.0038	0.0007
	25–29	0.8452	0.1237	0.0311	0.0000
	30–34	0.8009	0.1752	0.0231	0.0008
	35–39	0.7951	0.1829	0.0220	0.0000
	40–44	0.8388	0.1285	0.0327	0.0000
	45–49	0.7591	0.1887	0.0480	0.0041
	50–54	0.7674	0.2018	0.0307	0.0000
	55–59	0.7781	0.1691	0.0405	0.0123
	60–64	0.8170	0.1594	0.0235	0.0000
	65–69	0.8376	0.1570	0.0055	0.0000
	70–74	0.9039	0.0582	0.0379	0.0000
	75+	0.8383	0.1214	0.0403	0.0000

TABLE 8.4   Total Household Income (Distribution)

Year	Age	Earnings	Retirement income	Financial income	Welfare benefits	Other
1982	20–24	0.9043	0.0041	0.0154	0.0431	0.0331
	25–29	0.9236	0.0033	0.0085	0.0213	0.0434
	30–34	0.9261	0.0076	0.0105	0.0139	0.0419
	35–39	0.9031	0.0101	0.0159	0.0167	0.0543
	40–44	0.9323	0.0186	0.0165	0.0110	0.0216
	45–49	0.8944	0.0337	0.0231	0.0102	0.0385
	50–54	0.8594	0.0379	0.0358	0.0135	0.0534
	55–59	0.8138	0.0942	0.0538	0.0061	0.0320
	60–64	0.5437	0.3010	0.1094	0.0070	0.0388
	65–69	0.2244	0.5764	0.1446	0.0042	0.0505
	70–74	0.1607	0.6650	0.1544	0.0044	0.0156
	75+	0.1005	0.6406	0.2072	0.0054	0.0463
1983	20–24	0.9087	0.0043	0.0101	0.0349	0.0420
	25–29	0.9116	0.0040	0.0213	0.0253	0.0378
	30–34	0.9213	0.0055	0.0121	0.0204	0.0407
	35–39	0.9109	0.0106	0.0184	0.0135	0.0466
	40–44	0.8908	0.0238	0.0185	0.0160	0.0508
	45–49	0.9045	0.0262	0.0133	0.0147	0.0412
	50–54	0.8635	0.0467	0.0467	0.0090	0.0341
	55–59	0.8332	0.0926	0.0457	0.0134	0.0152
	60–64	0.5303	0.3317	0.1139	0.0118	0.0123
	65–69	0.2972	0.6110	0.1502	0.0039	−0.0622
	70–74	0.1916	0.6051	0.1367	0.0022	0.0644
	75+	0.0920	0.6452	0.1412	0.0019	0.1198
1984	20–24	0.9261	0.0053	0.0076	0.0208	0.0402
	25–29	0.9069	0.0022	0.0066	0.0171	0.0671
	30–34	0.9053	0.0052	0.0110	0.0122	0.0663
	35–39	0.9089	0.0168	0.0164	0.0098	0.0481
	40–44	0.9071	0.0206	0.0174	0.0095	0.0454
	45–49	0.8429	0.0288	0.0271	0.0101	0.0911
	50–54	0.8039	0.0505	0.0534	0.0143	0.0779
	55–59	0.7651	0.0814	0.0929	0.0094	0.0511
	60–64	0.5863	0.2470	0.0869	0.0110	0.0688
	65–69	0.3033	0.5166	0.1580	0.0126	0.0096

(*Continues*)

TABLE 8.4   (*Continued*)

Year	Age	Earnings	Retirement income	Financial income	Welfare benefits	Other
	70–74	0.2598	0.5773	0.0921	0.0021	0.0687
	75+	0.0977	0.5902	0.2095	0.0043	0.0983
1985	20–24	0.8997	0.0049	0.0033	0.0237	0.0684
	25–29	0.9327	0.0048	0.0126	0.0152	0.0347
	30–34	0.9522	0.0077	0.0104	0.0114	0.0183
	35–39	0.9250	0.0080	0.0086	0.0080	0.0504
	40–44	0.9012	0.0249	0.0243	0.0098	0.0398
	45–49	0.9070	0.0268	0.0178	0.0060	0.0425
	50–54	0.8906	0.0456	0.0371	0.0063	0.0205
	55–59	0.7730	0.0809	0.0824	0.0076	0.0562
	60–64	0.6567	0.2565	0.1182	0.0044	−0.0357
	65–69	0.2609	0.5728	0.1441	0.0051	0.0171
	70–74	0.1853	0.5850	0.1821	0.0033	0.0444
	75+	0.1216	0.6407	0.2187	0.0025	0.0165
1986	20–24	0.8958	0.0063	0.0116	0.0236	0.0627
	25–29	0.9245	0.0060	0.0057	0.0144	0.0494
	30–34	0.9302	0.0056	0.0159	0.0121	0.0361
	35–39	0.9232	0.0076	0.0166	0.0099	0.0427
	40–44	0.9226	0.0189	0.0207	0.0078	0.0301
	45–49	0.9151	0.0209	0.0193	0.0060	0.0386
	50–54	0.8823	0.0389	0.0307	0.0088	0.0393
	55–59	0.8204	0.0898	0.0624	0.0096	0.0178
	60–64	0.6337	0.2554	0.0864	0.0034	0.0211
	65–69	0.2731	0.5066	0.1608	0.0045	0.0550
	70–74	0.2451	0.5882	0.1555	0.0021	0.0091
	75+	0.1192	0.6407	0.1978	0.0031	0.0392
1987	20–24	0.8890	0.0045	0.0058	0.0372	0.0635
	25–29	0.9399	0.0049	0.0069	0.0161	0.0321
	30–34	0.9356	0.0076	0.0094	0.0143	0.0331
	35–39	0.9048	0.0100	0.0090	0.0085	0.0677
	40–44	0.9199	0.0152	0.0211	0.0117	0.0320
	45–49	0.9061	0.0212	0.0199	0.0109	0.0419
	50–54	0.8669	0.0522	0.0282	0.0093	0.0434

(*Continues*)

TABLE 8.4   (*Continued*)

Year	Age	Earnings	Retirement income	Financial income	Welfare benefits	Other
	55–59	0.8269	0.0773	0.0542	0.0085	0.0331
	60–64	0.5968	0.2864	0.0883	0.0021	0.0265
	65–69	0.3131	0.5399	0.1124	0.0018	0.0327
	70–74	0.1305	0.6727	0.1703	0.0033	0.0232
	75+	0.1244	0.6167	0.1875	0.0025	0.0688
1988	20–24	0.8945	0.0029	0.0211	0.0184	0.0631
	25–29	0.9245	0.0048	0.0043	0.0168	0.0496
	30–34	0.9331	0.0070	0.0129	0.0100	0.0370
	35–39	0.9138	0.0093	0.0112	0.0129	0.0527
	40–44	0.9170	0.0142	0.0173	0.0059	0.0456
	45–49	0.9090	0.0254	0.0141	0.0070	0.0446
	50–54	0.9102	0.0278	0.0140	0.0059	0.0421
	55–59	0.7617	0.0980	0.0557	0.0043	0.0802
	60–64	0.5901	0.2335	0.1001	0.0048	0.0716
	65–69	0.3161	0.5551	0.1142	0.0021	0.0124
	70–74	0.1401	0.6547	0.1654	0.0009	0.0389
	75+	0.0795	0.7129	0.2506	0.0006	−0.0435
1989	20–24	0.9150	0.0059	0.0055	0.0237	0.0498
	25–29	0.9305	0.0036	0.0078	0.0145	0.0436
	30–34	0.9303	0.0051	0.0072	0.0111	0.0464
	35–39	0.9208	0.0132	0.0221	0.0074	0.0364
	40–44	0.9234	0.0145	0.0178	0.0041	0.0402
	45–49	0.9035	0.0281	0.0230	0.0083	0.0371
	50–54	0.8706	0.0333	0.0341	0.0083	0.0538
	55–59	0.8351	0.0982	0.0538	0.0071	0.0057
	60–64	0.6112	0.2772	0.0917	0.0035	0.0163
	65–69	0.3208	0.5019	0.0878	0.0049	0.0846
	70–74	0.2146	0.6179	0.1422	0.0046	0.0208
	75+	0.0673	0.5378	0.2860	0.0035	0.1054
1990	20–24	0.8965	0.0027	0.0034	0.0280	0.0694
	25–29	0.9276	0.0036	0.0049	0.0180	0.0459
	30–34	0.9481	0.0050	0.0076	0.0096	0.0297
	35–39	0.9091	0.0114	0.0196	0.0112	0.0488

(*Continues*)

TABLE 8.4   (*Continued*)

Year	Age	Earnings	Retirement income	Financial income	Welfare benefits	Other
	40–44	0.9293	0.0105	0.0144	0.0068	0.0389
	45–49	0.9038	0.0263	0.0138	0.0065	0.0496
	50–54	0.9168	0.0354	0.0227	0.0087	0.0164
	55–59	0.7946	0.1050	0.0380	0.0080	0.0543
	60–64	0.6222	0.3004	0.0866	0.0065	−0.0156
	65–69	0.2719	0.5552	0.1027	0.0036	0.0666
	70–74	0.1497	0.6893	0.1763	0.0020	−0.0173
	75+	0.0777	0.6881	0.1892	0.0045	0.0405
1991	20–24	0.8739	0.0045	0.0109	0.0280	0.0828
	25–29	0.9087	0.0046	0.0081	0.0181	0.0604
	30–34	0.9253	0.0091	0.0071	0.0155	0.0430
	35–39	0.9236	0.0065	0.0130	0.0135	0.0434
	40–44	0.9444	0.0107	0.0162	0.0076	0.0210
	45–49	0.9176	0.0211	0.0250	0.0097	0.0266
	50–54	0.8895	0.0478	0.0265	0.0092	0.0271
	55–59	0.7961	0.0996	0.0456	0.0089	0.0497
	60–64	0.5969	0.2573	0.0720	0.0055	0.0683
	65–69	0.3394	0.5338	0.1251	0.0040	−0.0023
	70–74	0.1874	0.6290	0.1447	0.0022	0.0367
	75+	0.0674	0.7614	0.2185	0.0047	−0.0520
1992	20–24	0.8790	0.0025	0.0044	0.0318	0.0823
	25–29	0.8930	0.0068	0.0070	0.0244	0.0688
	30–34	0.9043	0.0108	0.0076	0.0194	0.0578
	35–39	0.9144	0.0101	0.0128	0.0120	0.0507
	40–44	0.8902	0.0139	0.0107	0.0136	0.0716
	45–49	0.9072	0.0216	0.0156	0.0140	0.0415
	50–54	0.8556	0.0484	0.0202	0.0127	0.0631
	55–59	0.7999	0.1313	0.0475	0.0124	0.0089
	60–64	0.5960	0.2991	0.0956	0.0091	0.0002
	65–69	0.3061	0.4993	0.1176	0.0064	0.0706
	70–74	0.1598	0.6516	0.1572	0.0030	0.0283
	75+	0.1487	0.6911	0.1302	0.0025	0.0274
1993	20–24	0.8649	0.0035	0.0029	0.0358	0.0929
	25–29	0.9153	0.0042	0.0074	0.0246	0.0485

(*Continues*)

TABLE 8.4   (*Continued*)

Year	Age	Earnings	Retirement income	Financial income	Welfare benefits	Other
	30–34	0.9305	0.0075	0.0055	0.0173	0.0392
	35–39	0.9168	0.0078	0.0059	0.0143	0.0552
	40–44	0.9306	0.0139	0.0103	0.0142	0.0310
	45–49	0.9259	0.0246	0.0273	0.0113	0.0108
	50–54	0.8811	0.0415	0.0167	0.0115	0.0492
	55–59	0.8367	0.1062	0.0301	0.0084	0.0187
	60–64	0.5773	0.3245	0.0684	0.0147	0.0150
	65–69	0.3948	0.4999	0.0918	0.0090	0.0046
	70–74	0.1795	0.6857	0.1443	0.0030	−0.0125
	75+	0.0640	0.7693	0.1405	0.0022	0.0240
1994	20–24	0.8781	0.0094	0.0018	0.0320	0.0788
	25–29	0.9143	0.0052	0.0031	0.0240	0.0534
	30–34	0.9262	0.0097	0.0077	0.0142	0.0422
	35–39	0.9370	0.0100	0.0142	0.0127	0.0262
	40–44	0.9218	0.0175	0.0186	0.0079	0.0343
	45–49	0.9239	0.0254	0.0141	0.0118	0.0248
	50–54	0.9216	0.0457	0.0167	0.0145	0.0015
	55–59	0.7953	0.1316	0.0467	0.0089	0.0175
	60–64	0.5892	0.3268	0.0388	0.0070	0.0382
	65–69	0.2885	0.5546	0.0583	0.0031	0.0955
	70–74	0.2106	0.6361	0.1268	0.0023	0.0242
	75+	0.1380	0.7178	0.1634	0.0029	−0.0220
1995	20–24	0.8705	0.0103	0.0059	0.0389	0.0743
	25–29	0.9352	0.0051	0.0045	0.0146	0.0405
	30–34	0.9480	0.0167	0.0080	0.0156	0.0118
	35–39	0.9276	0.0161	0.0127	0.0123	0.0313
	40–44	0.9406	0.0224	0.0055	0.0091	0.0224
	45–49	0.9432	0.0322	0.0097	0.0082	0.0068
	50–54	0.9132	0.0511	0.0275	0.0055	0.0027
	55–59	0.8320	0.0901	0.0278	0.0089	0.0412
	60–64	0.5819	0.3108	0.0592	0.0088	0.0393
	65–69	0.3276	0.5734	0.0663	0.0110	0.0217
	70–74	0.2773	0.5619	0.0711	0.0025	0.0871
	75+	0.1657	0.6821	0.1041	0.0089	0.0391

TABLE 8.5   Disposable Income (Aggregate)

Year	Age	Number of observations	Mean	Standard deviation	Median
1982	20–24	721	22,151	15,315	18,729
	25–29	883	30,102	20,423	25,655
	30–34	910	38,658	26,467	32,932
	35–39	673	39,536	28,954	35,011
	40–44	511	42,225	27,445	38,076
	45–49	475	40,432	27,117	38,003
	50–54	517	42,241	29,732	36,673
	55–59	499	37,634	26,583	32,319
	60–64	494	30,072	25,026	24,347
	65–69	432	24,272	19,817	18,793
	70–74	345	18,801	15,348	14,720
	75+	449	16,184	15,624	11,984
1983	20–24	534	21,678	18,037	17,590
	25–29	638	31,807	24,714	28,605
	30–34	617	36,666	24,590	32,579
	35–39	502	38,437	27,692	32,990
	40–44	351	45,580	32,802	38,822
	45–49	339	41,189	28,093	34,939
	50–54	315	42,550	32,803	36,146
	55–59	357	33,067	25,807	28,611
	60–64	335	28,893	22,990	23,906
	65–69	305	23,353	17,287	20,254
	70–74	235	20,605	18,943	14,865
	75+	289	16,169	18,538	10,729
1984	20–24	548	23,539	17,006	20,633
	25–29	672	32,494	22,675	27,848
	30–34	616	36,574	25,285	32,964
	35–39	543	40,185	28,160	34,868
	40–44	450	44,116	35,441	37,877
	45–49	338	41,493	32,061	35,331
	50–54	333	41,487	39,032	32,759
	55–59	344	39,581	38,802	28,475
	60–64	325	30,881	28,491	24,216

(*Continues*)

TABLE 8.5   (*Continued*)

Year	Age	Number of observations	Mean	Standard deviation	Median
	65–69	271	25,169	20,749	20,005
	70–74	217	24,041	27,508	15,291
	75+	330	19,640	31,442	12,992
1985	20–24	476	22,398	18,412	18,627
	25–29	664	30,397	22,287	26,684
	30–34	594	36,454	24,925	33,039
	35–39	545	43,225	32,071	35,036
	40–44	394	41,066	30,942	36,835
	45–49	335	43,008	33,948	37,934
	50–54	319	39,426	33,463	31,815
	55–59	302	36,331	39,685	24,630
	60–64	338	30,770	32,699	23,048
	65–69	286	24,463	22,256	19,304
	70–74	234	21,136	17,119	15,922
	75+	302	17,593	18,576	13,001
1986	20–24	818	22,629	16,658	19,917
	25–29	1,160	31,531	22,671	26,947
	30–34	1,172	37,718	26,922	32,214
	35–39	1,062	41,894	30,440	36,424
	40–44	792	44,071	31,550	41,336
	45–49	660	45,147	34,550	41,507
	50–54	622	43,295	33,062	37,153
	55–59	607	37,292	34,154	31,024
	60–64	646	31,606	28,880	23,520
	65–69	578	25,122	24,677	18,301
	70–74	431	23,107	20,368	17,061
	75+	643	17,679	17,288	12,477
1987	20–24	454	22,840	17,219	19,343
	25–29	703	32,123	21,965	28,446
	30–34	690	37,291	26,047	32,453
	35–39	641	43,383	33,110	37,356
	40–44	457	45,796	31,669	41,695
	45–49	357	44,544	33,139	38,759
	50–54	332	43,081	31,533	36,908

(*Continues*)

TABLE 8.5   (*Continued*)

Year	Age	Number of observations	Mean	Standard deviation	Median
	55–59	337	42,509	39,371	31,050
	60–64	364	31,200	29,450	22,562
	65–69	322	24,173	21,319	17,825
	70–74	256	22,088	21,936	15,289
	75+	380	17,892	16,718	12,465
1988	20–24	444	23,363	18,665	19,255
	25–29	626	31,657	20,363	27,986
	30–34	629	38,466	27,022	34,548
	35–39	579	41,418	27,847	36,872
	40–44	470	46,551	34,605	41,095
	45–49	388	43,975	29,697	40,126
	50–54	299	46,969	37,505	35,807
	55–59	295	39,212	35,344	30,806
	60–64	297	32,702	30,627	25,087
	65–69	285	24,747	21,132	20,464
	70–74	237	26,427	29,880	20,073
	75+	313	16,096	19,501	11,908
1989	20–24	411	22,115	13,993	19,215
	25–29	619	30,864	20,334	27,487
	30–34	592	40,033	27,904	35,246
	35–39	581	41,032	28,209	37,333
	40–44	489	49,566	33,071	42,397
	45–49	387	43,805	35,064	37,044
	50–54	310	45,276	40,251	34,327
	55–59	243	37,370	29,644	31,185
	60–64	282	33,880	27,361	26,899
	65–69	308	28,036	25,297	21,049
	70–74	224	25,917	28,458	18,256
	75+	282	23,111	26,576	14,100
1990	20–24	408	22,745	15,706	18,687
	25–29	618	31,261	20,555	28,448
	30–34	639	36,432	24,481	31,366
	35–39	556	40,692	29,634	34,230
	40–44	521	46,694	32,287	41,014

(*Continues*)

TABLE 8.5 (*Continued*)

Year	Age	Number of observations	Mean	Standard deviation	Median
	45–49	394	46,372	32,929	41,583
	50–54	291	42,461	30,326	37,488
	55–59	258	38,298	29,464	32,818
	60–64	319	32,682	38,421	23,503
	65–69	280	25,610	20,551	21,134
	70–74	240	20,608	16,017	16,639
	75+	358	16,600	14,742	12,110
1991	20–24	359	22,594	16,662	18,831
	25–29	581	32,541	21,742	28,147
	30–34	608	35,840	25,031	30,571
	35–39	583	38,474	27,740	33,128
	40–44	498	43,783	30,024	38,036
	45–49	391	43,618	32,944	37,088
	50–54	306	44,558	35,752	37,178
	55–59	278	39,840	31,212	32,507
	60–64	238	33,536	30,910	24,457
	65–69	298	25,232	25,064	18,923
	70–74	268	22,585	20,704	16,384
	75+	341	15,578	13,978	12,119
1992	20–24	411	21,470	16,016	17,291
	25–29	575	30,480	22,102	25,443
	30–34	621	35,341	23,448	31,125
	35–39	597	39,968	28,815	34,442
	40–44	542	42,606	32,691	37,037
	45–49	368	44,684	33,611	38,566
	50–54	297	41,130	32,310	35,887
	55–59	274	39,748	39,651	29,520
	60–64	282	30,538	27,367	23,107
	65–69	271	25,630	21,582	19,580
	70–74	219	23,071	18,797	17,455
	75+	382	19,119	17,000	14,416
1993	20–24	352	22,529	19,131	17,721
	25–29	524	28,948	20,647	25,481
	30–34	629	35,481	24,344	30,320

(*Continues*)

TABLE 8.5   (*Continued*)

Year	Age	Number of observations	Mean	Standard deviation	Median
	35–39	585	40,086	27,555	35,130
	40–44	468	43,661	29,503	37,466
	45–49	439	43,460	32,453	37,115
	50–54	336	43,657	35,037	37,056
	55–59	259	40,388	32,014	35,732
	60–64	274	27,430	23,404	21,478
	65–69	252	25,627	21,784	17,953
	70–74	217	22,903	19,686	17,416
	75+	392	17,134	12,482	14,245
1994	20–24	364	21,672	16,230	18,128
	25–29	500	29,038	20,141	24,627
	30–34	583	35,379	23,727	31,055
	35–39	568	39,842	29,707	33,232
	40–44	511	41,250	28,008	37,269
	45–49	450	41,216	32,165	34,535
	50–54	329	42,407	32,212	35,133
	55–59	257	37,246	31,751	29,524
	60–64	241	31,922	28,143	24,195
	65–69	242	24,772	26,739	17,463
	70–74	237	23,099	25,552	17,203
	75+	336	19,959	17,925	14,437
1995	20–24	337	21,782	17,507	17,306
	25–29	452	30,098	20,590	26,104
	30–34	553	32,059	23,528	27,728
	35–39	547	34,970	25,934	31,353
	40–44	515	40,988	30,805	35,226
	45–49	431	41,470	30,672	36,151
	50–54	320	38,748	31,539	30,632
	55–59	265	35,035	28,038	29,049
	60–64	247	28,306	25,928	21,480
	65–69	256	27,058	21,665	22,136
	70–74	228	27,504	25,229	20,139
	75+	314	18,040	16,417	13,240

TABLE 8.6   Total Household Income (Distribution)

Year	Age	Disposable income	Income tax	Social security contributions
1982	20–24	0.8351	0.1051	0.0597
	25–29	0.8288	0.1129	0.0583
	30–34	0.8305	0.1143	0.0552
	35–39	0.8378	0.1097	0.0525
	40–44	0.8234	0.1229	0.0537
	45–49	0.8198	0.1266	0.0536
	50–54	0.8376	0.1123	0.0501
	55–59	0.8289	0.1236	0.0475
	60–64	0.8704	0.0965	0.0331
	65–69	0.9355	0.0493	0.0152
	70–74	0.9317	0.0581	0.0102
	75+	0.9354	0.0576	0.0070
1983	20–24	0.8515	0.0921	0.0564
	25–29	0.8134	0.1298	0.0567
	30–34	0.8332	0.1096	0.0572
	35–39	0.8201	0.1250	0.0549
	40–44	0.8381	0.1100	0.0519
	45–49	0.8377	0.1091	0.0533
	50–54	0.8190	0.1310	0.0501
	55–59	0.8494	0.0975	0.0531
	60–64	0.8761	0.0922	0.0318
	65–69	0.9237	0.0554	0.0208
	70–74	0.9084	0.0768	0.0147
	75+	0.9521	0.0401	0.0078
1984	20–24	0.8543	0.0858	0.0599
	25–29	0.8415	0.0992	0.0593
	30–34	0.8258	0.1168	0.0574
	35–39	0.8519	0.0912	0.0569
	40–44	0.8357	0.1079	0.0564
	45–49	0.8341	0.1127	0.0532
	50–54	0.8495	0.0997	0.0508
	55–59	0.8631	0.0895	0.0473
	60–64	0.8702	0.0892	0.0406
	65–69	0.9118	0.0671	0.0211

(*Continues*)

TABLE 8.6   (*Continued*)

Year	Age	Disposable income	Income tax	Social security contributions
	70–74	0.9510	0.0297	0.0193
	75+	0.9328	0.0583	0.0089
1985	20–24	0.8697	0.0709	0.0595
	25–29	0.8368	0.1012	0.0620
	30–34	0.8433	0.0927	0.0640
	35–39	0.8526	0.0890	0.0584
	40–44	0.8438	0.0987	0.0575
	45–49	0.8495	0.0925	0.0581
	50–54	0.8592	0.0819	0.0590
	55–59	0.8493	0.0994	0.0514
	60–64	0.8682	0.0872	0.0446
	65–69	0.9293	0.0531	0.0176
	70–74	0.9102	0.0751	0.0148
	75+	0.9160	0.0723	0.0116
1986	20–24	0.8537	0.0889	0.0574
	25–29	0.8425	0.0995	0.0580
	30–34	0.8479	0.0939	0.0582
	35–39	0.8509	0.0959	0.0532
	40–44	0.8589	0.0850	0.0561
	45–49	0.8444	0.1021	0.0535
	50–54	0.8434	0.1020	0.0546
	55–59	0.8513	0.0998	0.0489
	60–64	0.8765	0.0847	0.0388
	65–69	0.9135	0.0668	0.0197
	70–74	0.9204	0.0644	0.0151
	75+	0.9405	0.0498	0.0097
1987	20–24	0.8559	0.0797	0.0644
	25–29	0.8382	0.0942	0.0676
	30–34	0.8491	0.0855	0.0654
	35–39	0.8513	0.0863	0.0624
	40–44	0.8348	0.1040	0.0612
	45–49	0.8474	0.0906	0.0620
	50–54	0.8359	0.1044	0.0597

(*Continues*)

TABLE 8.6 (*Continued*)

Year	Age	Disposable income	Income tax	Social security contributions
	55–59	0.8506	0.0952	0.0542
	60–64	0.8854	0.0722	0.0424
	65–69	0.9277	0.0482	0.0242
	70–74	0.9498	0.0367	0.0135
	75+	0.9537	0.0347	0.0117
1988	20–24	0.8644	0.0673	0.0683
	25–29	0.8495	0.0809	0.0696
	30–34	0.8404	0.0916	0.0680
	35–39	0.8463	0.0874	0.0663
	40–44	0.8322	0.1040	0.0638
	45–49	0.8428	0.0914	0.0658
	50–54	0.8520	0.0853	0.0627
	55–59	0.8561	0.0899	0.0539
	60–64	0.8682	0.0884	0.0434
	65–69	0.8958	0.0793	0.0249
	70–74	0.9483	0.0414	0.0103
	75+	0.9108	0.0811	0.0082
1989	20–24	0.8539	0.0767	0.0694
	25–29	0.8342	0.0941	0.0717
	30–34	0.8363	0.0939	0.0699
	35–39	0.8253	0.1064	0.0683
	40–44	0.8208	0.1132	0.0659
	45–49	0.8348	0.1010	0.0641
	50–54	0.8505	0.0887	0.0608
	55–59	0.8491	0.0885	0.0624
	60–64	0.8752	0.0791	0.0457
	65–69	0.9055	0.0693	0.0251
	70–74	0.9279	0.0565	0.0156
	75+	0.9238	0.0674	0.0087
1990	20–24	0.8583	0.0721	0.0696
	25–29	0.8415	0.0867	0.0718
	30–34	0.8331	0.0936	0.0733
	35–39	0.8402	0.0902	0.0695

(*Continues*)

TABLE 8.6   (*Continued*)

Year	Age	Disposable income	Income tax	Social security contributions
	40–44	0.8254	0.1072	0.0674
	45–49	0.8285	0.1057	0.0658
	50–54	0.8177	0.1153	0.0670
	55–59	0.8279	0.1074	0.0647
	60–64	0.8818	0.0700	0.0482
	65–69	0.9460	0.0264	0.0276
	70–74	0.9178	0.0660	0.0163
	75+	0.9271	0.0648	0.0081
1991	20–24	0.8733	0.0571	0.0697
	25–29	0.8209	0.1079	0.0712
	30–34	0.8345	0.0945	0.0710
	35–39	0.8352	0.0940	0.0708
	40–44	0.8169	0.1106	0.0725
	45–49	0.8157	0.1140	0.0703
	50–54	0.8143	0.1177	0.0680
	55–59	0.8490	0.0918	0.0591
	60–64	0.8663	0.0852	0.0485
	65–69	0.8880	0.0813	0.0308
	70–74	0.9393	0.0415	0.0193
	75+	0.8972	0.0956	0.0072
1992	20–24	0.8674	0.0644	0.0682
	25–29	0.8533	0.0775	0.0693
	30–34	0.8476	0.0828	0.0696
	35–39	0.8188	0.1104	0.0708
	40–44	0.8256	0.1039	0.0705
	45–49	0.8289	0.1012	0.0699
	50–54	0.8470	0.0847	0.0683
	55–59	0.8803	0.0595	0.0602
	60–64	0.8573	0.0935	0.0492
	65–69	0.9073	0.0620	0.0307
	70–74	0.9392	0.0459	0.0148
	75+	0.9457	0.0411	0.0132
1993	20–24	0.8631	0.0702	0.0668
	25–29	0.8416	0.0863	0.0721

(*Continues*)

TABLE 8.6   (*Continued*)

Year	Age	Disposable income	Income tax	Social security contributions
	30–34	0.8464	0.0822	0.0714
	35–39	0.8265	0.1042	0.0693
	40–44	0.8282	0.1028	0.0690
	45–49	0.8133	0.1162	0.0705
	50–54	0.8428	0.0898	0.0674
	55–59	0.8564	0.0800	0.0637
	60–64	0.8886	0.0627	0.0487
	65–69	0.8866	0.0777	0.0357
	70–74	0.9278	0.0551	0.0172
	75+	0.9614	0.0307	0.0079
1994	20–24	0.8689	0.0623	0.0688
	25–29	0.8471	0.0812	0.0717
	30–34	0.8474	0.0805	0.0722
	35–39	0.8392	0.0888	0.0720
	40–44	0.8317	0.0984	0.0698
	45–49	0.8220	0.1081	0.0699
	50–54	0.8329	0.0977	0.0694
	55–59	0.8385	0.0984	0.0631
	60–64	0.8944	0.0575	0.0481
	65–69	0.9122	0.0645	0.0232
	70–74	0.9253	0.0500	0.0246
	75+	0.9446	0.0423	0.0131
1995	20–24	0.8735	0.0565	0.0700
	25–29	0.8538	0.0722	0.0740
	30–34	0.8269	0.0975	0.0757
	35–39	0.8408	0.0840	0.0751
	40–44	0.8376	0.0866	0.0758
	45–49	0.8118	0.1113	0.0769
	50–54	0.8404	0.0849	0.0747
	55–59	0.8454	0.0880	0.0666
	60–64	0.8525	0.0957	0.0519
	65–69	0.9099	0.0567	0.0334
	70–74	0.9147	0.0534	0.0320
	75+	0.9320	0.0464	0.0216

TABLE 8.7   Total Retirement Income (Distribution)

Year	Age	Private pensions	Social security benefits
1982	20–24	0.1045	0.8955
	25–29	0.3126	0.6874
	30–34	0.4296	0.5704
	35–39	0.2541	0.7459
	40–44	0.3803	0.6197
	45–49	0.5141	0.4859
	50–54	0.4944	0.5056
	55–59	0.6231	0.3769
	60–64	0.4791	0.5209
	65–69	0.3224	0.6776
	70–74	0.2713	0.7287
	75+	0.2323	0.7677
1983	20–24	0.2004	0.7996
	25–29	0.4078	0.5922
	30–34	0.3167	0.6833
	35–39	0.3294	0.6706
	40–44	0.4448	0.5552
	45–49	0.3478	0.6522
	50–54	0.5735	0.4265
	55–59	0.5585	0.4415
	60–64	0.5024	0.4976
	65–69	0.3047	0.6953
	70–74	0.2523	0.7477
	75+	0.2120	0.7880
1984	20–24	0.6125	0.3875
	25–29	0.3789	0.6211
	30–34	0.3018	0.6982
	35–39	0.5437	0.4563
	40–44	0.4432	0.5568
	45–49	0.5597	0.4403
	50–54	0.5928	0.4072
	55–59	0.6988	0.3012
	60–64	0.4833	0.5167
	65–69	0.3072	0.6928

(*Continues*)

TABLE 8.7   (*Continued*)

Year	Age	Private pensions	Social security benefits
	70–74	0.1982	0.8018
	75+	0.2031	0.7969
1985	20–24	0.1517	0.8483
	25–29	0.3371	0.6629
	30–34	0.3712	0.6288
	35–39	0.3724	0.6276
	40–44	0.3737	0.6263
	45–49	0.5652	0.4348
	50–54	0.6625	0.3375
	55–59	0.7669	0.2331
	60–64	0.5118	0.4882
	65–69	0.2951	0.7049
	70–74	0.1949	0.8051
	75+	0.1461	0.8539
1986	20–24	0.4472	0.5528
	25–29	0.3492	0.6508
	30–34	0.2775	0.7225
	35–39	0.4012	0.5988
	40–44	0.6236	0.3764
	45–49	0.5653	0.4347
	50–54	0.5986	0.4014
	55–59	0.6183	0.3817
	60–64	0.4849	0.5151
	65–69	0.2993	0.7007
	70–74	0.2497	0.7503
	75+	0.2196	0.7804
1987	20–24	0.1808	0.8192
	25–29	0.3016	0.6984
	30–34	0.3362	0.6638
	35–39	0.4555	0.5445
	40–44	0.4250	0.5750
	45–49	0.5896	0.4104
	50–54	0.6708	0.3292
	55–59	0.6771	0.3229

(*Continues*)

TABLE 8.7   (*Continued*)

Year	Age	Private pensions	Social security benefits
	60–64	0.4919	0.5081
	65–69	0.3318	0.6682
	70–74	0.2876	0.7124
	75+	0.1593	0.8407
1988	20–24	0.0002	0.9998
	25–29	0.2249	0.7751
	30–34	0.5354	0.4646
	35–39	0.3054	0.6946
	40–44	0.5101	0.4899
	45–49	0.6774	0.3226
	50–54	0.4455	0.5545
	55–59	0.6792	0.3208
	60–64	0.4102	0.5898
	65–69	0.3572	0.6428
	70–74	0.3745	0.6255
	75+	0.2321	0.7679
1989	20–24	0.3093	0.6907
	25–29	0.2708	0.7292
	30–34	0.2900	0.7100
	35–39	0.2959	0.7041
	40–44	0.6377	0.3623
	45–49	0.5274	0.4726
	50–54	0.5976	0.4024
	55–59	0.8523	0.1477
	60–64	0.5204	0.4796
	65–69	0.4039	0.5961
	70–74	0.3157	0.6843
	75+	0.2706	0.7294
1990	20–24	0.8569	0.1431
	25–29	0.6028	0.3972
	30–34	0.2949	0.7051
	35–39	0.3763	0.6237
	40–44	0.4816	0.5184

(*Continues*)

TABLE 8.7 (*Continued*)

Year	Age	Private pensions	Social security benefits
	45–49	0.4308	0.5692
	50–54	0.5727	0.4273
	55–59	0.6608	0.3392
	60–64	0.4801	0.5199
	65–69	0.4005	0.5995
	70–74	0.3090	0.6910
	75+	0.2303	0.7697
1991	20–24	0.4638	0.5362
	25–29	0.3895	0.6105
	30–34	0.4892	0.5108
	35–39	0.2937	0.7063
	40–44	0.3794	0.6206
	45–49	0.4988	0.5012
	50–54	0.6655	0.3345
	55–59	0.7350	0.2650
	60–64	0.4874	0.5126
	65–69	0.3738	0.6262
	70–74	0.2931	0.7069
	75+	0.2440	0.7560
1992	20–24	0.0001	0.9999
	25–29	0.4321	0.5679
	30–34	0.3878	0.6122
	35–39	0.4419	0.5581
	40–44	0.3026	0.6974
	45–49	0.5420	0.4580
	50–54	0.6538	0.3462
	55–59	0.7085	0.2915
	60–64	0.4723	0.5277
	65–69	0.2561	0.7439
	70–74	0.3273	0.6727
	75+	0.2585	0.7415
1993	20–24	0.4632	0.5368
	25–29	0.2108	0.7892

(*Continues*)

TABLE 8.7   (*Continued*)

Year	Age	Private pensions	Social security benefits
	30–34	0.5023	0.4977
	35–39	0.1936	0.8064
	40–44	0.5099	0.4901
	45–49	0.4593	0.5407
	50–54	0.6531	0.3469
	55–59	0.7286	0.2714
	60–64	0.4554	0.5446
	65–69	0.3387	0.6613
	70–74	0.3157	0.6843
	75+	0.2418	0.7582
1994	20–24	0.1476	0.8524
	25–29	0.0842	0.9158
	30–34	0.1572	0.8428
	35–39	0.2588	0.7412
	40–44	0.4633	0.5367
	45–49	0.5714	0.4286
	50–54	0.6447	0.3553
	55–59	0.7607	0.2393
	60–64	0.4925	0.5075
	65–69	0.3667	0.6333
	70–74	0.2896	0.7104
	75+	0.3219	0.6781
1995	20–24	0.1661	0.8339
	25–29	0.2498	0.7502
	30–34	0.2791	0.7209
	35–39	0.2562	0.7438
	40–44	0.4984	0.5016
	45–49	0.5179	0.4821
	50–54	0.6489	0.3511
	55–59	0.6025	0.3975
	60–64	0.4654	0.5346
	65–69	0.3978	0.6022
	70–74	0.3800	0.6200
	75+	0.2376	0.7624

TABLE 8.8   Consumption Expenditure, Saving as Residual (Aggregate) and Saving Rate[a]

Year	Age	Number of observations	Consumption expenditure			Saving as residual			Saving rate
			Mean	Standard deviation	Median	Mean	Standard deviation	Median	
1982	20–24	721	20,749	17,941	16,764	1,402	18,349	2,163	0.0327
	25–29	883	29,048	41,248	19,616	1,054	41,409	4,786	0.0579
	30–34	910	32,069	45,721	23,674	6,589	45,460	7,862	0.1113
	35–39	673	32,167	32,659	25,264	7,369	35,842	8,580	0.1590
	40–44	511	31,667	23,274	26,587	10,558	25,252	10,157	0.2626
	45–49	475	35,267	37,164	26,493	5,165	36,053	8,797	0.0989
	50–54	517	29,624	27,607	23,782	12,617	28,983	10,929	0.3130
	55–59	499	25,732	21,916	20,849	11,902	28,697	11,498	0.2878
	60–64	494	24,326	44,410	17,728	5,746	43,391	4,927	0.2031
	65–69	432	17,815	17,896	14,827	6,457	21,788	4,094	0.2246
	70–74	345	14,857	10,222	12,449	3,944	14,056	2,952	0.1981
	75+	449	12,055	10,331	9,554	4,129	12,873	2,726	0.2347
1983	20–24	534	24,388	34,203	17,563	−2,710	32,562	1,329	−0.1714
	25–29	638	33,508	44,994	22,475	−1,701	44,027	3,328	−0.0570
	30–34	617	43,233	69,851	25,030	−6,567	66,646	4,449	−0.1999
	35–39	502	42,189	82,790	27,655	−3,751	85,402	5,181	−0.0735
	40–44	351	45,987	68,641	29,508	−407	64,311	6,916	0.0432
	45–49	339	36,463	44,411	25,934	4,726	42,211	6,504	0.1042
	50–54	315	33,033	39,453	23,865	9,517	42,632	11,675	0.2147
	55–59	357	26,424	30,783	20,283	6,643	29,174	6,457	0.1956
	60–64	335	24,672	20,255	20,001	4,220	22,706	2,345	0.1880
	65–69	305	22,316	16,995	17,798	1,038	20,190	1,973	0.0940
	70–74	235	17,205	15,371	12,866	3,400	16,977	2,151	0.1087
	75+	289	12,712	10,044	9,944	3,457	14,374	1,576	0.2543
1984	20–24	548	28,153	35,816	20,100	−4,614	35,882	771	−0.1663
	25–29	672	35,091	48,518	22,538	−2,597	46,754	3,750	−0.0981
	30–34	616	38,972	56,334	25,496	−2,397	54,371	5,624	−0.0619
	35–39	543	43,754	66,820	27,711	−3,569	66,360	6,924	−0.0258
	40–44	450	39,157	49,565	30,309	4,958	52,384	8,051	0.1180
	45–49	338	41,802	54,521	29,850	−309	51,779	5,125	−0.0155
	50–54	333	34,692	31,529	27,008	6,795	40,324	5,481	0.1785
	55–59	344	29,371	25,422	23,039	10,209	29,559	4,636	0.2227
	60–64	325	25,305	20,800	19,431	5,576	26,366	3,407	0.1939

(*Continues*)

TABLE 8.8   (*Continued*)

Year	Age	Number of observations	Consumption expenditure			Saving as residual			Saving rate
			Mean	Standard deviation	Median	Mean	Standard deviation	Median	
	65–69	271	21,854	15,261	17,837	3,315	16,804	2,695	0.1428
	70–74	217	20,139	41,524	14,376	3,903	46,331	3,482	0.1314
	75	330	14,067	12,904	10,707	5,574	31,211	2,987	0.2787
1985	20–24	476	27,319	34,659	18,190	−4,922	33,772	417	−0.2140
	25–29	664	36,924	55,048	22,764	−6,527	51,789	1,859	−0.2245
	30–34	594	40,923	58,275	27,246	−4,469	55,709	3,167	−0.1307
	35–39	545	48,941	85,327	29,191	−5,716	83,011	6,187	−0.1571
	40–44	394	40,547	55,447	28,268	519	52,459	5,381	0.0056
	45–49	335	39,252	44,689	29,532	3,756	46,605	6,648	0.0546
	50–54	319	40,113	58,663	24,163	−686	55,228	3,797	0.0543
	55–59	302	31,429	35,194	20,491	4,902	36,810	3,088	0.0992
	60–64	338	27,383	26,445	20,784	3,387	32,586	3,848	0.0994
	65–69	286	21,482	19,915	15,588	2,981	17,101	2,812	0.1543
	70–74	234	18,847	22,821	13,420	2,288	22,392	2,308	0.1440
	75+	302	14,842	17,780	11,112	2,752	15,081	2,189	0.1773
1986	20–24	818	27,520	50,361	17,927	−4,891	48,310	1,122	−0.2129
	25–29	1,160	37,797	66,072	21,976	−6,266	62,897	3,500	−0.1959
	30–34	1,172	37,828	51,679	24,181	−110	48,798	5,546	−0.0353
	35–39	1,062	41,144	62,868	26,339	750	58,647	7,735	0.0065
	40–44	792	43,854	52,131	29,571	217	52,452	7,398	0.0330
	45–49	660	45,321	74,551	28,028	−174	73,338	9,669	0.0420
	50–54	622	37,162	51,772	25,558	6,132	50,530	8,648	0.1933
	55–59	607	29,847	31,690	22,688	7,445	36,363	6,796	0.1991
	60–64	646	27,660	38,899	18,650	3,945	38,972	3,528	0.1117
	65–69	578	21,361	21,940	16,395	3,761	27,399	3,282	0.1662
	70–74	431	18,617	16,226	14,131	4,491	20,242	3,487	0.2073
	75+	643	14,371	17,032	10,749	3,308	19,678	2,669	0.2043
1987	20–24	454	29,392	41,068	19,526	−6,552	39,280	−86	−0.2436
	25–29	703	35,867	61,991	22,788	−3,743	60,720	4,646	−0.1899
	30–34	690	43,130	68,274	25,736	−5,838	63,917	4,203	−0.1373
	35–39	641	42,392	57,069	28,436	991	54,333	5,331	0.0029
	40–44	457	46,190	58,324	30,744	−394	54,297	7,938	−0.0032
	45–49	357	38,637	42,735	26,929	5,907	41,074	7,983	0.1393

(*Continues*)

TABLE 8.8   (*Continued*)

Year	Age	Number of observations	Consumption expenditure			Saving as residual			Saving rate
			Mean	Standard deviation	Median	Mean	Standard deviation	Median	
	50–54	332	32,099	28,073	25,065	10,982	31,576	10,032	0.2495
	55–59	337	28,872	24,235	21,753	13,637	33,273	7,659	0.3111
	60–64	364	30,233	46,883	18,951	967	43,921	3,352	0.0647
	65–69	322	24,763	31,691	16,929	−590	34,771	1,644	0.0041
	70–74	256	19,985	18,420	14,749	2,104	19,539	2,015	0.0961
	75+	380	13,581	12,461	10,231	4,311	15,927	2,843	0.2552
1988	20–24	444	25,467	29,360	18,715	−2,104	29,742	−289	−0.1207
	25–29	626	36,191	58,942	22,346	−4,534	54,569	3,666	−0.1545
	30–34	629	44,412	73,256	26,590	−5,946	70,747	4,962	−0.0891
	35–39	579	43,674	82,021	27,560	−2,257	80,961	7,680	−0.0580
	40–44	470	45,937	69,083	30,478	614	67,916	7,001	0.0092
	45–49	388	42,388	73,503	29,958	1,587	72,441	7,441	0.0426
	50–54	299	36,160	43,683	24,535	10,809	40,325	9,011	0.2282
	55–59	295	29,222	27,503	21,185	9,990	38,351	6,570	0.2450
	60–64	297	30,477	53,962	19,137	2,225	55,196	3,750	0.0439
	65–69	285	23,420	22,827	16,814	1,327	26,316	2,542	0.0621
	70–74	237	20,685	25,755	15,309	5,743	22,194	4,247	0.1657
	75+	313	15,220	17,424	10,727	876	25,582	2,238	0.0826
1989	20–24	411	29,116	43,701	19,056	−7,002	42,338	268	−0.3033
	25–29	619	35,312	54,135	22,056	−4,447	53,412	3,558	−0.0364
	30–34	592	43,249	98,996	25,931	−3,216	93,021	6,225	−0.0596
	35–39	581	42,575	57,719	28,609	−1,543	54,265	7,097	−0.0434
	40–44	489	44,995	47,713	33,630	4,571	48,549	8,682	0.0576
	45–49	387	38,106	47,147	25,661	5,699	44,267	7,181	0.0959
	50–54	310	36,814	42,593	26,494	8,462	44,774	7,321	0.1342
	55–59	243	33,085	38,598	22,288	4,285	39,703	5,992	0.1111
	60–64	282	26,084	23,629	19,726	7,796	26,884	6,596	0.2173
	65–69	308	22,791	19,118	17,764	5,245	25,297	3,507	0.1506
	70–74	224	27,004	92,509	15,055	−1,087	80,053	2,494	−0.0841
	75+	282	16,010	18,214	10,038	7,101	21,797	3,729	0.2410
1990	20–24	408	27,730	53,883	18,641	−4,985	50,706	992	−0.2134
	25–29	618	30,763	45,697	21,269	499	42,812	4,714	−0.0225
	30–34	639	38,735	55,588	23,847	−2,303	52,380	4,830	−0.0891
	35–39	556	44,050	68,961	26,879	−3,358	67,187	5,298	−0.0991

(*Continues*)

TABLE 8.8   (*Continued*)

Year	Age	Number of observations	Consumption expenditure			Saving as residual			Saving rate
			Mean	Standard deviation	Median	Mean	Standard deviation	Median	
	40–44	521	44,888	80,439	26,965	1,806	76,374	8,270	0.0199
	45–49	394	37,575	42,191	27,589	8,796	44,076	7,959	0.1719
	50–54	291	34,861	43,527	24,644	7,600	42,098	10,895	0.1580
	55–59	258	30,555	31,212	22,484	7,742	33,726	8,106	0.2250
	60–64	319	26,146	30,711	20,209	6,536	32,731	3,890	0.2129
	65–69	280	22,018	24,012	17,477	3,592	25,517	3,500	0.1616
	70–74	240	21,225	44,732	14,597	−618	42,374	2,997	0.0064
	75+	358	14,518	13,652	11,205	2,082	17,407	1,706	0.1384
1991	20–24	359	22,545	18,236	18,455	50	19,071	370	0.0099
	25–29	581	33,974	46,805	21,648	−1,433	44,736	5,122	−0.0670
	30–34	608	38,092	55,482	23,404	−2,252	51,874	5,136	−0.0297
	35–39	583	40,641	63,349	25,598	−2,168	59,851	5,341	−0.0530
	40–44	498	38,496	42,562	28,576	5,288	42,593	8,548	0.1302
	45–49	391	37,599	39,247	28,487	6,019	43,325	7,902	0.1437
	50–54	306	34,740	32,567	24,876	9,819	36,390	8,061	0.2321
	55–59	278	29,364	32,364	22,414	10,476	33,589	8,528	0.2565
	60–64	238	27,969	28,275	19,653	5,567	31,232	3,210	0.1831
	65–69	298	22,351	22,941	16,557	2,880	29,512	1,917	0.1769
	70–74	268	18,189	15,736	14,151	4,396	16,970	2,792	0.1890
	75+	341	14,477	14,488	11,066	1,101	16,281	1,820	0.1153
1992	20–24	411	22,037	19,853	17,302	−567	19,128	−294	−0.0435
	25–29	575	28,618	34,631	20,905	1,862	32,549	2,969	0.0283
	30–34	621	38,923	50,639	24,166	−3,581	48,675	3,117	−0.0779
	35–39	597	41,005	61,116	24,541	−1,037	59,755	5,648	−0.0550
	40–44	542	42,089	47,685	28,880	517	42,767	5,961	0.0071
	45–49	368	39,824	46,872	24,797	4,860	47,170	6,662	0.1365
	50–54	297	34,605	45,291	22,153	6,525	47,398	8,070	0.1670
	55–59	274	30,695	39,746	21,184	9,053	37,758	5,956	0.2386
	60–64	282	26,452	23,989	18,536	4,086	25,155	3,057	0.1305
	65–69	271	21,248	18,675	16,197	4,382	19,586	2,341	0.1814
	70–74	219	18,443	15,963	14,717	4,628	17,405	4,038	0.1684
	75+	382	16,284	17,999	12,026	2,835	18,750	2,137	0.1045
1993	20–24	352	25,240	35,077	16,353	−2,711	36,022	435	−0.1485
	25–29	524	31,577	51,778	20,733	−2,629	51,102	3,292	−0.0876

(*Continues*)

TABLE 8.8 (*Continued*)

Year	Age	Number of observations	Consumption expenditure			Saving as residual			Saving rate
			Mean	Standard deviation	Median	Mean	Standard deviation	Median	
	30–34	629	40,615	59,679	23,601	−5,134	57,160	3,873	−0.2070
	35–39	585	47,069	65,706	26,256	−6,983	60,465	4,727	−0.1821
	40–44	468	47,421	67,594	28,814	−3,760	62,748	6,898	−0.0800
	45–49	439	44,512	53,696	27,912	−1,052	52,777	4,956	−0.0394
	50–54	336	38,668	51,548	25,176	4,989	52,140	8,702	0.0808
	55–59	259	34,493	44,103	23,663	5,895	42,695	6,648	0.1023
	60–64	274	25,872	29,598	18,349	1,558	29,226	2,690	0.0450
	65–69	252	22,010	18,757	16,152	3,617	24,508	3,218	0.1685
	70–74	217	20,027	16,364	15,371	2,876	20,682	2,233	0.1042
	75+	392	15,108	12,464	11,638	2,026	12,292	2,536	0.1440
1994	20–24	364	23,842	22,402	17,634	−2,170	21,788	−402	−0.0323
	25–29	500	28,833	35,848	20,593	205	35,066	3,195	−0.0262
	30–34	583	31,618	36,746	22,809	3,761	36,961	6,168	0.0905
	35–39	568	38,285	58,990	25,048	1,557	58,674	6,138	0.0356
	40–44	511	40,680	53,549	27,026	570	52,827	7,879	0.0257
	45–49	450	40,886	57,080	25,949	330	57,738	5,408	−0.0005
	50–54	329	37,278	45,321	23,917	5,129	41,063	6,011	0.1084
	55–59	257	35,658	63,277	21,886	1,587	64,306	5,362	0.0392
	60–64	241	22,834	16,330	18,004	9,088	23,625	4,310	0.2778
	65–69	242	21,707	23,167	16,090	3,065	30,729	2,103	0.1117
	70–74	237	19,157	15,155	14,626	3,942	24,402	2,757	0.1339
	75+	336	16,123	14,828	11,833	3,837	17,392	2,544	0.1831
1995	20–24	337	25,222	44,890	16,421	−3,440	42,981	327	−0.1452
	25–29	452	33,401	48,635	20,010	−3,303	46,447	3,907	−0.0587
	30–34	553	33,638	51,144	22,071	−1,579	48,400	4,349	−0.0837
	35–39	547	37,080	65,854	22,973	−2,109	65,864	5,022	0.0080
	40–44	515	40,527	62,223	24,571	461	59,448	7,338	0.0847
	45–49	431	38,124	59,293	24,313	3,346	61,818	8,234	0.0181
	50–54	320	30,406	34,839	22,591	8,342	41,375	8,055	0.2091
	55–59	265	31,161	36,729	20,096	3,874	37,330	6,698	0.1676
	60–64	247	22,355	18,029	17,141	5,951	24,886	4,926	0.2190
	65–69	256	23,631	31,475	17,913	3,426	30,207	3,273	0.1520
	70–74	228	19,655	15,910	15,475	7,850	26,185	4,383	0.2800
	75+	314	14,427	15,655	11,381	3,613	18,762	2,214	0.2056

[a]The saving rate is computed as ratio of mean saving to mean disposable income.

TABLE 8.9   Median Saving Rates and Distribution

Year	Age	Number of observations	Median saving rate	Percentage of households with saving rates <−1%	Percentage of households with saving rates from −1% to +1%	Percentage of households with saving rates >+1%
1982	20–24	721	0.1482	0.38	0.01	0.62
	25–29	883	0.2194	0.31	0.02	0.67
	30–34	910	0.2729	0.29	0.01	0.70
	35–39	673	0.2654	0.28	0.01	0.71
	40–44	511	0.3129	0.24	0.01	0.74
	45–49	475	0.2634	0.31	0.00	0.68
	50–54	517	0.3080	0.21	0.01	0.78
	55–59	499	0.3302	0.25	0.01	0.74
	60–64	494	0.2688	0.27	0.01	0.71
	65–69	432	0.2505	0.28	0.01	0.71
	70–74	345	0.2364	0.26	0.03	0.71
	75+	449	0.2553	0.29	0.01	0.70
1983	20–24	534	0.0836	0.42	0.02	0.56
	25–29	638	0.1322	0.40	0.01	0.59
	30–34	617	0.1680	0.36	0.01	0.63
	35–39	502	0.1945	0.34	0.01	0.65
	40–44	351	0.2110	0.34	0.01	0.66
	45–49	339	0.2305	0.29	0.01	0.70
	50–54	315	0.3187	0.29	0.00	0.71
	55–59	357	0.2668	0.28	0.00	0.72
	60–64	335	0.1704	0.33	0.01	0.66
	65–69	305	0.1651	0.38	0.01	0.61
	70–74	235	0.1452	0.37	0.02	0.61
	75+	289	0.1722	0.34	0.02	0.64
1984	20–24	548	0.0081	0.49	0.01	0.50
	25–29	672	0.1539	0.38	0.01	0.61
	30–34	616	0.1983	0.35	0.01	0.64
	35–39	543	0.2163	0.34	0.01	0.65
	40–44	450	0.2305	0.35	0.01	0.65
	45–49	338	0.1860	0.39	0.00	0.61

(*Continues*)

TABLE 8.9   (*Continued*)

Year	Age	Number of observations	Median saving rate	Percentage of households with saving rates <−1%	Percentage of households with saving rates from −1% to +1%	Percentage of households with saving rates >+1%
	50–54	333	0.2357	0.33	0.02	0.65
	55–59	344	0.2114	0.32	0.00	0.67
	60–64	325	0.2058	0.33	0.01	0.66
	65–69	271	0.1447	0.33	0.01	0.66
	70–74	217	0.2372	0.33	0.01	0.66
	75+	330	0.2572	0.31	0.00	0.69
1985	20–24	476	0.0235	0.49	0.01	0.51
	25–29	664	0.0848	0.43	0.02	0.55
	30–34	594	0.1230	0.39	0.02	0.59
	35–39	545	0.1865	0.37	0.01	0.62
	40–44	394	0.1925	0.36	0.01	0.63
	45–49	335	0.2022	0.33	0.01	0.66
	50–54	319	0.1932	0.34	0.01	0.64
	55–59	302	0.1800	0.42	0.01	0.58
	60–64	338	0.1518	0.38	0.01	0.62
	65–69	286	0.2364	0.34	0.01	0.66
	70–74	234	0.1533	0.35	0.01	0.64
	75+	302	0.2159	0.30	0.01	0.70
1986	20–24	818	0.0604	0.46	0.01	0.52
	25–29	1,160	0.1748	0.39	0.01	0.60
	30–34	1,172	0.2145	0.35	0.01	0.63
	35–39	1,062	0.2428	0.33	0.01	0.66
	40–44	792	0.2259	0.34	0.01	0.65
	45–49	660	0.2788	0.32	0.01	0.67
	50–54	622	0.2787	0.29	0.02	0.69
	55–59	607	0.2611	0.33	0.01	0.67
	60–64	646	0.2071	0.35	0.00	0.64
	65–69	578	0.2094	0.32	0.02	0.66
	70–74	431	0.2591	0.31	0.01	0.68
	75+	643	0.2441	0.30	0.01	0.69

(Continues)

TABLE 8.9   (*Continued*)

Year	Age	Number of observations	Median saving rate	Percentage of households with saving rates <−1%	Percentage of households with saving rates from −1% to +1%	Percentage of households with saving rates >+1%
1987	20–24	454	0.0091	0.49	0.01	0.50
	25–29	703	0.1596	0.36	0.02	0.62
	30–34	690	0.1624	0.37	0.02	0.61
	35–39	641	0.1973	0.33	0.01	0.66
	40–44	457	0.2371	0.36	0.01	0.63
	45–49	357	0.2729	0.27	0.01	0.72
	50–54	332	0.3169	0.26	0.02	0.72
	55–59	337	0.2913	0.30	0.00	0.70
	60–64	364	0.1739	0.35	0.01	0.64
	65–69	322	0.1406	0.39	0.02	0.59
	70–74	256	0.1400	0.40	0.00	0.59
	75+	380	0.2502	0.29	0.01	0.70
1988	20–24	444	−0.0334	0.52	0.00	0.48
	25–29	626	0.1923	0.37	0.00	0.62
	30–34	629	0.1847	0.35	0.01	0.64
	35–39	579	0.2630	0.29	0.01	0.70
	40–44	470	0.2020	0.36	0.02	0.63
	45–49	388	0.2317	0.33	0.01	0.66
	50–54	299	0.3287	0.24	0.01	0.74
	55–59	295	0.2783	0.30	0.01	0.69
	60–64	297	0.1505	0.40	0.02	0.59
	65–69	285	0.1651	0.37	0.02	0.61
	70–74	237	0.2142	0.31	0.01	0.68
	75+	313	0.1954	0.35	0.00	0.65
1989	20–24	411	0.0328	0.46	0.01	0.52
	25–29	619	0.1753	0.35	0.02	0.64
	30–34	592	0.1968	0.32	0.01	0.67
	35–39	581	0.2204	0.33	0.02	0.64
	40–44	489	0.2512	0.30	0.00	0.70
	45–49	387	0.2063	0.32	0.01	0.67
	50–54	310	0.2581	0.32	0.01	0.67

(*Continues*)

TABLE 8.9   (*Continued*)

Year	Age	Number of observations	Median saving rate	Percentage of households with saving rates <−1%	Percentage of households with saving rates from −1% to +1%	Percentage of households with saving rates >+1%
	55–59	243	0.2359	0.30	0.01	0.69
	60–64	282	0.2443	0.33	0.01	0.66
	65–69	308	0.1903	0.35	0.01	0.64
	70–74	224	0.2008	0.33	0.00	0.67
	75+	282	0.2782	0.26	0.00	0.74
1990	20–24	408	0.0723	0.43	0.02	0.55
	25–29	618	0.1882	0.35	0.01	0.64
	30–34	639	0.1989	0.34	0.02	0.64
	35–39	556	0.2066	0.36	0.00	0.64
	40–44	521	0.2408	0.31	0.01	0.68
	45–49	394	0.2514	0.30	0.02	0.69
	50–54	291	0.2879	0.27	0.00	0.73
	55–59	258	0.2987	0.32	0.00	0.68
	60–64	319	0.2018	0.37	0.01	0.62
	65–69	280	0.2102	0.33	0.00	0.67
	70–74	240	0.1928	0.36	0.01	0.63
	75+	358	0.1768	0.36	0.01	0.63
1991	20–24	359	0.0079	0.48	0.03	0.50
	25–29	581	0.2008	0.34	0.01	0.65
	30–34	608	0.2043	0.34	0.01	0.65
	35–39	583	0.2298	0.34	0.01	0.65
	40–44	498	0.2555	0.29	0.01	0.70
	45–49	391	0.2651	0.28	0.01	0.71
	50–54	306	0.2809	0.28	0.01	0.71
	55–59	278	0.2970	0.29	0.00	0.71
	60–64	238	0.2019	0.34	0.02	0.65
	65–69	298	0.1750	0.34	0.01	0.65
	70–74	268	0.2248	0.31	0.01	0.68
	75+	341	0.1632	0.37	0.01	0.62

(*Continues*)

TABLE 8.9   (*Continued*)

Year	Age	Number of observations	Median saving rate	Percentage of households with saving rates $<-1\%$	Percentage of households with saving rates from -1% to $+1\%$	Percentage of households with saving rates $>+1\%$
1992	20–24	411	−0.0059	0.50	0.01	0.49
	25–29	575	0.1477	0.37	0.02	0.61
	30–34	621	0.1603	0.38	0.01	0.62
	35–39	597	0.2081	0.36	0.01	0.64
	40–44	542	0.2059	0.36	0.02	0.62
	45–49	368	0.2680	0.31	0.01	0.68
	50–54	297	0.2905	0.31	0.01	0.68
	55–59	274	0.2545	0.35	0.01	0.64
	60–64	282	0.1821	0.36	0.01	0.63
	65–69	271	0.1356	0.37	0.02	0.62
	70–74	219	0.2512	0.31	0.01	0.68
	75+	382	0.1739	0.35	0.02	0.63
1993	20–24	352	0.0263	0.48	0.01	0.52
	25–29	524	0.1560	0.38	0.01	0.61
	30–34	629	0.1473	0.41	0.01	0.58
	35–39	585	0.1896	0.35	0.02	0.63
	40–44	468	0.2296	0.35	0.01	0.64
	45–49	439	0.1963	0.34	0.01	0.65
	50–54	336	0.2857	0.31	0.01	0.68
	55–59	259	0.2592	0.33	0.01	0.66
	60–64	274	0.1752	0.38	0.02	0.61
	65–69	252	0.2030	0.35	0.02	0.63
	70–74	217	0.1350	0.39	0.01	0.60
	75+	392	0.2125	0.33	0.01	0.65
1994	20–24	364	−0.0155	0.50	0.01	0.48
	25–29	500	0.1560	0.39	0.01	0.60
	30–34	583	0.2272	0.33	0.01	0.66
	35–39	568	0.1902	0.34	0.01	0.65
	40–44	511	0.2514	0.31	0.01	0.68
	45–49	450	0.1939	0.37	0.01	0.62
	50–54	329	0.2092	0.31	0.01	0.69

(*Continues*)

TABLE 8.9   (*Continued*)

Year	Age	Number of observations	Median saving rate	Percentage of households with saving rates <−1%	Percentage of households with saving rates from −1% to +1%	Percentage of households with saving rates >+1%
	55–59	257	0.2538	0.35	0.00	0.65
	60–64	241	0.2714	0.32	0.01	0.67
	65–69	242	0.1552	0.38	0.02	0.60
	70–74	237	0.1213	0.38	0.02	0.60
	75+	336	0.2278	0.29	0.00	0.71
1995	20–24	337	0.0294	0.48	0.01	0.51
	25–29	452	0.1651	0.37	0.02	0.61
	30–34	553	0.1753	0.38	0.01	0.62
	35–39	547	0.2266	0.35	0.01	0.64
	40–44	515	0.2870	0.30	0.02	0.68
	45–49	431	0.2639	0.31	0.01	0.68
	50–54	320	0.2964	0.31	0.01	0.68
	55–59	265	0.2721	0.33	0.01	0.66
	60–64	247	0.1974	0.34	0.03	0.63
	65–69	256	0.2107	0.35	0.01	0.64
	70–74	228	0.2369	0.30	0.00	0.69
	75+	314	0.2063	0.31	0.02	0.67

TABLE 8.10   Cohort Composition

Cohort	Year of birth	Average cell size	Years in the sample	Ages observed
1	1911–1915	265	82–96	67–83
2	1916–1920	336	82–96	62–80
3	1921–1925	365	82–96	57–75
4	1926–1930	356	82–96	52–70
5	1931–1935	350	82–96	47–65
6	1936–1940	382	82–96	42–60
7	1941–1945	471	82–96	37–55
8	1946–1950	634	82–96	32–50
9	1951–1955	690	82–96	27–45
10	1956–1960	693	82–96	22–40
11	1961–1965	530	82–96	20–35